Cloud Computing with the Windows® Azure™ Platform

Cloud Computing with the Windows® Azure™ Platform

Roger Jennings

WILEY

Wiley Publishing, Inc.

Cloud Computing with the Windows® Azure™ Platform

Published by
Wiley Publishing, Inc.
10475 Crosspoint Boulevard
Indianapolis, IN 46256
www.wiley.com

This book is dedicated to my wife, Alexandra.
Looking forward to our twenty-fifth wedding anniversary.

About the Author

Roger Jennings is an author and consultant specializing in Microsoft .NET *n*-tier database applications and data-intensive Windows Communication Foundation (WCF) Web services with SQL Server. He's been a beta tester for most versions of Visual Basic, starting with the Professional Extensions for Visual Basic 2.0 (code-named Rawhide), SQL Server since version 4.21, and all versions of Visual Studio.

More than 1.25 million English copies of Roger's 26 computer-related books are in print, and they have been translated into more than 20 languages. He's the author of *Professional ADO.NET 3.5 with LINQ and the Entity Framework* and *Expert One-on-One Visual Basic 2005 Database Programming* for Wiley/Wrox, three editions of *Database Developer's Guide to Visual Basic* (SAMS Publishing), two editions of *Access Developer's Guide* (SAMS), 11 editions of *Special Edition Using Microsoft Access* (QUE Publishing), and two editions of *Special Edition Using Windows NT 4.0 Server* (QUE). He's also written developer-oriented books about Windows 3.1 multimedia, Windows 95, and Windows 2000 Server for QUE; Active Directory Group Policy and Visual Basic web services for Osborne McGraw-Hill; and Microsoft Office InfoPath 2003 SP-1 for Microsoft Press. Roger has been a contributing editor of Redmond Media Group's *Visual Studio Magazine* and its predecessor, Fawcette Technical Publications' *Visual Basic Programmer's Journal*, for more than 15 years. His articles also appear in *Redmond Magazine* and he writes "TechBriefs" and cover stories for *Redmond Developer News*.

Roger has more than 30 years of computer-related experience, beginning with real-time medical data acquisition and chemical process control systems driven by Wang 700 calculators and later Wang BASIC microcomputers. He's the principal developer for OakLeaf Systems, a Northern California software consulting firm and author of the OakLeaf Systems blog (http://oakleafblog.blogspot.com). His OakLeaf Code of Federal Regulations (CFR) ASP.NET Web service demonstration won the charter Microsoft .NET Best Award for Horizontal Solutions (http://bit.ly/Balng, www.microsoft.com/presspass/features/2002/aug02/08-07netwinners.mspx).

Credits

Executive Editor
Bob Elliott

Project Editor
Adaobi Obi Tulton

Technical Editors
Mike Amundsen
David Robinson

Production Editor
Daniel Scribner

Copy Editor
Paula Lowell

Editorial Director
Robyn B. Siesky

Editorial Manager
Mary Beth Wakefield

Production Manager
Tim Tate

**Vice President and Executive
Group Publisher**
Richard Swadley

Vice President and Executive Publisher
Barry Pruett

Associate Publisher
Jim Minatel

Project Coordinator, Cover
Lynsey Stanford

Proofreader
Nancy C. Hanger, Windhaven

Indexer
Robert Swanson

Cover Image
© Jupiter Images / Digital Vision

Acknowledgments

Many thanks to technical editors Dave Robinson and Mike Amundsen for corrections and suggestions as the chapters passed through numerous Community Technical Previews and SQL Azure Database's mid-course correction.

David Robinson is a Senior Program Manager on the SQL Azure Database (SADB) team. David is responsible for a multitude of things including driving product features, code samples, and most importantly demonstrating to customers the value that SADB and cloud computing provides. David enjoys getting out in the community, presenting on SADB, gathering feedback, and helping to ensure SADB meets whatever demands you throw at it. David has also written for *MSDN* magazine on developing solutions against SADB. Before joining the SADB team, David was a Solutions Architect on Microsoft's Health and Life Sciences team. Before joining Microsoft, David held various senior positions with a variety of software and consulting companies. David got his start as a developer at Computer Associates in the early '90s. When not working, David enjoys spending time with his wife and helping her corral their four young daughters. David blogs at `http://bit.ly/qIT1S`, `http://blogs.msdn.com/drobinson/default.aspx`.

Mike Amundsen is an internationally known author and lecturer who travels throughout the United States and Europe speaking about and teaching a wide range of topics including .NET, the Internet, team development, and other subjects. He has more than a dozen books to his credit; his most popular titles are *Teach Yourself Database Programming with Visual Basic in 21 Days*, *Using Visual InterDev*, and *ASP.NET for Developers*. When he's not traveling, Mike spends his time with his wife and three children at their home in Kentucky. Mike and Subbu Allamaraju are writing the *RESTful Web Services Cookbook* to be published by O'Reilly Media at the end of 2009. Mike's mca blog is at `www.amundsen.com/blog/`.

Wrox Executive Editor Bob Elliott convinced me to start writing .NET developer books for Wiley/Wrox. Adaobi Obi Tulton, project editor for this and my two earlier Wiley/Wrox titles, made sure that chapters didn't slip too far behind the schedule required to deliver this book before the official announcement of the Windows Azure Platform's release to the Web at Microsoft's Professional Developers Conference 2009.

Contents

Contents

Contents

Introduction

Cloud computing became a hot topic in mid-2008 and, by mid-2009, had achieved top buzzword status. As proof of its popularity, a mid-August 2009 search on Bing.com for "cloud computing" returned *92 million hits.* Hardly a week goes by that doesn't include at least one cloud computing conference somewhere around the globe. Mainstream business magazines, such as *Forbes* and *Business Week*, regularly run cloud-computing feature articles and comprehensive special reports, such as *Business Week*'s "Cloud Computing's Big Bang for Business" of June 5, 2009, which presented case studies of cloud usage by Serena Software, Optum Health, Genentech, Coca-Cola Enterprises, and Info Tech (`http://bit.ly/uecfb`, `www.businessweek.com/magazine/toc/09_24/B4135cloud_computing.htm`). Earlier that week, Microsoft CEO Ray Ozzie addressed Silicon Valley's Churchill Club on "The Potential of Cloud Computing" (`http://bit.ly/g2wqn`, `www.churchillclub.org/eventDetail.jsp? EVT_ID=820`). TechCrunchIT's Leena Rao quoted Ozzie in a June 4, 2009 post (`http://bit.ly/1h01j`, `www.techcrunchit.com/2009/06/04/liveblogging-microsofts-ray-ozzie-on-the-potential-of-cloud-computing`):

> In essence, the nature of Windows Azure … will enable people to wrap existing Windows Server workloads in a way with as little change as possible to move up in a public or private cloud environment. It's laying out program design patterns and infrastructure — this is what an idea[l] cloud computing structure looks like, this is how you build a program with the elastic ability to scale, etc ….

When asked by moderator Steven Levy, "How many companies can build big clouds?" Ozzie replied:

> Not too many. I don't know about Amazon. They are the leader. They have done amazing work. But the level of [Windows] Server enterprise deployments is substantial. We have so many companies who are using Exchange and SharePoint who want to get into this infrastructure … it's a big investment.

Amazon Web Services is today's "800-pound gorilla" of cloud computing, having been in the Infrastructure as a Service (IaaS) market for three years with its Elastic Computing Cloud (EC2), announced in November 2006, and Simple Storage Services (S3), which started operation in March 2006. Google was one of the first players in the Platform as a Service (PaaS) business with the Python-powered Google App Engine (GAE), which now supports Java as a programming language. GAE started with a limit of 10,000 developers in early April 2008 and opened to all comers in May 28, 2008. The poster-child of Software as a Service (SaaS), Salesforce.com, Inc., had 55,400 customer-relationship management (CRM) customers and more than 1.5 million subscribers in mid-2009, according to Wikipedia. Verizon was one of the first telecom firms to announce entry into cloud-based Computing as a Service (CaaS) business in June 2009. Sun Microsystems, which was in the process of being acquired by Oracle when this book was written, and IBM are potential PaaS competitors to Windows Azure.

Ozzie responded to Levy's question, "What's your competitive edge when it comes to cloud computing over other tech companies?" with the following list:

1. Technology: Microsoft Research has been doing tremendous things.

2. Operating systems.

3. Storage investments because of search.

4. Developer edge: Five to seven million developers working on the Microsoft stack. It's a great market opportunity. If we can prove to them that we have a great infrastructure for their software, they will deploy it. There's also opportunity with partners — there are going to be lots of opportunity for partners, like hardware partners to make money.

5. Enterprise: Exchange and SharePoint are great ways to save money.

This book concentrates on item 4 of the preceding list. Microsoft's competitive edge in cloud computing hinges on its capability to leverage the skills of cadres of .NET architects and developers who use Visual Studio (VS) 2008 and 2010 to move on-premises applications and services to Azure WebRoles, WorkerRoles, and .NET Services. Publishing to hosted staging in the Azure cloud from VS's Solution Explorer requires only a few mouse clicks. Moving from staging to production deployment is a single-click operation that automatically creates two data replicas for high availability. Provisioning additional service instances during traffic surges and retiring them when usage subsides also is automatic.

SQL Server DBAs and database architects can take advantage of their Transact-SQL chops with SQL Azure Database (SADB), Microsoft Synchronization Framework, and the newly christened Data Hub (formerly codenamed *Project Huron*). Data Hub syncs database schemas and table rows between on-premises, mobile, and Azure databases. SQL Server Management Studio on your development machine can connect to an SQL Server database simply by changing the server's DNS name in the logon dialog. Managing SADB runs T-SQL on the SQL Server's traditional Transport Data Stream (TDS) protocol on TCP port 1433 with the .NET SqlClient class. Alternatively, ADO.NET Data Services (formerly *Project Astoria*) provides RESTful access to SADB data with HTTP[S].

Cloud Computing with the Windows Azure Platform's early chapters briefly discuss the business justification for moving many IT operations to the cloud and deal with thorny cloud security issues. However, the book concentrates on hands-on programming of Windows Azure Storage services — tables, blobs, and queues — and web applications (WebRoles and WorkerRoles), as well as .NET Services, including Access Control Services, Service Bus queues and routers, and Workflows. The Azure team decided late in the game to move from SQL Server Azure Database's Authority-Container-Entity (ACE) data model to SADB's fully relational Account-Server-Database model and didn't release the first SADB Community Technical Preview (CTP) until after this book's printing deadline. Therefore, the book's last two chapters about managing and programming SADB and Data Hub are downloadable, along with the sample source code, from the Wrox web site at www.wrox.com. The Azure team removed Workflow Services from the .NET Services feature set starting with the .NET Services July 2009 CTP because .NET Framework 4 will ship with a substantially improved workflow engine. Workflow Services will be reinstated after the final release of .NET 4.

Who This Book Is For

.NET developers, software architects, and development managers are the primary audience for this book, but IT executives and managers are likely to find the detailed information about auditing governance and security for Windows Azure services useful. For example Chapter 5, "Minimizing Risk When Moving to Azure Cloud Services," observes the need for cloud governance and security audits, and then goes on to describe the Statement of Auditing Standards (SAS) 70 Type I and Type II attestations and ISO/IEC 27001:2005 certifications received by Microsoft's data centers in mid-2009.

Microsoft was the first major PaaS cloud service provider to obtain both SAS 70 Type I and Type II attestations and ISO/IEC 27001:2005 certifications for its data centers.

What This Book Covers

Cloud Computing with the Windows Azure Platform covers server-side and client-side programming with Visual Studio 2008, the .NET Framework 3.5, Windows Azure Software Development Kit (SDK), .NET Services SDK, SQL Azure SDK, and ADO.NET Data Services using the local Azure Development Fabric, where applicable, and the Azure Production Fabric for the cloud. Sample programs illustrate data storage and retrieval with Azure blobs, tables, and queues; authenticating and authorizing users with ASP.NET membership and Azure Access Control Services; interconnecting services and clients with the Service Bus and its queues and routers; and implanting workflows with .NET Services and VS's graphical Workflow Designer. Most of the sample code uses the sample `StorageClient` library to simplify programming with traditional .NET objects rather than raw HTTP requests and responses.

When this book was written, .NET 4 and VS 2010 were in the Beta testing stage and the Azure Fabric did not support projects that required .NET 4 features. There is no significant difference when using VS 2010 and 2008 to author or deploy Azure projects or services.

How This Book Is Structured

This book is divided into four parts with two to five chapters. Most chapters build on the knowledge you've gained from preceding chapters. Thus, it's recommended that you work your way through the chapters sequentially. Following is a brief description of each part and its chapters' contents.

Part I: Introducing the Windows Azure Platform

Part I is devoted to generic cloud computing topics, the Windows Azure infrastructure, and Azure Storage Services.

❑ **Chapter** 1, "Surveying the Role of Cloud Computing," starts with definitions of cloud computing and its estimated market size, discusses reasons for migrating applications and services to the cloud, outlines the history of cloud computing and its ancestors, such as Oracle's Network Computer, and then goes on to describe various *aaS variations, such as Data storage as a Service (DaaS), Software as a Service (SaaS), and Microsoft's Software + Services, as well as cloud computing ontologies. The chapter closes with details about the National Institute for Standards and Technology (NIST)'s "Draft NIST Working Definition of Cloud Computing v13" and "Presentation on Effectively and Securely Using the Cloud Computing Paradigm v22" (http://bit.ly/KQ2ZZ, http://csrc.nist.gov/groups/SNS/cloud-computing/index.html) publications.

❑ **Chapter** 2, "Understanding Windows Azure Platform Architecture" begins with a description of the Windows Azure Platform's components, the Azure Development Portal for managing hosted applications and services, and the Azure Development Platform, which implements the

Developer Fabric and Developer Storage to emulate the cloud-based services on developers' computers. A tour of the Windows Azure SDK and templates added to VS 2008 by Windows Azure Tools for Visual Studio follows, and the chapter continues with details about .NET Services, the Service Bus, Workflow services, and deploying solutions to the Azure cloud.

❏ **Chapter** 3, "Analyzing the Windows Azure Operating System," digs into the Azure Fabric Controller, which handles application/service deployment, load balancing, OS/data replication, and resource management. It then goes on to describe the relationships between physical nodes and logical roles, and the services they host, as well as how the host and guest virtual machine (VMs) are created for a new production project. A discussion of the roles of upgrade domains, which support rolling service software updates and patches to the Windows Azure operating system, and fault domains for high-availability services, as well as how the fabric maintains tenant privacy in a multitenancy environment follows. The chapter closes with details of virtualizing Windows Server for use by Azure.

❏ **Chapter** 4, "Scaling Azure Table and Blob Storage" explains how to create Azure storage accounts, describes how to use the Fiddler2 web debugger proxy to view HTTP request and response messages, analyzes how the sample C# `StorageClient` library simplifies storage programming, and then goes into detailed programming techniques for using Azure tables and blobs as data sources for WebRoles. The source code contains sample C# solutions for tables (`oakleaf.cloudapp.net`) and blobs (`oakleaf2.cloudapp.net`) that are deployed to the cloud.

Part II: Taking Advantage of Cloud Services in the Enterprise

Part II shows you how to overcome enterprise-scale business issues with transport and store data encryption, basic cloud authentication and authorization techniques, improving the scalability of and enabling transactions for Azure tables, and processing compute operations in parallel with Azure queues and WorkerRoles.

❏ **Chapter** 5, "Minimizing Risk When Moving to Azure Cloud Services," starts by discussing the "Top 10 Obstacles to and Opportunities for Growth of Cloud Computing" from the University of California Berkeley's "Above the Clouds: A Berkeley View of Cloud Computing" whitepaper, service-level agreements (SLAs), and NIST's definition of *IT-related risk*, as well as federal agency plans for deploying cloud services. An analysis of regulations, such as the Gramm-Leach-Bliley (GLB) Act, Sarbanes-Oxley Act (SOX), Health Insurance Portability and Accountability Act (HIPAA), and the Foreign Corrupt Practices Act, as well as the Payment Card Industry-Data Security Standard (PCC-DSS), which requires auditing, follows. Code for implementing Secure Sockets Layer (SSL) transmission encryption for WebRoles, TLS for Azure Data Services, and encrypting personal information in Azure Storage Services follows. The chapter concludes with sections about auditing conformance to regulatory and industry standards.

❏ **Chapter** 6, "Authenticating and Authorizing Service Users," shows you how to adapt ASP.NET authentication and role management to Azure WebRoles with the `AspProviders` class library and the `TableStorageMembershipProvider`, `TableStorageRoleProvider`, `TableStorageProfileProvider`, and `TableStorageSessionProvider` classes. The chapter ends with the details for integrating ASP.NET Membership services with an Azure service.

❑ **Chapter 7,** "Optimizing the Scalability and Performance of Azure Tables," describes how to choose the optimum combination of PartitionKey and RowKey values, which correspond to a relational table's composite primary key; handle associated (child or parent) entities; and take advantage of Entity Group Transactions, which the Azure team introduced in the Windows Azure May 2009 CTP. An example for using ADO.NET Data Services to upload homogeneous (parent *or* child entities) and heterogeneous (parent *and* child entities) tables with a comparison of performance follows. The chapter closes with code to display heterogeneous entities in linked parent/child ASP.NET DataGrid controls.

❑ **Chapter 8,** "Messaging with Azure Queues," explains the benefits of offloading computing services to one or more WorkerRoles and describes how to create and process Azure queues using the QueueStorage, MessageQueue, QueueProperties, and Message classes and the MessageReceivedEventHandler delegate. The chapter also describes how to enhance the Thumbnails.sln sample solution and minimize network traffic when polling for blob updates. The final Photo Gallery Azure Queue Test Harness sample project at oakleaf5.cloudapp.net/ includes a GridView of image blobs added by a queue from local graphics files.

Part III: Tackling Advanced Azure Service Techniques

Part III introduces programming .NET Services members — Access Control Services (ACS), .NET Service Bus (SB), and Workflow services (WF) — with the Microsoft .NET Services SDK.

❑ **Chapter 9,** "Authenticating Users with .NET Access Control Services," describes ACS as a security token service infrastructure hosted in Windows Azure that authenticates credentials and issues tokens. The chapter shows you how to provision and create a .NET Services solution, use Microsoft's FederatedIdentity.net web site to create federated Information Card credentials, use Geneva Server beta 2 to create Information Cards for your own organization, and use CardSpace Information Cards for user authentication and authorization with ACS.

❑ **Chapter 10,** "Interconnecting Services with the .NET Service Bus," explains how to use the SB and its various messaging patterns for traversing firewalls and Network Address Translation (NAT) devices while interconnecting Windows Azure and other applications via the Internet. Programming topics include relaying messages with SB, making services publicly discoverable by an Atom feed, and using the configuration file to specify WSHttpRelayBinding.

❑ **Chapter 11,** "Exploring .NET [Workflow Services and] Service Bus Queues and Routers," explains persisting messages in Service Bus queues (SBQs) with the QueueManagementClient class and delivering messages with Service Bus routers (SBR)s. The online version of this chapter, which will come after the release of .NET 4, will use the CheckScoreWorkflow.sln sample project to introduce WF cloud application architecture and the .NET Service Portal's Workflow Management pages.

Part IV: Working with SQL Azure Services (Online Only)

The Microsoft SQL Server team announced its intention to replace its original SQL Server Data Services (SSDS) implementation of a schemaless Entity-Attribute-Value (EAV) data model with fully relational SQL Data Services (SDS), also known as, "SQL Server in the Cloud," and introduced SDS with an invitation-only CTP in July 2009. The SDS team changed SDS's name to SQL Azure Database in early July 2009. The first (August 2009) SADB CTP was too late to include in the first printing of this book, so Part IV's chapters will be available for download from the same location as the source code and Workflow, the book's pages on the Wrox web site (www.wrox.com).

See the later "Source Code and Online Chapters" section for details about downloading the sample source code and these chapters.

❏ **Chapter** 12: "Managing SQL Azure Accounts, Databases, and Data Hubs"

❏ **Chapter** 13: "Exploiting SQL Azure Database's Relational Features"

Conventions

To help you get the most from the text and keep track of what's happening, Wrox uses a number of conventions throughout the book.

Notes, tips, hints, tricks, and asides to the current discussion are placed in italics like this.

As for styles in the text:

❏ New terms and important words are *highlighted* when introducing them.

❏ Keyboard strokes look like this: **Ctrl+A**.

❏ URIs and code within the text appear like so: persistence.properties.

❏ Long URLs are shortened by http://bit.ly to URIs like http://bit.ly/sJbNe to minimize typing and are followed by the item's original URI for use in the event of a mismatch.

❏ Replaceable values in code are italicized: *tableName.entityName*.

❏ Code is presented in two different ways:

```
A monospace font with no highlighting works for most code examples.
Gray highlighting emphasizes code that's particularly important in the present
context.
```

Source Code and Online Chapters

As you work through the examples in this book, you may choose either to type in all the code manually or to use the source code files that accompany the book. All the source code used in this book is available for download at www.wrox.com. Once at the site, simply locate the book's title (either by using the Search box or by using one of the title lists) and click the Download Code link on the book's detail page to obtain all the source code for the book.

Because many books have similar titles, you may find it easiest to search by ISBN; this book's ISBN is 978–0–470–50638–7.

After you download the code, just decompress it with your favorite archiving tool. Alternatively, you can go to the main Wrox code download page at www.wrox.com/dynamic/books/download.aspx to see the code available for this book and all other Wrox books. The online version of Chapter 11, and Chapters 12 and 13 can also be downloaded from the web site using the same method.

Errata

We make every effort to ensure that no errors are in the text or in the code. However, no one is perfect, and mistakes do occur. If you find an error in one of our books, like a spelling mistake or faulty piece of code, we would be very grateful for your feedback. By sending in errata you may save another reader hours of frustration and at the same time you will be helping us provide even higher quality information.

To find the errata page for this book, go to www.wrox.com and locate the title using the Search box or one of the title lists. Then, on the book details page, click the Book Errata link. On this page you can view all errata that have been submitted for this book and posted by Wrox editors. A complete book list including links to each book's errata is also available at www.wrox.com/misc-pages/booklist.shtml.

P2p.wrox.com

For author and peer discussion, join the P2P forums at p2p.wrox.com. The forums are a web-based system for you to post messages relating to Wrox books and related technologies and interact with other readers and technology users. The forums offer a subscription feature to e-mail you topics of interest of your choosing when new posts are made to the forums. Wrox authors, editors, other industry experts, and your fellow readers are present on these forums.

At p2p.wrox.com you will find a number of different forums that will help you not only as you read this book, but also as you develop your own applications. To join the forums, just follow these steps:

1. Go to p2p.wrox.com and click the Register link.
2. Read the terms of use and click Agree.
3. Complete the required information to join as well as any optional information you want to provide and click Submit.
4. You will receive an e-mail with information describing how to verify your account and complete the joining process.

You can read messages in the forums without joining P2P but in order to post your own messages, you must join.

After you join, you can post new messages and respond to messages other users post. You can read messages at any time on the Web. If you would like to have new messages from a particular forum e-mailed to you, click the Subscribe to this Forum icon by the forum name in the forum listing.

For more information about how to use the Wrox P2P, be sure to read the P2P FAQs for answers to questions about how the forum software works as well as many common questions specific to P2P and Wrox books. To read the FAQs, click the FAQ link on any P2P page.

Part I

Introducing the Windows Azure Platform

1

Surveying the Role of Cloud Computing

The term *cloud computing* implies access to remote computing services offered by third parties via a TCP/IP connection to the public Internet. The cloud symbol in a network diagram, which initially represented any type of multiuser network, came to be associated specifically with the public Internet in the mid-1990s. As an example, the following is the first paragraph of Wikipedia's definition of cloud computing as of mid-January 2009:

> Cloud computing is Internet ("cloud")-based development and use of computer technology ("computing"). It is a style of computing in which resources are provided "as a service" over the Internet to users who need not have knowledge of, expertise in, or control over the technology infrastructure ("in the cloud") that supports them.

Gartner defines cloud computing as

> Scalable, IT-related capabilities provided as a service on the Internet.

The preceding definitions encompass almost all common Internet-based activities, ranging from individuals sending e-mail messages and viewing Web pages to retailers processing credit and debit card charges for online purchases. Google CEO Eric Schmidt narrowed the definition a bit in an August 9, 2006 interview by Danny Sullivan at the Search Engine Strategies Conference (transcribed at http://bit.ly/wday4, www.google.com/press/podium/ses2006.html):

> What's interesting [now] is that there is an emergent new model, and you all are here because you are part of that new model. I don't think people have really understood how big this opportunity really is. It starts with the premise that the data services and architecture should be on servers. We call it *cloud computing* — they should be in a "cloud" somewhere. And that if you have the right kind of browser or the right kind of access, it doesn't matter whether you have a PC or a Mac or a mobile phone or a BlackBerry or what have you — or new devices still to be developed — you can get

access to the cloud. There are a number of companies that have benefited from that. Obviously, Google, Yahoo!, eBay, Amazon come to mind. The computation and the data and so forth are in the servers. [Emphasis added.]

Mr. Schmidt is considered by many to be the first user of the term *cloud computing* in the context of its embodiment in 2008 and later, but the term didn't reach the threshold for inclusion in Google's Trends service until about September 2007 (see Figure 1-1). Mr. Schmidt makes the assumption in the preceding quotation that data services provided by the cloud-computing servers were defined by the organizations that owned the servers, specifically Google, Yahoo!, eBay, and Amazon.

Figure 1-1: Worldwide traffic for the terms *cloud computing, Windows Azure, Amazon EC2*, and *Google App Engine* for the years 2000 through 2008 as reported by the Google Trends service.

Amazon released its Elastic Compute Cloud (EC2) web service, which was the first service to permit users to run their own custom programs — rather than host web sites only — in the Internet cloud, on August 23, 2006, just two weeks after the Schmidt interview.

IDC, a well-regarded technology market analysis firm, forecasted in late October 2008 that IT spending on cloud services will grow by a factor of almost three and reach $42 billion by 2012, at which time it would account for about nine percent of total software sales. IDC expects that spending on cloud computing will accelerate during the forecast period, ending up by capturing 25 percent of IT spending growth in 2012 and gaining nearly a third of that growth the following year.

Cloud Computing with the Windows Azure Platform covers the enterprise-oriented cloud computing services offered by Windows Azure Platform as illustrated by the logo of Figure 1-2, which introduced Azure-related technical sessions at the Professional Developers Conference (PDC) 2008, held in Los Angeles October 27–30, 2008. Microsoft released the first Community Technical Preview (CTP) of Azure, formerly known as "Project RedDog" and occasionally called "Stratus," at PDC 2008.

Figure 1-2: The Windows Azure Platform was called the Azure Services Platform until July 2009.

Specifically, this book covers

- ❑ *Windows Azure*, the operating system which implements the Windows Azure Fabric's production version in virtualized Windows Server 2008 clusters.

- ❑ *Azure Storage Services*, which provides scalable persistent storage of structured tables, arbitrary blobs, and queues.

- ❑ *SQL Services*: SQL Azure Database implements Microsoft SQL Server in the cloud with features commonly offered by enterprise-scale relational database management systems. SQL Reporting and SQL Analysis services are expected as future data-related SQL Services.

- ❑ *.NET Services*: Access Control, Service Bus, and Workflow services, as well as Server Bus Queues and Routers.

- ❑ *Windows Azure Software Development Kit (SDK)*, which implements the Azure Development fabric and Azure Storage Services on local development PCs.

- ❑ *Windows Azure Tools for Microsoft Visual Studio*, which provide Visual Studio 2008 and 2010 project templates and other support for developing applications that run on the Windows Azure Development and Production fabrics.

The book does not cover the Live Operating Environment (LOE, formerly Mesh Operating Environment, MOE) and its Live Services because these are consumer-oriented features. Nor does it dig into Microsoft SharePoint Services, Microsoft Dynamics CRM Services, or Office Business Applications (OBAs) because they are Microsoft proprietary applications that have been modified to run on the Azure Production Fabric and use Azure Storage Services to persist state. This book's content is directed to the Azure services that are not crossed out in Figure 1-3.

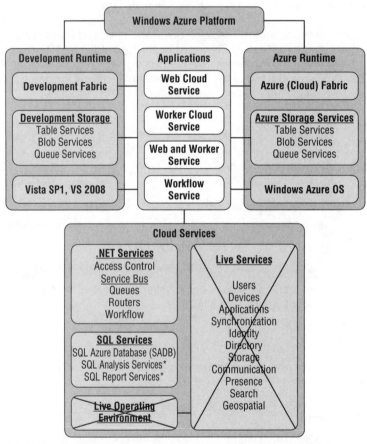

Figure 1-3: Enterprise-oriented Windows Azure Platform and SDK features. Features not covered in this book are crossed out.

This book was written with the fourth (May 2009) and later CTPs of the Windows Azure SDK and Windows Azure Tools for Microsoft Visual Studio.

Chapter 2, "Understanding Windows Azure Platform Architecture" and the remaining chapters of Part I, "Introducing the Windows Azure Platform," describe the underlying architecture and implementation of Windows Azure and its repertoire of enterprise-oriented features.

Why Migrate Applications and Services to the Cloud?

Cloud computing is receiving massive press coverage, generating an unending series of conferences, increasing IT management mindshare and substantial software developer resources because it enables small, medium, and large businesses to

❑ Get new products or services to market faster by minimizing time to deploy fixed IT assets, such as servers, switches, and routers, and by eliminating related incremental capital investment in these assets.

❑ Conduct market tests quickly and constrain losses by failing fast if the market, product, or service doesn't meet expectations.

❑ Defer long-term planning until results of initial market tests are known.

❑ Replace capital expenditures for unneeded capacity to accommodate periodic usage spikes, such as those that occur after announcing seasonal discounts or a new software version, with usage-based monthly payments.

If initial market tests succeed, serving software applications or services from the cloud lets business units deploy new products quickly and scale applications or services almost instantly to meet customer demands. For top management, the key to adopting cloud computing is its ability to trade IT capital investment for usage-based operating expenditures.

Cloud Computing's Ancestry

On the client side, many computer hardware and software suppliers took up the challenge of breaking the Microsoft/Intel hegemony in the PC market by designing and marketing networked diskless workstations, also known as *thin clients*. Microsoft offered its own thin Internet clients as Web TV set-tops and connected to intranets with Zero-Administration Windows (ZAW) for NetPC clients. These client designs reduced cost by eliminating local fixed disks and relied on networked servers to load applications and store user files. However, thin-client prices weren't low enough to capture significant market share from the ubiquitous Windows PC.

The new netbook platform, which appeared in the laptop PC market just as cloud computing gained widespread attention, appears to offer sufficient cost incentive to achieve volume manufacture. Netbooks usually offer conventional hard disks with less capacity than mainstream laptops or solid-state disks (SSDs).

Application service providers (ASPs) and web hosting firms were the first to rent server CPU cycles and storage space on an as-needed basis. The larger of these organizations are expected to participate in the cloud computing market.

Diskless Workstations and Thin Clients

Oracle's Network Computer (NC) concept of the mid-1990s probably is cloud computing's most direct ancestor. Oracle trademarked the *Network Computer* term in 1996 for a diskless network client for business use and established a Network Computer Reference Profile. The profile required all NC appliances to support HTML, HTTP, Java, and other Internet-related standards. The price advantage of NCs over PCs, if any, wasn't sufficient to create a significant market among businesses and the poor connectivity of dial-up connections discouraged consumer NetPC usage.

Microsoft and Intel produced a competing standard called "NetPC" to compete with the NC profile. In 1997 Dell Computer introduced a sealed-case PC with no floppy disk, CD drive, or other optional components, that ran Windows NT 4.0 Workstation. Compaq and HP introduced similar NetPC workstations that ran ZAW in mid-1997.

Sun Microsystems' trademarked "The Network is the Computer" motto led to its initiative to replace PCs with JavaStations, which used the Java operating system running on SPARC processors. IBM dipped its toe in the diskless workstation market with Network Stations. JavaStations and Network Stations had the same technology problems as NCs. Wyse Technology, Inc., originally a manufacturer of terminals for mainframes and minicomputers, entered the PC market and then branched into NCs in the 1990s.

These thin clients had sufficient computing power to run a web browser and a few simple applications downloaded from the Web on demand but relied on networked disc storage. Oracle CEO Larry Ellison abandoned the NC project and Sun gave up on the JavaStation in about 2000. NetPCs and ZAW fared no better; of these U.S. thin-client pilgrims, only Wyse was producing significant quantities of dedicated thin-client workstations for business use in 2009.

Thin clients might make a comeback with VMware Inc.'s release of VMware View Open Client, a recently open-sourced desktop infrastructure client that lets you connect a Linux desktop or laptop to hosted virtual Windows desktops managed by VMware View. Gartner predicts that

❑　Approximately 50 million user licenses for hosted virtual desktops will be purchased by 2013.

❑　Thin-client terminals will account for about 40 percent of user devices for hosted virtual desktop deployment.

Web TV and Its Clones or Descendants

Microsoft acquired WebTV Networks, which operated an online consumer web service and licensed the design of a diskless workstation that used a conventional TV set as the display, in August 1997. At the time, WebTV Networks had about 150,000 subscribers; both Sony and Philips were producing WebTV set-top boxes under license. Microsoft purchased WebTV Networks' subscribers in 2001 for the Microsoft Network (MSN), terminated Sony Electronics' and Philips Consumer Electronics' licenses, and rebranded WebTV as MSN TV. Thomson remains the sole U.S. set-top box licensee under the RCA brand.

America Online introduced AOL-TV, a WebTV lookalike, in 2000. In 1999 AOL teamed with Liberate Technologies, formerly known as NCI or Network Computers, Inc., a creator of thin-client systems such as the NetChannel, to write software for its set-top box. AOL reportedly had offered $65 million for NetChannel in December 1997, but negotiations broke down and AOL ceased financial support for NetChannel. AOL finally paid $29 million for NetChannel after it shut down service to its 10,000 subscribers on May 3, 1998. Thomson was the producer of NetChannel's set-top box but Philips made AOL-TV's set-top boxes, which sold for $249.95. The AOL-TV subscription cost $14.95 per month on top of AOL's then $21.95 per month PC service charge.

In 2004, when MSN TV 2 launched with set-top boxes that ran the Windows CE operating system and offered broadband access as well as dial-up Internet connectivity, analysts estimated that MSN TV had about one million subscribers.

As of early 2009, RCA MSN TV 2 Internet and Media Players had an MSRP of $199.95 and were available online through Amazon.com and a few other retailers but were on backorder from Microsoft. (Circuit City, the sole in-store MSN TV 2 box retailer, voluntarily liquidated in January 2009.) Microsoft's "MSN TV Services Fact Sheet" page on PressPass hasn't changed since May 2006, which might indicate a lack of Microsoft's interest in continuing to devote resources to MSN TV 2.

Netbook Clients

Netbooks are small laptop PCs that are designed for wireless networking and access to the Internet, long battery life, and physical robustness. The netbook platform grew out of Nicholas Negroponte's One Laptop per Child (OLPC) program whose mission is, "To create educational opportunities for the world's poorest children by providing each child with a rugged, low-cost, low-power, connected laptop with content and software designed for collaborative, joyful, self-empowered learning." The original OX-1 model, which went into large-scale production in late 2007, targeted a $100 cost to third-world governments by 2008. The OX-1 features an AMD CPU, 1200 x 900-pixel, 7.5-in. (diagonal) LCD display, 256MB DRAM, 1GB ROM for the Linux operating system and "Open Firmware," 1GB flash memory, a Secure Digital (SD) card slot, and 802.11b/g and 802.11s (mesh) wireless communication. The price in early 2009 for substantial quantities turned out to be about US$219 for the 50 least-developed countries and US$259 for other jurisdictions.

Intel's Classmate PC design, which like the OLPC OX-1 is designed for emerging markets, provides street cred to the almost US$300 actual selling price category. Acer Aspire One, Asus Eee PC, Dell Inspiron Mini, and HP Mini models offer prices ranging from about US$300 to US$400, depending on display size, SSD capacity and other specifications. In early 2009, AT&T offered a US$349 mail-in rebate to Dell Inspiron Mini 9 purchasers who sign up for an AT&T data plan, which reduces the cost of the netbook to US$99. Other carriers probably will join AT&T with iPhone-like hardware subsidies to gain cellular data subscribers.

> *Netbooks powered by Atom CPUs from Intel running Google's Chrome OS operating system are expected by 2010.*

Other assemblers add "Cloud" to their model names; for example, Everex introduced its US$399 Cloud-Book computer in early 2008. The *New York Times* writers Brad Stone and Ashlee Vance point out in their "$200 Laptops Break a Business Model" story of January 25, 2009:

> [M]ore experimental but lower-cost technologies like netbooks, Internet-based software services (called cloud computing) and virtualization, which lets companies run more software on each physical server, are on the rise . . .

> The only bright spot in the PC industry is netbooks. Analysts at the Gartner research company said shipments rose to 4.4 million devices in the third quarter of 2008, from 500,000 units in the first quarter of last year. Analysts say sales could double this year (2009) despite a deep worldwide recession.

Market researcher DisplaySearch projects sub-US$300 netbooks to increase from worldwide sales of one million units in 2007 to 14 million in 2009. Netbooks and smartphones probably will constitute the majority of clients connected to cloud-computing virtual servers by 2010.

Application Service Providers and Software as a Service

The ASP market fueled the late 1990s dot-com bubble but ASPs also were one of the largest market segments to survive the early 2000s burst. As Service-Oriented Architecture (SOA) gained traction with software developers and enterprise IT departments, ASPs gradually became known as *Software as a Service (SaaS)* providers. There are five generally accepted ASP market segments:

- ❑ *Specialty ASPs* usually deliver a single application, such as credit card or other payment processing, customer relationship management (CRM), human resources management system (HRMS), word processing, spreadsheet, database or timesheet services. Google Apps provide web-based email, calendar, word-processing, spreadsheet and presentation modules to business users for a fixed charge per user per year, while Salesforce.com rents CRM capabilities and Intuit provides its QuickBase RDBMS with per subscriber per month billing.

- ❑ *Enterprise ASPs* deliver a broad spectrum of specialty ASP solutions. For example, Microsoft rents Microsoft SharePoint Services, Microsoft Dynamics CRM Services, and Office Business Applications (OBAs), as well as Windows Live services online.

- ❑ *Vertical-market ASPs* deliver multiple software solutions for a specific customer category, such as medical or dental practice, insurance brokerage, church congregation, residential or commercial construction, or personal finance management.

- ❑ *Local-market ASPs* deliver geocoded marketing services to small service businesses, such as restaurants, pubs and bars, within a limited geographic region.

ASPs usually charge fixed monthly fees per subscriber, which include software license fees. "Excessive usage" surcharges aren't common, but providers often add disproportionate fees for ancillary "a la carte" services. Applications that require the provider to train customers' users commonly involve setup fees, yearly commitments, minimum payments, and the like.

Web Hosting Services

Web hosting services, which have been available since about 1991, are the most prolific of all cloud-computing forebears; it's estimated about 50,000 services in the U.S. host 100 or more web sites. Web hosting services provide operating systems, web server implementations, e-mail processing, content storage, high-speed Internet connectivity, and related services at monthly charges ranging from free to thousands of dollars, depending on resources consumed. Web hosting services fall into the following categories:

- ❑ *Shared server hosting* runs multiple sites from a single physical server and operating system instance. Relatively little protection exists for an individual web site's intellectual property with shared server hosting because several services run on shared resources, including the same operating system instance. Most free and low-cost (US$30.00 per month and lower) services use shared server hosting. It's common to include content storage up to about 1GB and Internet traffic to 1TB or so per month in the basic monthly charge with surcharges for added storage and traffic. Setup fees are uncommon.

❑ *Virtual Private Server* (VPS), also called *dedicated virtual server* hosting, isolates the operating system and web server in a virtualized instance, which allows a site to be logically partitioned from other sites on one or a cluster of physical machines. VPS hosting provides additional security and costs from about US$40 or more per month with increased storage and traffic limits. Small-scale e-commerce sites commonly use VPS hosting. Some firms charge small setup fees for VPS hosting.

❑ *Dedicated server hosting* leases a physical web server to the operator for increased security by content isolation at a cost of from about US$200 per month and up, with the monthly charge dependent on resources provided. Setup fees are common for dedicated server hosting.

❑ *Colocation facilities* house the web site operator's server and storage hardware in a data center building, often inside a fenced enclosure with restricted access. This is the only web hosting category in which the hosting firm doesn't own the Web and application servers. The colocation provider supplies Internet connectivity, power, cooling, fire protection, data backup, and other security services. Colocation commonly is used for large content-oriented web site and medium-size or larger e-commerce sites. Setup and monthly charges are based on floor area, power consumption, and Internet traffic.

Colocation facilities suffered mightily when the dot-com bubble burst and several such organizations declared bankruptcy. Exodus Communications, one of the early large dedicated server hosting and collocation facilities, captured a NASDAQ record for 13 consecutive quarters of more than 40 percent growth and then opted for Chapter 11 bankruptcy in September 2001 during the demise of the dot-com bubble.

Rackspace Hosting, Inc. is a large web hosting firm that offers VPS hosting (which it calls *cloud hosting*) and specializes in *managed hosting*, which includes dedicated server hosting and collocation, targeting small and medium-sized businesses (SMBs). Rackspace launched its Mosso division in February 2008 to compete in the cloud computing market. The company acquired in October 2008 JungleDisk, an online backup service, and Slicehost, a virtualized server provider, to enhance its competitive stance against Amazon Web Services' EC2, Simple Storage Services, and Elastic Block Storage. By early 2009, Rackspace was managing more than 40,000 servers and devices for customers around the globe.

Cloud Computing and Everything as a Service

Cloud computing services, like many other SOA implementations, are *composable*. Wikipedia defines a *highly composable system* as a system that "provides recombinant components that can be selected and assembled in various combinations to satisfy specific user requirements. The essential attributes that make a component composable are that it be: self-contained (modular), that is, it can be deployed independently ...; it may cooperate with other components, but dependent components are replaceable. It must also be stateless, which means it treats each request as an independent transaction, unrelated to any previous request."

Following are the generally accepted recombinant components that contribute to delivering cloud computing:

❑ *Files [storage] as a Service*: FaaS, often called *Data Storage as a Service* (DaaS), lets users store files of various data types in a highly scalable hierarchical file system and retrieve them over the Internet as various Multipurpose Internet Mail Extension (MIME) types. FaaS was one of the first cloud-based services. Several Internet start-ups, such as SmugMug, DropBox,

Ozmo, and HolaServers, use Amazon Web Services' Simple Storage Service (S3) to hold graphic images and other files, charging users a small or no access fee. Microsoft Live SkyDrive is a FaaS provider that gives users up to 25GB of free file storage at no charge.

The term *Data Storage* or *Database as a Service* implies structured storage with at least some relational database management system (RDBMS) features, such as query capabilities, primary and foreign key indexes, and entity associations through simulated JOINs. Commercial cloud services, such as Amazon Web Services (AWS), Google App Engine (GAE), and Windows Azure, offer indexed Entity-Attribute-Value (EAV) tables and query languages having some relationship to SQL. Microsoft says SQL Azure Database (SADB) "offer highly scalable and Internet-facing distributed database services in the cloud for storing and processing relational queries." SADB, Amazon SimpleDB, and GAE's DataStore offer advanced features that qualify them as Databases as a Service (DBaaS).

❑ *Software as a Service*: SaaS delivers a packaged or equivalent commercial software application to end users over the Internet with a subscription or usage-based pricing model, as opposed to a traditional lifetime license for a particular version. Examples include Microsoft Office Live, Microsoft Exchange Online, Microsoft SharePoint Online, Microsoft Dynamics CRM Online, and Salesforce.com. Microsoft was an early SaaS supporter with SOAP-based web services but has gradually migrated to promoting Software plus Services (S+S). *Application as a Service* is a synonym for SaaS.

❑ *Software plus Services*: S+S is Microsoft's marketing terminology for traditional licensed on-premises software offered as a hosted service by Microsoft or hosting partners. Hosting partners can offer virtualized private-labeled Microsoft server applications, such as Exchange or SQL Server, or value-added services to Microsoft-hosted applications, such as Dynamics CRM. The feature that distinguishes S+S is the ability for customers to run the equivalent services on premises. The most interesting example of S+S is Amazon Web Service's EC2 running Windows Server 2003 and SQL Server [Express] 2005 with Elastic Block Store data storage and S3 storage for Amazon Machine Images (AMIs) and EBS snapshot backups.

❑ *Infrastructure as a Service*: IaaS provides traditional data center resources, such as highly scalable virtualized computing power, memory and storage, over a network (typically, but not necessarily, the Internet) and usually with a subscription or per usage pricing model. IaaS is also called *utility computing*. Internet-delivered cloud examples include Amazon Web Services, GoGrid, and Flexiscale. IaaS or PaaS delivered over an intranet is called a *private cloud*.

❑ *Communication as a Service*: CaaS provides communication capability that is service-oriented, configurable, schedulable, predictable, and reliable, as well as network security, dynamic provisioning of virtual overlays for traffic isolation or dedicated bandwidth, guaranteed message delay, communication encryption, and network monitoring. CaaS is critical to meeting Service Level Agreements (SLAs) but usually is considered to be a component of SaaS, S+S, or IaaS.

❑ *Monitoring as a Service*: MaaS notifies the user of cloud computing or network outages, errors, or slowdowns. For example, Cloud Status is a simple iPhone application that monitors the status of Amazon Web Services, Google App Engine, and Twitter and reports whether service is normal, has problems, or is down. MaaS can contain auditing components for network vulnerability assessment or to verify SLA conformance and the accuracy of monthly usage charges. Some suppliers of MaaS services, such as RightScale, also provide instance deployment automation for increasing the number of running AMI instances during demand peaks and reducing the number as demand subsides.

❑   *Platform as a Service*: PaaS usually comprises at least these three distinct elements:

    ❑   *Tools as a Service* (TaaS), which provides Web-based development tools and languages, such as Microsoft Visual Studio (for Visual C#, Visual Basic, IronPython, and IronRuby) or open-source Eclipse (primarily for Java). The Windows Azure Tools for VS 2008 include templates for creating Web, Worker, Web and Worker, and Cloud Sequential Workflow Services that can run under a local (developer) or cloud (production) Windows Azure instance (fabric). Google App Engine offers a hosted Python variant as well as webapp and Django frameworks.

    ❑   *A virtualized runtime application platform* that enables running applications in the cloud, typically on top of an IaaS and delivered as SaaS. Amazon EC2 has pre-built AMIs for 32-bit and 64-bit Linux distributions, Windows Server 2003 R2 with SQL Server 2005, and Oracle databases, as well as 64-bit OpenSolaris. Windows Azure runs on Windows Server 2008 with a custom version of Microsoft's Hyper-V hypervisor. Google App Engine offers Python.

    ❑   *FaaS* to persist the state of the runtime application in Amazon's Elastic Block Store, SimpleDB or S3, Google's BigTable, or Windows Azure Storage Services' tables and blobs.

❑   *Everything as a Service*: EaaS, XaaS, or *aaS is a subset of cloud computing, according to Wikipedia, which calls EaaS "a concept of being able to call up re-usable, fine-grained software components across a network." What's missing in this definition is orchestrated interaction between the components to solve a business problem, which is often called *Integration as a Service*.

HP is one of the major proponents of Everything as a Service. "Topic 22: Creating a Business Operating Environment in the Global Services Ecosystem," one of HP Labs' 2008 Research Topics in its Innovative Research Programs, starts with these two paragraphs:

> In this applied research project, HP Labs is investigating what customer service lifecycles and experiences are possible in an "Everything as a Service" model and prototyping underlying intellectual property to enable them. HP Labs' goal in this research area is to address the technical challenges that must be overcome to move a business task to services over the Internet.

> Shane Robison, HP's Chief Strategy and Technology Officer, has detailed a set of "Everything as a Service" predictions that he believes will shape the IT industry in years to come. One of his predictions is that "by 2012, a Fortune 50 company will research, develop, and launch a major product using only Internet-based services." This opinion is supported by information available from industry analysts, such as Gartner and IDC. In this project, we ask: "What would a corporation wishing to move to an 'Everything as a Service' model need to do?"

The preceding component definitions incorporate concepts and content from Wikipedia, blog posts by Geva Perry, David Linthicum, and James Urquhart, as well as the "Toward a Unified Ontology of Cloud Computing" research paper (`http://bit.ly/12BPZD`*, *`www.cs.ucsb.edu/~lyouseff/CCOntology/`*
`CloudOntology.pdf`) by Lamia Youseff (University of California, Santa Barbara, California), and Maria Butrico and Dilma Da Silva (IBM T.J. Watson Research Center, Yorktown, New York).*

Cloud Computing Ontologies

The term *cloud computing* has yet to gain a meaning, set of technologies, or level of abstraction upon which all participants — observers, suppliers, and consumers — can agree. Catchall terminology, such as SOA, *utility computing,* or *open services,* isn't precise enough to identify the cloud-computing model accurately. This situation invites information scientists to attempt creating a cloud computing *ontology.* According to Wikipedia, "ontology deals with questions concerning what entities exist or can be said to exist, and how such entities can be grouped, related within a hierarchy, and subdivided according to similarities and differences."

Rising to the occasion, Lamia Youseff, a Ph.D candidate at the University of California, Santa Barbara, California, and Maria Butrico and Dilma Da Silva, researchers at the IBM T.J. Watson Research Center, Yorktown, New York, published in 2008 a "Toward a Unified Ontology of Cloud Computing" research paper that establishes the five-layer model shown in Figure 1-4 to define the relationships between SaaS, PaaS, IaaS, DaaS, CaaS, and HaaS.

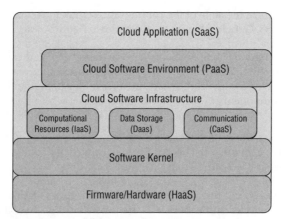

Figure 1-4: The five-layer structure of cloud computing as described in the "Toward a Unified Ontology of Cloud Computing" research paper.

Following is a high-level overview of Youseff's five-layer ontological model as used in this book:

❑ Youseff and her colleagues designate the top-level *Cloud Application Layer* as the access point for SaaS applications, such as Salesforce CRM and GAE, through Web portals.

❑ Cloud application developers use the *Cloud Software Environment Layer,* which provides support for a programming language and a set of application programming interfaces (APIs) "to facilitate the interaction between the environments and the cloud applications," which leads to the Platform as a Service moniker. The Cloud Software Environment Layer is built on the Software Kernel and Firmware/Hardware layers and provides Computational Services (IaaS), Data Storage (DaaS), and Communication (CaaS) services. Virtual machines (VMs) commonly deliver IaaS, although Windows Azure offers the option of a dedicated server running Windows Server 2008. However, it's arguable that CaaS capabilities belong at the lower Firmware/Hardware (HaaS) level because off-premises HaaS isn't practical without CaaS.

The authors classify Salesforce CRM with its Apex "on-demand" programming language and GAE, which supports Python, in the top two layers. Salesforce.com designates Force.com as a PaaS offering that supports 800+ applications from independent software vendors (ISVs) and 80,000+ custom applications as of early 2009. GAE requires at least some familiarity with Python programming to provide useful services, but promises to support other languages in the future. The Windows Azure Platform's name and its dependence on Visual Studio 2008 place Microsoft's cloud offering squarely in the PaaS category. Windows Azure supports any programming language that conforms to the Common Language Runtime (CLR). The Youseff research paper didn't include a reference to Azure as of early 2009.

❑ The *Software Kernel* can be implemented as an OS kernel, hypervisor, virtual machine monitor and/or clustering middleware, or various combinations of these systems. Although grid applications played a significant role in early cloud computing implementations, the grid has given way to the hypervisor as the preferred software kernel for cloud computing because the latter abstracts hardware idiosyncrasies from the service. Adding CaaS makes this layer equivalent to traditional VPS Web hosting.

❑ The *Firmware/Hardware* layer is the physical computing, switching, and routing hardware that forms the cloud's backbone. The HaaS provider operates, manages, and upgrades the hardware on behalf of its lessees, who supply their own operating system and application software, and charges by the GB for data ingress and egress, similar to web server colocation. Leasing eliminates users' need to invest in building and managing data centers and might reduce the cost of power and insurance.

Other recognized and self-anointed cloud computing "thought leaders" offer numerous cloud computing definitions and ontologies. For example, David Linthicum of Blue Mountain Labs proposes and briefly describes the following 10 major cloud computing components in his "Defining the Cloud Computing Framework" blog post of January 18, 2009 (`http://bit.ly/iYgXc`, `http://cloudcomputing.sys-con.com/node/811519`):

❑ Storage-as-a-Service

❑ Platform-as-a-Service

❑ Database-as-a-Service

❑ Integration-as-a-Service

❑ Information-as-a-Service

❑ Security-as-a-Service

❑ Process-as-a-Service

❑ Management/Governance-as-a-Service

❑ Application-as-a-Service

❑ Testing-as-a-Service

According to its CCIF Mission & Goals Web page, the Cloud Computing Interoperability Forum (`http://bit.ly/YAmDP`, `http://groups.google.com/group/cloudforum/web/ccif-mission-goals`) "was formed in order to enable a global cloud computing ecosystem whereby organizations are able to seamlessly work together for the purposes for wider industry adoption of cloud computing technology and related services. A key focus will be placed on the creation of a common agreed-upon framework/ontology that enables the ability of two or more cloud platforms to exchange information in a unified manner." The CCIF's Google Group had about 550 members in early 2009.

Attempts to create detailed taxonomies for cloud computing inevitably result in re-running the Red Queen's race: "It takes all the running you can do to keep in the same place." Youseff's five-level ontology is likely to suffice until cloud computing reaches adolescence or the CCIF produces an alternative.

The Red Queen in Lewis Carroll's Through the Looking-Glass and What Alice Found There said, "It takes all the running you can do to keep in the same place. If you want to get somewhere else, you must run at least twice as fast as that."

According to Wikipedia, the Red Queen Principle can be restated as: "For an evolutionary system, continuing development is needed just in order to maintain its fitness relative to the systems it is co-evolving with."

Cloud Computing Concerns

Privacy and security are the two primary governance issues that IT managers face when attempting to reduce project budgets and improve scalability with PaaS, IaaS, SaaS, or any combination of cloud computing services. An *InformationWeek* magazine poll of 456 "business technology professionals" conducted in late 2008 found only 18 percent were using cloud services and 34 percent had no interest in doing so (`http://bit.ly/SqcTY`, `www.internetevolution.com/document.asp?doc_id=170782`). More than half of the respondents expressed concern about security; performance, control, vendor lock-in, and support were the next four most-expressed doubts about cloud computing. SaaS has been subject to the same litany of doubt, but the successes of Salesforce.com and AWS prove that governance issues can be overcome.

Following are the "Five Fast Fixes" to secure data in the cloud recommended by Mike Fratto, the author of *InformationWeek*'s "Cloud Control" article of January 26, 2009 that delivered the poll's conclusions:

1. *Define Your Governance Needs*: Are they internal, external, legal? List the requirements and how they're satisfied.

2. *Classify Your Data*: Before you can determine what data you can safely put in the cloud, you first have to classify and label it according to sensitivity and type.

3. *Choose Wisely*: Identify cloud vendors that can satisfy your processing and governance needs. Direct business leaders to walk away from the rest, no matter how attractive pricing is.

4. *Set Limits*: Define what the service provider can do with your data. Prohibiting the outsourcing of processing to a third party without your consent is basic.

5. *Put Rules in Writing*: Publish policies and procedures stating which cloud vendors can receive which types of data.

One of the most important elements of cloud governance is ascertaining where data is located when it's in the cloud. As Fratto observes in his article, it's possible for SaaS and other cloud providers to store data on servers that are under the control of another organization. Outsourcing data storage or backup by the computational services vendor can lead to two or more degrees of separation between your organization and its original data or backups.

Industry groups, such as the Payment Card Industry (PCI) require banks, online merchants and Member Service Providers (MSPs) to protect cardholder information by compliance with a set of security standards, which include MasterCard's Site Data Protection (SDP) program and Visa's Cardholder Information Security Program (CISP). The United States Health Insurance Portability and Accountability Act of 1996 (HIPAA) establishes standardized mechanisms for electronic data interchange (EDI), security, and confidentiality of all healthcare-related data, as well as security mechanisms to ensure confidentiality and data integrity for any health information that identifies an individual. Not knowing who had physical possession of your charge card data would surely fail a PCI audit, which might preclude a merchant from accepting credit or debit card payment; it would certainly violate HIPAA confidentiality regulations, which can result in fines or other sanctions. However, these security and privacy issues also apply to outsourcing conventional data entry and processing operations, which is becoming increasingly commonplace, and aren't specific to cloud computing.

The Information Technology Laboratory of the U.S. National Institute of Standards and Technology (NIST) is contemplating the identification of minimal standards and architecture to enable federal agencies to create or purchase interoperable cloud computing capabilities. The ITL's Computer Security Division has the mission "to provide standards and technology to protect information systems against threats to the confidentiality of information, integrity of information and processes, and availability of information and services in order to build trust and confidence in Information Technology (IT) systems."

NIST's "Perspectives on Cloud Computing and Standards" presentation lists the following characteristics of a potential *Federal Cloud Infrastructure*:

❑   Agencies would own cloud instances or "nodes."

❑   Nodes would provide the same software framework for running cloud applications.

❑   Nodes would participate in the Federal cloud infrastructure.

❑   Federal infrastructure would promote and adopt cloud architecture standards (non-proprietary).

❑   "Minimal standards" refers to the need to ensure node interoperability and application portability without inhibiting innovation and adoption, thus limiting the scale of cloud deployments.

Subsequently, NIST issued their Draft NIST Working Definition of Cloud Computing v13 (`http://bit.ly/10TNdu`, `http://csrc.nist.gov/groups/SNS/cloud-computing/cloud-def-v14.doc`) *and Presentation on Effectively and Securely Using the Cloud Computing Paradigm v18* (`http://bit.ly/17PKbM`, `http://csrc.nist.gov/groups/SNS/cloud-computing/cloud-computing-v22.ppt`). *The Obama White House is expected to be the first major federal government user of cloud-computing services.*

When this book was written, there were no non-proprietary cloud architecture standards; node interoperability was the target of a CCIF spinoff called the Unified Cloud Interface (UCI) project (`http://bit.ly/EHRrp`, `http://code.google.com/p/unifiedcloud`) started by Enomaly (`http://bit.ly/16DldY`) founder and chief technologist, Reuven Cohen. According to Cohen, UCI's "concept is to provide a single interface that can be used to retrieve a unified representation of all multi-cloud resources and to control these resources as needed." Cohen writes in the project's UCI_Requirements Wiki:

> The key drivers of a Unified Cloud Interface (UCI) is "One Abstraction to Rule Them All" — an API for other APIs. [UCI would be a] singular abstraction that can encompass the entire infrastructure stack as well as emerging cloud centric technologies through a unified interface. What a semantic model enables for UCI is a capability to bridge both cloud-based APIs such as Amazon Web Services with existing protocols and standards, regardless of the level of adoption of the underlying API's or technology. The goal is simple, develop your application once, deploy anywhere at anytime for any reason.

Cohen posits that "you can't standardize what you can't define," so a cloud computing taxonomy/ontology will play an important role in UCI. The final goal appears to be to prevent cloud vendor lock-in by making it possible to migrate a deployed PaaS, IaaS, or SaaS project from an external to a private cloud or to another vendor's cloud infrastructure quickly and with minimal inconvenience or cost.

NIST promises to create these additional "Special Publications" in 2009 and later:

❑   Securing cloud architectures

❑   Securing cloud applications

❑   Enabling and performing forensics in the cloud

❑   Centralizing security monitoring in a cloud architecture

❑   Obtaining security from third-party cloud architectures through service-level agreements

❑   Security compliance frameworks and cloud computing (for example, HIPAA, FISMA, SOX)

You can expect to find draft versions of these publications from a link to the Special Publications (800 Series) on the Computer Security Division's Computer Security Resource Center Publications page (`http://bit.ly/17d9qq`, `http://code.google.com/p/unifiedcloud`).

If NIST can come up with a set of non-proprietary security features for an interoperable, non-proprietary cloud architecture, Information Technology Laboratory will make a substantial contribution to cloud computing's future.

Summary

Cloud computing is an emerging technology that threatens to reach "next best thing" status in 2009 and 2010 while throwing off the remnants of its Wild West ancestry. Spurred by tightened cost controls on fixed asset purchases, enterprise-scale IT departments will migrate beta deployments to full production on Windows Azure, Amazon EC2/EBS/S3, Google App Engine, GoGrid, or other commercial cloud platforms. IDC found cloud computing in October 2008 to be "accelerating adoption and poised to capture IT spending growth over the next five years." The key to cloud computing's growth is monthly charges based on usage instead of massive investment in on-premises server and networking facilities.

Off-premises web site hosting was an early precursor of cloud computing, but organizations such as Amazon.com and Google were the first purveyors of Platform as a Service with Amazon Web Services EC2 and the Google App Engine. Organizations that specialize in web site hosting, such as Rackspace Hosting, Inc., began to expand their traditional service repertoire to offer Everything as a Service in the last half of 2008. Microsoft was late to the cloud-computing party with its introduction of the Windows Azure Platform in late October 2008.

Defining generic cloud computing is difficult because there's no generally accepted ontology or taxonomy of its services. SOA introduced Software as a Service and Microsoft's Software+Services implementations, but Platform, Infrastructure, Computing, Storage, Communications, and Hardware as services also have their place in cloud computing's attempt to provide Everything as a Service. Three information scientists have proposed a five-layer model that includes SaaS, PaaS, IaaS, DaaS, CaaS, and HaaS.

The cloud symbology implies unlimited or restricted access via the public Internet. Therefore, security for cloud-based applications and data is one of upper management's primary governance concerns. Today's clouds rely primarily on token-based user authentication and authorization schemes, but federated access control integrated with enterprise directories is in most cloud purveyors' plans. Another issue is vendor lock-in because currently no standards exist for cloud interoperability and such standards might never be agreed upon. Organizations that don't trust existing Internet access control protocols can create their own on-premises "private clouds" behind corporate firewalls, but doing so requires capital investment in IT infrastructure and negates the primary justification for cloud computing.

2

Understanding Windows Azure Platform Architecture

The Windows Azure Platform is Microsoft's Windows Platform as a Service (PaaS) offering that runs on servers and related network infrastructure located in Microsoft data centers and is connected to the public Internet. The platform consists of a highly scalable (elastic) cloud operating system, data storage fabric and related services delivered by physical or logical (virtualized) Windows Server 2008 instances. The Windows Azure Software Development Kit (SDK) provides a development version of the cloud-based services, as well as the tools and APIs needed to develop, deploy, and manage scalable services in Windows Azure, including Visual Studio 2008 or 2010 templates for a standardized set of Azure applications. Figure 2-1 illustrates the platform's primary cloud and developer components.

According to Microsoft, the primary uses for Azure are to

- ❑ Add web service capabilities to existing packaged applications

- ❑ Build, modify, and distribute applications to the Web with minimal on-premises resources

- ❑ Perform services, such as large-volume storage, batch processing, intense or high-volume computations, and so on, off premises

- ❑ Create, test, debug, and distribute web services quickly and inexpensively

- ❑ Reduce costs and risks of building and extending on-premises resources

- ❑ Reduce the effort and costs of IT management

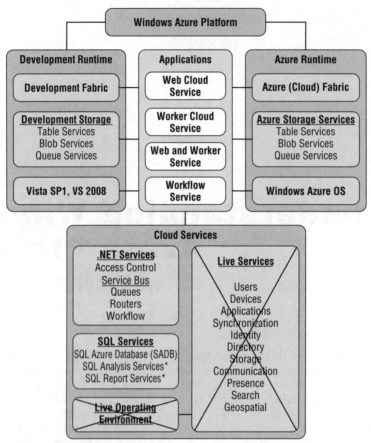

Figure 2-1: Components of the Windows Azure Platform and SDK.
Services marked with an asterisk (*) were not available when this book
was written in mid-2009.

The economic environment into which Microsoft released Azure in late October 2008 dictates that cost reduction — mentioned repeatedly in the preceding list — will be the primary motive for its adoption by small, medium, and enterprise-scale IT departments.

Microsoft designed the Azure Platform to enable .NET developers to leverage their experience with creating in Visual Studio 2008+ ASP.NET Web applications and Windows Communication Framework (WCF) services. Web application projects run in a sand-boxed version of Internet Information Services (IIS) 7; file-system-based web site projects aren't supported, but announcement of a "durable drive" is expected at PDC 2009. Web application and Web-based services run in partial trust Code Access Security, which corresponds approximately to ASP.NET's medium trust and limits access to some OS resources. The Windows Azure SDK (March 2009 CTP) enabled optional full trust Code Access security for invoking non-.NET code, using .NET libraries that require full trust, and inter-process communication using named pipes. Microsoft promises support for executing Ruby, PHP, and Python code in the cloud platform. The initial development platform release was restricted to Visual Studio 2008+ as the development environment with future support scheduled for Eclipse tools. The Azure Platform supports Web standards and protocols including SOAP, HTTP, XML, Atom, and AtomPub.

The Windows Azure Developer Portal

The initial entry point for Azure developers moving ASP.NET applications to the cloud is the Windows Azure Development Portal at `http://bit.ly/PbtOV (https://windows.azure.com/Cloud/ Provisioning/Default.aspx)`, which requires logging in with a Windows Live ID. Azure Community Technical Previews (CTPs) require separate GUID tokens for

- Windows Azure, which includes

  - Azure Hosted Services
  - Storage Accounts

- SQL Azure
- Live Services, which includes

  - Live Framework: Community Technology Preview
  - Live Services: Existing APIs

> *Live Services: Existing APIs isn't a CTP and doesn't require a token; you receive a Compute Only Live Services: Existing APIs account with each Windows Azure account. As of early 2009, a Windows Azure token entitles you to one Hosted Services account, two Storage Accounts, as well as one Hosted Deployment and Hosted Deployment Instance. You request Azure tokens through a Microsoft Connect page that you access by clicking the Billing link on the Development Portal's Summary - My Projects page.*

Figure 2-2 shows the Account page for the January 2009 CTP, which links to pages for setting up and managing SQL Azure, .NET Services and Live Services accounts. This page lets you redeem Azure and Live Framework CTP tokens provided by e-mail, and a Live Alerts page for specifying how and when to receive messages containing application-critical alerts, newsletters, and portal updates.

The March 2009 CTP introduced geolocation, which permits account holders to specify the data centers in which to store Hosted Services and Storage Accounts. Two choices were offered when this book was written: USA-Northwest (Quincy, WA) and USA-Southeast (San Antonio, TX.) You add sets of Hosted Services and Storage Accounts to an Affinity Group to assure that services and storage run in the same data center, which improves performance.

Figure 2-3 shows part of the Tokens page with several Windows Azure tokens redeemed. You paste the GUID received in a message from an Azure team member into the Resource Token ID text box and click Claim Token to add one or more entries for the appropriate entity or entities to the list.

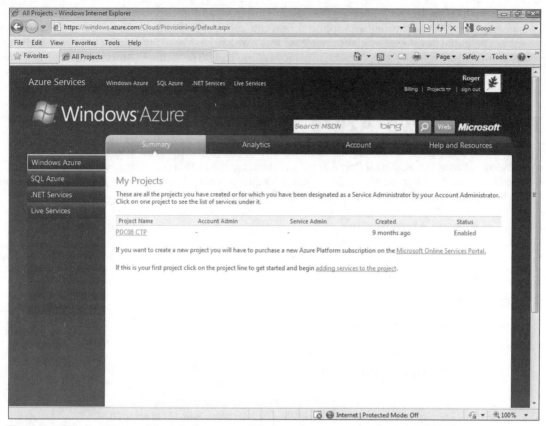

Figure 2-2: The Development Portal's Summary - Windows Azure page for the July 2009 CTP.

If you want to develop Live Framework-enabled web sites or Mesh-enabled web applications, request a Live Framework CTP token by e-mail from meshctpe@microsoft.com. After you receive and redeem the Live Framework token, download and install current CTPs of the Live Framework SDK and the Live Framework Tools for Visual Studio from links on the Live Services SDK page at http://bit.ly/oJIoz (http://dev.live.com/liveframework/sdk/). You must redeem a Live Framework token to download the Live SDK and Tools. As mentioned in Chapter 1, programming Live Services is beyond the scope of this book.

You don't need a Windows Azure account to test-drive Azure Hosted Services and Storage Services, because the Azure Development Platform emulates Azure's cloud services on your development computer, as you'll see in the following sections.

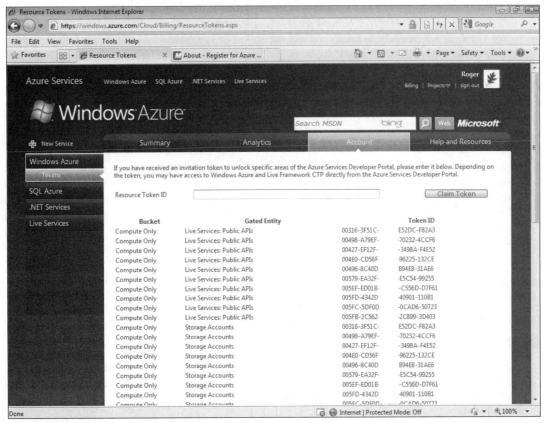

Figure 2-3: The Development Portal's Account - Azure Tokens page for the July 2009 CTP with GUIDs partially obscured.

Creating and Running Projects in the Azure Development Platform

Azure Cloud Fabric and Azure Storage Services don't support cloud-based development or debugging operations, so the Azure SDK provides on-premises clones in the form of the Development Fabric (DF) and Development Storage (DS) applications, which the Windows Azure SDK installs. The SDK also installs a Programs\Windows Azure SDK [*Month* 2009 CTP] menu, as well as a collection of sample applications and libraries of wrapper classes to simplify application programming.

.NET Framework 3.5 SP1 and SQL Express 2005 or 2008 must be present and you must enable ASP.NET and WCF HTTP Activation for IIS 7.0 under Windows Server 2008, Windows Vista SP2, or Windows 7 RC or later to install and run the SDK. The Windows Azure SDK CTP Release Notes include instructions for setting these options. The SDK isn't mandatory, because it's possible to use any operating system and programming language that supports HTTP requests and responses. However, you'll find using the SDK .NET APIs and libraries for applications and storage to be far simpler than working with HTTP directly.

Installing Windows Azure SDK and Tools for Visual Studio

After you install the Windows Azure SDK, you must download and install the Windows Azure Tools for Visual Studio to add templates for Web Cloud Service, Worker Cloud Service, Web and Worker Cloud Service, and Workflow Service projects. The later "Using Azure Application Templates for Visual Studio 2008" section describes differences between these templates.

You can download the current version of the Windows Azure SDK and Windows Azure Tools for Visual Studio from links at the bottom of Microsoft's main Windows Azure page at `http://bit.ly/A7Uza` (`www.microsoft.com/azure/windowsazure.mspx`).

Installing and Building the Windows Azure SDK Sample Applications

Installing the Windows Azure SDK doesn't install its sample applications, which are included in the \Program Files\Microsoft Windows Azure SDK\v1.0\samples.zip file. Install the sample files by unzipping samples.zip to a folder to which you have write access. This book uses samples extracted to the C:\Windows Azure SDK Samples folder.

The following table describes the sample applications.

Windows PowerShell is required to run the CloudDrive sample.

The folder to which you extract samples.zip will also contain the following three command files that you can run from the \Programs\Windows Azure SDK\Windows Azure SDK command prompt:

❑ *buildall.cmd* builds all sample projects without using Visual Studio; buildall.cmd runs the BuildAll project, which isn't a sample.

❑ *createtables.cmd* calls *buildall.cmd* and creates the database and tables required for the samples that employ Table Storage.

❑ *rundevstore.cmd* calls *createtables.cmd* and launches development storage, pointing it to the database created by *createtables.cmd*. Running development storage starts the Blob (binary large object), Queue, and Table services, as described in the later "Development Storage" section.

The simplest option is to execute *rundevstore.cmd*.

Project Name	Project Description
AspProviders Sample	Provides a sample library with implementations of the ASP.NET Membership, Role, Profile, and Session State providers.
AspProvidersDemo Sample	A simple service that makes use of the ASP.NET provider sample library.
CloudDrive Sample	A Windows PowerShell provider that enables command-line access to Blob Storage and Queue service resources as though they are file system resources available via a network drive.
DistributedSort Sample	A distributed sorting service that demonstrates the use of Blob Storage and the Queue service.
HelloFabric Sample	A simple service that demonstrates a WebRole and a WorkerRole and uses the Windows Azure runtime API to interact with the fabric from a running instance.
HelloWorld Sample	Demonstrates how to package a service for deployment to the fabric.
PersonalWebSite Sample	Demonstrates how to port an ASP.NET Web application to the Windows Azure environment.
StorageClient Sample	A sample client library that provides .NET wrapper classes for REST API operations for Blob, Queue, and Table Storage. The sample also includes a console application that can be used to test the library functionality.
Thumbnails Sample	A service that demonstrates a WebRole and a WorkerRole. The WebRole provides a front-end application for the user to upload photos and adds a work item to a queue. The WorkerRole fetches the work item from the queue and creates thumbnails in the designated directory.

The Development Fabric

DF comprises the following executables: DFAgent.exe, DFLoadBalancer.exe, DFMonitor.exe, and DFService.exe, which the Azure SDK setup program installs by default in the development PC's \Program Files\Windows Azure SDK\v1.0\bin\devfabric folder. The Task Manager's Processes page will show these four processes running after you start the DF by doing one of the following:

❑ Choose Programs\Windows Azure SDK\Development Fabric to start the Development Fabric service and its UI (DFUI.exe).

❑ Right-click the DF icon in the Taskbar's Notification Area, if present, and choose Start Development Fabric Service (see Figure 2-4).

❑ Compile and run an Azure-enabled application in Visual Studio.

Figure 2-4: Messages displayed by passing the mouse over (top) or right-clicking (bottom) the Taskbar's DF icon in the Notification Area after having started and stopped the DF.

Figure 2-5 shows the DFUI with two web applications (called *Service Deployments*) being debugged in VS 2008 concurrently. The fabric assigns sequential deployment numbers (616 and 617 in the figure) automatically. When you stop debugging, the corresponding application's entries disappear from DFUI's window.

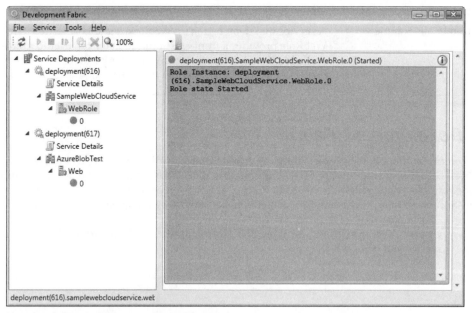

Figure 2-5: The Development Fabric UI application open with two sample Azure web applications (WebRoles) running in VS 2008.

Development Storage

The Windows Azure Platform supports three types of scalable persistent storage:

❑   *unstructured data* (blobs)

❑   *structured data* (tables)

❑   *messages* between applications, services, or both (queues)

Executing *rundevstore.exe* or building and running Azure user code in Visual Studio starts all three services, even if your project requires only one, and displays the Development Storage UI shown in Figure 2-6.

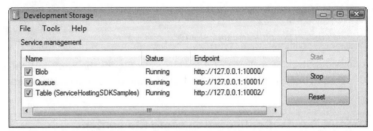

Figure 2-6: The Development Storage UI (DSUI) application open with the default ports assigned by the rundevstore.exe program to the three Azure Storage Services and the default table name for storing development schemas.

To protect against data loss, the Azure cloud stores blobs, tables, and queues in at least three separate containers in a single data center. Azure's geolocation features let you duplicate data in multiple Microsoft data centers for enhanced disaster recovery and to improve performance in specific geographic regions.

Azure Service Definition and Service Configuration Files

Azure applications that you run in the Development Framework can access data stored locally in Development Storage or uploaded to Azure cloud storage. The application looks for the port number and stored data in the location specified as endpoints in the project's ServiceConfiguration.cscfg file.

An Azure project's ServiceDefinition.csdef file defines a set of standard input endpoints and configuration settings whose values the ServiceConfiguration.cscfg file stores. Listing 2-1 shows the default content of the ServiceDefinition.csdef file when you create an Azure project based on one of the Windows Azure Tools for Visual Studio's standard templates with significant values emphasized:

Listing 2-1: Default ServiceDefinition.csdef file content

```
<ServiceDefinition name="SampleWebCloudService"
    xmlns="http://schemas.microsoft.com/ServiceHosting/2008/10/ServiceDefinition">
  <WebRole name="WebRole">
    <InputEndpoints>
      <!-- Must use port 80 for http and port 443 for https
```

Continued

Listing 2-1: Default ServiceDefinition.csdef file content *(continued)*

```
              when running in the cloud -->
         <InputEndpoint name="HttpIn" protocol="http" port="80" />
      </InputEndpoints>
      <ConfigurationSettings>
         <Setting name="AccountName"/>
         <Setting name="AccountSharedKey"/>
         <Setting name="BlobStorageEndpoint"/>
         <Setting name="QueueStorageEndpoint"/>
         <Setting name="TableStorageEndpoint"/>
      </ConfigurationSettings>
    </WebRole>
</ServiceDefinition>
```

`InputEndpoint` *values apply only to cloud storage.*

Listing 2-2 is the content of the ServiceConfiguration.cscfg file for the SampleWebCloudService Web application with default configuration values for Development Storage emphasized:

Listing 2-2: Default ServiceConfiguration.cscfg file content

```
<?xml version="1.0"?>
<ServiceConfiguration serviceName="SampleWebCloudService"
xmlns="http://schemas.microsoft.com/ServiceHosting/2008/10/ServiceConfiguration">
   <Role name="WebRole">
     <Instances count="1"/>
       <ConfigurationSettings>
         <Setting name="AccountName" value="devstoreaccount1"/>
         <Setting name="AccountSharedKey" value="Eby8vdM02xNOcqFlqUwJPLlmEtlCDXJ
            1OUzFT50uSRZ6IFsuFq2UVErCz4I6tq/K1SZFPTOtr/KBHBeksoGMGw=="/>
         <Setting name="BlobStorageEndpoint"       value="http://127.0.0.1:10000/"/>
         <Setting name="QueueStorageEndpoint"      value="http://127.0.0.1:10001/"/>
         <Setting name="TableStorageEndpoint"      value="http://127.0.0.1:10002/"/>
         <!--<Setting name="AccountName" value="oakleaf"/>
            <Setting name="AccountSharedKey" value="3elV1ndd ...  Coc0AMQA==" />
            <Setting name="BlobStorageEndpoint"
              value="http://blob.core.windows.net" />
            <Setting name="QueueStorageEndpoint"
              value="http://queue.core.windows.net" />
            <Setting name="TableStorageEndpoint"
              value="http://table.core.windows.net" />
         -->
       </ConfigurationSettings>
   </Role>
</ServiceConfiguration>
```

The emphasized values are for Development Storage and commented values are those for cloud data storage with a Windows Azure Storage Account. Using XML comments simplifies changing between Development and cloud storage during the development process.

Following are definitions of the default configuration elements in the ServiceConfiguration.csfg file:

❑ `Instances count` is the number of instances of your application that the cloud fabric will create when you deploy it.

❑ `AccountName` for cloud storage is the name you assigned to your Hosted Service with which you created the account; for Development Storage it's `devstoreaccount1` (a constant)

❑ `AccountSharedKey` for cloud storage encrypts several elements in the HTTP request message (called "Request Signing"), is confidential, is truncated in the preceding example, and isn't sent to the cloud. The value is a public constant for Developer Storage. In either case, the base64-encoded value must appear in the element as a single line of text.

❑ `BlobStorageEndpoint` for cloud storage is a public Universal Resource Identifier (URI) constant; for Developer Storage it's the development computer's loopback address (`localhost` = `127.0.0.1`) with `10000` as the default TCP port.

❑ `QueueStorageEndpoint` for cloud storage is a public URI constant; for Developer Storage it's the loopback address with `10001` as the default TCP port.

❑ `TableStorageEndpoint` for cloud storage is a public URI constant; for Development Storage it's the loopback address with `10002` as the default TCP port.

The Endpoint values appear in the Development Storage UI in Figure 2-6. You can specify custom TCP port numbers if the default values cause conflicts.

Azure Table Services

Choosing Tools, Table Service Properties in the DevelopmentStorage.exe application opens a dialog of the same name to let you change the SQL Server Express Edition database name that stores development schemas. (Cloud tables consist of metadata columns and property bags, and don't support schemas.) *ServiceHostingSDKSamples* is the default database name that *rundevstore.exe* creates; this chapter's OakLeaf Systems Azure Table Services Sample Project stores its schemas in the *SampleWebCloudService* database, as shown in Figure 2-7.

You can read the seven-part "Azure Table Storage Services Test Harness" blog series starting with "Part 1 — Introduction and Overview" at http://bit.ly/gPjQu, http://oakleafblog.blogspot. com/2008/11/azure-storage-services-test-harness.html. *The series describes in detail coding techniques for basic Azure projects. You might find the "Retire your Data Center" cover story from the February 2009 issue of* Visual Studio Magazine (http://bit.ly/gBIgk, http://visualstudiomagazine.com/articles/2009/02/01/retire-your-data-center.aspx), *which describes the same application, also of interest.*

Relational database management systems (RDBMSs) can be clustered to achieve high reliability. Running RDBMSs on high-performance servers, a process called *scaling up*, enables accommodating a large number of concurrent users. Serving data to thousands of Internet-facing servers in web farms requires *scaling out* tables by data replication, which conflicts with relational databases' reliance on immediate data consistency, referential integrity through foreign-key constraints, and ACID transactions. Entity-attribute-value (EAV) tables, such as those used by Google's BigTable storage system, which the Google App Engine uses, and Amazon Web Services' SimpleDB database, offer the capability to scale out easily and quickly by data replication at the expense of delayed data consistency (called *latency*) between replicas in multiple partitions. Scaling tables and other Azure Data Services data types is the topic of Chapter 4, "Scaling Azure Table and Blob Storage."

*ACID is an acronym for **a**tomic, **c**onsistent, **i**solated and **d**urable.*

*Eric Brewer's CAP Theorem (*http://bit.ly/18p9Ym, www.cs.berkeley.edu/~brewer/ cs262b-2004/PODC-keynote.pdf*) states that for the three properties of shared-data systems — data consistency, system availability, and network partitioning tolerance — only two can be achieved simultaneously. For example, a database that doesn't tolerate network partitions can achieve consistency and availability by using traditional RDBMS techniques, such as ACID transactions. Large distributed systems, such as those used by Amazon and Google, require network partitions so consistency can be achieved only by giving up availability or vice versa. Brewer proposes to substitute BASE for ACID; BASE is an acronym for **b**asically **a**vailable, **s**oft-state, and **e**ventual consistency.*

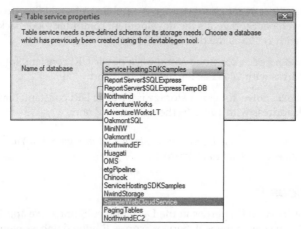

Figure 2-7: Changing the local table storage database in the DSUI application from the default *ServiceHostingSDKSamples* to *SampleWebCloudService*.

Figure 2-8 shows in SQL Server Management Studio 2005 the columns (attributes) of the Northwind sample database's Customers table imported into an Azure CustomerTable. The PartitionKey and RowKey attributes shown as a composite primary key in the bottom of the right pane form a composite entity (object) identifier that must be unique within a table; the RDBMS updates the Timestamp value for newly added or updated entities (rows). Azure considers PartitionKey, RowKey (string), and Timestamp (DataTime) values to be *metadata* and requires these attributes to be present in all tables; metadata values not shown include NextRowKey and NextPartitionKey, which applications use for data paging. The remaining nvarchar(1000) attributes are members of a *property bag*, which have optional user-supplied values. Data types for property bag entities can be Binary, Bool, DateTime, Double, GUID, Int, Long, or UTF-16-encoded String.

Entities may have up to 255 properties (attributes), including the three metadata (system) properties. The total size of an entity's data values is limited to 2MB.

Tables support HTTP GET, PUT, MERGE, POST, and DELETE operations. The base URI for the GET method to return a table from cloud storage is http://*AccountName*.table.core.windows.net/Tables ('*TableName*'). Query expressions return filtered entity sets with URIs, such as http://*AccountName*. table.core.windows.net/*TableName*$filter=*QueryExpression*). ADO.NET Data Services defines the query expression syntax. The .NET Client Library for ADO.NET Data Services (System.Data.Services.Client.dll) lets you use a subset of LINQ Standard Query Operators to generate URIs containing query expressions. The "Using the .NET Client Library with Table Storage" whitepaper (http://bit.ly/I37Ix, http://msdn.microsoft.com/en-us/library/dd179445.aspx) describes the client library classes and querying with LINQ. Queries return a maximum of 1,000 entities; paging with a combination of NextContainerKey and NextRowKey values (called a *continuation token*)enables returning more than 1,000 entities to an application.

Replace AccountName.table.core.windows.net *with* 127.0.0.1:10002/devstoreaccount1 *for Development Storage.*

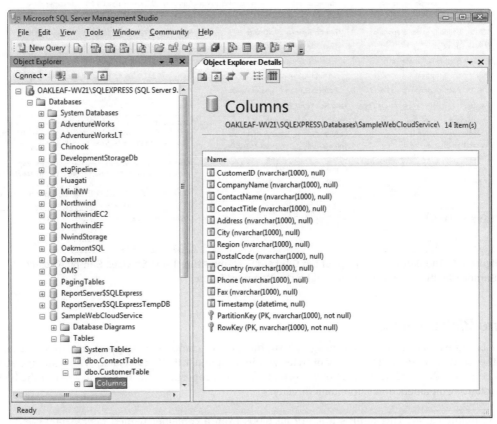

Figure 2-8: SQL Server Management Studio 2005 displaying columns (attributes) created from the Northwind Customers table and saved in an Azure table in Developer Storage.

Figure 2-9 is a screen capture of the OakLeaf Systems Azure Table Services Sample Project's web page displaying in the Development Fabric the first page of 12 CustomerTable entities and user-entered data for a new BOGUS customer entity to be inserted. You can test-drive the web application's production version at http://oakleaf.cloudapp.net/ and learn more about its structure in the later "Web Cloud Services" section and analyze its code in Chapter 7, "Optimizing the Scalability and Performance of Azure Tables."

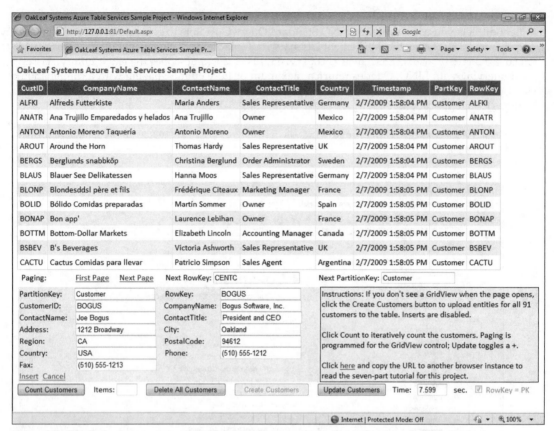

Figure 2-9: The Default.aspx page of the OakLeaf Systems Azure Table Services Sample Project (SampleCloudWebService) running in the Development Fabric.

Azure Blob Services

Blobs store binary data, such as images, XML documents, compressed (zipped or gzipped) files, and other content as an arbitrary array of bytes within a container that's associated with a storage account. A container is a user-defined set of blobs that has only properties, which include a list of the blobs it contains. Containers don't store data directly.

The following GET URI returns a list of all blobs from a container named *ContainerName*: http://*AccountName*.blob.core.windows.net/*ContainerName*$comp=list. Use http://*AccountName* .blob.core.windows.net/*ContainerName*/*BlobName* to read or download a specific blob, including metadata and user-defined properties.

> *Replace* AccountName.blob.core.windows.net *with* 127.0.0.1:10000/devstoreaccount1 *for Development Storage.*

You can upload a maximum of 64MB of data in a Put Blob operation to create a blob. You create blobs larger than 64MB by uploading a sequence of blocks, which are a maximum of 4MB in size, with Put Block operations.

Figure 2-10 shows the default page of the OakLeaf Systems Azure Blob Services Test Harness application after uploading two sets of three bitmap files and four zipped bitmap files from Windows Live SkyDrive plus an HTML file from a web page. HTTP headers, metadata, and user-defined property values provide the GridView control's data source. You can test-drive the AzureBlobTest application at `http://oakleaf2.cloudapp.net/`, learn more about its structure in the later "Web Cloud Services" section, and analyze its code in Chapter 4, "Scaling Azure Table and Blob Storage."

> *Upload Time is the time in seconds to stream the blob data to a filestream in the application; Create Time is the time in seconds to create the blob from the filestream. Upload times with cloud storage are much lower than those shown in Figure 2-10 because of better Internet connectivity between the application and SkyDrive, which might be colocated in a Microsoft data center. Microsoft promises filestream storage in future CTP releases.*

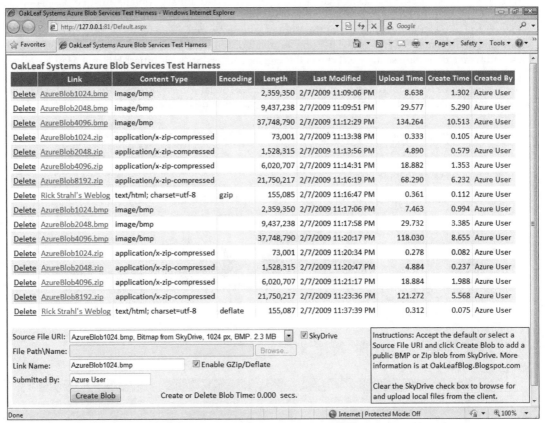

Figure 2-10: The Default.aspx page of the OakLeaf Systems Azure Blog Services Test Harness (AzureBlobTest) running in the Development Fabric.

Azure Queue Services

Azure queues are messages up to 8KB in size that any client or application with access to the storage account can access on a first-in, first-out basis. Azure queues have a REST API that's similar to that for blobs. For example, the following GET URI returns a list of all queues from a storage account named *AccountName*: `http://AccountName.queue.core.windows.net$comp=list`. Use `http://`*AccountName*`.queue.core.windows.net/`*QueueName* to retrieve one or more messages. Specify an optional `numofmessages` parameter to retrieve 2 to a maximum of 32 messages.

Replace AccountName`.queue.core.windows.net` *with* `127.0.0.1:10001/devstoreaccount1` *for Development Storage.*

The `Put Message` operation adds messages to a cloud queue by invoking the POST method with a URI such as `http://`*AccountName*`.queue.core.windows.net/`*QueueName*`/messages` with a Request Body consisting of one or more of the following XML fragments:

```
<QueueMessage>
    <MessageText>message-content</MessageText>
</QueueMessage>
```

where *message-content* is a string that can be UTF-8-encoded. Binary content must be Base64-encoded.

Figure 2-11 shows the default page of the Photo Gallery Azure Queue Services Test Harness application. Queue Name is a numeric date/time equivalent followed by a GUID to automatically sort in ascending creation date sequence. Type is the *message-content* 's Multipart Internet Mail Extensions (MIME) type. ETag is a date/time code that used to support optimistic consistency. You can test-drive the AzureQueueTest application at `http://oakleaf5.cloudapp.net/`, learn more about its structure in the later "Worker Cloud Services" section, and analyze its code in Chapter 8.

Figure 2-11: The Default.aspx page of the Photo Gallery Azure Queue Services Test Harness running in the Development Fabric.

Using Azure Application Templates for Visual Studio 2008

Downloading Windows Azure Tools for Visual Studio adds a Cloud Service template node to the New Project dialog. Double-clicking the Cloud Service node opens the New Cloud Service Project dialog, which enables adding ASP.NET Web Roles, Worker Roles or CGI Web Roles to the project. Figure 2-12 shows Visual Studio 2008 displaying a new project with two WebRoles and two WorkerRoles added. The Windows Azure SDK (July 2009 CTP) added the capability to add more than one role of each type to a Cloud Service. Each role is a separate Windows Azure CPU instance, so the minimum cost to run the project in the cloud would be 4 × $0.12 = $0.48 per hour.

Figure 2-12: Visual Studio 2008's New Project dialog overlaid with the New Cloud Service Project dialog displaying a solution with four Cloud Service roles.

The Live Framework node appears in the New Project dialog's Project Types pane only if you install Windows Azure Tools for Visual Studio, Live Framework SDK, and Live Framework Tools. Live Framework templates are Mesh-Enabled Web Application and Silverlight Mesh-Enabled Web Application.

Clicking OK twice with the roles shown in Figure 2-12 opens a new solution with WebRole and Worker-Role projects in Solution Explorer, as shown in Figure 2-13.

The solution's Roles node contains items that point to each WebRole project, which provides the ASP.NET UI for the application, and each WorkerRole for computing operations that don't require a UI or use the WebRole's ASP.NET pages as its UI.

References for Cloud Service projects include the `Microsoft.ServiceHosting.ServiceRuntime` namespace, which contains the classes listed in the following table:

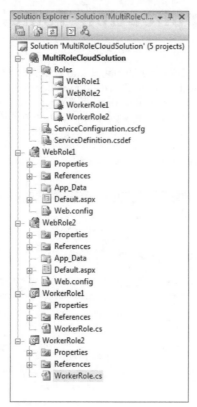

Figure 2-13: Solution Explorer
displaying the five projects added by
two WebRoles and two
WorkerRoles.

Class or Enum	Description of Class or Enumeration
RoleEntryPoint	Provides methods to manage the initialization, starting, and stopping of a service, as well as for monitoring the health of the service
RoleException	Raises an error when an invalid operation occurs within a role
RoleManager	Provides methods to log messages and raise alerts, retrieve service configuration settings, and return the location of the local storage resource
RoleStatus	An enumeration providing information about the current status of a role: Healthy, NonExistent, Started, Starting, Stopped, Stopping, or Unhealthy

Web Cloud Services and Client Wrapper Class Libraries

Projects that use the WebRole template provide an ASP.NET Default.aspx web page as the starting point for a default cloud application UI. Figure 2-14 shows the SampleWebCloudService project, which has a single WebRole project, open in VS 2008.

This service incorporates a Common class library from the HelloFabric sample application to assist in logging application problems. Application logs are the only practical means of debugging applications running in the Cloud Fabric. To read logs, you must copy them to blobs with a feature provided by the Developer portal.

The StorageClient sample project includes the sample StorageClient class library that provides, in conjunction with the .NET Client Library for ADO.NET Data Services, Microsoft .NET wrapper classes for HTTP operations on Azure Blob, Queue, and Table Storage Services. The sample project also includes a console application that lets you test the library's capabilities. The C# console application runs in the Development Fabric with Development Storage. The WebCloudService project uses the StorageClient's table-related classes.

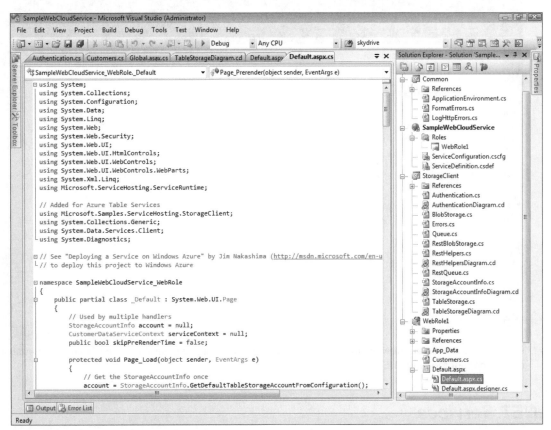

Figure 2-14: VS 2008 displaying the two default projects for a Web Cloud Service and the Common and StorageClient wrapper class libraries.

Taking Advantage of Auxiliary Cloud Services

The Windows Azure Platform incorporates three sets of auxiliary services .NET Services, SQL Azure Database, and Live Services. Early CTPs of .NET Services and SQL Azure Database (SADB) required an invitation code, which was valid for both services

The requirement for an invitation for a .NET Services account was lifted as of CTP 3, so go to the .NET Services My Subscriptions page at `http://bit.ly/e3knd (https://portal.ex.azure.microsoft.com/View.aspx)`, click the Sign Up link to open the Create Solution page, assign a unique Solution Name (see Figure 2-15), click the Create Solution button, and you're good to go with .NET Services and SQL Azure Database.

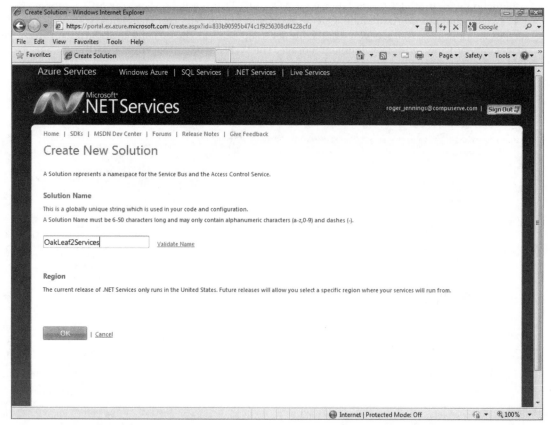

Figure 2-15: This Create New Solution page for .NET Services lets you create a service "solution" containing one or more of the three .NET Services.

.NET Services

Microsoft .NET Services are a set of scalable, developer-oriented services that are hosted by Windows Azure alongside Azure Storage Services in Microsoft data centers. .NET Services provide key infrastructure components for cloud-based Web and Worker applications.

.NET Access Control, Service Bus, and Workflow services take advantage of Web-standard Atom, AtomPub, SOAP, WS-*, and HTTP protocols, so any application that has reliable Internet access can use them and they're compatible with other popular programming languages, such as Java and Ruby. The MSDN Developer Center's home page for .NET Services is `http://bit.ly/bhAKT` (`http://msdn.microsoft.com/en-us/azure/netservices.aspx`.) The .NET Services – Technical Discussions Forum is at `http://bit.ly/V9TOj` (`http://social.msdn.microsoft.com/Forums/en-US/netservices/threads/`.)

The Microsoft .NET Services SDK (March 2009 CTP) provides class libraries, samples, and documentation for building connected applications with the .NET platform. You can download Java and Ruby .NET Services SDKs in addition to the .NET version from the .NET Services Developer Center page.

Access Control Services

Microsoft claims that Access Control Services (ACS) "provide an easy way to control web applications and services while integrating with standards-based identity providers, including enterprise directories and web identity systems such as Windows Live ID." Service Bus Services rely on a claims-based identity model for user authentication and role-based access control. The advantage of ACS is that you can write a set of declarative rules that can transform incoming security claims into a claims-based, federated identity to minimize developer effort. ACS relies on well-known user account stores, such as Live ID, Active Directory, or other stores that support Atom, AtomPub, SOAP or WS-*, and HTTP protocols.

The Windows Azure Platform Portal provides the administrative UI for ACS. The .NET Access Control Service page at `http://bit.ly/Co8NG` (`www.microsoft.com/azure/accesscontrol.mspx`) provides links to additional ACS resources.

You can learn more about ACS from these documents:

❑ "Microsoft .NET Access Control Service" help topic of the MSDN Library at `http://bit.ly/17IjY` (`http://go.microsoft.com/fwlink/?LinkID=131222`.)

❑ The Introduction to Microsoft .NET Access Control.docx file and "A Developer's Guide to the Microsoft .NET Access Control Service" from the Download White Papers link on `http://bit.ly/bhAKT` (`http://msdn.microsoft.com/en-us/azure/netservices.aspx`.)

Chapter 6, "Authenticating and Authorizing Service Users," includes sections that describe how to secure a WebRole application and Chapter 9, "Authenticating Users with .NET Access Control Services" is devoted to ACS.

Service Bus

Microsoft states that the .NET Service Bus (SB), which was originally known as *BizTalk Services*, "makes it easy to connect applications together over the Internet. Services that register on the Bus can easily be discovered and accessed, across any network topology." SB implements that Enterprise Service Bus (ESB) application pattern with Windows Communication Foundation (WCF). However, it reduces the programming effort ordinarily required to configure and code SaaS projects that use WCF to create bidirectional connectivity between the cloud and on-premises applications. When a new service connects to the bus all other applications and services on the bus can connect with it, even if they could not connect directly with one another. SBS provides a centralized and load-balanced relay service that supports industry-standard transport protocols and web services standards, including SOAP, SOAP, and WS-*.

The .NET Services SDK (March 2009 CTP) added Service Bus Queues (SBQs) and Routers (SBRs), which are discoverable, persisted SB objects that are independent of listeners' lifetimes. Like the other .NET Services, the basic API takes advantage of HTTP GET and POST methods and AtomPub extensions to define SBQs, which are a lightweight version of Queue Storage Services. SBRs forward messages from one or more publishers to one or more subscribers to create a pub/sub messaging model with optional multicasting to all subscribers. Publishers send messages using HTTP, HTTPS, or the SB's "NetOneway" protocol as plain HTTP messages or SOAP 1.1/1.2 envelopes. Subscribers can subscribe to a Router either using a NetOnewayBinding listener or listen to any publicly reachable HTTP endpoint. Chapter 11, "Exploring .NET Workflow Services and Service Bus Queues and Routers" provides detailed information about and sample programs for SBQs and SBRs.

Following are additional sources of information about SBS:

❑   "Microsoft .NET Service Bus" help topic of the MSDN Library at http://bit.ly/9timH (http://msdn.microsoft.com/en-us/library/dd129877.aspx).

❑   The Introduction to Microsoft .NET Service Bus.docx file and "A Developer's Guide to the Microsoft .NET Service Bus" from the Download White Papers link on http://bit.ly/bhAKT (http://msdn.microsoft.com/en-us/azure/netservices.aspx).

Chapter 10, "Interconnecting Services with the .NET Service Bus" covers SBS exclusively.

Workflow Services

Microsoft describes the .NET Workflow Services (WFS) as "a high-scale host for running workflows in the cloud." WFS orchestrates the sending, receiving, and manipulating of HTTP and Service Bus messages. It also provides hosted tools to deploy, manage, and track the execution of workflow instances, as well as a group of management APIs. You can construct workflows declaratively with WFS and the Visual Studio 2008 Workflow Designer.

You can learn more about WFS from these documents:

❑   "Microsoft .NET Workflow Service" help topic of the MSDN Library at http://bit.ly/3gaCF (http://msdn.microsoft.com/en-us/library/dd129879.aspx).

❑   The Introduction to Microsoft .NET Workflow Service.docx file and "A Developer's Guide to the Microsoft .NET Workflow Service" from the Download White Papers link on http://bit.ly/bhAKT (http://msdn.microsoft.com/en-us/azure/netservices.aspx.)

The electronic version of Chapter 11 (available from Wrox Website for this book, at www.wrox.com) will detail the development of a simple Cloud Sequential Workflow solution after .NET 4 releases to manufacturing and the .NET Services team provides a CTP with the new Workflow runtime implemented.

SQL Azure

SQL Services are highly scalable, on-demand relational database management, business intelligence (BI), and reporting utility services based provided by SQL Server 2008 and later. SQL Server Integration Services (SSIS), SQL Analysis Services (SSAS) and Reporting Services (SSRS) were scheduled for implementation in 2010 when this book was written.

SQL Data Services and SQL Azure Database (SADB)

SQL Azure Database (SADB) was originally called SQL Server Data Services (SSDS) when Microsoft announced SSDS as a standalone Database as a Service (DaaS) at the MIX08 conference in early 2008.

SSDS's initial architecture implemented schemaless EAV tables similar to Azure's Table Services in a non-relational Authority, Container, Entity (ACE) model. The SSDS team believed that potential Azure adopters wanted the simplicity of the EAV model rather than the relational features of SQL Server tables and other database objects. Microsoft had trumpeted the capability to leverage .NET and Visual Studio skills with the Windows Azure Platform. Therefore, .NET developers testing SSDS wanted a fully scalable, highly available version of SQL Server for the cloud.

In advance of Microsoft's Professional Developers Conference (PDC) in late October 2008, Amazon Web Services announced on September 20, 2008 support by Elastic Computing Cloud (EC2) for Windows Server 2003 R2 and the Express and Standard editions of SQL Server 2005 (`http://bit.ly/yXPPi`.) This new offering resulted in an even greater hue and cry by.NET developers for "SQL Server in the cloud" with full support for Transact-SQL and SQL Server datatypes.

The SSDS team ultimately saw the error of their ways and decided in early 2008 to abandon schemaless databases and the EAV model. First news about the change in direction came at the MSDN Developer Conference's visit to San Francisco on February 23, 2009 in conjunction with 1105 Media's Visual Studio Live! conference at the Hyatt Regency (see "A Mid-Course Correction for SQL Azure Database" at `http://bit.ly/85YOa`, `http://oakleafblog.blogspot.com/2009/02/mid-course-correction-for-sql-data.html`.) The newly named SQL Azure Database (SADB) team revealed more SADB details in March 2009 with presentations at MIX '09 and in May at Tech*Ed 2009 (see "Ten Slides from the 'What's New in Microsoft SQL Azure Database' (DAT202) Tech*Ed 2009 Session" at `http://bit.ly/nPLUB`, `http://oakleafblog.blogspot.com/2009/05/ten-slides-from-whats-new-in-microsoft.html`.)

According to Microsoft SADB evangelist David Robinson's May 6, 2009 presentation to Microsoft's Enterprise Developer and Solutions Conference, SADB will offer the following SQL Server features:

❑ Tables, indexes, and views

❑ Stored procedures and triggers

❑ Constraints

❑ Table variables

❑ Session temporary tables (#t)

The following features will be out-of-scope for v1:

❑ Distributed transactions

❑ Distributed queries

❑ CLR support

❑ Service Broker

❑ Spatial data types

❑ Physical server access or catalog DDL and views

David Robinson is this book's technical editor.

SADB hadn't been released as a public CTP when this book went to press, so the two SADB chapters are available for download from the book's page at `www.wrox.com`: Chapter 12, "Managing SQL Azure Accounts, Databases, and DataHubs" and Chapter 13, "Exploiting SQL Azure Database' Relational Features."

Obtaining an SADB v1 Private CTP Account

To obtain an invitation to the SADB v1 private CTP, click the Join the Mailing List link (`http://bit.ly/YDtQJ`, `go.microsoft.com/fwlink/?LinkID=149681&clcid=0x09`) on the SADB SQL Azure Database (SADB) page (`http://bit.ly/VdpIn`, `http://msdn.microsoft.com/en-us/sqlserver/dataservices/default.aspx`), which takes you to a Microsoft Connect page, and complete the survey. If you completed a survey for an SSDS account with your currently active Windows Live ID, the original survey (read-only) opens; in this case, the SADB team states that you'll receive an invitation automatically.

   SSDS beta accounts aren't valid for SADB v1 databases.

Deploying Applications and Services to the Azure Cloud

One of the primary benefits of the Windows Azure Platform is the ease of deployment of applications you create with the Development Storage and Fabric services to Azure (cloud) services. Most cloud applications and services will require access to data, persisted state, or both as tables, blobs, or queues. Most highly scalable applications will require similarly scalable data.

When you create a data-intensive application, it's likely that your application will include code to enable importing data from traditional sources, such as on-premises or online databases, image files, web pages, productivity application documents, or all of these data types, to Azure Storage Services. For example, the OakLeaf Systems Azure Blob Services Test Harness sample application contains code to import sets of specific image (*.bmp) and archive (*.zip) files stored in Windows Live SkyDrive public folders or any file from the client's file system to Azure Blobs.

   The OakLeaf Systems Azure Table Services Sample Project contains object initialization code to generate entities that emulate the Northwind Customers table's records.

Azure Storage Services

Changing from Development to Azure cloud storage requires only modifying the ServiceConfiguration .cscfg to change the `AccountName` value to the cloud storage project name and change the `BlogStorageEndpoint, QueueStorageEndpoint, TableStorageEndpoing` or all three values to `http://blob.core.windows.net, http://queue.core.windows.net,` or `http://table.core.windows.net,` as illustrated in the earlier "Azure Service Definition and Service Configuration Files" section. An original and at least two copies of all data stored in the cloud assure data reliability and continuity.

   The preceding paragraph assumes that your application can upload appropriate data to or generate data in the cloud.

Publishing Projects to the Azure Services Developer Portal

When you create a new hosting project in the online Windows Azure Development Portal, Windows Azure assigns it a GUID as a Private Deployment ID. Prior to the May 2009 CTP, Windows Azure also assigned a unique 16-character hexadecimal Application ID, such as 000000004C002F22. Previously, you would find that value in the Live Services and Active Directory Federation section of the Summary page for your hosted project, as shown in Figure 2-16.

Windows Azure runs hosted projects in Staging mode for private testing with a GUID as part of the IP and lets you migrate a staged project to Production mode with a single click, as described in the next section. This migration technique supports Azure's rolling upgrade process, which eliminates downtime when repairing or upgrading applications or services if you have more than one instance available.

Figure 2-16: An early version of the Azure Services Developer Portal's Summary page for a hosted project displayed the Application ID number.

You could synchronize your Visual Studio development project with the live version by opening the Properties window for the master project node and selecting the Portal Provisioning page to expose the Application ID text box. You could copy the ID value from the portal page and paste it to the Portal properties page's text box, as shown in Figure 2-17. When this book was written, the Azure Team was planning a workaround to provide a substitute for the Application ID link between VS 2008 and the Azure cloud instance.

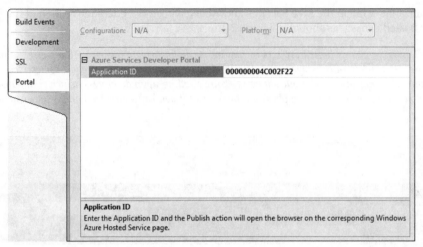

Figure 2-17: The Application ID from the Azure Services Developer Portal's Summary page pasted into the project's Portal properties page's Application ID page.

The following table describes the purpose of the three other properties pages:

Page	Purpose
Build Events	Enables specifying Azure-specific pre-build and post-build events, and when to run the post-build event
Development	Lets you specify the Development Storage database name and if you want to start Development Storage Services when you run the application from Visual Studio
SSL	Enables selecting Secure Sockets Layer (SSL) for Development Storage and publishing operations

Publishing the Project to the Cloud Fabric

Publishing the project requires copying a *package* (*ProjectName*.cspkg) and a configuration file (*ServiceConfiguration.cscfg) to your Windows Azure instance. A *package* for the cloud consists of a zipped and encrypted version of the development package file (*.csx) created when you run the project in the Development Fabric.

With the Application ID pasted into the Portal properties page, right-clicking the master project node and choosing Publish opens an Explorer window for the project's . . . \bin\Debug\Publish folder that displays the *ProjectName*.cspkg and ServiceConfiguration.cscfg files, and Windows Azure's Staging Deployment page (see Figure 2-18).

You can use the same label for the Staging and Production versions of a project, but different labels are recommended for clarity.

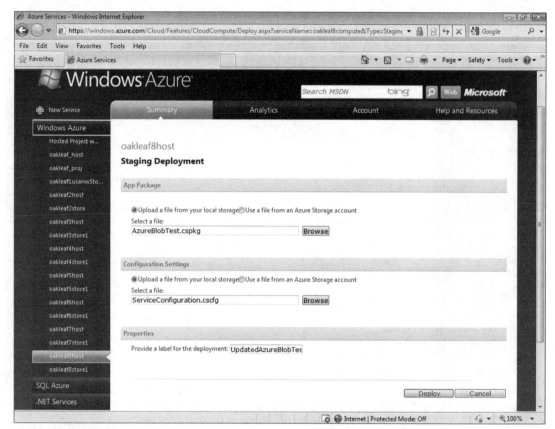

Figure 2-18: Deploying a hosted Azure project from the Development Fabric to the Cloud Fabric's Staging service requires specifying package and configuration files, typing a label for the project, and clicking the Deploy button.

After a few minutes or longer, depending on your project's package size and Internet connectivity, the Staging WebRole will be Allocated. Click Run to place the project in the Started mode. (see Figure 2-19).

Clicking Configure lets you edit the ServiceConfiguration.cscfg file or import a replacement. For example, you can increase or decrease the number of instances deployed by changing the Instance count *value. Microsoft recommends running two instances of your projects to assure maximum availability, even with light traffic.*

Figure 2-19: After deploying your project to the Staging service, click Run to place it in the Started role and then click the Web Site URL link to test it under the Windows OS operating system.

Click Run to instantiate the project in Staging mode, which starts an Initializing WebRole, and after a minute or two, place the Staging project in the Started WebRole. Click the Staging Private Web Site URL link to test the WebRole in your browser (see Figure 2-20).

Exchange the Staging for the Production version by clicking the button between the two package icons and clicking OK when you're asked "Are you sure you want to swap with the production deployment?"

Suspend Staging instances after placing them in production to avoid incurring running time charges on both Staging and Production instances when Microsoft releases Windows Azure.

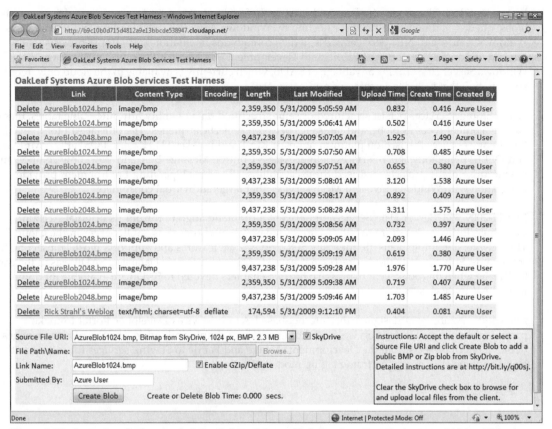

	Link	Content Type	Encoding	Length	Last Modified	Upload Time	Create Time	Created By
Delete	AzureBlob1024.bmp	image/bmp		2,359,350	5/31/2009 5:05:59 AM	0.832	0.416	Azure User
Delete	AzureBlob1024.bmp	image/bmp		2,359,350	5/31/2009 5:06:41 AM	0.502	0.416	Azure User
Delete	AzureBlob2048.bmp	image/bmp		9,437,238	5/31/2009 5:07:05 AM	1.925	1.490	Azure User
Delete	AzureBlob1024.bmp	image/bmp		2,359,350	5/31/2009 5:07:50 AM	0.708	0.485	Azure User
Delete	AzureBlob1024.bmp	image/bmp		2,359,350	5/31/2009 5:07:51 AM	0.655	0.380	Azure User
Delete	AzureBlob2048.bmp	image/bmp		9,437,238	5/31/2009 5:08:01 AM	3.120	1.538	Azure User
Delete	AzureBlob1024.bmp	image/bmp		2,359,350	5/31/2009 5:08:17 AM	0.892	0.409	Azure User
Delete	AzureBlob2048.bmp	image/bmp		9,437,238	5/31/2009 5:08:28 AM	3.311	1.575	Azure User
Delete	AzureBlob1024.bmp	image/bmp		2,359,350	5/31/2009 5:08:56 AM	0.732	0.397	Azure User
Delete	AzureBlob2048.bmp	image/bmp		9,437,238	5/31/2009 5:09:05 AM	2.093	1.446	Azure User
Delete	AzureBlob1024.bmp	image/bmp		2,359,350	5/31/2009 5:09:19 AM	0.619	0.380	Azure User
Delete	AzureBlob2048.bmp	image/bmp		9,437,238	5/31/2009 5:09:28 AM	1.976	1.770	Azure User
Delete	AzureBlob1024.bmp	image/bmp		2,359,350	5/31/2009 5:09:38 AM	0.719	0.407	Azure User
Delete	AzureBlob2048.bmp	image/bmp		9,437,238	5/31/2009 5:09:46 AM	1.703	1.485	Azure User
Delete	Rick Strahl's Weblog	text/html; charset=utf-8	deflate	174,594	5/31/2009 9:12:10 PM	0.404	0.081	Azure User

Figure 2-20: A staging deployment of the OakLeaf Azure Blob Services Test Project at a hidden URL of http://b9c10b0d715d4812a9e13bbcde538947.cloudapp.net/.

Summary

Microsoft introduced in late October 2008 the Windows Azure cloud operating system and other services provided by the Windows Azure Platform at the Professional Developers Conference (PDC) 2008. Windows Azure, which runs in Microsoft's rapidly expanding collection of data centers, competes directly with Amazon Web Services and the Google App Engine. The Azure team designed the systems and APIs to leverage .NET developers experience with C#, VB, and Visual Studio 2008 and later.

Windows Azure was in a private Community Technical Preview stage when this book was written, so those wanting access to Microsoft's cloud operating system required GUID tokens or invitation codes that were redeemable for Azure Hosted Projects, Azure Storage Projects, .NET Services, SQL Azure Database, or Windows Live Services. The Byzantine process for obtaining most Azure tokens starts at Microsoft Connect, but often requires intervention by Microsoft representative in Windows Azure forums. Windows Live ID provides authentication and authorization of Azure CTP users.

If you don't have the required tokens and invitations for cloud computing, you can test drive projects, blobs, queues, and tables destined for hosting by Windows Azure by downloading and installing the Windows Azure and .NET Services SDKs, which contain documentation and sample projects that you can run under the Development Fabric with Development Storage on a PC running Windows Vista or Windows Server 2008. Taking advantage of SADB, which currently is available in the cloud only, requires an invitation that includes a username and password.

Azure Storage Services persist structured or semi-structured data as entity-attribute-value tables, files of varying content types as blobs, and messages between projects as queues. The official API for managing the storage services is based on platform-agnostic REST and invokes HTTP GET, POST, PUT, MERGE, and DELETE methods. .NET Services deliver Access Control, Message Bus, and Workflow components to enterprise-grade projects that need these capabilities. The Live Operating Environment provides integration with Windows Live and Mesh services that target individual consumers.

In mid-2009 SQL Server Data Services underwent a dramatic migration from its original Account, Container, Entity architecture to SQL Azure Database v1, also known as "SQL Server in the Cloud." The new version implements all but a few SQL Server 2008 features and supports most Transact-SQL commands. Subsequently the Azure Team renamed SDS as SQL Server Database. SADB was in the early CTP stage when this book went to press, so the two chapters devoted to SADB are available for download from the Wrox web site.

Microsoft's Azure team designed the Internet-based Azure Services Developer Portal to make provisioning of new Hosted Services and Storage Projects simple and quick. The Portal also manages deployment of projects from the Development Storage and Fabric to Staging services for testing in the cloud and one-click migration from Staging mode to Production.

3

Analyzing the Windows Azure Operating System

Windows Azure is a "cloud layer" operating system that runs on thousands of Windows Server 2008 physical instances in Microsoft data centers. It's not required that you know how the Azure operating system (OS) works to develop and deploy applications or services to the Windows Azure Platform. However, a basic understanding of Windows Azure's architecture can aid you in designing complex applications that take advantage of OS features to achieve maximum performance, scalability, and security.

A Quick Tour of the Windows Azure OS

The data center's physical servers run an advanced, custom version of Microsoft's Hyper-V hypervisor technology that virtualizes the physical instances to deliver a clustered runtime fabric, called the Azure Fabric Controller (FC), which handles application/service deployment, load balancing, OS/data replication, and resource management. The FC deploys projects, adds instances automatically to meet demand, manages project software upgrades, and handles server failures to maintain project availability.

> *Early Azure CTPs don't implement dynamic service instance management in response to changes in demand. You specify the number of instances in the ServiceConfiguration.cscfg file and then redeploy the modified file to the project in the Azure Service Portal.*

The host virtual machine (host VM) controls access to the hardware of the physical server and supports multiple guest VMs in a multitenanted environment. Guest VMs (tenants) access physical server resources through the host VM. Early Community Technical Previews (CTPs) allocated to each guest VM the resources described in the following table:

> *The later "Virtualizing Windows Servers" section describes Windows Azure's virtualization process in greater detail.*

Resource Description	Resource Allocation
Host and guest operating system	64-bit Windows Server 2008
Central processing unit	1.5–1.7 GHz, 1 core x64 equivalent
RAM	1.7GB
Network connectivity	100Mbs
Transient local storage	250GB (not persistent)
Windows Azure Storage	50GB (persistent and replicated)

Roles are runnable components of an application; role instances run on the fabric's nodes and channels connect roles. WebRole instances accept HTTP or HTTPS requests via Internet Information Services (IIS) 7 and respond with an ASP.NET, ASP.NET MVC, or Silverlight UI. WorkerRoles provide batch computing services in response to request messages received from WebRoles or .NET Services in Azure Queues. Each WebRole or WorkerRole is assigned to its own guest VM and server core to isolate the tenant's data, as shown in Figure 3-1.

WorkerRoles can't accept inbound connections from external networks so they must use Azure Queues to communicate with WebRoles or .NET Services. WorkerRoles can send outbound messages on the external network.

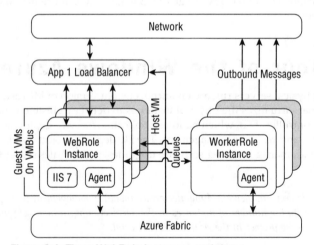

Figure 3-1: Three WebRole instances and three WorkerRole instances deployed by Azure to two physical servers with FC agents to manage load balancing for each set of instances.

According to Erick Smith's "Under the Hood: Inside the Cloud Computing Hosting Environment" (ES19) presentation to the Microsoft Professional Developer Conference (PDC) 2009 (http://bit.ly/16xSNH, http://channel9.msdn.com/pdc2008/ES19/), the FC maintains a graph of the inventory of physical and virtual machines, load balancers, routers, and switches it manages in a Microsoft data center. Edges of the graph are interconnections of various types; for example, network, serial, and power cables. The developer specifies with a declarative service model the topology of the service — the number and connectivity of roles, the attributes and locations of the various hardware components, as well as the quantity of fault/update domains and maximum instances of each role required. Smith says, "The FC manages the service lifecycle from the bare metal." Windows Azure's management features are similar to those employed by the Google App Engine (GAE) for its web applications and offered by RightScale for Amazon Web Services (AWS); as noted in earlier chapters, GAE and AWS are Azure's primary competitors.

> *Azure CTP's limit projects to a maximum of 2,000 runtime instance-hours with up to eight instances of a single production application as well as one Web and, optionally, one WorkerRole in a single fault and update domain. Testers can request exemptions from these limits by sending mail to* azquotas@microsoft.com.

Early CTPs limited applications to running managed .NET 3.5 code under a custom version of ASP.NET's medium trust Code Access Security (CAS). Microsoft promises future support for Python, Ruby, PHP, native code, and Eclipse tools. The May 2009 CTP introduced the option to run applications in full trust.

Azure fault domains for role instances represent a single point of failure, such as a rack; update domains for performing rolling software upgrades; or patches run across multiple fault domains (see Figure 3-2). Ultimately, you'll be able to specify your Service Model with Oslo's domain-specific language tools and store the model in the Oslo repository.

> *The initial CTP released at PDC 2008 didn't expose the Service Model; instead the Windows Azure Tools for Microsoft Visual Studio add-in contributes common Azure application-role templates for WebRole, WorkerRole, and Workflow, as described in Chapter 2.*

The Lifecycle of a Windows Azure Service

The Windows Azure infrastructure consists of physical nodes provided by individual servers or virtual machines (VMs) running on servers. Figure 3-3 shows the relationships between physical nodes and logical roles, and the services they host.

> *Figures 3-3 through 3-5 are based on PDC 2008's "Under the Hood: Inside the Cloud Computing Hosting Environment" session.*

Constraints on logical nodes, roles, and services include

- ❏ Only roles from a single service can be assigned to a node.
- ❏ Only a single instance of a role can be assigned to a node.
- ❏ A node must contain a compatible hosting environment.
- ❏ A node must have enough resources available to run a logical service.
- ❏ Nodes for a service must be located in an appropriate fault domain.
- ❏ Nodes must be healthy to host logical services.

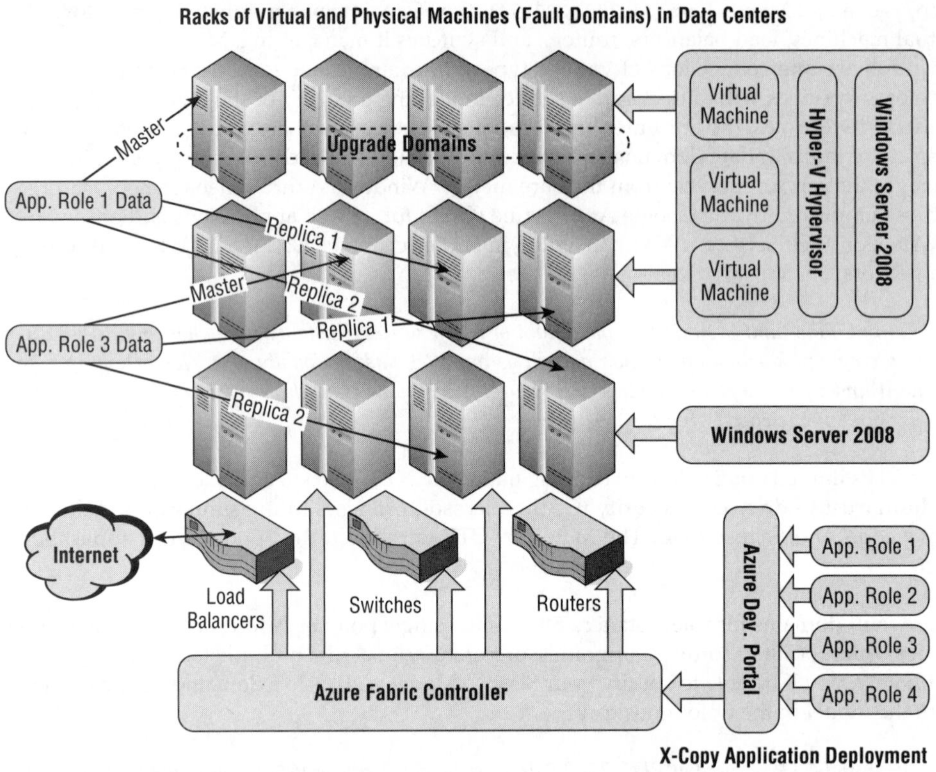

Racks of Virtual and Physical Machines (Fault Domains) in Data Centers

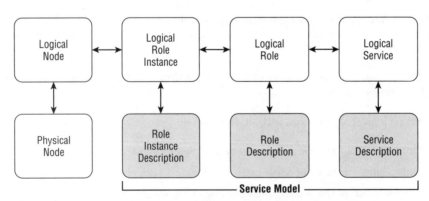

Figure 3-2: Fault domains consist of physical servers that share common hardware, such as a rack of servers. Azure stores a master and a minimum of two replica copies of all data for reliability. Upgrade domains consist of a group of servers from multiple fault domains.

Figure 3-3: The data structures that the FC uses to create a logical node, logical role instance, logical role, and logical service on a virtual physical node. The Service Model contributes the descriptions to the process.

Creating the Host VM and the First Guest VM on a Physical Server

When you add a Production instance of a new project and no uncommitted guest VMs are available to run its role(s), the Azure FC Agent boots an available physical server by downloading a maintenance operating system (MOS), which connects to the FC. The FC instructs the MOS's agent to create a partition for the host OS, load a virtual hard disk (VHD) OS, and restart the physical server. On initial startup, the server boots from the VHD OS, loads a guest OS image for the first guest VM, creates a copy of the guest OS image to add more guest VMs, and deploys a Customer Role to the first guest VM. The FC Agent then configures the infrastructure for the server and its VMs, such as load balancers, external (dedicated) and internal (virtual) IP addresses, switches, and routers. Redundant network components provide high reliability and availability.

> *The process of adding new VMs is wrapped in a transaction. If any operation in the process fails, all previous operations are rolled back. According to the Azure Team, the FC is implemented "mostly by managed code."*

Adding Guest VMs to a Host VM

If the new project's ServiceConfiguration.cscfg file's `<Instances count="n">` element has a number greater than 1 or the FC Agent has detected an impending inability of existing instances to handle increasing load, the FC Agent notifies the AFC to add another guest VM. The host VM copies the local guest OS image to create a new guest VM, which receives the appropriate Customer Role. The FC Agent repeats the process of configuring the infrastructure for new VMs. New guest VMs for a particular Customer Role ordinarily are added to physical servers in different Fault Domains.

> *All provisioning and deprovisioning operations occur in parallel throughout the data center to enable rapid response to demand fluctuations, hardware failures, or both. Early CTPs don't automate dynamic VM allocation and logical role instance addition or deletion. Future releases will support specifying minimum and maximum numbers for role instances.*

Maintaining Role Instance Health

The FC is responsible for keeping services running by inspecting their state and adding or removing role instances. Following are the primary FC responsibilities for maintaining service availability:

- ❏ The FC maintains a state machine for each node.
- ❏ A Role Instance Description determines a node's *goal state*.
- ❏ Internal or external events cause nodes to move to a different state.
- ❏ The FC maintains a cache of last state of each node.
- ❏ Load balancers probe the nodes to determine that each is operable and reports failures to the FC.
- ❏ The FC Agent reconciles the cached and actual state in response to heartbeat events.
- ❏ If the actual and goal states differ, on heartbeat events the FC Agent attempts to move the node closer to its goal state.
- ❏ The FC detects when the node reaches its goal state.

❑   If a failed node goes offline, the FC attempts to recover it.

❑   If the FC can't recover a failed node, it finds or creates a suitable replacement on other hardware and notifies other role instances of the configuration change.

Service state isn't maintained when a node fails. If saving the state of a failed logical role instance is important, your application should periodically persist the state, such as a cache, to Azure tables or blobs.

Upgrading Service Software and Windows Azure

Rolling service software upgrades and patches to the Windows Azure OS take place within transactions on running services in one Upgrade Domain at a time. The FC deploys resources to all nodes of the Upgrade Domain in parallel, so all updated services in the Upgrade Domain go offline temporarily during the upgrade while new logical role instances bind to physical nodes. The number of upgrade domains determines the service loss percentage during the upgrade, which usually occurs very quickly. Minimizing the upgrade's performance impact requires a substantial number of Upgrade Domains; this implies many role instances for each service.

Service software upgrades are automatic when you move the upgraded project from Staging to Production; some server upgrades and patches require intervention by data center personnel.

Securing and Isolating Services and Data

In the late 1990s and even into the first five years or so of the twenty-first century, enterprise IT departments had the power to deny ordinary workers access to the Internet from the organizations' networks. In many cases the restriction even applied to top management. IT managers simply said that the threat to network security and data privacy presented an outrageous risk to the organizations' survival. Executive managers, having witnessed repeated compromise of sensitive data by hackers, accepted the IT gurus' judgment at face value. Branch offices connected to central data centers by T-1 or slower lines leased from telcos at considerable expense. Mobile users were more hampered by the speed limitations of dial-up connections to branch or home offices. IT departments' focus was on *perimeter security* to "keep the bad guys out" of the corporate network by using stringent Network Access Control (NAC) parameters. Preventing office workers from connecting to the Internet with the organization's intranet led to many surreptitious dial-up connections and network hacks that managed to stay below the IT departments' radar for long periods.

According to Forrester Research, "NAC is a mix of hardware and software technology that dynamically controls client system access to networks based on their compliance with policy."

The need to accommodate an increasingly mobile sales force, support telecommuting employees, and acquiesce to on-premises workers' demands for high-speed Internet access to business-related information gradually overcame IT departments' nay-saying. Firewalls that permitted users and their applications to connect to the Internet with a limited number of open TCP ports provided the illusion of security to IT and corporate management. Firewalls enabled SaaS customer relationship management (CRM) applications, such as Salesforce.com, and third-party SOAP-based web services to thrive. Today very few sizable organizations exist whose internal network isn't connected, knowingly or unwittingly, to the Internet.

Reliance on Cloud-Computing Vendors' Security Claims

Surveys of potential cloud-computing adopters indicate that lack of security is a primary deterrent to moving at least a part of an organizations' computing and data storage operations to the cloud. The February 2009 "Above the Clouds: A Berkeley View of Cloud Computing" whitepaper by a team from the University of California – Berkeley's Reliable Adaptive Distributed (RAD) Systems Laboratory (`http://bit.ly/iSOer`, `http://d1smfj0g31qzek.cloudfront.net/abovetheclouds.pdf`) list the following as the first three of the "Top 10 Obstacles for Growth of Cloud Computing":

1. Availability of Service

2. Data Lock-In

3. Data Confidentiality and Auditability

Most IT departments currently view that allowing services to be delivered by third parties means they lose control over how data is secured, audited, and maintained and they can't enforce what they can't control. However, James Niccolai of IDG News Service writes in a "Cloud security fears are overblown, some say" article of February 19, 2009 (`http://bit.ly/C12l1`, `http://oakleafblog.blogspot.com/2009/02/security-issues-receive-main-focus-at.html`):

> It may sound like heresy to say it, but it's possible to worry a little too much about security in cloud computing environments, speakers at IDC's Cloud Computing Forum said on Wednesday.
>
> Security is the No. 1 concern cited by IT managers when they think about cloud deployments, followed by performance, availability, and the ability to integrate cloud services with in-house IT, according to IDC's research.
>
> "I think a lot of security objections to the cloud are emotional in nature, it's reflexive," said Joseph Tobolski, director for cloud computing at Accenture, [a global management consulting, technology services and outsourcing company]. "Some people create a list of requirements for security in the cloud that they don't even have for their own data center."

The key to acceptance of third-party security, auditing, and maintenance of customers' data in the cloud is *transparency*. Cloud-computing vendors, such as Microsoft, must fully detail their security-related practices and incorporate guaranteed levels of data security, auditing, availability, and reliability in their service-level agreements (SLAs.)

Microsoft's Charlie McNerney announced that "Microsoft's cloud infrastructure achieved both Statement of Auditing Standards (SAS) 70 Type I and Type II attestations and ISO/IEC 27001:2005 certification" for their data centers in his Securing Microsoft's Cloud Infrastructure post of 5/27/2009 (`http://bit.ly/VeAWD`, `http://blogs.technet.com/gfs/archive/2009/05/27/securing-microsoft-s-cloud-infrastructure.aspx`). Chapter 5, "Minimizing Risk When Moving To Azure Cloud Services," describes SAS 70 and ISO/IEC 27001:2005 requirements and the significance of the attestations and certifications.

Microsoft announced its SLA for Windows Azure, SQL Azure and .NET Services in mid-July 2009 (`http://bit.ly/16lKsY`, www.microsoft.com/azure/pricing.mspx)

Isolating Private Data of Multiple Tenants

Security for applications' data against access by unauthorized users from other organizations using the same service is one of the most important incentives for adopting virtualization in cloud computing by independent software vendors (ISVs). Windows Azure implements some *multitenant computing* also called *multitenancy* features. Wikipedia describes the features as follows (`http://bit.ly/bbgGH,` `http://en.wikipedia.org/wiki/Multi-tenant`):

> Multitenancy refers to a principle in software architecture where a single instance of the software runs on a software-as-a-service (SaaS) vendor's servers, serving multiple client organizations (tenants). Multitenancy is contrasted with a multi-instance architecture where separate software instances (or hardware systems) are set up for different client organizations. With a multitenant architecture, a software application is designed to virtually partition its data and configuration so that each client organization works with a customized virtual application instance.

Gianpaulo Carrara, a Microsoft architect who works with Azure, introduced the problem with multiple tenants' comingled data in his "Multi-Tenancy, metadata driven everything and you are my #1 customer" blog post of February 26, 2006 (`http://bit.ly/gbmKG,` `http://blogs.msdn.com/gianpaolo/archive/` `2006/02/26/539717.aspx`):

> In a pure multi-tenant architecture a single instance of the hosted application is capable of servicing all customers (tenants). Unlike more classical web applications or web services "in the cloud" which behave the same way for each requests, a multi-tenant architecture is designed to allow tenant-specific configurations at the UI (branding), business rules, business processes and data model layers. This is has to be enabled without changing the code as the same code is shared by all tenants, therefore transforming customization of software into configuration of software. As you can imagine, this drives the clear need for "metadata driven everything." The other main challenge is being able to co-locate (mingle and "de-mingle") persistent data of multiple tenants in the same data infrastructure.
>
> In other words, the challenge for the multi-tenant application is to behave as if it was fully dedicated to a single tenant but is actually serving all of them in parallel on the same code base. I call this "you are my #1 customer" approach; which means every customer believes they are the #1 customer but in reality they are all served by a talented customer rep.
>
> The main advantage of this architecture is (at least) twofold (a) the underlying infrastructure is shared, allowing massive economy of scale with optimal repartition of load and (b) because the very costly infrastructure and application development costs are shared, the "enterprise grade" application can be offered to very small businesses as well, permitting [it] to address the long tail of the market.

Carraro's "Software + Services for Architects" webcast (`http://bit.ly/1addvS,` `http://msdn` `.microsoft.com/en-us/architecture/aa699384.aspx`) of July 2008 discusses the control of SLA trade-offs between "do it yourself" and adopting a Software + Services approach with private and public cloud computing.

In early 2008 Eugenio Pace, another Microsoft architect, wrote a multitenant ASP.NET project with SQL Server Data Services (SSDS), the predecessor of SQL Azure Database (SADB), substituted for

SQL Server 200x as the data source. Pace's five-part "Litware HR on SSDS" tutorial blog posts, which began in March 2008, describes how a conventional (not cloud) multitenanted Web application can implement generic, multitenant data access with cloud S[S]DS data storage. The tutorial ends with an 11-minute "End to end demo of LitwareHR on SSDS" (http://bit.ly/7BHKI, http://blogs.msdn.com/eugeniop/archive/2008/04/27/end-to-end-demo-of-litwarehr-on-ssds.aspx), which demonstrates customizing and using an individual tenant site that has a dedicated S[S]DS container for data storage.

Designing a multitenant Azure application isn't an intuitive process, because the ServiceConfiguration.cscfg file for an Azure Hosted Service specifies the storage service and number of instances. When this book was written Microsoft had not provided official architectural guidance for writing multitenant projects to run on Windows Azure.

Assuring Fabric Controller Availability

The Azure FC is a high-availability failover cluster of replicas running on five to seven machines, each of which runs a simplified core version of the Azure OS.

The FC cluster implements

❑   Replicated state with automated failover

❑   Seamless transition to a new primary FC node from a failed primary or secondary FC node

❑   Service continuation when all FC replicas fail

❑   Rolling cluster software upgrades from a "root FC" utility, which also manages the cluster

Figure 3-4 is a diagram of an FC cluster with two secondary FC nodes (three fewer than the minimum).

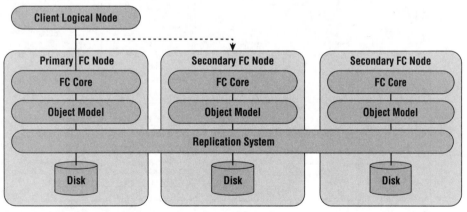

Figure 3-4: A diagram of an Azure Fiber Controller with a primary and two secondary FC nodes.

Following are descriptions of the components shown in Figure 3-4:

❑   *FC Core* runs the heartbeat, state machine, and resolver for resource allocation constraint problems.

- ❑ *Object Model* provides the logic for implementing roles and services.
- ❑ *Replication* system is dedicated to the FCs and is distributed across all FCs.
- ❑ *Disks* are partitions of the system disk for a machine running an FC cluster member.

Virtualizing Windows Servers for Azure

The objective of server virtualization is to maximize server utilization, which often is less than 50 percent in many of today's data centers. Utilization would be expected to decrease as the use of commodity server hardware becomes more common were it not for server virtualization. Multitenancy enables improving performance per dollar and per watt by running multiple applications and services on a single physical server. Initial VMs of Azure CTPs have a designated CPU core; therefore the maximum number of VMs created from a physical server is the number of CPU cores –1; the host partition also requires a core.)

Figure 3-5 illustrates the components of Windows Server 2008's Hyper-V hypervisor v1; Azure runs five to seven guest partitions in a server cluster.

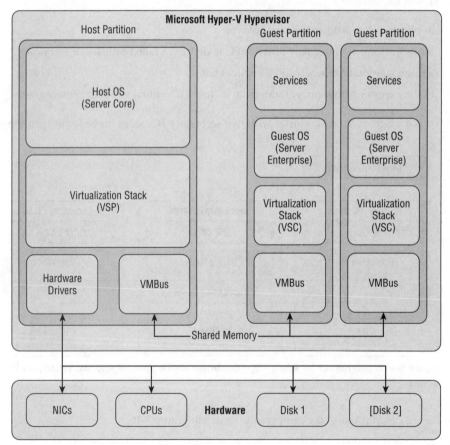

Figure 3-5: A diagram of Microsoft's Hyper-V hypervisor v1 with one host VM and two of five to seven guest VMs.

Following are descriptions of the components shown in Figure 3-5:

❑ *Host partition*, also called the parent partition, is dedicated to running the Host OS. In Hyper-V v1, the host partition is the root (boot) partition and there can be only one host partition.

❑ *Host OS* is a lightweight server operating system (Windows Server 2008 Core for Azure) controls access to the hardware of the underlying server, and provides a mechanism for other guest VMs (where our customers applications are deployed) to safely communicate with the outside world.

❑ *Guest partitions*, also called child partitions, are created and owned by the host OS and are dedicated to running guest OSes.

❑ *Guest OS* is a server operating system for applications and services (Windows Server 2008 Enterprise with IIS 7, .NET Fx 3.5, and other extensions for Azure).

❑ *Services* are custom-written (Azure) applications and services that run on the guest OS.

❑ *Virtualization Stack* (VSP, virtualization service provider) is a provider exposed by the virtualization stack that provides resources or services such as I/O to a child partition.

❑ *Virtualization Stack* (VSC, virtualization service client or consumer) is a software module that a guest loads to consume a resource or service. For I/O devices, the virtualization service client can be a device driver that the operating system kernel loads.

❑ *VMBus* is a shared-memory I/O bus that enables high-performance communication between VMs.

❑ *NICs* are physical network interface card(s).

❑ *CPUs* are physical central processing units, which have one or usually more cores.

❑ *Disk*(s) are the physical fixed disk(s) for the root and guest partitions.

The home page for Hyper-V is `http://bit.ly/DnJtW`, `www.microsoft.com/virtualization/` `default.mspx.`

Deploying the Azure Hypervisor in Non-Microsoft Data Centers

IT and general management has serious reservations about cloud-based application and service lock-in to a single vendor and the difficulty or impossibility of deploying applications, services, data, or all three on multiple Platform as a Service (PaaS) or Infrastructure as a Service (IaaS) clouds. For example, GAE supports Python as its only programming language. AWS supports Windows Server 2003 and probably will accommodate Windows Server 2008 in the future, but you can't emulate multitenanting of server instances without an appropriate hypervisor. The Azure hypervisor is a Microsoft internal-only product, as is the FC, so moving a project from Azure to AWS requires major modifications to the underlying source code and deployment methodology. Migrating large amounts of data from one vendor's cloud to another is even more challenging.

Reuven Cohen started a Cloud Computing Interoperability Forum Google Group (`http://bit.ly/` `DBcJQ`, `http://groups.google.com/group/cloudforum`) *to "define an organization that would enable interoperable enterprise-class cloud computing platforms through application integration and stakeholder cooperation."*

In late January 2009 Hoi Vo, a director on Microsoft's Cloud Infrastructure Services (Azure) team, wrote a blog post (`http://bit.ly/pfQSu`, `http://blogs.msdn.com/windowsazure/archive/2009/01/29/design-principles-behind-the-windows-azure-hypervisor.aspx`) that listed the three principles of the Windows Azure hypervisor's design:

1. *Efficient*: Push work to hardware as much as possible. Any percentage gain once multiplied to tens of thousands of machines will be very significant for us. Consequently we can bet on new processor features to save CPU cycles for the hosted application.

2. *Small footprint*: Any features not applicable to our specific cloud scenarios are removed. This guarantees that we do not have to worry about updating or fixing unnecessary code, meaning less churning or required reboots for the host. All critical code paths are also highly optimized for our Windows Azure scenarios.

3. *Tight integration*: The Windows Azure hypervisor is tightly optimized with the Windows Azure kernel. This is required to achieve the level of scalability and performance we want for our stack.

Vo states that because the Azure hypervisor is optimized for the data center's standard server hardware design, it isn't suitable for deployment outside of Microsoft data centers. However, performance-improving features of the Azure hypervisor, such as Second-Level Address Translation (SLAT) will find their way into future Hyper-V releases.

Summary

The Windows Azure operating system is based on Windows Server 2008 Enterprise Edition running on a Fabric Controller that's created by a customized version of Microsoft's Hyper-V hypervisor. The Azure Fabric provides each Hosted Service with a minimum of one core of the server's CPU, 1.7GB RAM, 100Mbs network connectivity, 250GB of transient storage, which doesn't persist during reboot, and an Azure Storage Service account with 50GB persistent storage in early Community Technical Previews. Hosted Services will be able to request and obtain additional resources and service instances at a surcharge in the release version.

The FC handles application/service deployment, load balancing, OS/data replication, and resource management. It also deploys projects, and in the release version, will add instances automatically to meet demand, manage project software upgrades, and handle server failures to maintain project availability. The FC assigns each role to its own virtual machine; role instances run on the fabric's nodes and channels connect roles. WebRole instances accept HTTP or HTTPS requests and respond with an ASP.NET, ASP.NET MVC, or Silverlight UI. WorkerRoles provide batch computing services in response to request messages received from WebRoles or .NET Services in Azure Queues. The FC runs on a high-availability cluster of five to seven servers to assure maximum reliability.

Services and storage are deployed to Failure Domains whose members have a common point of failure. Storage occupies master nodes, which are replicated to at least two other nodes in different Failure Domains. Rolling service software upgrades and patches to the Windows Azure OS take place on running services in a single Upgrade Domain at a time. The FC deploys resources to all nodes of the Upgrade Domain in parallel, so all updated services in the Upgrade Domain go offline temporarily during the upgrade.

Concerns about security and availability are uppermost in management's reservations about moving on-premises computing and data storage to the cloud. Application and storage security rely on the cloud's data center components, which are likely to provide greater resistance to attacks and unauthorized access than most premises data centers. Cloud vendors must provide service-level agreements that dispel potential customers' doubts about migrating to cloud computing and data storage.

Cloud vendor lock-in is another issue facing IT departments considering public cloud computing. Platforms as a Service, such as the Windows Azure Platform, has a higher lock-in quotient than Infrastructure as a Service, typified by Amazon Web Services' EC2, because Microsoft doesn't offer the customized Azure hypervisor for use on-premises. The Windows Azure SDK's Development Fabric isn't intended for high-reliability production deployment on intranets.

4

Scaling Azure Table and Blob Storage

Achieving high scalability requires cloud-based applications and services to be stateless so as not to rely on the data center's load balancing devices or software to route successive requests from a specific client to a particular logical node. However, most applications and services require access to data persisted in tables that share some characteristics of relational database tables, as well as individual binary large objects (blobs) for storing unstructured data such as images and text documents.

Azure Storage Services consist of highly scalable and available persistent storage for the following three types of data:

❑ *Tables* are structured tabular data stored in an Entity-Attribute-Value (EAV) data model; the maximum size of all attribute values of an entity is 1MB. Entities can be grouped into storage partitions, which are maintained in a single location.

❑ *Blobs* consist of unstructured file-based data stored in an array of bytes; containers store sets of individual blobs up to 50GB in size in hierarchical groups, which emulate a directory structure. Only blob containers and their content are available for public access.

❑ *Queues* contain an unlimited number of messages stored in tables for processing by global services (often Worker Cloud services); messages have a maximum size of 8KB. Messages usually are deleted after the process that reads them handles them. Queues are the subject of Chapter 8, "Messaging with Azure Queues."

To assure availability and reliability, all stored data consists of a master and two or more replicas stored on different Fault Domains. When Microsoft makes the Azure Services Platform available for general use, data can be replicated to multiple data centers to assure access in the event of a data center's destruction.

> *SQL Azure Database (SADB, formerly SQL Data Services, SDS, and SQL Server Data Services, SSDS) is an alternative to Azure Tables that offers many features of relational tables. Microsoft charges a premium for SADB storage and network ingress/egress traffic. SADB is the subject of Chapter 12, "Managing SQL Azure Database Accounts, Databases and DataHubs," and 13, "Exploiting SQL Azure Database' Relational Features."*

Creating Storage Accounts

Early Azure CTPs provided testers with two Storage Accounts with each Hosted Service account. A single Storage Account provides a separate URI for tables, blobs, and queues. When you receive a token GUID as the result of a request to sign up for an Azure beta account and create a Hosted Service account as described in Chapter 2's "The Windows Azure Developer Portal" section, the token enables you to create two Storage Accounts with different prefix names.

Create the First Storage Account with a Hosted Service Token

To create a Storage Account with a token, click the Account tab and its Manage My Tokens link to open the Tokens page, copy and paste the token GUID into the Resource Token ID text box, and click Claim Token to add a Compute Only bucket for the GUID to the Gated Entity's Storage Accounts group, as shown in Figure 4-1.

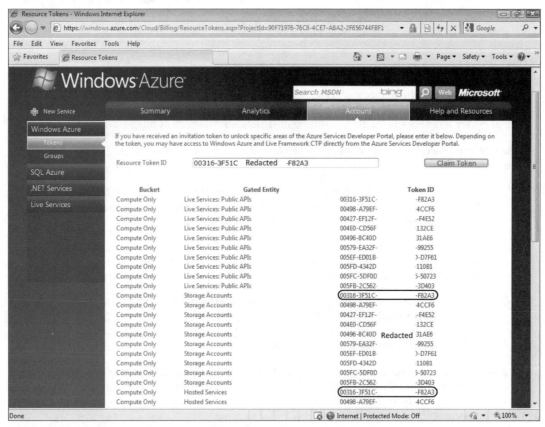

Figure 4-1: The Azure Developer Portal's Tokens page with the initial Storage Account for a Hosted Service token.

Clicking the Claim Token and Continue buttons opens the My Projects page. Click the Project Name link to open the project page and click the New Service link to open the Project | Create a new service component page with choices for Storage Account and Hosted Services (see Figure 4-2).

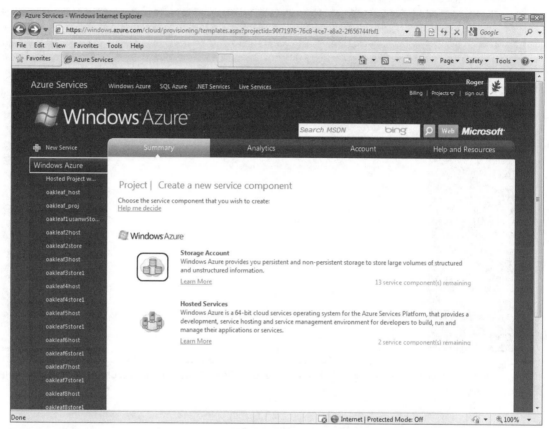

Figure 4-2: Clicking the Tokens Page's Claim Token button with a token valid for the first Storage Account leads to the Project page.

The Storage Account selection displays the number of Storage Accounts available (project(s) remaining) for the Hosted Service tokens you've redeemed. Click the Storage Account icon to open the Create a Project – Project Properties page. Type a unique Project Label and add a Project Description as shown in Figure 4-3.

Click the Next button to open the Create a Project – Storage Account page, add a unique Service Name DNS prefix consisting of lowercase letters and numerals, and click the Check Availability button to ensure the prefix is globally unique for Storage Accounts within all Azure data centers). To keep data in the same data center as the related hosted service, mark the "Yes, this service is related..." and "Create a new Affinity Group" buttons, select from the list of available data centers (regions) and type a name for the region in the text box (see Figure 4-4.) When this book was written, only the USA - Northwest (Quincy, WA) and USA - Southwest (San Antonio, TX) data centers were active.

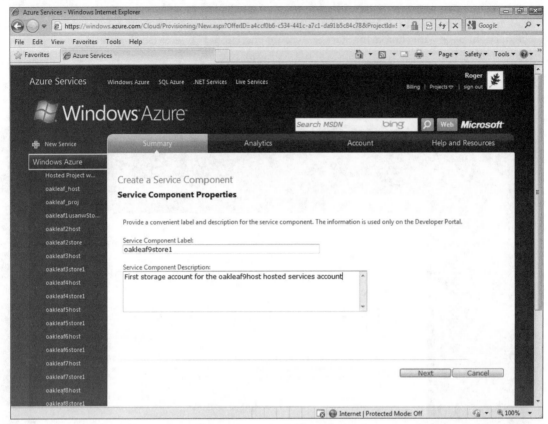

Figure 4-3: Assigning a unique Project Label to a new blob Storage Account in the Create a Project – Project Properties page.

Click Create to generate the new Storage Account and open the *Service Name* page, which displays an `http://dns_prefix.data_type.core.windows.net` endpoint for each of the three data types and displays Primary Access Key and Secondary Access Key values for the three endpoints (see Figure 4-5.)

> *Keep the Primary Access Key and Secondary Access Key values confidential because either of the two keys permits access to your storage services when added to the ServiceConfiguration.cscfg file.*

Create an Additional Storage Account with a Hosted Service Token

To create the second Storage Account for a Hosted Service, click the New Project link in the Development Portal's left panel to open the Project–Create a New Service Component page, which contains links for new Storage Accounts (refer to Figure 4-2) and proceed with the steps shown in Figures 4-3 through 4-5.

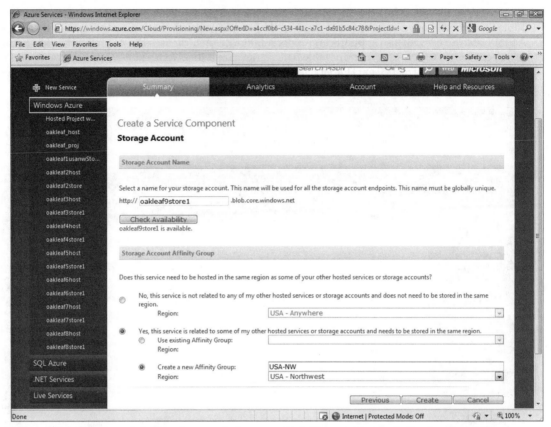

Figure 4-4: Assigning a globally unique prefix for a new blob Storage Account in the Create a Project –
Storage Account page.

Using or Wrapping the Azure Storage Services' REST APIs

You don't need to use a Hosted Service to take advantage of Azure's scalable storage features. In fact, you can access Storage Accounts and their data with any popular computer language, such as PHP, Python, IronPython, Ruby, IronRuby, Java, C#, or Visual Basic, that's capable of interacting with web resources by invoking HTTP's GET, POST, PUT, and other standard methods. Azure Storage Services provides official Representational State Transfer (REST) APIs for the Storage Account and each storage type. REST methods create, retrieve, update, or delete resources that are identified by Uniform Resource Identifiers (URIs). As you'll see in the sections that follow, using the official REST APIs directly requires passing many HTTP header value strings to System.Net.HttpWebRequest methods and parsing header strings returned in System.Net.HttpWebRequest objects.

Programming with "magic strings" rather than CLR objects is contrary to .NET's strongly typed object-oriented methodology. Therefore, Azure Tables support a restricted feature set of the .NET Client

Library for ADO.NET Data Services (formerly code-named and still called *Astoria*) to access data in Table Storage with queries composed with the LINQ to REST dialect that return .NET collections. SQL Azure Database (SADB) also supports and Astoria interface. Astoria uses the Atom Syndication Format (www.ietf.org/rfc/rfc4287.txt) for table data retrieval and the Atom Publishing Protocol (AtomPub, www.ietf.org/rfc/rfc5023.txt) for table insertions, updates, and deletions, as mentioned in Chapter 2.

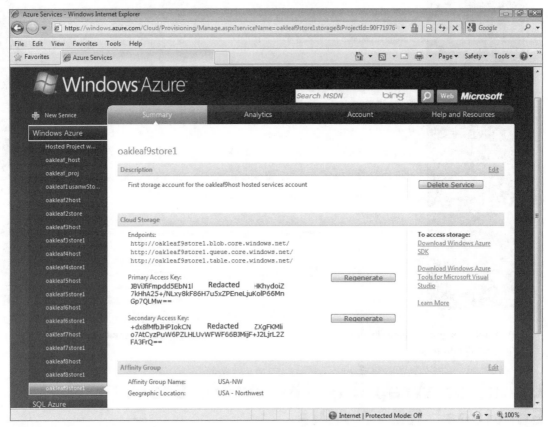

Figure 4-5: The last (*Service Name*) page in the process of creating a Storage Account.

Using Fiddler2 to Display HTTP Request and Response Headers and Content

A logging tool that captures HTTP header and body traffic between an Azure project running in the Development Fabric and Azure Data Storage's production data stores is essential for debugging data manipulation code. The examples in this book use IE 7 and the Fiddler2 proxy for monitoring and debugging data access code. According to its developer, Eric Lawrence (a member of Microsoft's Internet Explorer team):

> Fiddler is a Web Debugging Proxy which logs all HTTP(S) traffic between your computer and the Internet. Fiddler lets you inspect HTTP(S) traffic, set breakpoints,

and "fiddle" with incoming or outgoing data. Fiddler includes a powerful event-based scripting subsystem, and can be extended using any .NET language. Fiddler is free-ware and can debug traffic from virtually any application, including Internet Explorer, Mozilla Firefox, Opera, and thousands more.

Fiddler isn't a Microsoft product but two Internet Explorer Development Technical Articles are available for it: "Fiddler PowerToy – Part 1: HTTP Debugging" (`http://bit.ly/zZJjz`, `http://msdn.microsoft.com/en-us/library/bb250446.aspx`,) and "Fiddler PowerToy – Part 2: HTTP Performance" (`http://bit.ly/H9dAD`, `http://msdn.microsoft.com/en-us/library/bb250442.aspx`). You can download Fiddler2, which enables fiddling with HTTPS and requires .NET 2.0 or later, at no charge from `http://bit.ly/6qKe`, `www.fiddler2.com/Fiddler2/version.asp`. Running the installation program adds a Fiddler2 choice to IE's Tools menu; choosing Fiddler2 opens the application in its own window.

Figure 4-6 shows Fiddler2 capturing HTTP request and response headers for a MERGE request to add a plus symbol (+) to the CompanyName property value of a Customer entity in an Azure CompanyName table.

> *The Entity is the unit of Azure Tables, so changing a property value requires replacing all property values rather than updating only the property (attribute) value(s) that changed. Entities don't support projections;* GET *operations return — and* POST *or* PUT *operations create — complete entities only.*

To capture packets between your computer and Azure Storage Services running in the Microsoft Data Center, you must run your Azure project on the local Development Fabric. Specify production Data Services(s) in the project's ServiceConfiguration.cscfg file, as described in Chapter 2's "Azure Service Definition and Service Configuration Files" section, with entries similar to these:

```
<Setting name="AccountName" value="oakleaf"/>
<Setting name="AccountSharedKey" value="3elV1nddZEYv...Coc0AMQA==" />
<Setting name="BlobStorageEndpoint" value="http://blob.core.windows.net" />
<Setting name="QueueStorageEndpoint" value="http://queue.core.windows.net" />
<Setting name="TableStorageEndpoint" value="http://table.core.windows.net" />
```

> *Fiddler doesn't support capturing packets to or from the loopback (*localhost*) address,* `http://127.0.0.1`, *directly. To enable local packet logging, add a period after the IP address, as in the following:* `http://127.0.0.1.:8000.Default.aspx`.

Click the buttons at the bottom left of the window to turn on Capturing and All Processes, shown empha-sized in Figure 4-6. Click RAW to view HTTP request headers and request body, if applicable, in the Inspectors page's upper window; the lower window displays response headers and the response body, if applicable. The + symbol added to the entity made by the HTTP MERGE method is emphasized at the bottom of Figure 4-6's upper-right window.

Fiddler2's Request Builder window lets you create custom HTTP requests and, if you mark the Inspect Session check box, view the response headers and the response body, if applicable. Dragging a session item from the Web Sessions list to the upper-right window clones the original request when you click Execute, as shown in Figure 4-7.

Chapter 2's "Azure Table Services" section describes the composite primary key for entities, which con-sists of string PartitionKey and RowKey values. For example, if you replace MERGE with the GET method and remove the `If-Match` header, the `http://oakleaf.table.core.windows.net/CustomerTable` `(PartitionKey='Customer',RowKey='ALFKI')` URL returns the Alfreds Futterkiste entity. The `http://oakleaf.table.core.windows.net/CustomerTable()?$top=5` URL returns the first five CustomerTable entities and `http://oakleaf.table.core.windows.net/CustomerTable()?(PartitionKey` `='Customer',Country='Germany')` returns all Customer entities in Germany.

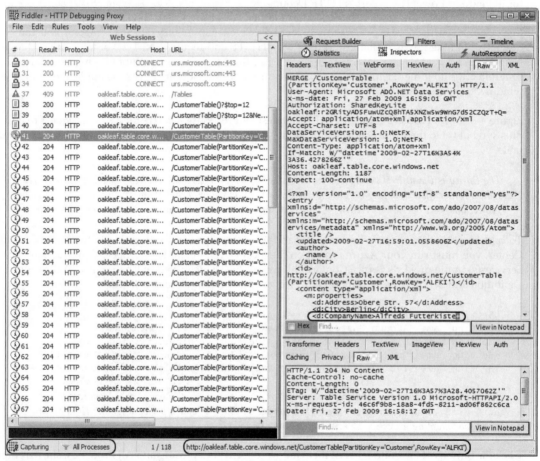

Figure 4-6: Fiddler2 capturing HTTP packets for a MERGE Table update from the SampleWebCloudService project.

C# Wrappers for RESTful Storage and Authentication Operations

The Azure team provides a set of C# wrappers for RESTful storage and authentication operations in the StorageClient.dll class library that you create from files in the \StorageClient folder of the \Program

Files\Windows Azure SDK\v1.0\Sample.zip file. The `StorageClient` library includes the class files shown in the following table:

> *Microsoft classifies the C# wrappers for Azure Data Service's REST API as "high-level .NET wrappers," not members of an official Microsoft API. This means there is no guarantee that future versions of these wrappers will be version-compatible with previous versions. If you're using Visual Studio 2008+ to write projects that access Azure Storage Services, you should copy these files to your project's folder and include them in a StorageClient.dll class library. The following sections contain more details about the wrapper classes contained in the preceding files.*

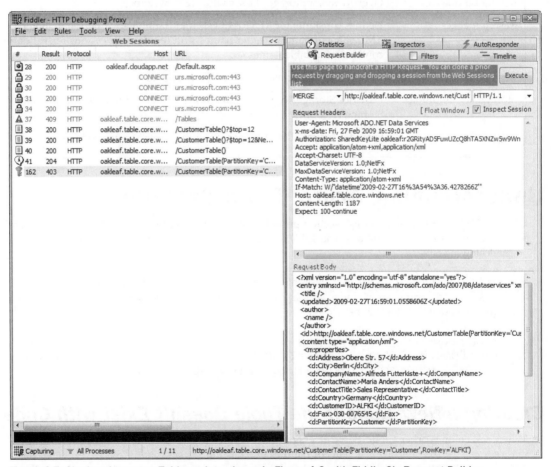

Figure 4-7: Cloning the MERGE Table update shown in Figure 4-6 with Fiddler2's Request Builder.

The following sections provide examples of the use of Astoria and REST wrapper classes for CRUD operations on Azure Table, Blob, and Queue services.

Class File	Description
Authentication.cs	Provides classes to support user authentication and authorization for Storage Services
BlobStorage.cs	Provides classes for accessing containers and their blob contents
Errors.cs	Provides error code enumerations and storage-side exceptions with HTTP response codes
Queue.cs	Provides QueueStorage and Message classes and related event handlers
RestBlobStorage.cs	Overrides BlobStorage classes with REST wrappers
RestHelpers.cs	Defines constants for REST requests and parameters, query parameters, XML element names, header names, and regular expressions for validating container and table names
RestQueue.cs	Overrides Queue classes with REST wrappers
StorageAccountInfo.cs	Provides StorageAccountInfo methods for retrieving and working with Storage Accounts
TableStorage.cs	Provides helper classes for accessing the Table Storage Service

Understanding Azure Table Storage

Chapter 2's ''Azure Table Services'' section provides an introduction to Azure's structured and semi-structured data storage capabilities. The TableStorage.cs file includes source code for the classes shown in the following table.

Figures 4-8, 4-9, and 4-10 are VS 2008 class diagrams for the classes contained in the TableStorage.cs file. These class diagrams are included in the \WROX\Azure\Chapter04\SampleWebCloudService\ StorageClient\TableStorageDiagram.cd file.

> *The sample code in the following sections is based on Jim Nakashima's ''Windows Azure Walkthrough: Simple Table Storage'' blog post of October 28, 2008 (*`http://bit.ly/g6c8z`*,* `http://blogs.msdn` `.com/jnak/archive/2008/10/28/walkthrough-simple-table-storage.aspx`*).*

Creating a New Table If the Table Doesn't Exist with Code

When a Web or Worker Cloud Service session that requires access to a table starts, the Global class's `Application_BeginRequest` event handler invokes the `FirstRequestInitialization` class's `Initialize()` method, which in turn invokes the `ApplicationStartUponFirstRequest()` method.

This method executes the `StorageAccountInfo.GetDefaultTableStorageFromConfiguration()` and `TableStorage.CreateTablesFromModel()` methods to generate the table from its class definition if it doesn't exist. Listing 4-1 is code from the Global.asax.cs file that makes sure that the methods are called only once per session at application startup:

> *Development Storage doesn't support creating tables dynamically from project code. Instead you must right-click the Cloud Service and select the Create Test Storage Tables command to create the SQL Server Express tables by reflection.*

Class	Description
TableStorage	The entry point for Azure's structured or semi-structured storage API. `TableStorage` objects provide methods for creating, listing, and deleting tables.
TableStorageTable	Creates a table with a specified name.
TableStorageEntity	Adds an entity with specified `PartitionKey` and `RowKey` values.
TableStorageDataServiceQuery	Defines a query that can handle continuation tokens for paging results.
TableStorageDataServiceContext	Creates a `DataServiceContext` object for a table with security information (`AccountName` and `SharedKey`).
TableStorageHelpers	Contains error-handling helpers and methods for testing whether properties can be inserted into a table.
ContextRef	A helper class to avoid long-lived references to context objects.
TableRetryWrapperException	A wrapper for `StorageClient` and `StorageServer` exceptions indicating retries are needed.
ParameterValidator	Throws an `ArgumentException` if the parameter is null or zero-length.
TableStorageConstants	Contains constants for testing properties, table names and table queries.
DataServiceUtilities	Support special requirements of ADO.NET Data Services conventions.

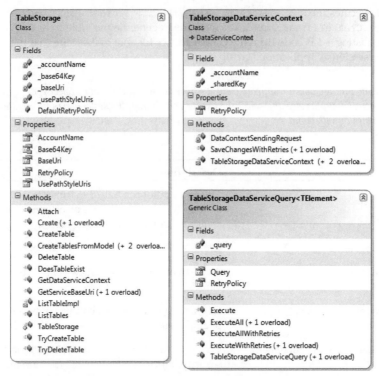

Figure 4-8: TableStorage, TableStorageDataServiceContext, and TableStorageDataServiceQuery class diagrams.

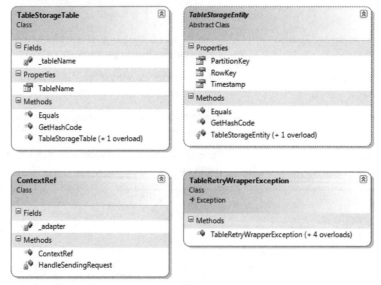

Figure 4-9: TableStorageTable, TableStorageEntity, ContextRef, and TableRetryWrapperException class diagrams.

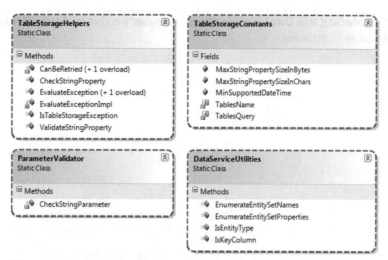

Figure 4-10: TableStorageHelpers, ParameterValidator,
TableStorageConstants, and DataServiceUtilities class diagrams.

Listing 4-1: Creating the CustomerTable if it doesn't exist in Azure Storage (Global.asax.cs)

```
namespace SampleWebCloudService_WebRole
{
    public class Global : System.Web.HttpApplication
    {
        void Application_BeginRequest(object sender, EventArgs e)
        {
            HttpApplication app = (HttpApplication)sender;
            HttpContext context = app.Context;

            // Attempt to perform first request initialization
            FirstRequestInitialization.Initialize(context);
        }

        class FirstRequestInitialization
        {
            private static bool s_InitializedAlready = false;
            private static Object s_lock = new Object();

            // Initialize only on the first request
            public static void Initialize(HttpContext context)
            {
                if (s_InitializedAlready)
                {
                    return;
                }

                lock (s_lock)
```

Continued

Listing 4-1: Creating the CustomerTable if it doesn't exist in Azure Storage (Global.asax.cs) *(continued)*

```
            {
                if (s_InitializedAlready)
                {
                    return;
                }

                ApplicationStartUponFirstRequest(context);
                s_InitializedAlready = true;
            }
        }
    }

    private static void ApplicationStartUponFirstRequest(HttpContext context)
    {
        // Make sure the tables exist before we use them.
        StorageAccountInfo account =
            StorageAccountInfo.GetDefaultTableStorageAccountFromConfiguration();
        TableStorage.CreateTablesFromModel(typeof(CustomerDataServiceContext),
            account);
    }
    }
}
```

For more detailed information about the preceding code, see the "Azure Storage Services Test Harness: Table Services 7 – Testing for Table Existence at App Startup Only" blog post (http://bit.ly/16iS6b, http://oakleafblog.blogspot.com/2008/11/azure-storage-services-test-harness_231.html). *Invoking this method consumes substantial resources, so it's important not to execute it more than once per session.*

The Customers.cs class file contains the code for the model, which creates the table from the CustomerDataModel class that implements IQueryable<T>. The class's default constructor accepts a GUID as the RowKey value and assigns the class name to PartitionKey; the parameterized constructor accepts PartitionKey and RowKey string values to create the composite primary key.

Any class that implements IQueryable<T> is a candidate source for the CreateTablesFromModel() method. The TableStorage class reflects over the following listing's CustomerDataServiceContext class and creates a table for each IQueryable<T> property. The table's entities have properties generated from the IQueryable<T>'s type T. Listing 4-2 is code in the Customers.cs file that creates the CustomerTable and CustomerDataService objects.

Listing 4-2: Creating the CustomerTable if it doesn't exist in Azure Storage (Customers.cs)

```
namespace SampleWebCloudService_WebRole

    #region CustomerDataModel class generated by LIMOG v2
    public class CustomerDataModel : TableStorageEntity
    {
        // Default parameterless constructor
```

```
    public CustomerDataModel()
        : base()
    {
        RowKey = Guid.NewGuid().ToString();
        PartitionKey = "CustomerDataModel";
    }
    // Partial parameterized constructor
    public CustomerDataModel(string partitionKey, string rowKey)
        : base(partitionKey, rowKey)
    {
    }

    public string CustomerID { get; set; }
    public string CompanyName { get; set; }
    public string ContactName { get; set; }
    public string ContactTitle { get; set; }
    public string Address { get; set; }
    public string City { get; set; }
    public string Region { get; set; }
    public string PostalCode { get; set; }
    public string Country { get; set; }
    public string Phone { get; set; }
    public string Fax { get; set; }
}
#endregion
#region EntityNameDataServiceContext (implementing IQueryable generates table)
internal class CustomerDataServiceContext : TableStorageDataServiceContext
{
    internal CustomerDataServiceContext(StorageAccountInfo accountInfo)
        : base(accountInfo)
    {
    }

    internal const string CustomerTableName = "CustomerTable";

    public IQueryable<CustomerDataModel> CustomerTable
    {
        get
        {
            return this.CreateQuery<CustomerDataModel>(CustomerTableName);
        }
    }

    public class CustomerDataSource
    {
        private CustomerDataServiceContext serviceContext = null;

        public CustomerDataSource()
        {
            // Get the settings from the Service Configuration file
            StorageAccountInfo account =

StorageAccountInfo.GetDefaultTableStorageAccountFromConfiguration();
```

Continued

77

**Listing 4-2: Creating the CustomerTable if it doesn't exist in Azure Storage
(Customers.cs)** *(continued)*

```
            // Create tables for public properties that implement IQueryable
            TableStorage.CreateTablesFromModel(typeof(CustomerDataServiceContext)
                , account);

            // Create the service context to query against
            serviceContext = new CustomerDataServiceContext(account);
            serviceContext.RetryPolicy =
                RetryPolicies.RetryN(3, TimeSpan.FromSeconds(1));
        }

        public IEnumerable<CustomerDataModel> Select()
        {
            // Page.Prerender event-handler populates GridView
            // This method is required for ObjectDataSource
            return null;
        }

        public void Delete(CustomerDataModel itemToDelete)
        {
            serviceContext.AttachTo(CustomerDataServiceContext.
                CustomerTableName, itemToDelete, "*");
            serviceContext.DeleteObject(itemToDelete);
            serviceContext.SaveChanges();
        }

        public void Insert(CustomerDataModel newItem)
        {
            serviceContext.AddObject(CustomerDataServiceContext.
                CustomerTableName, newItem);
            serviceContext.SaveChanges();
        }
    }
}
#endregion
}
```

The `CreateTablesFromModel()` method adds the `PartitionKey`, `RowKey`, and `Timestamp` properties (attributes) to those specified by the class's properties.

As noted in Chapter 2, Azure Tables support properties having the following .NET data types shown in the following table:

Data Type	Description
Binary	Array of bytes up to 64KB in size
Bool	Boolean value
DateTime	64-bit value expressed as UTC time ranging from 1/1/1600 to 12/31/9999

Data Type	Description
Double	64-bit floating point value
GUID	128-bit globally unique identifier
Int	32-bit integer
Long	64-bit integer
String	UTF-16-encoded value up to 64KB in size

Creating a New Table If the Table Doesn't Exist with the HTTP POST Method

In Listing 4-3 are the HTTP header and AtomPub-formatted body of the POST request captured by Fiddler2 upon generation by Listings 4-1 and 4-2 when starting the WebRole or WorkerRole.

Listing 4-3: HTTP POST request to create a new CustomerTable if it doesn't exist

```
POST /Tables HTTP/1.1
User-Agent: Microsoft ADO.NET Data Services
x-ms-date: Thu, 26 Feb 2009 22:03:42 GMT
Authorization: SharedKeyLite oakleaf:i8WF7XrpHgB9IYHM7EBcTqUCgI9XSFLjaDJhuMtVQMg=
Accept: application/atom+xml,application/xml
Accept-Charset: UTF-8
DataServiceVersion: 1.0;NetFx
MaxDataServiceVersion: 1.0;NetFx
Content-Type: application/atom+xml
Host: oakleaf.table.core.windows.net
Content-Length: 499
Expect: 100-continue
Connection: Keep-Alive

<?xml version="1.0" encoding="utf-8" standalone="yes"?>
<entry xmlns:d="http://schemas.microsoft.com/ado/2007/08/dataservices"
       xmlns:m="http://schemas.microsoft.com/ado/2007/08/dataservices/metadata"
       xmlns="http://www.w3.org/2005/Atom">
  <title />
  <updated>2009-02-26T22:03:42.2336961Z</updated>
  <author>
    <name />
  </author>
  <id />
  <content type="application/xml">
    <m:properties>
      <d:TableName>CustomerTable</d:TableName>
    </m:properties>
  </content>
</entry>
```

All three Azure data service types utilize SharedKey authorization, but Azure Tables accept an alternative SharedKeyLite authorization format from code such as .NET wrappers that employ the .NET Client Library for ADO.NET Data Services. To prevent unauthorized access to the Primary or Secondary Authorization Key value, code creates SharedKey and SharedKeyLite values by creating a string value from the request headers encoded by a Hash-based Method Authentication Code using the SHA-256 hash algorithm (HMAC-SHA256, http://msdn.microsoft.com/en-us/library/system.security .cryptography.hmacsha256.aspx). The `StorageClient` class library's Authentication.cs file contains code to generate the key values.

Listing 4-4 is the HTTP POST response header and HTTP 409 error body in AtomPub format returned when the table exists.

Listing 4-4: HTTP POST response if the CustomerTable already exists

```
<?xml version="1.0" encoding="utf-8" standalone="yes"?>
<entry xmlns:d="http://schemas.microsoft.com/ado/2007/08/dataservices"
       xmlns:m="http://schemas.microsoft.com/ado/2007/08/dataservices/metadata"
       xmlns="http://www.w3.org/2005/Atom">
  <title />
  <updated>2009-02-26T22:03:42.2336961Z</updated>
  <author>
    <name />
  </author>
  <id />
  <content type="application/xml">
    <m:properties>
      <d:TableName>CustomerTable</d:TableName>
    </m:properties>
  </content>
</entry>

HTTP/1.1 409 The table specified already exists.
Cache-Control: no-cache
Content-Length: 258
Content-Type: application/xml
Server: Table Service Version 1.0 Microsoft-HTTPAPI/2.0
x-ms-request-id: 16e8aa5c-f37c-4333-a543-cac68628c739
Date: Thu, 26 Feb 2009 22:02:03 GMT

<?xml version="1.0" encoding="utf-8" standalone="yes"?>
<error xmlns="http://schemas.microsoft.com/ado/2007/08/dataservices/metadata">
  <code>TableAlreadyExists</code>
  <message xml:lang="en-US">The table specified already exists.</message>
</error>
```

Adding Entities to a Table

Uploading data from on-premises relational database tables to Azure Tables is one of the primary tasks that IT organizations face when moving to cloud data storage. When this book was written, there were no Microsoft-supported utilities, such as SQL Server Integration Services (SSIS) packages, for uploading tables to Azure Tables. Therefore cloud application developers are likely to need to write their own Web or WorkerRoles for uploading and validating tabular data. Figure 4-11 shows the Sample-WebCloudService project running from a production deployment to the first OakLeaf Hosted Service (http://oakleaf.cloudapp.com) and initial Storage Service (http://oakleaf.table.core.windows.net) with 91 customers loaded into the CustomerTable table as it appears after clicking the Count Customers button to verify that 91 entities were added.

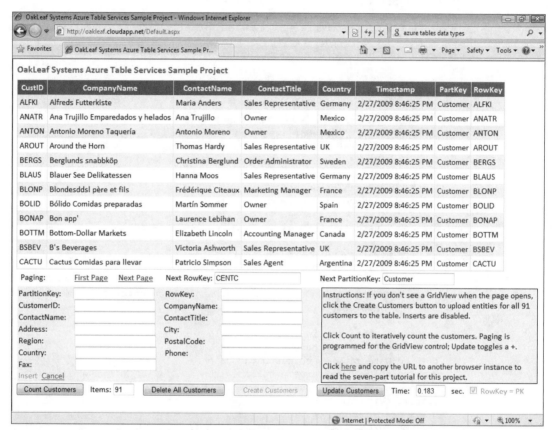

Figure 4-11: The Default.aspx page of the SampleWebCloudService Project when connected to Azure cloud services.

Adding New Entities with Code

Listing 4-5 is the code from the Create Customers button's Click event handler from the SampleWebCloudService project. The btnCreateCustomers_Click() method adds 91 Northwind Customer entities (rows) to the CustomerTable using the _Default class's CreateCustomerListWithRowKey() function from the LimogListFunctions.cs file.

> *Limog is an acronym for LINQ in-Memory Object Generator, a project from WROX's Professional ADO.NET 3.5 with LINQ and the Entity Framework book. You can learn more about Limog in the "Azure Storage Services Test Harness: Table Services 5 – Generating Classes/Collection Initializers with LIMOG v2" blog post* (http://bit.ly/RIJrs, http://oakleafblog.blogspot.com/2008/11/azure-storage-services-test-harness_21.html).

Listing 4-5: Code to add 91 entities from a Collection<T> to a table

```
namespace SampleWebCloudService_WebRole
{
    public partial class _Default : System.Web.UI.Page
        {
        // Creates all CustomerTable entities individually from an object initializer
        // Sets the customersView GridView's DataSource
         protected void btnCreateCustomers_Click(object sender, EventArgs e)
        {
            Stopwatch timer = new Stopwatch();
            timer.Start();

            List<CustomerDataModel> custDataModel = null;
            if (chkRowKeyPK.Checked)
                // Object initializer includes PartitionKey and RowKey values
                custDataModel = CreateCustomerListWithRowKey();
            else
                // Use default constructor
                custDataModel = CreateCustomerList();

            foreach (CustomerDataModel newItem in custDataModel)
            {
                if (newItem.CustomerID == null)
                    newItem.CustomerID = newItem.RowKey;

                serviceContext.AddObject(CustomerDataServiceContext.CustomerTableName
                    , newItem);
            }
            // Persist entities in the Azure Table
            serviceContext.SaveChanges();
            // Bind DataGridView to custDataModel
            customersView.DataSource = null;
            customersView.DataSourceID = "customerData";
            customersView.DataBind();

            txtTime.Text = (timer.ElapsedMilliseconds / 1000D).ToString("0.000");
            btnCreateCustomers.Enabled = false;
            btnUpdateCusts.Enabled = true;
        }
    }
}
```

The serviceContext.AddObject() method adds the current member of the custDataModel list to the serviceContext. Invoking the serviceContext.SaveChanges() method saves the cached entities to the CustomerTable.

If you need the equivalent of a relational JOIN, you must upload dependent records, such as the last few orders for each customer and all order details for each order you upload. The Azure team promises secondary indexes on entity values other than the primary key in a future version.

Adding a New Entity with the HTTP POST Method and AtomPub Body

Listing 4-6 is the HTTP POST request header and AtomPub body required to add the first of 91 Customer entities to the CustomerTable:

Listing 4-6: HTTP POST request header and body to add a new CustomerTable entity

```
POST /CustomerTable HTTP/1.1
User-Agent: Microsoft ADO.NET Data Services
x-ms-date: Thu, 26 Feb 2009 22:15:12 GMT
Authorization: SharedKeyLite oakleaf:yndp7wnZBl5nfHl39C9Yjd9lpetuGE3Q0Hr+3dArRNE=
Accept: application/atom+xml,application/xml
Accept-Charset: UTF-8
DataServiceVersion: 1.0;NetFx
MaxDataServiceVersion: 1.0;NetFx
Content-Type: application/atom+xml
Host: oakleaf.table.core.windows.net
Content-Length: 1083
Expect: 100-continue

<?xml version="1.0" encoding="utf-8" standalone="yes"?>
<entry xmlns:d="http://schemas.microsoft.com/ado/2007/08/dataservices"
xmlns:m="http://schemas.microsoft.com/ado/2007/08/dataservices/metadata"
xmlns="http://www.w3.org/2005/Atom">
  <title />
  <updated>2009-02-26T22:15:12.8647523Z</updated>
  <author>
    <name />
  </author>
  <id />
  <content type="application/xml">
    <m:properties>
      <d:Address>Obere Str. 57</d:Address>
      <d:City>Berlin</d:City>
      <d:CompanyName>Alfreds Futterkiste</d:CompanyName>
      <d:ContactName>Maria Anders</d:ContactName>
      <d:ContactTitle>Sales Representative</d:ContactTitle>
      <d:Country>Germany</d:Country>
      <d:CustomerID>ALFKI</d:CustomerID>
      <d:Fax>030-0076545</d:Fax>
      <d:PartitionKey>Customer</d:PartitionKey>
      <d:Phone>030-0074321</d:Phone>
      <d:PostalCode>12209</d:PostalCode>
      <d:Region m:null="true" />
      <d:RowKey>ALFKI</d:RowKey>
      <d:Timestamp m:type="Edm.DateTime">0001-01-01T00:00:00</d:Timestamp>
    </m:properties>
  </content>
</entry>
```

The <entry xmlns:d="http://schemas.microsoft.com/ado/2007/08/dataservices" xmlns:m="http://schemas.microsoft.com/ado/2007/08/dataservices/metadata" xmlns="http://www.w3.org/

`2005/Atom">` element verifies that Azure Table Services is to use ADO.NET Data Services conventions, such as the AtomPub format, to process the entity insert operation. The `Timestamp` property value is the minimum `DateTime` value. Lack of a `<feed>` parent element indicates that the `<entry>` is a singleton.

Listing 4-7 Is the HTTP POST response header and AtomPub body for the successful addition of a new entity to the CustomerTable.

Listing 4-7: HTTP POST response after adding a new CustomerTable entity

```
Cache-Control: no-cache
Transfer-Encoding: chunked
Content-Type: application/atom+xml;charset=utf-8
ETag: W/"datetime'2009-02-26T22%3A13%3A35.4152565Z'"
Location: http://oakleaf.table.core.windows.net/CustomerTable(PartitionKey=
'Customer',
RowKey='ALFKI')
Server: Table Service Version 1.0 Microsoft-HTTPAPI/2.0
x-ms-request-id: 4da35e6c-6598-406c-aa45-856f1085fdd3
Date: Thu, 26 Feb 2009 22:13:34 GMT


5DB
<?xml version="1.0" encoding="utf-8" standalone="yes"?>
<entry xml:base="http://oakleaf.table.core.windows.net/"
       xmlns:d="http://schemas.microsoft.com/ado/2007/08/dataservices"
       xmlns:m="http://schemas.microsoft.com/ado/2007/08/dataservices/metadata"
       m:etag="W/&quot;datetime'2009-02-26T22%3A13%3A35.4152565Z'&quot;"
       xmlns="http://www.w3.org/2005/Atom">
  <id>http://oakleaf.table.core.windows.net/CustomerTable(PartitionKey='Customer',
      RowKey='ALFKI')</id>
  <title type="text"></title>
  <updated>2009-02-26T22:13:35Z</updated>
  <author>
    <name />
  </author>
  <link rel="edit" title="CustomerTable"
    href="CustomerTable(PartitionKey='Customer',RowKey='ALFKI')" />
  <category term="oakleaf.CustomerTable"
    scheme="http://schemas.microsoft.com/ado/2007/08/dataservices/scheme" />
  <content type="application/xml">
    <m:properties>
      <d:PartitionKey>Customer</d:PartitionKey>
      <d:RowKey>ALFKI</d:RowKey>
      <d:Timestamp m:type="Edm.DateTime">2009-02-26T22:13:35.4152565Z</d:Timestamp>
      <d:Address>Obere Str. 57</d:Address>
      <d:City>Berlin</d:City>
      <d:CompanyName>Alfreds Futterkiste</d:CompanyName>
      <d:ContactName>Maria Anders</d:ContactName>
      <d:ContactTitle>Sales Representative</d:ContactTitle>
      <d:Country>Germany</d:Country>
      <d:CustomerID>ALFKI</d:CustomerID>
      <d:Fax>030-0076545</d:Fax>
      <d:Phone>030-0074321</d:Phone>
      <d:PostalCode>12209</d:PostalCode>
```

```
      </m:properties>
    </content>
  </entry>
  0
```

The ETag header value is the Timestamp property value with colons (:) escaped; ETag header values are compared with a Timestamp property value for concurrency conflict management.

Taking Advantage of Entity Group Transactions

The Windows Azure SDK (May 2009 CTP) introduced Entity Group Transactions (EGTs), which enable transacted Insert Entity, Update Entity, Merge Entity, and Delete Entity operations on entities in the same Entity Group. An Entity Group is a set of entities in the same Azure Table that have the same PartitionKey value.

EGTs require specifying a new x-ms-version request header with a value of 2009-04-14 or later and accept a maximum of 100 entities in a single ADO.NET Data Services client change set. The change set also can contain a single query. Online help for EGTs is available at http://bit.ly/kfWtD, http://msdn .microsoft.com/en-us/library/dd894038.aspx.

The May 2009 CTP version of the SDK's development environment doesn't support EGTs in Development Storage. The May 2009 CTP's implementation of the sample StorageClient wrapper doesn't support EGTs, so you can't execute EGTs with conventional .NET code that uses StorageClient objects.

Steve Marx's "Sample Code for Batch Transactions in Windows Azure Tables" post (http://bit.ly/ j2VXy, http://blog.smarx.com/posts/sample-code-for-batch-transactions-in-windows- azure-tables) includes an updated StorageClient library and a simple test program to demonstrate EGTs.

Querying for a Specific Entity or Entities

Querying probably will be the most common operation on production Azure Tables. The following sections describe C# code and HTTP GET methods to return paged LINQ to REST query result sets and display them in the SampleWebCloudService project's GridView control.

Paging code is adapted from Steve Marx's "Paging Over Data in Windows Azure Tables" November 12, 2008 blog post (http://bit.ly/bShh, http://blog.smarx.com/posts/paging-over-data-in- windows-azure-tables).

Querying for Pages of Entities with Code

As mentioned earlier, ADO.NET Data Services clients use LINQ to REST syntax to generate the HTTP GET method. LINQ to REST encodes query strings with a small subset of Astoria's query options, operators, and functions. The following table shows ADO.NET Data Services' methods, properties, standard query operators, comparison operators, and Boolean operators supported by LINQ to REST queries:

LINQ to REST is an unofficial abbreviation for LINQ to ADO.NET Data Services.

Conspicuous by their absence are Order By, Group By, Skip, and many other LINQ Standard Query Operators. Select must return complete entities; as mentioned earlier, projections aren't supported.

Queries return a maximum of 1,000 items, so Take(1000) *is the upper limit.* NextPartitionKey *and* NextRowKey *property values provide the starting position for paging operations that apply the* Take() *method. ADO.NET Data Services v1 doesn't support aggregate functions, such as* Count() *or* Sum().

Category	Supported Methods, Properties, Query Operators, or Comparison Operators
Data Service Query Methods	AddQueryOption, BeginExecute, EndExecute, GetEnumerator.
Data Service Query Properties	All ADO.NET DataServiceQuery properties are supported.
Standard Query Operators	From, In, Where, Select (no projections), Take (with limitations), First, FirstOrDefault.
Comparison Operators	Equal, GreaterThan, GreaterThanOrEqual, LessThan, LessThanOrEqual, NotEqual.
Boolean Operators	And, AndAlso, Not, Or.

Listing 4-8 populates a 12-row GridView with pages of 12 or fewer Customer entities with code contained in event handlers of the Default.aspx.cs code-behind file.

Listing 4-8: Code to populate the GridView with 12-entity pages

```
namespace SampleWebCloudService_WebRole
{
    public partial class _Default : System.Web.UI.Page
    {
        // Used by multiple handlers
        StorageAccountInfo account = null;
        CustomerDataServiceContext serviceContext = null;
        public bool skipPreRenderTime = false;

        protected void Page_Load(object sender, EventArgs e)
        {
            // Get the StorageAccountInfo once
            account =
                StorageAccountInfo.GetDefaultTableStorageAccountFromConfiguration();
            serviceContext = new CustomerDataServiceContext(account);
            serviceContext.RetryPolicy =
                RetryPolicies.RetryN(3, TimeSpan.FromSeconds(1));
        }

        protected void Page_Prerender(object sender, EventArgs e)
        {
            // This query gets a page of 12 customers at a time
            Stopwatch timer = new Stopwatch();
            timer.Start();

            // Write a LINQ to REST query
```

```
            int pageSize = 12;
            var query = (DataServiceQuery<CustomerDataModel>)
                (new
CustomerDataServiceContext(account).CustomerTable.Take(pageSize));

            // Request a continuation token
            var continuation = Request["ct"];
            if (continuation != null)
            {
                // ct param looks like "<partitionKey>/<rowKey>"
                string[] tokens = continuation.Split('/');
                var partitionToken = tokens[0];
                var rowToken = tokens[1];

                // These become continuation token (ct) query parameters in the
                          request.
                query = query.AddQueryOption("NextPartitionKey", partitionToken)
                          .AddQueryOption("NextRowKey", rowToken);
            }
            var result = query.Execute();

            // Cast to a QueryOperationResponse and read the custom headers
            var qor = (QueryOperationResponse)result;
            string nextPartition = null;
            string nextRow = null;
            qor.Headers.TryGetValue("x-ms-continuation-NextPartitionKey",
                out nextPartition);
            qor.Headers.TryGetValue("x-ms-continuation-NextRowKey",
                out nextRow);

            if (nextPartition != null && nextRow != null)
            {
                nextLink.NavigateUrl = string.Format("?ct={0}/{1}", nextPartition,
                    nextRow);
                txtNextPartitionKey.Text = nextPartition;
                txtNextRowKey.Text = nextRow;
                btnCreateCustomers.Enabled = false;
                btnDeleteAll.Enabled = true;
            }
            else
            {
                txtNextPartitionKey.Text = null;
                txtNextRowKey.Text = null;
                nextLink.Visible = false;
            }
            // Change the customersView DataView's DataSource to the query response
            customersView.DataSourceID = null;
            customersView.DataSource = result;
            customersView.DataBind();
        }
    }
}
```

The var query = (DataServiceQuery<CustomerDataModel>)(new CustomerDataServiceContext (account).CustomerTable.Take(pageSize)); instruction is method syntax for the LINQ to REST query, which returns a DataServiceQuery<CustomerDataModel> type that you must execute to retrieve the entity collection. Cast the result to the QueryOperationResponse type, which supports continuation tokens for paging.

The serviceContext.RetryPolicy = RetryPolicies.RetryN(3, TimeSpan.FromSeconds(1)) instruction specifies a maximum of three retries at one-second intervals to obtain the query result set. The continuation variable holds two continuation tokens that contain the NextPartitionKey and NextRowKey values to define the starting point for the next page of values. You must explicitly request continuation tokens as named QueryOperationResponse.QueryOptions.

Querying for the Second Page of 12 Entities with the HTTP GET Method

Clicking the sample Default.aspx page's Next Page link button fires another Page_Prerender event, which executes a GET request that includes the NextPartitionKey and NextRowKey values in the query string, as shown in Listing 4-9.

Listing 4-9: HTTP GET request for the second page of 12 CustomerTable entities

```
GET /CustomerTable()?$top=12 &NextPartitionKey=Customer&NextRowKey=CENTC HTTP/1.1
User-Agent: Microsoft ADO.NET Data Services
x-ms-date: Thu, 26 Feb 2009 22:15:07 GMT
Authorization: SharedKeyLite oakleaf:htCsBgNfPtm0u+jY56ozC/pZqw6c/25j17CElzFjdoo=
Accept: application/atom+xml,application/xml
Accept-Charset: UTF-8
DataServiceVersion: 1.0;NetFx
MaxDataServiceVersion: 1.0;NetFx
Host: oakleaf.table.core.windows.net
```

Clicking the First Page link button resets the NextPartitionKey and NextRowKey values to null. If you want to implement a Previous Page button, you must persist a last-in, first-out stack of NextRowKey values in Global.asax.cs or ViewState and add appropriate code to pop the appropriate token.

Listing 4-10 shows the GET response for the second page with the continuation token values for the third page.

Listing 4-10: HTTP GET response for the second page of 12 CustomerTable entities

```
HTTP/1.1 200 OK
Cache-Control: no-cache
Transfer-Encoding: chunked
Content-Type: application/atom+xml;charset=utf-8
Server: Table Service Version 1.0 Microsoft-HTTPAPI/2.0
x-ms-request-id: 8ff7440f-7419-40eb-9910-74e99602f666
x-ms-continuation-NextPartitionKey: Customer
x-ms-continuation-NextRowKey: FRANK
Date: Thu, 26 Feb 2009 22:13:29 GMT

200
<?xml version="1.0" encoding="utf-8" standalone="yes"?>
<feed xml:base="http://oakleaf.table.core.windows.net/"
```

```
        xmlns:d="http://schemas.microsoft.com/ado/2007/08/dataservices"
        xmlns:m="http://schemas.microsoft.com/ado/2007/08/dataservices/metadata"
        xmlns="http://www.w3.org/2005/Atom">
  <title type="text">CustomerTable</title>
  <id>http://oakleaf.table.core.windows.net/CustomerTable</id>
  <updated>2009-02-26T22:13:29Z</updated>
  <link rel="self" title="CustomerTable" href="CustomerTable" />
</feed>
```

Querying for the First Eight Customer Entities Located in the USA

Listing 4-11 contains an example of a LINQ to REST expression that combines LINQ's where and take() Standard Query Qperators to retrieve the first eight Customer entities with USA as the Country property value. The Page_Load event handler assigns the serviceContext instance.

Listing 4-11: Code to retrieve and display the first eight Customer entities in the USA

```
// Retrieve and display first eight Customer entities in the USA
var results = (from c in serviceContext.CustomerTable
              where c.Country == "USA"
              select c).Take(8);
TableStorageDataServiceQuery<CustomerDataModel> query =
    new TableStorageDataServiceQuery<CustomerDataModel>
        (results as DataServiceQuery<CustomerDataModel>);
IEnumerable<CustomerDataModel> result = query.ExecuteAllWithRetries();
customersView.DataSourceID = null;
customersView.DataSource = result;
customersView.DataBind();
```

Executing the preceding code generates the HTTP GET request and response of Listings 4-12 and 4-13. The following table describes the four Execute ... () methods supported by TableStorageDataServiceQuery objects:

Listing 4-12: HTTP GET request for the first eight Customer entities in the USA

```
GET /CustomerTable()?$filter=Country%20eq%20'USA'&$top=8 HTTP/1.1
User-Agent: Microsoft ADO.NET Data Services
x-ms-date: Sun, 01 Mar 2009 18:10:19 GMT
Authorization: SharedKeyLite oakleaf:RzHMRAy/Hj/Dn/Z7UZKacAY2Y4LnVC6MMvOt7YF+Xtc=
Accept: application/atom+xml,application/xml
Accept-Charset: UTF-8
DataServiceVersion: 1.0;NetFx
MaxDataServiceVersion: 1.0;NetFx
Host: oakleaf.table.core.windows.net
```

URL encoding substitutes %20 for the space characters required to separate LINQ to REST comparison operators and their arguments in query strings.

Listing 4-13: HTTP GET response for the request in Listing 4-12.

```
HTTP/1.1 200 OK
Cache-Control: no-cache
```

Continued

Listing 4-13: HTTP GET response for the request in Listing 4-12. *(continued)*

```
Transfer-Encoding: chunked
Content-Type: application/atom+xml;charset=utf-8
Server: Table Service Version 1.0 Microsoft-HTTPAPI/2.0
x-ms-request-id: 2eb64479-9245-4cbe-affd-a06459a5e4c5
Date: Sun, 01 Mar 2009 18:09:49 GMT
```

The response body is omitted for brevity.

`Execute ... ()` Method	Action When Invoked
`Execute()` or `ExecuteWithRetries()`	Return up to the first 1,000 entities.
`ExecuteAll()` or `ExecuteAllWithRetries()`	Return all entities with continuation tokens as you enumerate over groups of 1,000 entities.
`ExecuteWithRetries()` and `ExecuteAllWithRetries()`	Use the retry policy set on the `TableStorageData ServiceContext` object for the queries.

Updating Entities by Replacing Their Property Values

The Update Customers button toggles adding or removing a plus sign (+) suffix to or from the `CompanyName` property value of all 91 Customer entities. As mentioned earlier, entities are the basic units of Azure Tables, so the REST API defines a new HTTP `MERGE` method that requires the request body to contain values for all entity properties, not just those properties whose values are to be changed. `PartitionKey` and `RowKey` values are immutable and can't be updated.

The ADO.NET Data Services client library uses verb tunneling with `POST` and a header for cases where custom methods, such as `MERGE`, aren't allowed. You can learn more about the differences between `MERGE` and `PUT` methods from Pablo Castro's "Merge vs. Replace Semantics for Update Operations" post of May 20, 2008 (`http://blogs.msdn.com/astoriateam/archive/2008/05/20/merge-vs-replace-semantics-for-update-operations.aspx`).

Updating Entities with Code

For ease of use, the SampleWebCloudService project has an Update Customers button that executes the code of Listing 4-14 to toggle the change to the `CompanyName` property value.

Listing 4-14: Code to toggle a + suffix to the CompanyName property value

```
// Updates all CustomerTable entities individually
// Sets the customersView GridView's DataSource
protected void btnUpdateCusts_Click(object sender, EventArgs e)
{
    Stopwatch timer = new Stopwatch();
    timer.Start();
```

```
skipPreRenderTime = true;

CustomerDataServiceContext serviceContext = null;

// Create the service context to query against
serviceContext = new CustomerDataServiceContext(account);
serviceContext.RetryPolicy = RetryPolicies.RetryN(3,
    TimeSpan.FromSeconds(1));

var results = from c in serviceContext.CustomerTable
              select c;
TableStorageDataServiceQuery<CustomerDataModel> query =
    new TableStorageDataServiceQuery<CustomerDataModel>
    (results as DataServiceQuery<CustomerDataModel>);
IEnumerable<CustomerDataModel> queryResults =
    query.ExecuteAllWithRetries();

// Toggle them as updated
foreach (var result in results)
{
    if (result.CompanyName.Contains("+"))
        result.CompanyName =
            result.CompanyName.Substring(0, result.CompanyName.Length - 1);
    else
        result.CompanyName += "+";
    serviceContext.UpdateObject(result);
}
serviceContext.SaveChanges();

// Display the current page of changed entities
customersView.DataSource = null;
customersView.DataSourceID = "customerData";
customersView.DataBind();
txtTime.Text = (timer.ElapsedMilliseconds / 1000D).ToString("0.000");
}
```

Updating Entities with the HTTP MERGE Method

Listing 4-15 contains the MERGE request header and body and Listing 4-16 contains the response header for an update that adds a + symbol to the first CustomerTable entity on the first page.

Listing 4-15: HTTP MERGE request header and body for an update to the first CustomerTable entity

```
MERGE /CustomerTable(PartitionKey='Customer',RowKey='ALFKI') HTTP/1.1
User-Agent: Microsoft ADO.NET Data Services
x-ms-date: Thu, 26 Feb 2009 22:27:48 GMT
Authorization: SharedKeyLite oakleaf:rQwBAjjf2A2rTVJGXtgUzePpqZbIUS6ScK03ehVAI2s=
Accept: application/atom+xml,application/xml
Accept-Charset: UTF-8
DataServiceVersion: 1.0;NetFx
```

Continued

Listing 4-15: HTTP MERGE request header and body for an update to the first CustomerTable entity *(continued)*

```
MaxDataServiceVersion: 1.0;NetFx
Content-Type: application/atom+xml
If-Match: W/"datetime'2009-02-26T22%3A13%3A35.4152565Z'"
Host: oakleaf.table.core.windows.net
Content-Length: 1187
Expect: 100-continue

<?xml version="1.0" encoding="utf-8" standalone="yes"?>
<entry xmlns:d="http://schemas.microsoft.com/ado/2007/08/dataservices"
xmlns:m="http://schemas.microsoft.com/ado/2007/08/dataservices/metadata"
xmlns="http://www.w3.org/2005/Atom">
  <title />
  <updated>2009-02-26T22:27:48.0812664Z</updated>
  <author>
    <name />
  </author>
  <id>http://oakleaf.table.core.windows.net/CustomerTable(PartitionKey='Customer',
      RowKey='ALFKI')</id>
  <content type="application/xml">
    <m:properties>
      <d:Address>Obere Str. 57</d:Address>
      <d:City>Berlin</d:City>
      <d:CompanyName>Alfreds Futterkiste+</d:CompanyName>
      <d:ContactName>Maria Anders</d:ContactName>
      <d:ContactTitle>Sales Representative</d:ContactTitle>
      <d:Country>Germany</d:Country>
      <d:CustomerID>ALFKI</d:CustomerID>
      <d:Fax>030-0076545</d:Fax>
      <d:PartitionKey>Customer</d:PartitionKey>
      <d:Phone>030-0074321</d:Phone>
      <d:PostalCode>12209</d:PostalCode>
      <d:Region m:null="true" />
      <d:RowKey>ALFKI</d:RowKey>
      <d:Timestamp m:type="Edm.DateTime">2009-02-26T22:13:35.4152565Z</d:Timestamp>
    </m:properties>
  </content>
</entry>
```

Listing 4-16: HTTP MERGE response after an update to the first CustomerTable entity

```
HTTP/1.1 204 No Content
Cache-Control: no-cache
Content-Length: 0
ETag: W/"datetime'2009-02-26T22%3A26%3A09.7397062Z'"
Server: Table Service Version 1.0 Microsoft-HTTPAPI/2.0
x-ms-request-id: e61443a9-7f12-41a9-bd08-dd726dee52c2
Date: Thu, 26 Feb 2009 22:26:09 GMT
```

Notice that the response contains the generated ETag *header value for the updated values for use by subsequent concurrency conflict detection code.*

Deleting Entities

The final CRUD operation is deleting entities. The .NET Client Library doesn't support wildcards in Where expressions, so deletions must iterate the collection of entities to be deleted and mark them to be deleted individually, as shown in Listing 4-17.

Listing 4-17: Code to delete all Customer entities in the CustomerTable

```
// Deletes all CustomerTable entities individually
// Resets the customersView GridView's DataSource
protected void btnDeleteAll_Click(object sender, EventArgs e)
{
    Stopwatch timer = new Stopwatch();
    timer.Start();
    skipPreRenderTime = true;
    var results = from c in serviceContext.CustomerTable
                  select c;
    TableStorageDataServiceQuery<CustomerDataModel> query =
        new TableStorageDataServiceQuery<CustomerDataModel>
            (results as DataServiceQuery<CustomerDataModel>);
    IEnumerable<CustomerDataModel> queryResults = query.ExecuteAllWithRetries();

    foreach (var result in results)
    {
        serviceContext.DeleteObject(result);
    }
    serviceContext.SaveChanges();
    customersView.DataSource = null;
    customersView.DataSourceID = "customerData";
    customersView.DataBind();

    btnCreateCustomers.Enabled = true;
    btnUpdateCusts.Enabled = false;
    txtTime.Text = (timer.ElapsedMilliseconds / 1000D).ToString("0.000");
}
```

Invoking the SaveChanges() method deletes the entities from their table with multiple DELETE requests and responses similar to those in Listings 4-18 and 4-19:

Listing 4-18: HTTP DELETE request for a CustomerTable entity

```
DELETE /CustomerTable(PartitionKey='Customer',RowKey='ALFKI') HTTP/1.1
User-Agent: Microsoft ADO.NET Data Services
x-ms-date: Thu, 26 Feb 2009 22:14:57 GMT
Authorization: SharedKeyLite oakleaf:y/UUPazLiQK2ULhjJnBxOT5FxtM0ofM3S+f2qESvWJo=
Accept: application/atom+xml,application/xml
Accept-Charset: UTF-8
DataServiceVersion: 1.0;NetFx
MaxDataServiceVersion: 1.0;NetFx
Content-Type: application/atom+xml
If-Match: W/"datetime'2009-02-26T16%3A00%3A55.7667062Z'"
Host: oakleaf.table.core.windows.net
Content-Length: 0
```

Listing 4-19: HTTP DELETE response after deleting a CustomerTable entity

```
HTTP/1.1 204 No Content
Cache-Control: no-cache
Content-Length: 0
Server: Table Service Version 1.0 Microsoft-HTTPAPI/2.0
x-ms-request-id: 138a7375-20ca-47a0-8257-6dbe6d4f8253
Date: Thu, 26 Feb 2009 22:13:19 GMT
```

Storing and Retrieving Blobs

Working with Azure Blob Services is considerably simpler than manipulating Azure Tables and entities. Figure 4-12 shows the AzureBlobTest project running on the Developer Fabric after the download of seven BMP and eight ZIP blobs from Windows Live SkyDrive public folders and the upload of them to Azure Blob Services in the cloud.

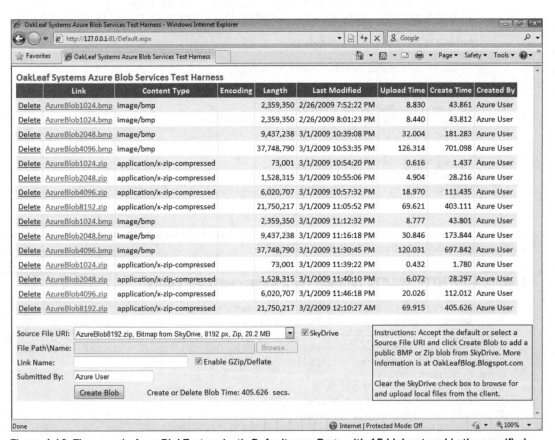

Figure 4-12: The sample AzureBlobTest project's Default.aspx Page with 15 blobs stored in the specified Container.

The SkyDrive check box is marked by default, making SkyDrive the source for BMP and ZIP blobs that you select in the Source File URI drop-down list. Selecting a blob from this list fills the Link Name text box with "AzureBlob" plus the width of the bitmap in pixels and the file type extension. To order the list in the addition sequence, blobs are named with UTC date and time in ISO 8601 format. Clicking a Link item with a `bmp` extension generates a URL, such as `http://oakleaf2.blob.core.windows .net/oakleaf2store/2009-02-26T19:53:07.7481188Z.bmp Target="_Blank"`, to open a BMP file in a new window. Blob URIs use the `http://servicename.blob.core.windows.net/containername/ [path/]blobname.ext` format. The `containername` is the Project Label you gave to an Azure Storage Account you created from a Hosted Service token in the Azure Services Developer Portal.

> *The Create a Project – Project Properties page of early Windows Azure CTPs states that Project Label and Project Description "information is used only on the developer panel." This statement isn't correct.*

Clicking a Link item with a `zip` extension opens a File Download dialog with buttons to open or save the ZIP file, or cancel the operation.

Clearing the SkyDrive check box disables the drop-down list and enables the File Path/Name text box and Browse button, which lets users update files from the local file system when running the project in the Development Framework.

> *The Upload Times shown in Figure 4-12 are the time in seconds to retrieve the files from SkyDrive; Create Times are the times in seconds required to stream the blobs to Azure Blob Services in the cloud. These operations were conducted over an AT&T DSL connection that tested 2,544 kbps download and 429 kbps upload immediately before the preceding operations. The ratio of Upload to Create times reflects the approximate 6:1 ratio of download to upload network speed.*
>
> *The "Initial Azure Blob Generation Time vs. File Size Graph" post (`http://bit.ly/12lsCq`, `http://oakleafblog.blogspot.com/2009/01/initial-azure-blob-generation-time-vs.html`) provides a graphical and tabular representation of the much shorter times required to perform the same operations with cloud storage.*

Blob Content Types

Blobs are byte arrays, so they can contain any type of data that can be expressed as a series of octets. The maximum length of an Azure blob is 50GB in the latest CTP. A blob's data type is defined by its `Content-Type` HTTP header value, which uses a `type/subtype` format defined by IETF RFC 2046, "Multipurpose Internet Mail Extensions (MIME) Part Two: Media Types" (`www.ietf.org/rfc/ rfc2046.txt`). RFC 2046 defines the top-level media types listed in the following table.

RFC 2046's authors anticipated that many additional subtypes would be required and designated the Internet Assigned Numbers Agency (IANA) as the registrar of media types. IANA's MIME Media Types page (`http://bit.ly/nnCIb`, `www.iana.org/assignments/media-types/`) lists current content types with links to current subtypes. When this book was written, IANA had added `example`, which cannot be used in a `Content-Type` header, and `model` as registered MIME media types, and a large number of subtypes for most types.

Media types and subtypes that begin with x- are classified as experimental (private) values to be used by consenting systems by mutual agreement. The use of experimental values as top-level types is strongly discouraged; most x- values are `application` subtypes. Most Azure-specific metadata uses x-ms-* or similar experimental HTTP headers, such as x-ms-date: Thu, 26 Feb 2009 21:05:25 GMT.

Class	Type	RFC 2046 Description
Discrete	Text	Textual information; the subtype plain indicates that the data contains no formatting commands.
Discrete	Image	Image data, which requires a display device to view the information; RFC 2046 defines initial jpeg and gif subtypes.
Discrete	Audio	Audio data, which requires an audio output device to "display" the data; RFC 2046 defines an initial basic subtype.
Discrete	Video	Video data, which requires the capability to display moving images; RFC 2046 defines an initial mpeg subtype.
Discrete	application	Discrete data that do not fit any other category. RFC 2046 defines initial octet-stream and PostScript subtypes.
Composite	Multipart	Data consisting of multiple entities of independent data types.
Composite	Message	An encapsulated message.

Figure 4-13: Diagrams of the BlobContainer and BlobStorage
abstract classes and BlobContents class in the BlobStorage.cd file.

The StorageClient Class Library's Blob Storage and REST Blob Storage Classes

The StorageClient class library has fewer Blob than Table classes because Blobs have one fewer levels in their hierarchy than Tables. Figures 4-13 through 4-15 show the class diagrams from StorageClient's BlobStorage.cd and RestBlobStorage.cd files.

The `BlobContainerRest` and `BlobStorageRest` classes, which are used extensively in the code sections that follow, inherit from `BlobContainer` and `BlobStorage`.

Obtaining a File from Windows Live SkyDrive and Uploading It to Azure Blob Storage with Code

Listing 4-20 contains the code that downloads blobs from Windows Live SkyDrive and uploads them or files from the client's file system to Azure Blob Storage. The blob and log account and container names are stored with other related metadata in the ServiceConfiguration.cscfg file's `ConfigurationSettings` section. There's little that users can do about errors when running the project in production, so error-handling consists of writing messages to a `statusMessage` text box invoking the `RoleManager.WriteToLog()` method to add blobs with error information to the `oakleaf2log` container.

Figure 4-14: Diagrams of the ContainerProperties, BlobProperties, and RetryProperties classes in the BlobStorage.cd file.

Figure 4-15: Diagrams of the BlobContainerRest, BlobStorageRest, and ListContainersResult classes and the XPathQueryHelper static class in the RestBlobStorage.cd file.

Listing 4-20: Code to download a file in 4,096-byte chunks to a MemoryStream and upload it in 1MB blocks to an Azure Blob Services Container

```
{
    public partial class _Default : System.Web.UI.Page
    {
        // Attempt to add a blob from a SkyDrive file or from the local file system
        protected void insertButton_Click(object sender, EventArgs e)
        {
            // Clear the status message
            statusMessage.Text = null;
            requestId = null;

            try
            {
                // Set fileUpload validation
                string extension = null;
                if (chkSkyDrive.Checked)
                {
                    fileUploadValidator.Enabled = false;
                    extension = lstURLs.SelectedValue;
                    extension = extension.Substring(extension.LastIndexOf("."));
                    if (extension.Contains(".com"))
                        // Special-case for HTML page/blog downloads
                        extension = ".html";
                }
                else
                {
                    fileUploadValidator.Enabled = true;
                    extension = return
                        System.IO.Path.GetExtension(fileUploadControl.FileName);
                }

                // Use high-resolution ISO8601 UTC DateTime string to order entries
                string utcDate = DateTime.Now.ToUniversalTime().ToString("o");
                BlobProperties properties = new BlobProperties(utcDate + extension);

                // Create metadata to be associated with the blob
                NameValueCollection metadata = new NameValueCollection();
                metadata["FileName"] = fileNameBox.Text;
                metadata["CreateTime"] = "0.000";
                metadata["Submitter"] = submitterBox.Text;

                // Time upload operation
                sw.Reset();
                sw.Start();

                // Get the blob data
                BlobContents fileBlob = null;

                long contentLength = 0;
                if (chkSkyDrive.Checked)
                {
```

Continued

Listing 4-20: Code to download a file in 4,096-byte chunks to a MemoryStream and upload it in 1MB blocks to an Azure Blob Services Container *(continued)*

```
                    // Create a web request allowing common/all MIME types
                    HttpWebRequest request =
                        (HttpWebRequest)WebRequest.Create(lstURLs.SelectedValue);
                    request.Accept =
                        "image/gif, image/jpeg, image/pjpeg, image/png, " +
                        "image/bmp, application/x-gzip, application/x-zip, " +
                        "application/x-zip-compressed, application/octet-stream, " +
                        " */*";

                    if (chkEnableGZip.Checked)
                        // Support GZip, deflate
                        request.Headers.Add(HttpRequestHeader.AcceptEncoding,
                            "gzip, deflate");

                    // Set GetResponse and GetRequestStream timeout to 300 seconds
                    // for large blobs
                    request.Timeout = 300 * 1000;
                    // Set timeout for writing to or reading from a stream to 300
                    // seconds for large blobs
                    request.ReadWriteTimeout = 300 * 1000;

                    // Get response header values for writable properties
                    WebHeaderCollection headers = request.GetResponse().Headers;
                    properties.ContentType = headers["Content-Type"];
                    properties.ContentEncoding = headers["Content-Encoding"];

                    // For logging
                    requestId = headers["x-ms-request-id"];

                    if (long.TryParse(headers["Content-Length"], out contentLength))
                    {
                        Stream respStream =
                            request.GetResponse().GetResponseStream();
                        if (chkEnableGZip.Checked
                            && properties.ContentEncoding != null)
                        {
                            // Decompress gzip/deflate streams
                            if (properties.ContentEncoding.ToLower()
                                .Contains("gzip"))
                            {
                                respStream = new GZipStream(respStream,
                                    CompressionMode.Decompress);
                            }
                            else if

                                (properties.ContentEncoding.ToLower()
                                    .Contains("deflate"))
                            {
                                respStream = new DeflateStream(respStream,
                                    CompressionMode.Decompress);
                            }
                        }
```

```
        headers = request.GetResponse().Headers;
        // Chunking to blocks requires streams that support seeking
        // (.CanSeek = true)
        using (MemoryStream memStream = new MemoryStream())
        {
            // Use a 4-kB buffer
            byte[] buffer = new byte[4096];
            int count = 0;
            do
            {
                count = respStream.Read(buffer, 0, buffer.Length);
                memStream.Write(buffer, 0, count);
            } while (count != 0);
            fileBlob = new BlobContents(memStream.ToArray());
        }
        respStream.Close();
    }
}
else
{
    properties.ContentType =
        fileUploadControl.PostedFile.ContentType;
    contentLength = fileUploadControl.PostedFile.ContentLength;
    fileBlob = new BlobContents(fileUploadControl.FileBytes);
}
metadata["UploadTime"] = (sw.ElapsedMilliseconds /
    1000D).ToString("#,##0.000");

if (contentLength > 0)
{
    // Add metadata to properties
    properties.Metadata = metadata;

    // Time blob creation
    sw.Reset();
    sw.Start();
    blobContainer.CreateBlob(properties, fileBlob, true);
    lblTime.Text = (sw.ElapsedMilliseconds /
        1000D).ToString("#,##0.000");
    metadata["CreateTime"] = lblTime.Text;

    properties.Metadata = metadata;
    blobContainer.UpdateBlobMetadata(properties);

    if (doWriteLogs)
    {
        string logEntry = properties.Name + ";" +
            metadata["FileName"] +
            ";" + properties.ContentType + ";" +
            properties.ContentEncoding + ";" +
            contentLength.ToString("#,##0") + ";" +
            properties.LastModifiedTime + ";" +
            metadata["UploadTime"] + ";" +
            metadata["CreateTime"] + ";" +
```

Continued

101

Listing 4-20: Code to download a file in 4,096-byte chunks to a MemoryStream and upload it in 1MB blocks to an Azure Blob Services Container *(continued)*

```
                                metadata["Submitter"] + ";" +
                                DateTime.Now.ToString();
                        RoleManager.WriteToLog("Verbose", logEntry);
                    }

                    // Update the UI
                    UpdateFileList();
                    fileNameBox.Text = "";
                    statusMessage.Text = "";
                }
                else
                {
                    statusMessage.Text = "Zero-length blob not created.";
                    // x-ms-request-id included in logs per Jai Haridas, 1/3/2009
                    if (requestId == null)
                        RoleManager.WriteToLog("Error",
                            "Attempt to add zero-length blob.");
                    else
                        RoleManager.WriteToLog("Error",
                            "Attempt to add zero-length blob (x-ms-request-id = " +
                            requestId + ").");
                }
            }
            catch (WebException webExcept)
            {
                statusMessage.Text = "Web Exception uploading blob: " +
                    webExcept.Message;
                if (requestId != null)
                    statusMessage.Text += " (x-ms-request-id = " + requestId +
                        ").";

                if (doWriteLogs)
                    RoleManager.WriteToLog("Error", statusMessage.Text);

            }
            catch (Exception ex)
            {
                statusMessage.Text = "Exception uploading blob: " + ex.Message;
                if (requestId != null)
                    statusMessage.Text += " (x-ms-request-id = " + requestId + ").";

                if (doWriteLogs)
                    RoleManager.WriteToLog("Error", statusMessage.Text);
            }
        }
    }
}
```

Persisting Log Blobs to Containers

The RoleManager.WriteToLog() method writes messages to the virtual operating system's event log, which isn't accessible to Azure or .NET Services. Log entries are the only method for debugging services running in the Azure Fabric, so the Azure team provides a means to persist event log entries to blobs. To copy the logs to blobs contained in a designated container name (oakleaf2logs for this example), open the Hosted Service (oakleaf2host), click the Production service's Configure button to open the *ServiceName* – Production Deployment – Azure Blob Test Harness – Service Tuning page, type the Container Name, and click the Copy Logs button (see Figure 4-16). The copying process occurs within a minute or two under normal conditions.

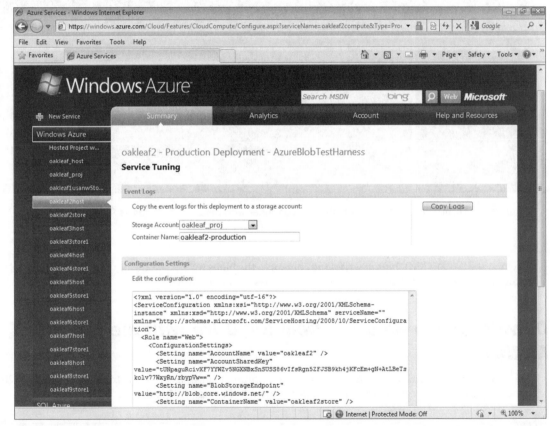

Figure 4-16: Copying logs from the virtual operating system's event logs to the designated container name.

Viewing Content and Log Blobs with Utilities

Several utilities exist for viewing and copying Azure Hosted Services' XML log data. Many have operating system or other limitations, which makes them less useful. Bill Lodin's Windows Azure Log Viewer project works under Windows Vista and filters blobs to list only log files; more information and source code for the project is available at `http://bit.ly/WykNP`, `http://msdn.microsoft.com/en-us/azure/dd637760.aspx`. Figure 4-17 shows error logs that occurred when SkyDrive was temporarily out of commission on January 5, 2009.

Azure creates log blobs for each 15-minute period in which at least one log entry occurs.

Figure 4-17: Displaying a list of error blobs in a container with Bill Lodin's Windows Azure Log Viewer.

Clicking the Save to XML button writes the content of the blobs to an XML file of your choice. Figure 4-18 shows IE 8 displaying the content of the error log files list in Figure 4-18.

Downloading a Blob File from SkyDrive with the HTTP GET Method

The `Stream respStream = request.GetResponse().GetResponseStream();` instruction in Listing 4-20 generates the GET request and response headers shown in Listings 4-21 and 4-22.

Listing 4-21: HTTP GET request for uploading a 2.36MB public bitmap blob from Windows Live SkyDrive

```
GET
/y1pmIyIHdmdh72WYsCNJpCXaDrO4l0byEZYgC6nTVoc2WwoLb1rMSvvB8LO70Itetoy8s1PWwo9rwOga_D
iyzaA_w/AzureBlob1024.bmp HTTP/1.1
Accept: image/gif, image/jpeg, image/pjpeg, image/png, image/bmp,
application/x-gzip,  application/x-zip, application/x-zip-compressed,
application/octet-stream, */*
Accept-Encoding: gzip, deflate
Host: fjhpug.bay.livefilestore.com
```

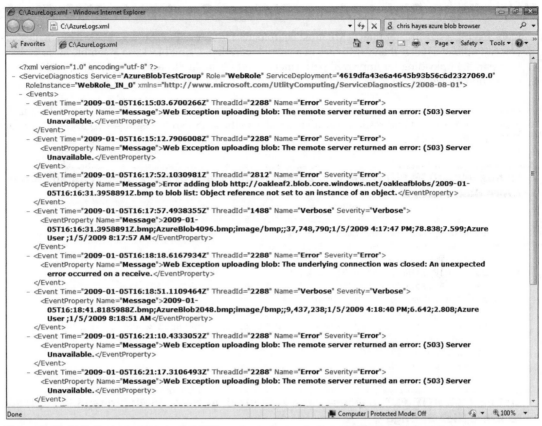

Figure 4-18: IE 8 displaying the partial XML content of error logs copied from a blob container.

Listing 4-22: HTTP GET response for uploading a 2.36MB public bitmap blob from Windows Live SkyDrive

```
HTTP/1.1 200 OK
Date: Thu, 26 Feb 2009 21:04:55 GMT
Server: Microsoft-IIS/6.0
P3P: CP="BUS CUR CONo FIN IVDo ONL OUR PHY SAMo TELo"
X-Powered-By: ASP.NET
X-MSNSERVER: BY2STRWBA260
X-AspNet-Version: 2.0.50727
Content-Location:
http://fjhpug.bay.livefilestore.com/y1pAalNawB0iSRMtfpb09bdujbj6ejuC1T6
jCNp7pXQM8ZAFTG7gYJEjFztfT68gAY04JVEa9UbLS8
Content-Length: 2359350
X-SqlDataOrigin: S
X-StreamOrigin: B
Cache-Control: private
Expires: Wed, 27 May 2009 21:04:55 GMT
Last-Modified: Sun, 28 Dec 2008 16:46:11 GMT
Content-Type: image/bmp
```

Uploading a Blob to Azure Storage Services in 1MB Blocks

Blobs having a size greater than 64MB must be uploaded to Azure Blob Storage in 4MB or smaller blocks; you can upload smaller than 64MB files in a single operation. Using blocks to assemble large blobs permits parallel uploading for improved performance and the ability to resume uploading in the event of connection problems.

Executing the `blobContainer.CreateBlob(properties, fileBlob, true);` instruction in Listing 4-20 generates PUT request and response headers similar to those shown in Listings 4-23 and 4-24 for each 1MB or smaller block.

Listing 4-23: HTTP PUT request to upload a 1MB block of the 2.36MB bitmap blob to Azure Blob Storage

```
PUT /oakleaf2store/2009-02-26T21%3a04%3a55.8384887Z.bmp?comp=block
&blockid=AQAAAA%3d%3d&timeout=30 HTTP/1.1
x-ms-date: Thu, 26 Feb 2009 21:05:25 GMT
Content-Type: image/bmp
x-ms-meta-FileName: AzureBlob1024.bmp
x-ms-meta-CreateTime: 0.000
x-ms-meta-Submitter: Azure User
x-ms-meta-UploadTime: 8.932
Authorization: SharedKey oakleaf2:frBWGtgXfH8bjaexWvBm5Z+wpFnWtrS5TKduk4wrzL0=
Host: oakleaf2.blob.core.windows.net
Content-Length: 1048576
Expect: 100-continue
```

Listing 4-24: HTTP PUT response for a 1MB block of the 2.36MB bitmap blob uploaded to Azure Blob Storage

```
HTTP/1.1 201 Created
Transfer-Encoding: chunked
Content-MD5: m10f0+eN72dLslV53O6qpQ==
Server: Blob Service Version 1.0 Microsoft-HTTPAPI/2.0
x-ms-request-id: 33363ac5-daf7-4ced-8194-b6d15bde008c
Date: Thu, 26 Feb 2009 21:04:06 GMT
```

Downloading a Selected Blob

As mentioned earlier, clicking a filename for a blob of the `image` media type in the GridView's Link column opens the image in its own window. Blobs of the `application` media type usually open a File Download dialog.

Opening a Selected Blob in a Browser or Dialog with Code

The emphasized lines of the Default.aspx page's source code in Listing 4-25 generate the FileURI for the blob, such as `http://oakleaf2.blob.core.windows.net/oakleaf2store/2009-02-26T19:53:07 .7481188Z.bmp Target="_Blank"`, to open a BMP file in a new window.

Listing 4-25: ASP.NET source code to open the selected file in a new window or display a file download dialog

```
<asp:GridView ID="fileView"
    AutoGenerateColumns="False" DataKeyNames="BlobName"
    Runat="server" onrowcommand="RowCommandHandler" BackColor="White"
    BorderColor="#DEDFDE" BorderStyle="None" BorderWidth="1px" CellPadding="4"
    ForeColor="Black" GridLines="Vertical" onrowdeleted="fileView_RowDeleted"
    onrowdeleting="fileView_RowDeleting" AllowSorting="True"
    EnableSortingAndPagingCallbacks="True">
    <RowStyle BackColor="#F7F7DE" />
    <Columns>
        <asp:ButtonField Text="Delete" CommandName="DeleteItem"/>
        <asp:HyperLinkField
            HeaderText="Link"
            DataTextField="FileName"
            DataNavigateUrlFields="FileUri" Target="_blank" />
        ...
    </Columns>
    ...
</asp:GridView>
```

Displaying a Selected Bitmap Blob in a Browser with a GET Request

The emphasized ASP.NET source code of Listing 4-25 generates the HTTP GET request and response shown in Listings 4-26 and 4-27 for a blob that has the image media type.

Listing 4-26: HTTP GET request for the 2.36MB bitmap blob from Azure Blob Storage

```
GET /oakleaf2store/2009-02-26T21:04:55.8384887Z.bmp HTTP/1.1
Accept: */*
Referer: http://127.0.0.1:82/Default.aspx
Accept-Language: en-us
User-Agent: Mozilla/4.0 (compatible; MSIE 8.0; Windows NT 6.0; Trident/4.0; SLCC1;
.NET CLR 2.0.50727; Media Center PC 5.0; .NET CLR 3.5.21022; .NET CLR 3.5.30428;
.NET CLR 3.5.30729; .NET CLR 3.0.30618; MS-RTC LM 8; InfoPath.2;
OfficeLiveConnector.1.3; OfficeLivePatch.1.3)
Accept-Encoding: gzip, deflate
Host: oakleaf2.blob.core.windows.net
Connection: Keep-Alive
```

Listing 4-27: HTTP GET response for the 2.36MB bitmap blob from Azure Blob Storage

```
HTTP/1.1 200 OK
Content-Length: 2359350
Content-Type: image/bmp
Last-Modified: Thu, 26 Feb 2009 21:04:12 GMT
ETag: 0x8CB666CE8A66E7D
Server: Blob Service Version 1.0 Microsoft-HTTPAPI/2.0
x-ms-request-id: 56fdeb2e-9e83-45b8-84ed-2eb944457acf
```

Continued

Listing 4-27: HTTP GET response for the 2.36MB bitmap blob from Azure Blob Storage
(continued)

```
x-ms-meta-FileName: AzureBlob1024.bmp
x-ms-meta-CreateTime: 45.332

x-ms-meta-Submitter: Azure User
x-ms-meta-UploadTime: 8.932
Date: Thu, 26 Feb 2009 21:18:24 GMT
```

Deleting a Specified Blob

You can't update blob content directly in the CTP used to write this book, so the only remaining CRUD operation on CTP blobs is deletion. The Azure group promises to enable replacing, adding, or removing a blob's blocks, and copying blobs to a new blob name in future versions.

You can update blob metadata with code in the CTP.

Deleting a Blob Selected in a GridView Control with Code

Listing 4-28 contains the code to find the blob selected for deletion from a current list and delete it by invoking the DeleteBlob() method.

Listing 4-28: Deleting a blob belected in a GridView control with code (not scalable)

```
// Process DeleteItem command
protected void RowCommandHandler(object sender, GridViewCommandEventArgs e)
{
    if (e.CommandName == "DeleteItem")
    {
        // Clear the status message
        statusMessage.Text = null;

        // Get blob count
        IEnumerable<object> blobList = blobContainer.ListBlobs(String.Empty, false);

        if (blobList.Count() > 3)
        {
            // Multiple users can have out-of-range index values
            try
            {
                int index = Convert.ToInt32(e.CommandArgument);
                if (index < fileView.DataKeys.Count)
                {
                    string blobName = (string)fileView.DataKeys[index].Value;
                    if (blobContainer.DoesBlobExist(blobName))
                    {
                        // Start deletion elapsed time
                        sw.Reset();
                        sw.Start();
                        blobContainer.DeleteBlob(blobName);
                        lblTime.Text = (sw.ElapsedMilliseconds /
                            1000D).ToString("#,##0.000");
```

```
                    }
                }
            }
            catch (Exception ex)
            {
                statusMessage.Text = "Can't delete selected item. " + ex.Message;

                if (doWriteLogs)
                        RoleManager.WriteToLog("Error", statusMessage.Text);
            }
        }
        else
            statusMessage.Text =
                "You must leave at least 3 blobs in the GridView for other users.";
    }
    UpdateFileList();
}
```

The approach used for deletion in listing isn't scalable because it depends on the blobList being immutable during the interval between selection and execution of the DeleteBlob() method. The interval might be a microsecond or less, but it introduces unacceptable uncertainty in the process. If e.Command returned the GridView's index value instead of index position, the value could be used with the DoesBlobExist test to delete the blob without the uncertainty.

Deleting a Blob Selected in a GridView Control with an HTTP DELETE Request

Executing the DeleteBlob() method generates the HTTP DELETE request and response headers of Listings 4-29 and 4-30.

Listing 4-29: HTTP DELETE request for the 2.36MB bitmap blob from Azure Blob Storage

```
DELETE /oakleaf2store/2009-02-26T20%3a10%3a00.7204059Z.bmp?timeout=30 HTTP/1.1
x-ms-date: Thu, 26 Feb 2009 20:38:27 GMT
Authorization: SharedKey oakleaf2:o4KZgoYFlaUymMACWp7NTmx81PzVR3Ydg5bHErVDUVQ=
Host: oakleaf2.blob.core.windows.net
Content-Length: 0
```

Listing 4-30: HTTP DELETE response for the 2.36MB bitmap blob from Azure Blob Storage

```
HTTP/1.1 202 Accepted
Server: Blob Service Version 1.0 Microsoft-HTTPAPI/2.0
x-ms-request-id: 03717cbb-dc34-4b97-b7aa-a3f3d8e353a3
Date: Thu, 26 Feb 2009 20:38:47 GMT
Content-Length: 0
```

Taking Advantage of New Copy Blob and Get Blob List Methods

The Windows Azure SDK (May 2009 CTP) introduced new Copy Blob PUT and Get Blob List GET request methods. Like the new EGTs for tables Copy Blob, you must specify an x-ms-version request header with a value of `2009-04-14`. Copy Blob copies a blob to a destination within the storage account; Get Blob List retrieves the list of blocks that have been uploaded as part of a blob; the May 2009 CTP version lets you specify lists of committed, uncommitted, or all blocks.

Online help for Copy Blob is available at `http://bit.ly/u0e5y`, `http://msdn.microsoft.com/en-us/library/dd894037.aspx` and for Get Blob List at `http://bit.ly/sQxbA`, `http://msdn.microsoft.com/en-us/library/dd179400.aspx`.

The May 2009 CTP's development environment and implementation of the sample `StorageClient` *wrapper don't support Copy Blob or Get Blob List operations, so you can't execute these methods with conventional .NET code that uses* `StorageClient` *objects.*

Steve Marx's "Sample Code for New Windows Azure Blob Features" post (`http://bit.ly/JjRuS`, `http://blog.smarx.com/posts/sample-code-for-new-windows-azure-blob-features`) includes an updated `StorageClient` *library and a simple test program to demonstrate these two methods.*

Late Changes to Azure Blobs

The Azure Team announced on August 11, 2009 the following three new features for `x-ms-version: 2009-7-17` of Azure Blobs:

- ❑   **Update Blob with PutBlockList**. Update the contents of a blob with `PutBlockList`, which lets you add blocks, remove blocks, replace blocks, shuffle the order of existing blocks, or any combination of these for an existing blob. You only need to upload the blocks you want to add or change.

- ❑   **Root Blob Container**. All storage accounts now can have a single root blob container. This enables applications to store and reference blobs with the domain address, such as in this sample:

- ❑   `http://myaccount.blob.core.windows.net/picture.jpg`

- ❑   This version also changes the way applications perform operations on containers to make it explicit that it is a container operation instead of a blob operation. For example, to create a container named `pictures`, issue the following PUT request:

- ❑   `PUT http://myaccount.blob.core.windows.net/pictures?restype=container`

- ❑   **Shared Access Signatures for Signed URLs**. You can create signatures, with an expiration date, that you can give to users to provide access to Azure Blobs without needing to disclose your private key value or make the blob container public. Following is a URL example with a signature (starting after the `?` query character) that allows read access to all blobs in the pictures container until July 20, 2009 and access to the `profile.jpg` blob in the `pictures` container.

    `GET http://myaccount.blob.core.windows.net/pictures/profile.jpg?`

    `se=2009-07-20&sr=c&sp=r&sig=xUXi%2f%2fxnETUHQoVOMGS06OkEiTo%3d`

    You create a signature computing a hash over a canonicalization of the request using your storage account secret key. The signature can then be used as part of the URL to provide read, write, or delete access for blob requests. Azure evangelist Steve Marx's "New Storage Feature: Signed Access Signatures" post of August 11, 2009 (`http://bit.ly/WFjlU`, `http://blog.smarx.com/posts/new-storage-feature-signed-access-signatures`) offers a sample application that lets you upload a file and specify the duration of its availability.

This operation returns a special URL that others can use to access the uploaded file until the expiration time.

The Update Blog with PutBlockList and Root Blob Container operations require you to specify `x-ms-version: 2009-7-17` in the header; Shared Access Signatures don't. The update also includes three minor semantic changes for blobs and one for tables. When this book was written, only the Windows Azure Storage REST interface supported these new features; support by the Windows Azure SDK and the `StorageClient` sample class library were scheduled to follow. Documentation for the new features is available at `http://bit.ly/t5VcY`, `http://msdn.microsoft.com/en-us/library/dd135733.aspx`.

Summary

Azure Storage Services provides scalable persistent stores for semi-structured or structured data in Azure Tables, file-based byte arrays in Azure Blobs, and messages containing text or serialized objects in Azure Queues. To assure data reliability, each instance of an Azure data type is stored as a master and two replicas, which are located in different failure domains. Ultimately, data can be replicated to two or more data centers for increased data security. Access to tables and queues requires knowledge of the storage account name and primary or secondary account shared key for security; blobs in containers designated as public can be accessed by anyone who knows the blob's URL. During Azure's test period, redeeming an access token for a free Hosted Service enables creating two no-charge Storage Accounts. Hosted Azure .NET applications as well as conventional applications written in any popular computer language can access Tables, Blobs, and Queues with the Web-standard REST API. The Azure SDK includes a .NET 3.5 SP1 `StorageClient` class library of wrappers for the REST API to simplify .NET programming with CLR objects.

Azure Tables use a schemaless Entity-Attribute-Value data model instead of the more common relational model because relational tables with fixed schema are notoriously difficult to scale to terabytes or petabytes and restructure after growing to these sizes. All tables contain three system properties (attributes): PartitionKey, RowKey, and Timestamp. Partitions define the unit of table consistency; PartitionKey and RowKey values define the equivalent of a composite primary key for the table. Custom attributes are a property bag whose members can vary within the table. The Google App Engine's Data Store and Amazon Web Service's SimpleDB use the EAV data model with query languages that emulate a SQL subset to return result sets. Azure uses LINQ to REST queries in conjunction with ADO.NET Data Services and the `StorageClient` classes to return entity collections. The chapter provided examples of CRUD operations on Azure Tables with LINQ or the REST API.

Azure Blobs consist of octets (named byte arrays) up to 50GB in length of any registered or experimental media type. Arrays of 64MB or fewer can be stored directly to a blob; large arrays are created by uploading multiple blocks up to 4MB in length. Assembling blobs from blocks permits uploading blocks in parallel and resuming block assembly after an interruption. Named containers store an unlimited number of blobs and may be designated as publically or privately readable. The chapter included examples for creating, retrieving, and deleting blobs with the REST API or .NET code that accesses the `StorageClient` classes.

Part II

Taking Advantage of Cloud Services in the Enterprise

5

Minimizing Risk When Moving to Azure Cloud Services

Earlier chapters observed that the Windows Azure Platform's capability to leverage developers' C# or VB programming expertise with Visual Studio is a primary selling point for the Windows Azure Platform, which must compete with entrenched cloud-computing rivals — such as Amazon Web Services' Elastic Computing Cloud (EC2) and the Google App Engine. You might infer from Azure marketing materials that you can simply take an existing ASP.NET Web site, tweak its Web.config settings and SQL Server connection string, and upload it to a Microsoft data center for deployment to Windows Azure.

As usual, reality differs greatly from marketing hype. As you'll see in this chapter, obtaining management buy-in might take more time and energy than developing a completely new project or upgrading an existing one. Other impediments include

❑   Moving from an ASP.NET web site to web application projects

❑   Migrating data to Azure Tables, Blobs, or SQL Data Services databases

❑   Moving the Web Application projects to Azure Hosted Services and connecting to Azure or SQL Azure Database

❑   Convincing IT and enterprise management that hosting applications in Windows Azure doesn't impose significant risk of business interruption or regulatory infraction

At least during Azure's early days, you'll find the last item to be by far the most difficult issue to overcome.

Bypassing Barriers to Cloud Computing

Your first step to an Azure development is convincing IT and top management that the cloud is a suitable hosting environment for an existing or new project. The initial objections probably will relate to entrusting a third party to provide application availability that's better than your on-premises IT department delivers. Maintaining complete confidentiality of valuable business information while in storage and in transit is a top concern in all management surveys of cloud-computing intentions. Although Microsoft-only or Microsoft-mostly shops are accustomed to Windows lock-in, management undoubtedly will be interested in portability of applications between clouds of multiple providers.

"Above the Clouds: A Berkeley View of Cloud Computing," is a whitepaper published in February 2009 by the UC Berkeley Reliable Adaptive Distributed Systems Laboratory (also known as RADLab; http://radlab.cs.berkeley.edu/), which received widespread attention from the computer press at least in part because of its vendor neutrality. "Above the Clouds" includes the following table to illustrate the 10 most important concerns of IT executives and top management when considering adopting cloud computing for their organizations:

Top 10 Obstacles to and Opportunities for Growth of Cloud Computing	
Obstacle	Opportunity
1 Availability of service	Use multiple cloud providers; use elasticity to prevent distributed denial of service attacks
2 Data lock-in	Standardize APIs; use compatible software to enable surge computing
3 Data confidentiality and auditability	Deploy encryption, VLANs, firewalls; geographical data storage
4 Data transfer bottlenecks	Using overnight courier for disks; data backup/archiving; higher bandwidth switches
5 Performance unpredictability	Improved VM support; flash memory; gang-schedule VMs
6 Scalable storage	Invent a scalable store
7 Bugs in large distributed systems	Invent a debugger that relies on distributed VMs
8 Scaling quickly	Invent an auto-scaler that relies on ML; use snapshots for conservation
9 Reputation/fate sharing	Offer reputation-guarding services like those for e-mail
10 Software licensing	Pay-for-use licenses; bulk-use sales

The following sections deal with obstacles from the preceding list that most cloud computing observers consider the most intransigent.

ML is a general-purpose functional programming language and an abbreviation for metalanguage.

Bernard Golden's "Cloud Computing: What UC Berkeley Can Teach You" article for the CIO web site (http://bit.ly/PCLZA, www.cio.com/article/483390/Cloud_Computing_What_UC_Berkeley_Can _Teach_You?taxonomyId=168354) *is a review of the whitepaper from an IT management perspective.*

Maximizing Data Availability and Minimizing Security Risks

Today's cloud-based infrastructures are likely to exhibit better availability than most enterprise on-premises IT services. Availability is usually measured in *nines*; for example, *four nines* represents services being available 99.99% of the time. There are 43,200 minutes in a 30-day month, so achieving four nines availability would permit a maximum of 4.32 minutes (0.01% of 43,200) of scheduled or unscheduled downtime per month.

It's common for telecommunications systems and data centers to be designed to achieve five nines availability, which corresponds to less than 30 seconds downtime per month. Cloud-computing vendors ultimately must enter into service-level agreements (SLAs) that specify competitive application availability. Customers want five nines, but it appears that vendors might offer only three nines; for example, Microsoft announced in mid-July 2009 that its SLA would cover 99.95% uptime guarantee for two or more Azure service instances and 99.9% availability for storage services. Similarly, Amazon Web Services warrants 99.95% uptime for EC2 and 99.9% for S3. Google hadn't announced an SLA for Google App Engine when this book was written. Cloud-computing SLAs offer rebates or credits for downtime but don't cover business interruption losses.

Regardless of the applicable SLA, it might take your application much longer than the downtime to recover from a catastrophic failure that requires restoring the application, data, or both from a backup copy. Azure provides failover clustering of thrice-replicated data and the Hosted Application instances running when failure occurs. Real-world recovery time for clustered applications and replicated data remains to be measured.

The "Above the Clouds" authors recorded outages for Amazon Simple Storage Service (S3), Google App Engine, and Gmail in 2008, and listed explanations for the outages in the publication's Table 7 with the following comment: "Note that despite the negative publicity due to these outages, few enterprise IT infrastructures are as good."

An IT-Related Risk Definition

The National Institute of Standards and Technology (NIST), formerly the National Bureau of Standards, defines *IT-Related Risk* as

> The net mission impact considering (1) the probability that a particular threat-source will exercise (accidentally trigger or intentionally exploit) a particular information system vulnerability and (2) the resulting impact if this should occur. IT-related risks arise from legal liability or mission loss due to:

1. Unauthorized (malicious or accidental) disclosure, modification, or destruction of information.

2. Unintentional errors and omissions.

3. IT disruptions due to natural or man-made disasters.

4. Failure to exercise due care and diligence in the implementation and operation of the IT system.

The preceding definition is part of National Institute of Standards and Technology Special Publication (NIST SP) 800-53 Revision 2, which provides guidelines for securing information systems within the federal government by employing security controls. The guidelines apply to all aspects of information systems that process, store, or transmit federal information, except national security systems as defined by 44 United States Code (U.S.C), Section 3542. NIST 800-53 Rev. 2 is intended to provide guidance to federal agencies in achieving a Federal Information Processing Standard (FIPS) 200, Minimum Security Requirements for Federal Information and Information Systems, baseline.

The federal government has a mixed history with IT initiatives with many notable failed attempts to adopt new technology. However, successful deployment of cloud computing and concomitant development of governance systems that minimize IT risk for the public sector will ameliorate availability and security concerns and spur adoption by the private sector. The federal contribution to private-sector cloud computing probably will center on formal standards for maintaining data availability and security. Federal and many state governments have privacy regulations for data that identifies individuals.

The Obama administration is likely to be more favorable to cloud computing proposals than its predecessors. For example, *ComputerWorld* magazine writer Patrick Thibodeau reported on March 5, 2009 in his "New federal CIO Vivek Kundra wants a Web 2.0 government" article:

> The U.S. government's first CIO, Vivek Kundra, introduced himself today as someone who will act aggressively to change the federal government's use of IT by adopting consumer technology and ensuring that government data is open and accessible.
>
> Kundra also wants to use technology such as cloud computing to attack the government's culture of big-contract boondoggles and its hiring of contractors who end up "on the payroll indefinitely."

Azure Web Services ensure application availability by replicating stored data at least three times and offering optional geolocation of replicas in separate Microsoft data centers to provide disaster recovery services.

NIST's Idea for Federal Cloud Computing Standards

Chapter 1's "Cloud Computing Concerns" section introduced "Perspectives on Cloud Computing and Standards" (http://bit.ly/x054z, http://csrc.nist.gov/groups/SMA/ispab/documents/minutes /2008-12/cloud-computing-standards_ISPAB-Dec2008_P-Mell.pdf), a presentation by Peter Mell and Tim Grance of NIST's Information Technology Laboratory. The presentation begins with a federal definition of standards-based cloud computing and continues with an "idea: Federal government identifies minimal standards and an architecture to enable agencies to create or purchase interoperable cloud capabilities." It then goes on with brief lists of benefits and approaches to adopting cloud computing, which apply equally to the private sector.

The presentation concludes with the following list of NIST Special Publication (SPs) to be created in fiscal year 2009:

❑   Overview of cloud computing

❑   Cloud computing security issues

❑   Securing cloud architectures

❑   Securing cloud applications

❑   Enabling and performing forensics in the cloud

❑   Centralizing security monitoring in a cloud architecture

❑   Obtaining security from third-party cloud architectures through service-level agreements

❑   Security compliance frameworks and cloud computing (for example, HIPAA, FISMA, and SOX)

Subsequently, NIST issued their Draft NIST Working Definition of Cloud Computing v13 (http://bit.ly/10TNdu, http://csrc.nist.gov/groups/SNS/cloud-computing/cloud-def-v14 .doc) *and Presentation on Effectively and Securely Using the Cloud Computing Paradigm v18* (http://bit.ly/17PKbM, http://csrc.nist.gov/groups/SNS/cloud-computing/cloud-computing -v22.ppt).

When this book was written in early 2009, only a few of the preceding SPs were available in draft form or final form from NIST's Publications web pages (http://bit.ly/sJECD, http://csrc.nist.gov/publications/). *Watch these pages for pending standards; NIST updates its publication lists frequently.*

Potential Cloud Computing Deployment by the Department of Defense

The National Security Agency's "DoD Cloud Computing Security Challenges" briefing by Chris Kubic, Chief Architect, Information Assurance Architecture and Systems Security Engineering Group, describes potential military cloud applications (http://bit.ly/171BzF, http://csrc.nist.gov/groups/SMA/ispab/documents/minutes/2008-12/cloud-computing-IA -challenges_ISPAB-Dec2008_C-Kubic.pdf), which consist, in part, of the following:

❑   *Cyber Network Defense*: Sensor data storage, analysis, situational awareness

❑   *Battlespace Awareness* with the Common Operating Picture: status of troops, missions, vehicles, weapons, supplies; in the future — autonomous (unmanned) weapons systems

❑   *Storage/processing of tactical Intelligence, Surveillance, Reconnaissance (ISR) feeds*; creating a tailored picture based on a user's access privileges

❑   *Simulation and Visualization*: Mission planning and training

Tactical use of cloud computing by the military and other security-intensive agencies will reduce IT organizations' apprehension that cloud computing is, by its very nature, unreliable and insecure.

Gaining and Auditing Regulatory Compliance

Several laws and regulations related to data security and privacy are currently in effect in the United States. These include the Gramm-Leach-Bliley (GLB) Act, Sarbanes-Oxley Act (SOX, also known as the

119

Public Company Accounting Reform and Investor Protection Act of 2002), Health Insurance Portability and Accountability Act (HIPAA), and the Foreign Corrupt Practices Act. The UK's London Stock Exchange Combined Code and South Africa's Report on Corporate Governance for South Africa (King II) regulate transparency in financial reporting. The European Community's Directive 95/46/EC is on the protection of personal data targets protecting individual privacy in digital information and its communication.

Following are three of the most important federal regulatory compliance mandates and a critical private-sector standard that involve identity management, risk assessment, or both. Most organizations implement a plan that ensures the security, confidentiality (or privacy when the information involves personal identification of employees or consumers), and integrity of sensitive data. These plans usually are subject to periodic tests by independent security auditors to ensure compliance.

Gramm-Leach-Bliley Act

The GLB Act defines non-public information as including a consumer's name, address, telephone number, date of birth, social security number, and any other information that was derived from any sort of application or form wherein the consumer provided such information to a financial institution. The GLB Act considers at least the following types of institutions to be financial institutions: non-bank mortgage lenders, loan brokers, some financial or investment advisers, debt collectors, tax return preparers, banks, and real estate settlement service providers.

According to Wikipedia, GLB's Safeguards Rule (Subtitle A: Disclosure of Nonpublic Personal Information, codified at 15 U.S.C. Sections 6801–6809) "requires financial institutions to develop a written information security plan that describes how the company is prepared for, and plans to continue to protect clients' nonpublic personal information. (The Safeguards Rule also applies to information of those no longer consumers of the financial institution.)"

The information security plan must include

❑   Developing, monitoring, and testing a program to secure the information

❑   Change the safeguards as needed with the changes in how information is collected, stored, and used

❑   Constructing a thorough [risk management] on each department handling the nonpublic information

❑   Denoting at least one employee to manage the safeguards

Obviously, moving such information from an on-premises data center to a third-party's cloud data center will involve changes to GLB reporting and compliance auditing procedures.

Sarbanes-Oxley Act

SOX, which applies only to publicly owned companies, was enacted by congress in response to a series of large corporate frauds, primarily those committed by Enron, WorldCom, and Tyco during the years 2000 through 2004. SOX was intended to make corporate reporting more transparent. Its provisions aim to

- ❏ Reduce or eliminate conflicts of interest of independent financial auditors who also provide consulting services, as well as those of securities analysts who receive compensation from investment bankers

- ❏ Improve oversight by boards of directors' audit committees of independent financial auditors

- ❏ Increase oversight by the Securities and Exchange Commission (SEC) by increasing its budget substantially

- ❏ Require accounting for employee stock option compensation as an operating expense

According to Wikipedia (http://bit.ly/skaSn, http://en.wikipedia.org/wiki/Sarbanes-Oxley_Act), the Public Company Accounting Oversight Board (PCAOB) approved Auditing Standard No. 5 for public accounting firms on July 25, 2007. The SEC also released its interpretive guidance on June 27, 2007. The latter is generally consistent with the PCAOB's guidance but is intended to provide guidance for management. Both management and the independent auditor are responsible for performing their assessment in the context of a top-down risk assessment, which requires management to base both the scope of its assessment and evidence gathered on risk. This gives management wider discretion in its assessment approach. These two standards together require management to

- ❏ Assess both the design and operating effectiveness of selected internal controls related to significant accounts and relevant assertions, in the context of material misstatement risks

- ❏ Understand the flow of transactions, including IT aspects, sufficient enough to identify points at which a misstatement could arise

- ❏ Evaluate company-level (entity-level) controls, which correspond to the components of the Committee of Sponsoring Organizations of the Treadway Commission (COSO) framework (www.coso.org/)

- ❏ Perform a fraud risk assessment

- ❏ Evaluate controls designed to prevent or detect fraud, including management override of controls

- ❏ Evaluate controls over the period-end financial reporting process

- ❏ Scale the assessment based on the size and complexity of the company

- ❏ Rely on management's work based on factors such as competency, objectivity, and risk

- ❏ Conclude on the adequacy of internal control over financial reporting

A key tenet of SOX is data integrity. Moving financial transactions and associated data from the corporation's premises to a cloud data center doesn't necessarily increase risk. However, it does affect the flow of transactions and can influence the adequacy of internal control over financial reporting.

Health Information Technology and HIPAA

The Obama administration's intention to have all U.S. residents move to electronic health records (EHRs) in five years received a US$19 billion earmark for Health Information Technology (HIT) in the American Recovery and Reinvestment Act (ARRA) of 2009 that President Obama signed into law on February 17, 2009. On the whole, Federal privacy/security laws (HIPAA) are expanded to protect patient health information and HIPAA privacy and security laws would apply directly to business associates of covered entities. ARRA also prohibits the sale of a patient's health information without the patient's written authorization, except in limited circumstances involving research or public health activities, or "otherwise determined by the secretary in regulations to be similarly necessary and appropriate."

The secretary's unlimited right to sell patients' health information has aroused serious objections from privacy advocates.

HIPAA's Privacy Rule establishes regulations for the use and disclosure of *Protected Health Information* (PHI). PHI is any information held by a covered entity that concerns health status, provision of health care, or payment for health care that can be linked to an individual. PHI has been interpreted to include any part of an individual's electronic medical record (EMR) or payment history, but HIPAA specifies 18 PHI identifiers in the following list. Covered entities include health plans, health-care clearinghouses, and health care providers who transmit any health information in electronic form in connection with a transaction covered by this subchapter (45 CFR Section 164.501).

The 18 types of identifiers of PHI were, when this book was written, as follows:

1. Names.

2. All geographical subdivisions smaller than a state, including street address, city, county, precinct, zip code, and their equivalent geocodes, except for the initial three digits of a zip code, if according to the current publicly available data from the Bureau of the Census: (1) the geographic unit formed by combining all zip codes with the same three initial digits contains more than 20,000 people; and (2) the initial three digits of a zip code for all such geographic units containing 20,000 or fewer people is changed to 000.

3. Dates (except year) for dates directly related to an individual, including birth date, admission date, discharge date, date of death; and all ages over 89 and all elements of dates (including year) indicative of such age, except that such ages and elements may be aggregated into a single category of age 90 or older.

4. Phone numbers.

5. Fax numbers.

6. Electronic mail addresses.

7. Social Security numbers.

8. Medical record numbers.

9. Health plan beneficiary numbers.

10. Account numbers.

11. Certificate/license numbers.

12. Vehicle identifiers and serial numbers, including license plate numbers.

13. Device identifiers and serial numbers.

14. Web Universal Resource Locators (URLs).

15. Internet Protocol (IP) address numbers.

16. Biometric identifiers, including finger and voice prints.

17. Full face photographic images and any comparable images.

18. Any other unique identifying number, characteristic, or code (note this does not mean the unique code assigned by the investigator to code the data).

Any code used to replace the identifiers in datasets cannot be derived from any information related to the individual and the master codes, nor can the method to derive the codes be disclosed. For example, the unique code cannot include the last four digits (in sequence) of the social security number.

It's clear from the length of the preceding list that a substantial amount of the data in the master header record of the EHR or EMR must be encrypted to conform to HIPPA requirements for making *personally identifiable information* anonymous.

NIST Special Publication 800-122, "Guide to Protecting the Confidentiality of Personally Identifiable Information (PII)" (`http://bit.ly/sc2G3, http://csrc.nist.gov/publications/drafts/800-122 /Draft-SP800-122.pdf`)*, defines PII as*

> *Information which can be used to distinguish or trace an individual's identity, such as their name, social security number, biometric records, etc. alone, or when combined with other personal or identifying information which is linked or linkable to a specific individual, such as date and place of birth, mother's maiden name, etc.*

EU directive 95/46/EC, "Protection of Individuals with Regard to the Processing of Personal Data and on the Free Movement of Such Data," (`http://bit.ly/188e0N, www.cdt.org/privacy/eudirective /EU_Directive_.html`) *defines PII as*

> *Article 2a: 'personal data' shall mean any information relating to an identified or identifiable natural person ('data subject'); an identifiable person is one who can be identified, directly or indirectly, in particular by reference to an identification number or to one or more factors specific to his physical, physiological, mental, economic, cultural or social identity.*

The American Recovery and Reinvestment Act of 2009 (ARRA), which President Obama signed into law on February 17, 2009, includes Title XIII, the Health Information Technology for Economic and Clinical Health Act (HITECH Act), which dedicates $22 billion in federal funding to advance the use of health information technology. Subtitle D of the HITECH Act modifies applicability of HIPAA's security and privacy regulations that govern health-related information as follows:

❑ Business associates of HIPAA-covered entities are now independently subject to HIPAA.

❑ Business associates are now subject to the same civil and criminal penalties as covered entities.

❑ Requirements for notification of unsecured data breaches have been added.

Requirements for notification of data breaches are similar to those for personal information of California residents as described in the later "California Senate Bill 1386" section. "Unsecured" personal health information generally means information that is not encrypted or secured in such as manner as to make it unreadable to an unauthorized person. However, the Department of Health and Human Services is instructed to issue guidance on the meaning of "unsecured" and other key terms.

Payment Card Industry-Data Security Standard (PCC-DSS)

The Payment Card Industry (PCI) has a Data Security Standard (PCI-DSS) that's administered by the PCI Security Standards Council (PCI-SSC), whose five founding members are American Express, Discover Financial Services, JCB International, MasterCard Worldwide, and Visa Inc. PCI-DSS v1.2 became effective on October 1, 2008 v1.1 had a sunset date of December 31, 2008.

According to Wikipedia (http://bit.ly/W7pv2, http://en.wikipedia.org/wiki/PCI_DSS) and the PCI's web site (http://bit.ly/139Lrk, https://www.pcisecuritystandards.org/security _standards/pci_dss.shtml), PCI-DSS v1.2 defines the Control Objectives and Requirements for Compliance for merchants that process, store. or transmit payment cardholder data shown in the following table:

Control Objectives	PCI DSS Requirements
Build and Maintain a Secure Network	1. Install and maintain a firewall configuration to protect cardholder data.
	2. Do not use vendor-supplied defaults for system passwords and other security parameters.
Protect Cardholder Data	3. Protect stored cardholder data.
	4. Encrypt transmission of cardholder data across open, public networks.
Maintain a Vulnerability Management Program	5. Use and regularly update anti-virus software on all systems commonly affected by malware.
	6. Develop and maintain secure systems and applications.
Implement Strong Access Control Measures	7. Restrict access to cardholder data by business need-to-know.
	8. Assign a unique ID to each person with computer access.
	9. Restrict physical access to cardholder data.
Regularly Monitor and Test Networks	10. Track and monitor all access to network resources and cardholder data.
	11. Regularly test security systems and processes.
Maintain an Information Security Policy	12. Maintain a policy that addresses information security.

The preceding requirements apply only to merchants who store a cardholder's Primary Account Number, which usually is 16 digits in length. If the merchant uses a payment gateway organization, which eliminates the need for the merchant to process payment card transactions, the requirements don't apply. PCI's List of Validated Payment Applications page (`http://bit.ly/GtX16`, `https://www.pcisecuritystandards.org/security_standards/vpa/vpa_approval_list.html?mn=&vn=0&ap=1&rg=0`) listed 24 gateway vendors and 26 payment applications on March 13, 2009, of which 25 applications were noted as "Acceptable for new deployments."

PCI's Self-Assessment Questionnaire (SAQ)

The PCI provides merchants who aren't required to undergo an onsite data security assessment by a Qualified Security Assessor (QSA) with Self-Assessment Questionnaire (SAQ), which is a validation tool that's intended to assist merchants and service providers in self-evaluating their compliance with the PCI DSS. The following table lists the five SAQ validation types, their descriptions, and the applicable SAQ version.

SAQ Validation Type	Description	SAQ
1	Card-not-present (e-commerce or mail/telephone-order) merchants with all cardholder data functions outsourced. (This would never apply to face-to-face merchants.)	A
2	Imprint-only merchants with no electronic cardholder data storage.	B
3	Stand-alone dial-up terminal merchants, no electronic cardholder data storage.	B
4	Merchants with payment application systems connected to the Internet, no electronic cardholder data storage.	C
5	All other merchants (not included in preceding descriptions for SAQs A-C) and all service providers defined by a payment brand as eligible to complete an SAQ.	D

Stores that use a secure payment gateway that's recognized by the major payment-card firms to handle credit card transactions don't process, store, or transmit any credit card information on the servers; nor do they have access to payment card ID numbers. Such merchants can use SAQ Validation Type 1 and SAQ version A, which only requires certification that

❑ Merchant does not store, process, or transmit any cardholder data on merchant premises but relies entirely on third-party service provider(s) to handle these functions.

❑ The third party service provider(s) handling storage, processing, and/or transmission of cardholder data is confirmed to be PCI DSS compliant.

❑ Merchant does not store any cardholder data in electronic format.

❑   If merchant does store cardholder data, such data is only in paper reports or copies of receipts and is not received electronically.

PCI's Prioritized Approach Framework

Merchants with a small or no IT organization have indicated the need for a road map for gaining compliance with PCI-DSS. In response, the PCI issued in March 2009 a Prioritized Approach framework to help merchants who are not yet fully compliant with the PCI DSS understand and reduce risk while on the road to compliance. The framework focuses on security milestones outlined in the following list for protecting against the highest risk factors and escalating threats facing cardholder data security:

❑   If you don't need it, don't store it.

❑   Secure the perimeter.

❑   Secure applications.

❑   Monitor and control access to your systems.

❑   Protect stored cardholder data.

❑   Finalize remaining compliance efforts, and ensure all controls are in place.

The PCI's Prioritized Approach for DSS 1.2 page (`http://bit.ly/14AS9p`, `https://www .pcisecuritystandards.org/education/prioritized.shtml`) provides links to a guide document and Excel worksheet to aid in use of the framework.

California Senate Bill 1386

California Senate Bill 1386, also called the California Information Practice Act or California Security Breach Notification Act, requires that anyone who conducts business within the state of California and licenses or owns computerized personal information about any California residents, comply with the specified standards of regulation of data security, which include

❑   Defining personal data as an individual's first initial or name and last name in conjunction with that individual's social security number, driver's license number or California identification card number, an account number, credit, or debit card number in combination with any required security code, access code, or password that would permit access to an individual's financial account

❑   Notifying any resident of California whose unencrypted personal data has been acquired by an unauthorized entity and disclosing to the resident the personal data exposed by the breach

Any affected firms or agencies that encrypt *all instances* of personal data are not subject to the notification requirements of SB 1386.

> SB 1386 does not define the terms encrypt or encryption, so the degree of security offered by the encryption method employed probably is subject to judicial determination.

Massachusetts' and Nevada's Data Privacy Laws

In 2008 Nevada and Massachusetts passed data privacy laws that require encryption of personal data. Nevada Revised Statutes 597.970 (`http://bit.ly/xzeIJ`, `www.leg.state.nv.us/NRs/NRS-597.html`

`#NRS597Sec970`) requires all businesses to encrypt personally-identifiable customer data that are transmitted electronically. Massachusetts' 201 CMR 17.00: Standards for The Protection of Personal Information of Residents of the Commonwealth (`http://bit.ly/jZTxA`, `www.mass.gov/?pageID=ocaterminal&L=4&L0=Home&L1=Consumer&L2=Privacy&L3=Identity+Theft &sid=Eoca&b=terminalcontent&f=reg201cmr17&csid=Eoca`) requires encryption of personal information on laptops and other portable data devices. The laws apply to out-of-state companies with operations or customers in those two states as well as resident businesses. All organizations doing business in all 50 states must comply with the data encryption requirements.

The laws define personal information as the combination of an individual's name with a driver's license, credit card information, or social security number (SSN). The *Wall Street Journal*'s "New Data Privacy Laws Set For Firms" article of October 16, 2008 provides additional details on the new legislation. Like California's SB 1386, Nevada's law defines the encryption method's cryptographic strength. Massachusetts' law requires use of a "128-bit or higher algorithmic process."

It's only a matter of time before all U.S. states enact data privacy laws or the federal government enacts privacy legislation that overrides the states' regulations.

Implementing Secure Sockets Layer Transmission Encryption for Web Roles

Azure services can enable Transport Layer Security (TLS) to use the Secure HTTP protocol (HTTPS) for transmission of encrypted requests to and responses from production Hosted Services and Storage Accounts for Web Roles. To enable HTTPS with TLS, add the line emphasized in Listing 5-1 to your service's ServiceDefinition.csdef file:

Listing 5-1: Enabling TLS for Secure HTTP WebRole transport

```
<!-- Must use port 80 for http and port 443 for https when running in the
cloud -->
<InputEndpoint name="HttpIn" protocol="http" port="80" />
<InputEndpoint name="HttpsIn" protocol="https" port="443" />
```

If you enable HTTPS transmission you must create a self-signed SSL certificate for the Development Fabric, add it to your Personal certificate store, and then Enable SSL Connections in the project's SSL properties page. To avoid warning messages about lack of trust of the certificate, add the certificate to your Trusted Root Certificate Authorities. The later "Creating a Self-Signed Certificate for the Development Fabric" section describes how to create, store, and enable such a certificate.

A self-signed certificate is required because the certificate's private key isn't secure in the development environment.

To request TLS in production, change `http://servicename.cloudapp.net/` to `https://servicename .cloudapp.net/` in the service URL. To *require* HTTPS transmission with TLS, remove the line in Listing 5-1 containing `HttpIn`.

Listing 5-2 contains the request headers to establish TLS for a production Web Role that has a server certificate created by a test Root Certificate Authority that you create. TCP port 443, which specifies TLS/SSL is emphasized.

Listing 5-2: Request headers to establish a TLS connection for a WebRole

```
CONNECT oakleaf3.cloudapp.net:443 HTTP/1.0
User-Agent: Mozilla/4.0 (compatible; MSIE 8.0; Windows NT 6.0; Trident/4.0; GTB6;
SLCC1; .NET CLR 2.0.50727; Media Center PC 5.0; .NET CLR 3.5.21022;
.NET CLR 3.5.30428; .NET CLR 3.5.30729; .NET CLR 3.0.30618; MS-RTC LM 8;
InfoPath.2; OfficeLiveConnector.1.3;
OfficeLivePatch.1.3)
Proxy-Connection: Keep-Alive
Content-Length: 0
Host: oakleaf3.cloudapp.net
Pragma: no-cache
```

Listing 5-3 shows the response headers trapped by Fiddler2 from the oakleaf3 production Hosted Service with the TLS security protocol specified by the highlighted Tls characters.

Listing 5-3: Response headers establishing a TLS connection for a WebRole with your certificate

```
HTTP/1.1 200 Connection Established
Timestamp: 11:06:30:0857
FiddlerGateway: Direct

This is a HTTPS CONNECT Tunnel.  Secure traffic flows through this connection.

Secure Protocol: Tls
Cipher: Aes 128bits
Hash Algorithm: Sha1 160bits
Key Exchange: RsaKeyX 1024bits

== Client Certificate ==========
None.
== Server Certificate ==========
[Subject]
  CN=oakleaf3.cloudapp.net
[Issuer]
  CN=OakLeaf CA, O=OakLeaf Systems, OU=Development, L=Oakland, S=CA, C=US
[Serial Number]
  8A6ED385CA220E9942CCDD3960F4ADC6
[Not Before]
  3/20/2009 4:05:42 PM
[Not After]
  3/20/2017 4:05:41 PM
[Thumbprint]
  248187B259A5BDCFEDE23843FC1E66D4239C59D2
```

The Issuer (Root Certificate Authority) is OakLeaf CA and the test server certificate's common name (CN) is the URI of the production service. You'll probably find that a test certificate, rather than a commercial server certificate from a commercial Certificate Authority (CA), such as Go Daddy, Comodo, or Thawte, is more convenient during service development. All users of the secure service must add the test Root Certificate Authority to their Trusted Root Certificate Authorities list.

Commercial CAs require evidence of ownership of the domain for which you seek a certificate. In most cases, proof of ownership is represented by an e-mail address within the domain, such as alias@cloudapp.net *for the preceding example, to which the CA sends the response to a certificate request. Obviously, this procedure won't work for Azure, so you must obtain a commercial certificate for the domain name you own and then specify* servicename.cloudapp.net *as a DNS* CNAME *record.*

TLS v1.1 is the successor to SSLv3, and is the subject of IETF RFC 4346, "The Transport Layer Security (TLS) Protocol Version 1.1," of April 2006. SSLv3 commonly uses the 128-bit RC4 (also called ARC4 or ARCFOUR) encryption algorithm; TLS v1.1 negotiates a CipherSuite that the web server and browser support. HTTPS with TLS v1.1 or SSLv3 encryption and 128-bit keys are considered sufficiently secure to protect Internet *transmission* of consumer banking and payment card transactions. Qualifying for exemption from SB 1386 requires that personal information be *stored* as encrypted data also.

The term 128-bit specifies the length of the encryption key. As noted in RFC 4346, the United States restricted the export of cryptographic software containing certain strong encryption algorithms when SSLv3 and TLS 1.0 were designed. A series of cipher suites were designed to operate at reduced (40-bit) key lengths in order to comply with those regulations. Due to advances in computer performance, these algorithms are now unacceptably weak, and export restrictions have since been loosened to allow 128-bit keys.

Figure 5-1 shows the AzureTableTestHarness service's SSL page with a self-signed certificate for the https://127.0.0.1/ loopback (localhost) URL of the Development Fabric and the test certificate for the https://oakleaf3.cloudapp.net production URL.

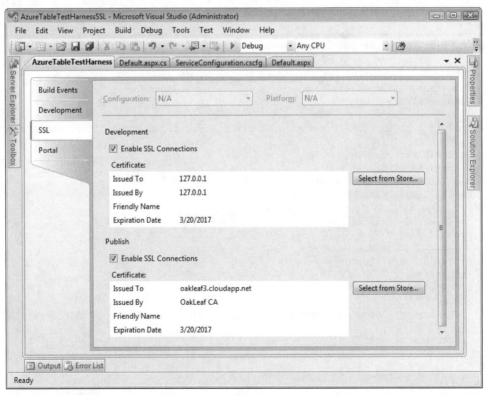

Figure 5-1: Specifying self-signed and test certificates for the Development and Azure Fabrics in the project's SSL properties page.

Enabling TLS for Azure Data Services

HTTPS for data transport is required to secure mixed-mode services during development with personally identifiable data but probably will not be required in a full production service where the Hosted and Data Services are located in the same data center. Enabling TLS for transporting Azure Blobs, Tables, and Queues requires changing http to https in the project's ServiceConfiguration,cscfg file, as shown by the emphasized characters in Listings 5-4 and 5-5.

Listing 5-4: Enabling SSL for secure HTTP Blob, Table, and Queue transport

```
<Setting name="BlobStorageEndpoint"      value="https://blob.core.windows.net" />
<Setting name="QueueStorageEndpoint"     value="https://queue.core.windows.net" />
<Setting name="TableStorageEndpoint"     value="https://table.core.windows.net" />
```

Listing 5-5: Request headers to establish an SSL connection for Tables

```
CONNECT oakleaf3.table.core.windows.net:443 HTTP/1.1
Host: oakleaf3.table.core.windows.net
Proxy-Connection: Keep-Alive
```

You don't need your own certificates for Data Services because certificates issued by the Microsoft Secure Service Authority are valid for https://servicename.table.core.windows.net by virtue of the wild-card (*) in the Subject header's CN, as illustrated in Listing 5-6.

Listing 5-6: Response headers to establish an SSL connection for Tables

```
HTTP/1.1 200 Connection Established
Timestamp: 10:21:13:4337
FiddlerGateway: Direct

This is a HTTPS CONNECT Tunnel.  Secure traffic flows through this connection.

Secure Protocol: Tls
Cipher: Aes 128bits
Hash Algorithm: Sha1 160bits
Key Exchange: RsaKeyX 1024bits

== Client Certificate ==========
None.

== Server Certificate ==========
[Subject]
  CN=*.table.core.windows.net
[Issuer]
  CN=Microsoft Secure Server Authority, DC=redmond, DC=corp, DC=microsoft, DC=com
[Serial Number]
  5A501E5F00050000E869
```

```
[Not Before]
  10/7/2008 1:32:39 PM
[Not After]
  10/7/2009 1:32:39 PM
[Thumbprint]
  708BFA75C5EFADD0DA55E88C75352CD6E4E2562F
```

The Microsoft Secure Server Authority is an Intermediate Certification Authority issued by the Microsoft Internet Authority, which in turn is issued by the GTE CyberTrust Global Root authority. Notice the brief (one-year) lifespan of the preceding Microsoft certificate compared with the eight-year duration of Listing 5-3's test certificate.

Creating a Self-Signed Certificate for the Development Fabric

Internet Explorer's Internet Options dialog's Content page has a Certificates button that opens a Certificates dialog. Mozilla Firefox offers a similar View Certificates button on its Options, Advanced, Encryption page. Server Authentication certificates must be issued by an organization listed in the Certificates dialog's Trusted Root Certificate Authority list to avoid messages questioning authenticity. For a production service, you need a certificate for a domain name you own, such as *mydomain*.com that's issued by one of the organizations on the list and a CNAME DNS record that points to *servicename*.cloudapp.net. For the Development Fabric, you must create a self-signed certificate for the Cassini Development Web server.

> *The "Enabling SSL Connections on Windows Azure" whitepaper* (http://bit.ly/GbnSh, http://msdn.microsoft.com/en-us/library/dd203056.aspx) *by Jim Nakashima explains how to set up SSL connections for both production and development servers. Scott Guthrie's "Tip/Trick: Enabling SSL on IIS 7.0 Using Self-Signed Certificates" blog post* (http://bit.ly/2pJ3xG, http://weblogs.asp.net/scottgu/archive/2007/04/06/tip-trick-enabling-ssl-on-iis7 -using-self-signed-certificates.aspx) *shows you how to use IIS 7.0 to create a self-signed certificate for* localhost. *Neither of these articles explains how to use MakeCert.exe to create a certificate with a customized domain name.*

As mentioned earlier, the default URL for secure services running in the Development Fabric is https://127.0.0.1/ but IE8's Certificates dialog doesn't let you specify a CN other than the default localhost or your machine's account name. If you use the localhost certificate, you must dismiss a warning message each time you compile and run the project. To specify a custom CN, you must use VS 2008's MakeCert.exe command-line utility with the Visual Studio 2008 Command Prompt to create the certificate with these parameters:

```
makecert.exe -n "CN=127.0.0.1" -pe -ss My -sr CurrentUser -sky exchange -m 96 -a sha1
-eku 1.3.6.1.5.5.7.3.1 -r
```

The following table explains the preceding parameter values:

Parameter	Description
-n "CN=127.0.0.1"	The x509 name of certificate, usually a web server URL
-pe	Marks the generated private key as exportable
-ss My	Specifies the certificate store to hold output certificate
-sr CurrentUser	Specifies the certificate store location (CurrentUser or LocalMachine)
-sky exchange	Key type (exchange or signature)
-m 96	Duration of the certificate's validity period in months
-a sha1	Algorithm (md5 default or sha1)
-eku 1.3.6.1.5.5.7.3.1	Enhanced key object identifiers (all uses)
-r	Creates a self-signed certificate

The Development web server requires the self-signed certificate to be located in the CurrentUser *store.*

After you run the preceding command, opening the Certificates dialog displays the self-signed certificate in your Personal certificates list, as shown in Figure 5-2.

Exporting and Importing the Issuer to the Trusted Root Certificate Authorities List

To add the issuer of a certificate to the Trusted Root Certificate Authorities List, do the following:

1. Click the Certificates dialog's Export button to start the Certificate Export Wizard and click Next to open the Export Private Key dialog.

2. Select the Yes, Export the Private Key option and click Next to open the Export File Dialog.

3. Select the Personal Information Exchange – PKCS #12 (.PFX) option, mark the Include All Certificates in the Certification Path if Possible and Export All Extended Properties check boxes, and click Next to open the Password dialog.

4. Type and confirm a password to encrypt the private key, and click Next to open the File to Export dialog.

5. Click Browse and navigate to your Users*UserName*\\Documents folder, add a *ServerCerts* or similar folder, name the file *127-0-0-1DevCert*.pfx or the like, and click Save to export the certificate and open the Completing the Certificate Export Wizard dialog.

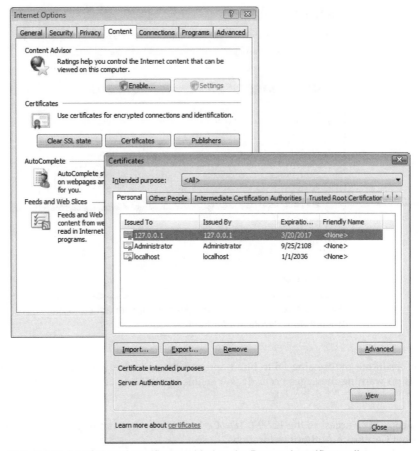

Figure 5-2: A self-signed certificate added to the Personal certificates list.

6. Click Finish to dismiss the wizard.

7. Click the Certificates dialog's Trusted Root Certificate Authorities tab and the Import button to open the Certificate Import Wizard and click Next to open the File to Import dialog.

8. Select Personal Information Files (*.pfx) in the list, browse to and open the file you saved in step 5, and click Next to open the Password dialog.

9. Type the password you assigned in step 4, mark the Mark This Key as Exportable and Generate All Extended Properties check boxes, and click Next to open the Certificate Store dialog.

10. Accept the Place All Certificates in the Following Store option with Trusted Root Certificate Authorities in the Certificate Store list, and click Next to open the Completing the Certificate Import Wizard.

11. Click Finish to create the new Trusted Root Certificate Authority (see Figure 5-3).

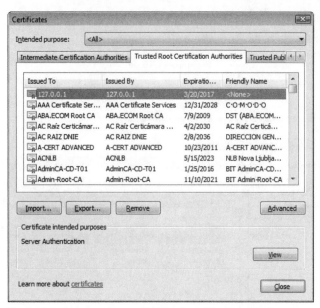

**Figure 5-3: An entry for a self-signed certificate added to the
Trusted Root Certificate Authorities list.**

Test your certificate by pressing F5 to build and run the service in the Development Fabric to
verify that no warning messages occur. If you enabled both ports 80 and 443, change the URL to
`https://127.0.0.1/`.

Provide a copy of or access to the *127-0-0-1DevCert*.pfx file so they can import it into their Personal and
Trusted Root Certificate Authorities locations.

Creating a Test Root Certificate Authority and Using It to Sign a Test Certificate

You receive authenticity warnings if you use a self-signed certificate with a production service, so it's
a good practice to create a test Root Certificate Authority and Certificates based on the authority. The
process is similar to that for self-signed certificates but has an additional step. You can combine both
commands in a single batch; the second command refers to the OakLeaf CA created by the first command,
as shown in Listing 5-7.

Listing 5-7: Response headers to establish an SSL connection for Tables

```
makecert.exe -n "CN=OakLeaf CA,O=OakLeaf
Systems,OU=Development,L=Oakland,S=CA,C=US"
-pe -ss Root -sr LocalMachine -sky exchange -m 96 -a sha1 -len 2048 -r

makecert.exe -n "CN=oakleaf3.cloudapp.net" -pe -ss My -sr CurrentUser -sky exchange
-m 96 -in "OakLeaf CA" -is Root -ir CurrentUser -a sha1 -eku 1.3.6.1.5.5.7.3.1
```

The following table lists descriptions of MakeCert.exe parameters not included in the previous table:

Parameter	Description
-n "O= ... "	The x509 organization name
-n "OU= ... "	The x509 organizational unit (department) name
-n "L= ... "	The x509 location (city) name
-n "S= ... "	The x509 state abbreviation or region name
-n "C= ... "	The x509 country abbreviation or name
-in OakLeaf CA	The name of the issuer (Root Certification Authority)
-len 2048	Specifies a 2,048-bit key length

You must export *.pfx files of both certificates and provide them for import to developers or users of your secure service.

Encrypting Personal Information in Azure Storage Services

Storing encrypted personally identifiable and other highly confidential information requires encrypting the data before storing it as an entity to an Azure Table or adding it as the payload of an Azure Blob or Queue. .NET 3.5 provides implementations of many standard cryptographic algorithms, including symmetrical (shared secret key) and asymmetrical (Public Key Infrastructure, PKI). Symmetrical encryption for data streams consumes far fewer resources than asymmetrical encryption. Employing symmetrical encryption contributes to the scalability of hosted services, especially for large Azure Blobs. .NET 3.5's managed symmetric cryptography classes in the System.Security.Cryptography namespace include special stream class called a CryptoStream that encrypts data read into the stream.

❑ AesManaged provides a managed implementation of the Advanced Encryption Standard (AES) symmetric algorithm. AES was established as Federal Information Processing Standard (FIPS) 197 by the NIST on November 26, 2001.

❑ DESCryptoServiceProvider defines a wrapper over the cryptographic service provider (CSP) version of the Data Encryption Standard (DES) algorithm.

❑ RC2CryptoServiceProvider defines a wrapper over the CSP implementation of the RC2 algorithm.

❑ RijndaelManaged accesses the managed version of the Rijndael algorithm, on which AES is based. AES has a fixed block size of 128 bits (16 bytes) and a key size of 128, 192, or 256 bits;

Rijndael can be specified with block and key sizes in any multiple of 32 bits, with a minimum of 128 bits and a maximum of 256 bits.

❏ `TripleDESCryptoServiceProvider` defines a wrapper over the CSP version of the TripleDES algorithm.

AES is a federal standard so it is likely to be accepted by both federal and state agencies as an adequate means of securing personally identifiable information. You can learn more about the preceding cryptographic algorithms from their Wikipedia entries.

Encrypting and Decrypting Strings with AES

The AzureTableTestHarnessSSL.sln project in the \WROX\Azure\Chapter05 folder is based on Chapter 4's SampleWebCloudService.sln project. The project encrypts PII from the Northwind Customers table with `AesManaged` when creating or updating entities, and decrypts it for presentation in the GridView control and bulk updates. The AesManagedEncryption.cs file contains the `EncryptDecrypt` class, which provides `Encrypt` and `Decrypt` methods for UTF-8-encoded strings, which the StorageClient's HTTP request header specifies as the `Accept-Charset` header and the response delivers as Content-Type: `application/atom+xml;charset=utf-8`. The encrypted bytes are delivered as a Base64-encoded string.

Encrypting Plaintext to Ciphertext

The Password-Based Key Derivation Function (PBKDF2) creates a shared secret (encryption/decryption) key from a combination of password and *salt* byte arrays. Salt bytes represent an index into a large set of keys derived from the password. It need not be kept secret. In the example that follows, the password and salt are embedded literal strings. Encrypting the password with a public-private key pair could be used to increase security and the Windows Data Protection API (DPAPI) can provide secure storage for the private key.

> PBKDF2 is part of RSA Laboratories' Public-Key Cryptography Standards (PKCS) #5 v2.0, which is published by the IETF as RFC 2898 also (www.ietf.org/rfc/rfc2898.txt). For more information about DPAPI see the "Windows Data Protection" whitepaper on MSDN (http://msdn.microsoft.com/en-us/library/ms995355.aspx).
>
> When this book was written the Azure Fabric did not support DPAPI security.

Listing 5-8 contains the encryption code, which returns the Base64-encoded ciphertext.

Listing 5-8: Method for encrypting a plaintext UTF8 string with the AesManaged encryption class

```
public static string Encrypt(string input)
{
    try
    {
        // Plaintext string input
        string data = input;
        // Convert to an array of UTF-8 bytes
```

```
        byte[] utfData = UTF8Encoding.UTF8.GetBytes(data);

        byte[] saltBytes = UTF8Encoding.UTF8.GetBytes("S0d1umChl0r1de");
        // Use the PBKDF2 standard for password-based key generation
        Rfc2898DeriveBytes rfc = new Rfc2898DeriveBytes("K3yPassw0rd!", saltBytes);

        // Advanced Encryption Standard symmetric encryption algorithm
        AesManaged aes = new AesManaged();

        // Set AES parameters
        aes.BlockSize = aes.LegalBlockSizes[0].MaxSize;
        aes.KeySize = aes.LegalKeySizes[0].MaxSize;
        aes.Key = rfc.GetBytes(aes.KeySize / 8);
        aes.IV = rfc.GetBytes(aes.BlockSize / 8);

        // Encryption
        ICryptoTransform encryptTransf = aes.CreateEncryptor();

        // Output stream, can be also a FileStream
        MemoryStream encryptStream = new MemoryStream();
        CryptoStream encryptor =
            new CryptoStream(encryptStream, encryptTransf, CryptoStreamMode.Write);

        // Write, flush, clear and close the encryptor
        encryptor.Write(utfData, 0, utfData.Length);
        encryptor.Flush();
        encryptor.Clear();
        encryptor.Close();

        // Create a byte array and convert it to a Base64-encoded string
        byte[] encryptBytes = encryptStream.ToArray();
        string encryptedString = Convert.ToBase64String(encryptBytes);

        return encryptedString;
    }
    catch (Exception exEncr)
    {
        string msg = "AES Encryption error: " + exEncr.Message;
        if (RoleManager.IsRoleManagerRunning)
            RoleManager.WriteToLog("Critical", msg);
        return input;
    }
}
```

Invoking the CryptoStream.Clear() *method is a call to* IDisposable.Dispose, *which removes the stream from memory to provide additional security and lets its resources be reallocated for other purposes.*

Listing 5-9 shows the HTTP request header for the ALFKI entity with CompanyName, ContactName, ContactTitle, Address, PostalCode, Phone, and Fax attribute values encrypted and emphasized. Employer names other than for sole proprietorships generally aren't considered to be PII, but are encoded to demonstrate techniques for decrypting, modifying, and encrypting data updates.

Listing 5-9: HTTP request headers and payload to add an encrypted entity to the OakLeaf3 table

```
POST /CustomerTable HTTP/1.1
User-Agent: Microsoft ADO.NET Data Services
x-ms-date: Sun, 22 Mar 2009 23:02:36 GMT
Authorization: SharedKeyLite oakleaf3:Uz0M8ww4jzDdmEkFvC3t2rITMWQZ02almi3oPfpfBAE=
Accept: application/atom+xml,application/xml
Accept-Charset: UTF-8
DataServiceVersion: 1.0;NetFx
MaxDataServiceVersion: 1.0;NetFx
Content-Type: application/atom+xml
Host: oakleaf3.table.core.windows.net
Content-Length: 1181
Expect: 100-continue

<?xml version="1.0" encoding="utf-8" standalone="yes"?>
<entry xmlns:d="http://schemas.microsoft.com/ado/2007/08/dataservices"
    xmlns:m="http://schemas.microsoft.com/ado/2007/08/dataservices/metadata"
    xmlns="http://www.w3.org/2005/Atom">
  <title />
  <updated>2009-03-22T23:02:36.6079953Z</updated>
  <author>
    <name />
  </author>
  <id />
  <content type="application/xml">
    <m:properties>
      <d:Address>or2WWgWMlRYh0uHlmpxeDQ==</d:Address>
      <d:City>Berlin</d:City>
      <d:CompanyName>3AsJUvWGgaFxQts7R0jQXV8ow1tEMu0HCdhzq2XSS54=</d:CompanyName>
      <d:ContactName>RYcJfx+StUtjayIUR3u1RQ==</d:ContactName>
      <d:ContactTitle>CUWrBpIJKUstOSrs070KVho8dSkjUc+5z4rkk8qQXPY=</d:ContactTitle>
      <d:Country>Germany</d:Country>
      <d:CustomerID>ALFKI</d:CustomerID>
      <d:Fax>KoVXBXayW6A9C2B3nDwjuA==</d:Fax>
      <d:PartitionKey>Customer</d:PartitionKey>
      <d:Phone>o5XG1kwxVOu7OVZoiJAVGg==</d:Phone>
      <d:PostalCode>t5/s0kjSCVQo7OD0jw896w==</d:PostalCode>
      <d:Region m:null="true" />
      <d:RowKey>ALFKI</d:RowKey>
      <d:Timestamp m:type="Edm.DateTime">0001-01-01T00:00:00</d:Timestamp>
    </m:properties>
  </content>
</entry>
```

Listing 5-10 contains the HTTP response headers and confirming Atom <entry> element as the payload.

Listing 5-10: Response headers and payload from adding an encrypted entity to the OakLeaf3 table

```
HTTP/1.1 201 Created
Cache-Control: no-cache
```

```
Transfer-Encoding: chunked
Content-Type: application/atom+xml;charset=utf-8
ETag: W/"datetime'2009-03-22T23%3A02%3A01.2831774Z'"
Location:
http://oakleaf3.table.core.windows.net/CustomerTable(PartitionKey='Customer',
    RowKey='ALFKI')
Server: Table Service Version 1.0 Microsoft-HTTPAPI/2.0
x-ms-request-id: cd745998-27fe-47a6-8194-e51d0aaae7ee
Date: Sun, 22 Mar 2009 23:02:00 GMT

640
<?xml version="1.0" encoding="utf-8" standalone="yes"?>
<entry xml:base="http://oakleaf3.table.core.windows.net/"
    xmlns:d="http://schemas.microsoft.com/ado/2007/08/dataservices"
    xmlns:m="http://schemas.microsoft.com/ado/2007/08/dataservices/metadata"
    m:etag="W/&quot;datetime'2009-03-22T23%3A02%3A01.2831774Z'&quot;"
    xmlns="http://www.w3.org/2005/Atom">
  <id>http://oakleaf3.table.core.windows.net/CustomerTable(PartitionKey='Customer',
    RowKey='ALFKI')</id>
  <title type="text"></title>
  <updated>2009-03-22T23:02:01Z</updated>
  <author>
    <name />
  </author>
  <link rel="edit" title="CustomerTable"
    href="CustomerTable(PartitionKey='Customer',RowKey='ALFKI')" />
  <category term="oakleaf3.CustomerTable"
    scheme="http://schemas.microsoft.com/ado/2007/08/dataservices/scheme" />
  <content type="application/xml">
    <m:properties>
      <d:PartitionKey>Customer</d:PartitionKey>
      <d:RowKey>ALFKI</d:RowKey>
      <d:Timestamp m:type="Edm.DateTime">2009-03-22T23:02:01.2831774Z</d:Timestamp>
      <d:Address>or2WWgWMlRYh0uHlmpxeDQ==</d:Address>
      <d:City>Berlin</d:City>
      <d:CompanyName>3AsJUvWGgaFxQts7R0jQXV8ow1tEMu0HCdhzq2XSS54=</d:CompanyName>
      <d:ContactName>RYcJfx+StUtjayIUR3u1RQ==</d:ContactName>
      <d:ContactTitle>CUWrBpIJKUstOSrs070KVho8dSkjUc+5z4rkk8qQXPY=</d:ContactTitle>
      <d:Country>Germany</d:Country>
      <d:CustomerID>ALFKI</d:CustomerID>
      <d:Fax>KoVXBXayW6A9C2B3nDwjuA==</d:Fax>
      <d:Phone>o5XG1kwxVOu7OVZoiJAVGg==</d:Phone>
      <d:PostalCode>t5/s0kjSCVQo7OD0jw896w==</d:PostalCode>
    </m:properties>
  </content>
</entry>
0
```

Decrypting Ciphertext to Plaintext

Symmetrical encryption implies that decrypting the encrypted Base64 string parallels the encryption process, as Listing 5-11 demonstrates.

139

Listing 5-11: Method for decrypting an encrypted string with the AesManaged encryption class

```
public static string Decrypt(string base64Input)
{
    try
    {
        //byte[] encryptBytes = UTF8Encoding.UTF8.GetBytes(input);
        byte[] encryptBytes = Convert.FromBase64String(base64Input);

        byte[] saltBytes = UTF8Encoding.UTF8.GetBytes("S0d1umCh10r1de");
        // Use the PBKDF2 standard for password-based key generation
        Rfc2898DeriveBytes rfc = new Rfc2898DeriveBytes("K3yPassw0rd!", saltBytes);

        // Advanced Encryption Standard symmetric encryption algorithm
        AesManaged aes = new AesManaged();

        // Set AES parameters
        aes.BlockSize = aes.LegalBlockSizes[0].MaxSize;
        aes.KeySize = aes.LegalKeySizes[0].MaxSize;
        aes.Key = rfc.GetBytes(aes.KeySize / 8);
        aes.IV = rfc.GetBytes(aes.BlockSize / 8);

        // Decryption
        ICryptoTransform decryptTrans = aes.CreateDecryptor();

        // Output stream, can be also a FileStream
        MemoryStream decryptStream = new MemoryStream();
        CryptoStream decryptor =
            new CryptoStream(decryptStream, decryptTrans, CryptoStreamMode.Write);

        // Write, flush, clear and close the encryptor
        decryptor.Write(encryptBytes, 0, encryptBytes.Length);
        decryptor.Flush();
        decryptor.Clear();
        decryptor.Close();

        // Create UTF string from decrypted bytes
        byte[] decryptBytes = decryptStream.ToArray();
        string decryptedString =
            UTF8Encoding.UTF8.GetString(decryptBytes, 0, decryptBytes.Length);

        return decryptedString;
    }
    catch (Exception exDecr)
    {
        string msg = "AES Decryption error: " + exDecr.Message;
        if (RoleManager.IsRoleManagerRunning)
            RoleManager.WriteToLog("Critical", msg);
        return base64Input;
    }
}
```

Listings 5-9 and 5-11 are based on a C# example by H. W. Soderlund (Encrypt / Decrypt in Silverlight, `http://bit.ly/128fNZ, http://silverlight.net/forums/p/14449/49982.aspx`).

The sample project decrypts pages of 12 or fewer entities. Listing 5-12 is the HTTP request for the first 12 entities.

Listing 5-12: Request headers for the first 12 entities from the OakLeaf3 table

```
GET /CustomerTable()?$top=12 HTTP/1.1
User-Agent: Microsoft ADO.NET Data Services
x-ms-date: Mon, 23 Mar 2009 18:03:12 GMT
Authorization: SharedKeyLite oakleaf3:WpVjGB/HrOReR62rLV7PphAHpvg4ZsqPReY2V0+Jmpg=
Accept: application/atom+xml,application/xml
Accept-Charset: UTF-8
DataServiceVersion: 1.0;NetFx
MaxDataServiceVersion: 1.0;NetFx
Host: oakleaf3.table.core.windows.net
```

Listing 5-13 shows the response headers and encrypted payload for the first of 12 entities, which the client decrypts. Intercepting the response with a web debugger, such as Fiddler2, proves that the PII has been stored as encrypted data in the table.

Listing 5-13: Response headers for the first of 12 encrypted Entities from the OakLeaf3 table

```
HTTP/1.1 200 OK
Cache-Control: no-cache
Transfer-Encoding: chunked
Content-Type: application/atom+xml;charset=utf-8
Server: Table Service Version 1.0 Microsoft-HTTPAPI/2.0
x-ms-request-id: e7d863f7-0aa3-4b75-bc91-da82b54be9bf
x-ms-continuation-NextPartitionKey: Customer
x-ms-continuation-NextRowKey: CENTC
Date: Mon, 23 Mar 2009 18:02:41 GMT

4377
<?xml version="1.0" encoding="utf-8" standalone="yes"?>
<feed xml:base="http://oakleaf3.table.core.windows.net/"
xmlns:d="http://schemas.microsoft.com/ado/2007/08/dataservices"
xmlns:m="http://schemas.microsoft.com/ado/2007/08/dataservices/metadata"
xmlns="http://www.w3.org/2005/Atom">
  <title type="text">CustomerTable</title>
  <id>http://oakleaf3.table.core.windows.net/CustomerTable</id>
  <updated>2009-03-23T18:02:42Z</updated>
  <link rel="self" title="CustomerTable" href="CustomerTable" />
  <entry m:etag="W/&quot;datetime'2009-03-23T17%3A44%3A15.1933594Z'&quot;">
    <id>http://oakleaf3.table.core.windows.net/CustomerTable(PartitionKey=
      'Customer', RowKey='ALFKI')</id>
    <title type="text"></title>
    <updated>2009-03-23T18:02:42Z</updated>
    <author>
      <name />
```

Continued

141

Listing 5-13: Response headers for the first of 12 encrypted Entities from the OakLeaf3 table *(continued)*

```
        </author>
        <link rel="edit" title="CustomerTable"
          href="CustomerTable(PartitionKey='Customer',RowKey='ALFKI')" />
        <category term="oakleaf3.CustomerTable"
          scheme="http://schemas.microsoft.com/ado/2007/08/dataservices/scheme" />
        <content type="application/xml">
          <m:properties>
            <d:PartitionKey>Customer</d:PartitionKey>
            <d:RowKey>ALFKI</d:RowKey>
            <d:Timestamp
              m:type="Edm.DateTime">2009-03-23T17:44:15.1933594Z
            </d:Timestamp>
            <d:Address>or2WWgWMlRYh0uHlmpxeDQ==</d:Address>
            <d:City>Berlin</d:City>
            <d:CompanyName>3AsJUvWGgaFxQts7R0jQXV8ow1tEMu0HCdhzq2XSS54=</d:CompanyName>
            <d:ContactName>RYcJfx+StUtjayIUR3u1RQ==</d:ContactName>
            <d:ContactTitle>
              CUWrBpIJKUstOSrs070KVho8dSkjUc+5z4rkk8qQXPY=
            </d:ContactTitle>
            <d:Country>Germany</d:Country>
            <d:CustomerID>ALFKI</d:CustomerID>
            <d:Fax>KoVXBXayW6A9C2B3nDwjuA==</d:Fax>
            <d:Phone>o5XG1kwxVOu7OVZoiJAVGg==</d:Phone>
            <d:PostalCode>t5/s0kjSCVQo7OD0jw896w==</d:PostalCode>
          </m:properties>
        </content>
      </entry>
  ...
</feed>
0
```

Orchestrating Encryption and Decryption in a TableStorageEntity Instance

The sample project's Customers.cs file contains the CustomerDataModel class, which represents the table's object model, is the central object to whose members you apply the Encrypt and Decrypt methods for CRUD operations. The CustomerDataModel class inherits from the StorageClient class library's TableStorageEntity abstract class.

Listing 5-14 shows the code for the CustomerDataModel class members getters and setters, including those that handle PII. The emphasized getArg and setArg method calls and methods handle decryption and encryption, respectively. Set the _Default.isCreateCusts flag to true to prevent decryption when a Get operation closely precedes a Set operation, which occurs when adding new or updating entities.

Listing 5-14: Code for encrypting and decrypting CustomerDataModel members

```
public class CustomerDataModel : TableStorageEntity
{
    public string base64Regex =
```

```csharp
            "^(?:[A-Za-z0-9+/]{4})*(?:[A-Za-z0-9+/]{2}==|[A-Za-z0-9+/]{3}=)?$";

    // Default parameterless constructor
    public CustomerDataModel() : base()
    {
        RowKey = Guid.NewGuid().ToString();
        PartitionKey = "Customers";
    }
    // Partial parameterized constructor
    public CustomerDataModel(string partitionKey, string rowKey)
        : base(partitionKey, rowKey)
    {
    }

    public string CustomerID { get; set; }

    // Encrypted personally identifiable information
    private string companyName;
    public string CompanyName
    {
        get
        {
            return getArg(companyName);
        }
        set
        {
            companyName = setArg(value);
        }
    }

    // Process getter
    public string getArg(string getVar)
    {
        if (getVar != null)
            if (Regex.IsMatch(getVar, base64Regex))
                if (_Default.isCreateCusts)
                    // Get encrypted value from object
                    return getVar;
                else
                    // Decrypt value from object
                    return EncryptDecrypt.Decrypt(getVar);
            else
                // Get plaintext value
                return getVar;
        else
            return null;
    }

    // Process setter
    public string setArg(string setVar)
    {
        if (Regex.IsMatch(setVar, base64Regex))
            return setVar;
        else
```

Continued

143

Listing 5-14: Code for encrypting and decrypting CustomerDataModel members
(continued)

```
            return EncryptDecrypt.Encrypt(setVar);
    }

    private string contactName;
    public string ContactName
    {
        get
        {
            return getArg(contactName);
        }
        set
        {
            contactName = setArg(value);
        }
    }

    private string contactTitle;
    public string ContactTitle
    {
        get
        {
            return getArg(contactTitle);
        }
        set
        {
            contactTitle = setArg(value);
        }
    }

    private string address;
    public string Address
    {
        get
        {
            return getArg(address);
        }
        set
        {
            address = setArg(value);
        }
    }

    private string postalCode;
    public string PostalCode
    {
        get
        {
            return getArg(postalCode);
        }
        set
        {
            postalCode = setArg(value);
```

```
        }
    }

    private string phone;
    public string Phone
    {
        get
        {
            return getArg(phone);
        }
        set
        {
            phone = setArg(value);
        }
    }

    private string fax;
    public string Fax
    {
        get
        {
            return getArg(fax);
        }
        set
        {
            fax = setArg(value);
        }
    }

    // Not personally identifiable data
    public string City { get; set; }
    public string Region { get; set; }
    public string Country { get; set; }

}
```

Analyzing Encryption's Performance Hit

As you would expect, encryption exacts a serious toll on table CRUD performance, although deletions are only slightly affected. The following table lists the times in seconds to execute the sample project's five operational features in the Azure Fabric (production) and Developer Fabric with and without encryption.

Encrypting with AES's 128-bit block size increases data payload by two bytes average. Base64 encoding increases payload by four bytes for each group of three bytes encoded; the formula is Base64Bytes = ((UTF8Bytes + 3 − (UTF8Bytes MOD 3)) /3) × 4. CPU cycles to encrypt and decrypt data contribute more performance loss by far than payload size increase.

You can increase the speed of Count *operations by adding a flag to prevent decryption and encryption when counting instances iteratively.*

Operation	Azure Fabric HTTP Plain	Azure Fabric HTTPS Encr	Dev. Fabric HTTP Plain	Dev. Fabric HTTPS Encr
Create 91 and display 12 Customer entities	5.716 s.	36.9 s.	15.7 s.	69.7 s.
Count 91 Customer entities	0.219 s.	2.11 s.	0.298 s.	4.37 s.
Delete 91 Customer entities	5.51 s.	6.81 s.	10.3 s.	11.2 s.
Update 91 Customer entities	5.66 s.	24.9 s.	16.0 s.	91.5 s.
Display page of 12 Customer entities	0.473 s.	2.35 s.	0.307 s.	4.54 s.

Salt values prevent encoded literal values for LINQ `where` constraints from working with encoded columns because salt causes encrypting the same value twice to produce different cipher text. LINQ `orderby` operations on encrypted attribute values won't result in the desired sequence of items, so you can't conduct range searching. Behavior of secondary indexes, which Microsoft said were planned for v1 of Azure Tables but weren't available for testing when this book was written, is likely to be adversely affected by encryption.

You can add attributes to hold hash values of the original cleartext values and then perform an equality search. To prevent dictionary attacks, you can add a secret hash-based message authentication code (HMAC). The `System.Security.Cryptography.HMAC` class has `ComputeHash()` and `Create()` members for HMACs.

The Azure team defines secondary indexes as indexes on attributes that aren't part of the primary key.

Comparing Client-Side Encryption with SQL Server's Column-Based Server Encryption

SQL Server 2005 introduced column-level and row-level encryption, often called *cell-level* encryption, as well as key management services. My "Encrypt and Decrypt Data in Yukon" article (`http://bit.ly/OseDw, http://visualstudiomagazine.com/features/article.aspx?editorialsid =1296`) in *Visual Studio Magazine*'s August 2005 issue describes how SQL Server's first self-contained encryption processes work and offers a downloadable VB.NET 2005 sample project. Encrypted columns must use the `varbinary` data type.

Column-level cryptographic operations don't reduce performance as dramatically as client-side operations, but they can interfere with the performance of indexes. T-SQL `WHERE` and `ORDER BY` clauses on encrypted columns require HMACs and exhibit issues similar to those for Azure Tables. Range searches aren't possible with hashed-value columns. Laurentiu Cristofor's December, 2005 "SQL Server 2005: searching encrypted data" blog post (`http://bit.ly/M16qG, http://blogs.msdn.com/lcris/archive/2005/12/22/506931.aspx`) describes these and other issues with cell-level encryption.

The SQL Azure Database team answered my "Will SDS support Database Encryption, certificate and key management?" question on March 12, 2009 with the following statement: "Database encryption? Not initially, but it's on the list and as we have demonstrated — if there is sufficient customer demand, it will be one of the first things we add after v1." (`http://bit.ly/cTWjP,` `http://blogs.msdn.com/ssds/archive/2009/03/12/9471765.aspx`).

Understanding SQL Server 2008's Transparent Data Encryption

When this book was written Microsoft was in the process of upgrading SDS from a customized version of SQL Server 2005 that used an Entity-Attribute-Value data model to fully relational SQL Server 2008. SQL Server 2008 added Transparent Data Encryption (TDE), which imposes a cryptographic layer between the SQL Server data engine and the file system. The primary advantages of TDE, which encrypts the entire database (including backup and log files), over cell level are that it encrypts and decrypts data at the page level as it moves between files and memory and doesn't increase data size. TDE moots issues of what data is PII and what is not; *everything* is encrypted.

One of TDE's primary architectural criteria was to meet the requirements of PCI-DSS, SB 1386, and other legislation in process when SQL Server 2008 was in development with minimum effort by database administrators (DBAs). Unfortunately, SDS won't support TDE.

You can learn more about TDE from the "Database Encryption in SQL Server 2008 Enterprise Edition" technical article (`http://bit.ly/3wcuXw, http://msdn.microsoft.com/en-us/library/cc278098` `.aspx`*), Laurentiu Cristofor's October 2007 "SQL Server 2008: Transparent data encryption feature — a quick overview" blog post (*`http://bit.ly/zf9Uk, http://blogs.msdn.com/lcris` `/archive/2007/10/03/sql-server-2008-transparent-data-encryption-feature-a-quick-` `overview.aspx`*), and Joe Yong's "SQL Server 2008 TDE: Encryption You Can Use!" January 2008 blog post (*`http://bit.ly/ACOKb, http://blog.scalabilityexperts.com/2008/01/08/93/`*).*

Auditing Conformance to Regulatory and Industry Standards

SOX Section 404 requires "an assessment, as of the end of the most recent fiscal year of the Company, of the effectiveness of the internal control structure and procedures of the issuer for financial reporting." According to Wikipedia, the SEC's interpretive guidance makes "both management and the external auditor responsible for performing their assessment in the context of a top-down risk assessment, which requires management to base both the scope of its assessment and evidence gathered on risk." As noted in the earlier "Sarbanes-Oxley Act" section, management must "[u]nderstand the flow of transactions, including IT aspects, sufficient enough to identify points at which a misstatement could arise."

An unreported violation of the HIPAA regulations for protecting PII in PHI or failure to encrypt all stored PII related to credit card transactions greatly increases risk of enforcement actions that could threaten the firm's financial stability. Data center or network outages that interrupt access to cloud-based application, storage, or both for a substantial period of time could cause serious adverse financial affects. Management and independent auditors who vouch for the accuracy of financial statements share liability for misstatements. The firm's current internal IT controls and procedures presumably meet the adequacy requirements of the SOX "internal control report" for on-premises applications and data. However, it's not likely that management or independent auditors will have access to a cloud service provider's facilities and operating personnel in order to make such an assessment of off-premises IT operations.

Statement on Auditing Standards No. 70 (SAS 70)

The American Institute of Certified Public Accountants (ICPA) Statement on Auditing Standards No. 70: Service Organizations (SAS 70), "The Effect of Information Technology on the Auditor's Consideration of Internal Control in a Financial Statement Audit," requires independent financial auditors to consider information technology as part of overall internal control.

SAS 70 Type I or II governs an examination of a service organization, such as a cloud services provider, that represents that the organization has been through an in-depth audit of its control objectives and activities with respect to the services provided. SAS 70 Wikipedia (http://en.wikipedia.org/wiki/SAS_70) defines the two SAS 70 audit types as follows:

❑ A *Type I* service auditor's report includes the service auditor's opinion on the fairness of the presentation of the service organization's description of controls that had been placed in operation and the suitability of the design of the controls to achieve the specified control objectives.

❑ A *Type II* service auditor's report includes the information contained in a Type I service auditor's report and also includes the service auditor's opinion on whether the specific controls were operating effectively during the period under review.

SOX representations as to the adequacy of internal controls are for a period of one year, so a Type II report is required. If you have sufficient leverage, you should request that the SAS 70 audit specify the extent of GLB, SOX, HIPAA, and PCI-DSS compliance and describe how the service firm has instituted control objectives to meet the SLAs it offers.

SAS 70 (www.sas70.com/index2.htm) is a web site dedicated to the SAS 70 auditing standard and third-party assurance for service organizations.

Frederick Green's "Compliance with Sarbanes-Oxley and SAS 94: The Critical Role of Application Security in Internal Control" paper (http://bit.ly/AMVgr, www.nysscpa.org/committees/emergingtech /sarbanes_act.htm) explains how SAS 94 relates to SOX.

The ISO/IEC 27001:2005 Standard

ISO/IEC 27001 (Information technology–Security techniques–Information Security Management Systems–Requirements) is an international standard for Information Security Management Sysems (ISMSs). According to the ISO 27001 web site (www.27001.com):

An ISO/IEC 27001 compliant system will provide a systematic approach to ensuring the availability, confidentiality and integrity of corporate information. Using controls based on indentifying and combating the entire range of potential risks to the organization's information assets.

The standard draws on the expertise and knowledge of experienced information security practitioners in a wide range of significant organizations across more than 40 countries, to set out the best practice in information security. And is increasingly used by firms to demonstrate regulatory compliance and effective business risk management, as well as helping them to prepare and position themselves for all new and emerging regulations.

An ISO/IEC 27001-certificated ISMS will ensure that you are in compliance with the whole range of information-related legislation, including (as applicable) HIPAA, GLBA, SB 1386 and other State breach laws, PIPEDA, FISMA, EU Safe Harbor regulations, and so on.

An ISO/IEC 27001-certificated ISMS will ensure that you have in place the general control environment on which a successful SOX s404 report depends.

ISO/IEC 27001:2005 is intended to be used in conjunction with ISO/IEC 27002:2005 ("Information technology–Security techniques–Code of practice for information security management"), which was formerly identified as ISO/IEC 17799. ISO/IEC 27002:2005 lists security control objectives and recommends a range of specific security controls.

Azure's SAS 70 and ISO/IEC 27001:2005 Audits and Certifications

Charlie McNerney, Microsoft's General Manager, Business and Risk Management, Global Foundation Services posted "Securing Microsoft's Cloud Infrastructure" (http://bit.ly/VeAWD, http://blogs.technet.com/gfs/archive/2009/05/27/securing-microsoft-s-cloud-infrastructure.aspx) to the Global Foundation Services Team Blog on May 27, 2009. The post announced the release of a "Security Microsoft's Cloud Infrastructure" whitepaper published in May 2009 (http://bit.ly/18TKFy, www.globalfoundationservices.com/security/documents/SecuringtheMSCloudMay09.pdf) and "Independent, third-party validation of ... Microsoft's cloud infrastructure achieving both SAS 70 Type I and Type II attestations and ISO/IEC 27001:2005 certification."

Although McNerney wrote, "We are proud to be one of the first major online service providers to achieve ISO 27001 certification for our infrastructure," searches for claims by other cloud vendors of ISO/IEC 27001 certification for their PaaS or IaaS services returned no hits when this book was written.

Service-Level Agreements and Business Interruption Risk

The "Maximizing Data Availability and Minimizing Security Risks" topic near the beginning of the chapter briefly described typical SLAs. SLAs are de rigueur for off-premises IT providers of computing, web, and storage services. When this book was written, obtaining coverage by cloud computing users for business interruption risk was very problematic. As cloud computing becomes an accepted business practice and actuaries can predict the probability of provider outages of various durations, casualty carriers undoubtedly will compete to provide business interruption coverage.

Summary

Migrating from on-premises data centers to cloud computing and data storage services, such as those offered by the Windows Azure Platform, require a substantial amount of up-front analysis that's well beyond the realm of traditional application development and database administration. Top management and the IT staff are likely to be the major hurdle to moving selective computing and data storage operations off premises because of data security and integrity concerns. Data centers run by organizations with major Internet presences, such as Microsoft, Amazon, and Google, are likely to be as or more secure than those of prospective enterprise-grade customers.

A common goal of government agencies and established firms is risk avoidance; thus interest in and, ultimately, adoption of cloud computing by government agencies will validate private-sector decisions to take advantage of cloud services. NIST's Information Technology Laboratory is in the forefront of developing cloud computing standards for federal agencies. Standards developed by NIST probably will become the baseline for future industry specifications.

The GLB Act and HIPAA contain federal regulations to protect U.S. residents' non-public and personally identifiable information; California's SB 1386 requires notification of unauthorized access of California residents' PII. PCI-DSS dictates procedures for minimizing the risk of exposure of credit- and debit-card holders' PII in conjunction with card ID numbers. SOX requires implementation of internal controls to minimize the misstatements of financial risks; breaching any governmental regulation or PCI-DSS standard certainly implies financial peril, which might be unknown to management or independent auditors when issuing a yearly SOX compliance report.

Data is at the greatest risk of exposure while it's transiting the Internet. The secure HTTPS protocol with SSL or TLS encryption has proven safe for conducting personal banking and credit card purchase operations over the Internet. HTTPS is reasonably easy to implement for Azure Hosted Services by using Visual Studio's MakeCert.exe command-line utility and IE 8's Certificates dialog. Enabling HTTPS for Data Services within or between data centers involves only a change to a few characters in the project's ServiceConfiguration.cscfg file.

The chapter's AzureTableTestHarness.sln sample application demonstrates techniques for client-side symmetrical encryption and decryption of PII in Azure Tables with .NET 3.5's `AesManaged` cryptography provider class. Encrypting PII, such as CompanyName, ContactName, ContactTitle, Address, PostalCode, Phone, and Fax attributes of the Northwind Customers table doesn't involve a substantial amount of added code but it does exact a major-scale performance penalty for most CRUD operations.

If the Azure team is able to implement SQL Server 2005's server-side cell-level encryption in SQL Azure Database v1, you'll be able to encrypt and decrypt PII for HIPAA, PCI-DSS, and SB 1386 compliance with much less development and testing time and better performance than for client-side encryption. Availability of SQL Server 2008's Transparent Data Encryption will make compliance even simpler by encrypting and decrypting entire databases on the fly.

Microsoft appears to be the first PaaS provider that offers both SAS 70 attestation and ISO/IEC 27001:2005 certification by an independent auditor. These audits will compensate, at least in part, for Microsoft's late entrance to the cloud computing services market.

Authenticating and Authorizing Service Users

The pages of sample projects in Chapters 4, "Scaling Azure Table and Blob Storage" and 5, "Minimizing Risk When Moving to Azure Cloud Services" are available to anyone who knows the name of the cloud service; they require no user authentication or role-based authorization whatsoever. Few real-world services are likely to allow public access other than to simple demonstration versions. At the least, they'll require all production users to log into the Hosted Service as a member of one or more predefined role(s), such as user, reader, writer, supervisor, or administrator. A common method of securing access to a WebRole running on Windows Azure is to use an implementation of ASP.NET Membership Services that's customized to accommodate the cloud-computing infrastructure.

An alternative to a full-scale implementation of ASP.NET Membership Services and role management is basic Windows Live ID (WLID) authentication. A May 2009 update to the Azure Services Development Portal simplified WLID authentication by automatically adding a Live Services Existing APIs project for each existing and new Hosted Services project you create. The Windows Live ID Web Authentication SDK 1.2 and Windows Live Tools for Microsoft Visual Studio 2008 provide sample code and ASP.NET server controls that you can use to implement WLID authentication for Azure projects in production.

Taking Advantage of ASP.NET Membership Services

The "Introduction to Membership" online help topic (http://bit.ly/4iCzDz, http://msdn.microsoft.com/en-us/library/yh26yfzy.aspx) describes a prebuilt set of facilities for validating user credentials, which are stored in SQL Server [Express] tables, for access to web sites. ASP.NET Membership Services enable

❑   Creating new users and passwords.

❑   Storing membership information (user names, passwords, and supporting data). By default membership uses SQL Server but can accommodate Active Directory or an alternative data store.

❑   Changing and resetting passwords.

❑   Identifying authenticated users to applications.

❑   Specifying a custom membership provider, such as one designed for use with WebRoles running under the Development Fabric with locally stored or cloud-based data, or under the Azure Fabric with Azure Tables and Blobs.

You can review and post membership questions and answers in the ASP.NET Security Forum (`http://forums.asp.net/25.aspx`).

ASP.NET Login Controls

The following ASP.NET login controls let you create a complete authentication system that requires little code:

❑   *ChangePassword* lets a user change her password by supplying the original password, and then creating and confirming the new password.

❑   *CreateUserWizard* control collects user name, password, password confirmation, e-mail alias, security question, and security answer information from new users. By default, the wizard adds the new user to the system.

❑   *Login* contains text boxes for entering the user name and password and a check box that enables users to store their identity using ASP.NET membership for automatic authentication the next time they start the service.

❑   *LoginStatus* displays a login link for unauthenticated users and a logout link for authenticated users.

❑   *LoginName* displays a user's login name if the user has logged in using ASP.NET membership or a Windows account name with Windows authentication.

❑   *LoginView* lets you display different information to anonymous and logged-in users with the `AnonymousTemplate` or `LoggedInTemplate`, which you can customize.

❑   *PasswordRecovery* lets a user retrieve her password by sending a message to the e-mail address that she used when creating the account.

User Role and Profile Management

You can integrate ASP.NET Membership Services with ASP.NET role management services for authorizing authenticated users. The "Managing Authorization Using Roles" online help topic (`http://bit.ly/12DSA6, http://msdn.microsoft.com/en-us/library/9ab2fxh0.aspx`) describes how to take advantage of ASP.NET role management features. The default role provider store is SQL Server.

Similarly, you can integrate ASP.NET Membership Services with user profiles to enable application-specific customization for individual users. The "ASP.NET Profile Properties Overview" online help topic (`http://bit.ly/FkAby, http://msdn.microsoft.com/en-us/library/2y3fs9xs.aspx`) describes how to integrate the user's profile.

The . . .\AspProvider folder includes an ASP.NET Providers Sample: ASP.NET Application Providers for Windows Azure page (providers-extended-readme.mht) that explains the differences between the Windows Azure and SQL Server membership providers.

Adapting ASP.NET Authentication and Role Management to Windows Azure Web Roles

Deploying your Web Role under Windows Azure in data centers enables storing user data in Azure Data Services or SADB tables. It's a common practice to create or specify Azure Blob, Table, and Queue Storage Services when creating a new Hosted Service, so Azure Storage Services are the preferable default. If you take advantage of geolocation services, tables and blobs of multiple Hosted Service instances can easily access the same role and profile data stored as Storage Services in the same or different data centers.

Load balancing can cause HTTP requests from a single user to be forwarded to different machines in one or more data centers. Therefore, the session state provider must keep session data inside a single, replicated session blob to keep session state consistent for the user during the entire session.

The Windows Azure SDK includes two membership-related sample projects: AspProviders.sln, which includes ASPProviders.dll and StorageClient.dll class libraries, and AspProvidersDemo.sln, which adds the AspProvidersDemo and AspProvidersDemo_WebRole projects to demonstrate adding membership services to a Web Role.

The \Program Files\Windows Azure SDK\v1.0\Samples.zip file contains 11 sample projects that demonstrate many advanced Windows Azure Platform features. The following sections assume that you extract the files to an unprotected location, C:\Azure Samples.

Running the Windows Azure SDK's AspProvidersDemo Service Locally

To build and run the AspProvidersDemo.sln project for the first time, execute buildme.cmd and runme.cmd to open the Default.aspx page, as shown in Figure 6-1.

Clicking the Login link in the headline or the first item in the pages list displays the message shown in Figure 6-2.

Clicking OK dismisses the message, creates the AspProvidersDemoDB database and opens the Login page (see Figure 6-3).

If you receive an error at this or a later step, right-click Solution Explorer's AspProviderDemo node and choose Create Test Storage Tables to create the local storage database.

Click the Create New User link to open the CreateNewWizard.aspx page and add all required fields for a new account in the `CreateUserWizardStep1` form, as shown in Figure 6-4.

Unlike most authentication systems, user names are case sensitive. Passwords and answers to lost-password questions are encrypted in the table with a salted hash.

153

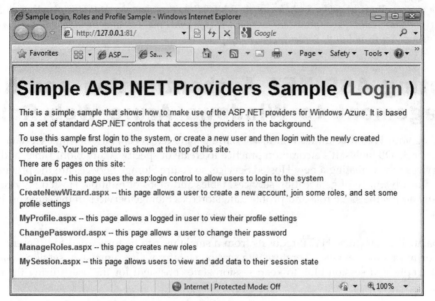

Figure 6-1: The default page of the AspProvidersDemo service with a list of six available pages.

Figure 6-2: This message appears when you start using the form but haven't created the project's database for local storage.

Click Create User to move to the next step, which offers three default built-in roles: Countrymen, Family, and Friends (see Figure 6-5). Select one of the built-in roles and click Finish to add the new member to the Members and Roles tables and return to the Default.aspx page.

> *AspProvidersDemo lets you add, but not delete, a user's role(s) in the* `wsAssignUserToRoles` *step, which is the only point in the demo where you can assign role(s) to a user.*

You can add new roles, but not delete roles, in the ManageRoles.aspx page. For this chapter's sample project, add DbAdmin, DbReader, and DbWriter roles, which will correspond to SQL Server's built-in db_owner, db_datareader, and db_datawriter database roles (see Figure 6-6).

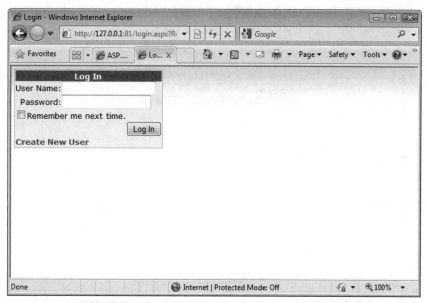

Figure 6-3: The Login page of the AspProvidersDemo service for registered and unregistered users.

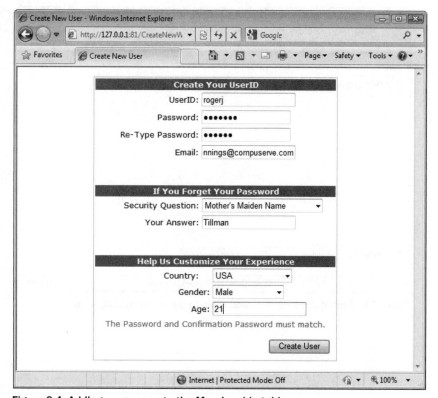

Figure 6-4: Adding a new user to the Membership table.

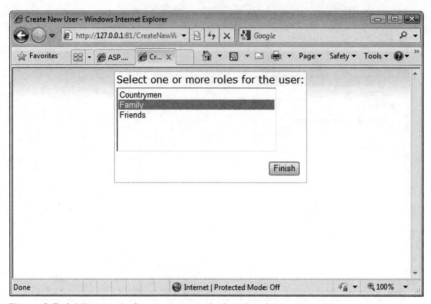

Figure 6-5: Adding a role for a new user during the signup process.

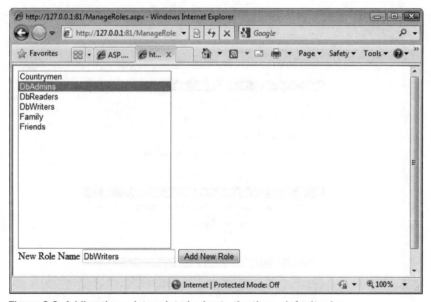

Figure 6-6: Adding three data-related roles to the three default roles.

Working with the AspProvidersDemoDB Database

The easiest way to get rid of unwanted roles, such as Countrymen, Family, and Friends, is to open the AspProvidersDemoDB database in SQL Server Management Studio [Express]. The database contains three user tables: dbo.Membership, dbo.Roles, and dbo.Sessions, as shown in the database diagram of Figure 6-7. Each table has a clustered composite index on the PartitionKey and RowKey columns.

Figure 6-7: The database diagram for the Membership, Roles, and Sessions tables.

Although obvious relationships exist between the UserName values of the Membership and Roles tables and the BlobName values of the Membership or Sessions tables, by default no referential integrity constraints are enforced in the database.

To remove the Countrymen, Family, and Friends roles and the initial user you added in the preceding section, do the following:

1. Right-click Object Explorer's Roles node and choose Open Table to display a datasheet containing the six roles. Select the Countrymen, Family, and Friends rows and delete them.

2. Right-click Object Explorer's Members node, choose Open Table, note the UserID `uniqueidentifier`, and encrypted Password, PasswordSalt, and PasswordAnswer cells, and then delete the user you added in the preceding section.

3. Repeat the preceding section's process for your administrative account but add the DbAdmin, DbReader, and DbWriter roles in the final step.

Exploring Azure-Specific Membership Elements and Attributes in the Web.config File

The AspProviderDemo_WebRole project's Web.config file includes several groups under the `<system.web>` section with default attribute values specific to ASP.NET Web Cloud Service projects.

Membership Section

Listing 6-1 shows the `<membership>` section with Cloud Service-specific attribute values emphasized:

Listing 6-1: Default elements and attribute values for the web.config file's `<membership>` section

```
<system.web>
   <membership defaultProvider="TableStorageMembershipProvider"
       userIsOnlineTimeWindow = "20">
     <providers>
       <clear/>
       <add name="TableStorageMembershipProvider"
         type="Microsoft.Samples.ServiceHosting.AspProviders. _
           TableStorageMembershipProvider"
         description="Membership provider using table storage"
         applicationName="AspProvidersDemo"
         enablePasswordRetrieval="false"
         enablePasswordReset="true"
         requiresQuestionAndAnswer="false"
         minRequiredPasswordLength="1"
         minRequiredNonalphanumericCharacters="0"
         requiresUniqueEmail="true"
         passwordFormat="Hashed"
       />
     </providers>
   </membership >
</system.web>
```

Line-continuation characters indicate attribute values that exceed the number of printable code characters on a monospace line.

The `userIsOnlineTimeWindow` value is the number of minutes after the `LastActivityDateUtc` timestamp value during which the user is considered to be online.

The default `minRequiredPasswordLength` value of 1 is clearly inappropriate and should be set to a value between 6 and 8.

Role Manager, Profile, and Session State Sections

Role Manager, Profile, and Session storage is theoretically optional, but most projects will require at least
`<roleManager>` and `<sessionState>` sections (see Listing 6-2).

**Listing 6-2: Default elements and attribute values for the web.config file's
`<roleManager>`, `<profile>`, and `<sessionState>` sections**

```
<system.web>
   <roleManager enabled="true" defaultProvider="TableStorageRoleProvider"
       cacheRolesInCookie="true" cookieName=".ASPXROLES" cookieTimeout="30"
       cookiePath="/" cookieRequireSSL="false" cookieSlidingExpiration = "true"
       cookieProtection="All" >
     <providers>
       <clear/>
       <add name="TableStorageRoleProvider"
         type="Microsoft.Samples.ServiceHosting.AspProviders. _
           TableStorageRoleProvider"
         description="Role provider using table storage"
         applicationName="AspProvidersDemo"
      />
     </providers>
   </roleManager>

   <profile enabled="true" defaultProvider="TableStorageProfileProvider"
       inherits="UserProfile">
     <providers>
       <clear/>
       <add name="TableStorageProfileProvider"
         type="Microsoft.Samples.ServiceHosting.AspProviders. _
           TableStorageProfileProvider"
         description="Profile provider using structured storage"
         applicationName="AspProvidersDemo"
       />
     </providers>

     <! —
     <properties>
       <add name="Country" type="string"/>
       <add name="Gender" type="string"/>
       <add name="Age" type="Int32"/>
     </properties>
     — >
   </profile>

   <sessionState mode="Custom" customProvider="TableStorageSessionStateProvider">
     <providers>
       <clear />
       <add name="TableStorageSessionStateProvider"
           type="Microsoft.Samples.ServiceHosting.AspProviders. _
             TableStorageSessionStateProvider"
           applicationName="AspProvidersDemo"
       />
     </providers>
   </sessionState>
</system.web>
```

Optional Data Services and Default Settings in Web.Config

You can add the settings shown in Listing 6-3 to Web.config to specify Data Services endpoints and account information as well as default table names, provider application name, and blob container names for profile and session data.

Listing 6-3: Optional Web.config elements to specify Data Services endpoints and account data plus default names for tables, application, and profile and session containers

```
<appSettings>
    <add key = "TableStorageEndpoint" value="http://127.0.0.1:10002"/>
    <add key = "BlobStorageEndpoint" value="http://127.0.0.1:10000"/>
    <add key = "AccountName" value="devstoreaccount1"/>
    <add key = "AccountSharedKey" value="Eby8vdM02xNOcqFlqUwJPLlmEtlCDXJ1 .."/>

    <add key = "DefaultMembershipTableName" value="Membership"/>
    <add key = "DefaultRoleTableName" value="Roles"/>
    <add key = "DefaultSessionTableName" value="Session"/>
    <add key = "DefaultProviderApplicationName" value="ProviderTest"/>
    <add key = "DefaultProfileContainerName" value="profile"/>
    <add key = "DefaultSessionContainerName" value="session"/>
</appSettings>
```

Corresponding <Setting> elements in the ServiceConfiguration.cscfg file override values specified in the Web.config file or the default values supplied by code in the AspProviders project's Configuration class.

Adding <Setting> elements to the ServiceConfiguration.cscfg file is the preferred approach because you can edit that file in the Azure Services Portal. Editing Web.config requires recompiling and redeploying the service. <Setting> elements added to the ServiceConfiguration.cscfg file require adding corresponding elements to the ServiceDefinition.csdef file.

Listing 6-4 shows the Configuration class's code for the lowest priority default values.

Listing 6-4: Code to provide default names for tables, application, and profile and session containers

```
internal const string DefaultMembershipTableName = "Membership";
internal const string DefaultRoleTableName = "Roles";
internal const string DefaultSessionTableName = "Sessions";
internal const string DefaultSessionContainerName = "sessionprovidercontainer";
internal const string DefaultProfileContainerName = "profileprovidercontainer";
internal const string DefaultProviderApplicationName = "appname";
```

If you change one or more table names, you must regenerate the local Data Services database.

Data Services and Default Settings in ServiceConfiguration.cscfg

Listing 6-5 shows the ServiceConfiguration.cscfg file for the modified AspProviderDemo.sln project in the WROX\Azure\Chapter06\AspProviderDemo folder:

Listing 6-5: Service configuration settings for local storage endpoints

```xml
<?xml version="1.0"?>
<ServiceConfiguration serviceName="AspProvidersDemo"
xmlns="http://schemas.microsoft.com/ServiceHosting/2008/10/ServiceConfiguration">
  <Role name="WebRole">
    <Instances count="2" />
    <ConfigurationSettings>
      <! — For local storage — >
      <Setting name="AccountName" value="devstoreaccount1"/>
      <Setting name="AccountSharedKey" value="Eby8vdM02xNOcqFlqUwJP .."/>
      <Setting name="BlobStorageEndpoint" value="http://127.0.0.1:10000"/>
      <Setting name="QueueStorageEndpoint" value = "http://127.0.0.1:10001"/>
      <Setting name="TableStorageEndpoint" value="http://127.0.0.1:10002"/>
      <Setting name="allowInsecureRemoteEndpoints" value=""/>
  </Role>
</ServiceConfiguration>
```

The later section,"Moving the AspProvidersDemo's Data Source to the Cloud," explains use of the `allowInsecureRemoteEndpoints` *setting, which doesn't apply to local storage.*

Analyzing the AspProviders Library's Classes

The AspProviders sample class library contains seven Azure-specific class files, which serve as the starting point for adding ASP.NET membership features to Cloud Web applications. Three of these classes, `TableStorageMembershipProvider`, `TableStorageRoleProvider`, and `TableStorageSessionProvider`, include *TableName*`DataServiceContract` classes, which inherit from the `TableStorageDataServiceContract` class. Therefore these classes automatically generate `Membership`, `Role`, and `Session` tables with the structures defined by the derived class.

The `TableStorageMembershipProvider` *manages user profiles, so a* `Profile` *table isn't required.*

The TableStorageMembershipProvider Class

The `TableStorageMembershipProvider` class stores user data inside a membership table managed by Azure Table Services. To prevent downtime during web application or data center software updates, web applications are hosted on a minimum of two web service instances in one or more data centers. The `TableStorageMembershipProvider` instances running on these two (or more) web service instances access the same user data (state) in the membership table. Figure 6-8 shows part of the content of a typical `MembershipRow` item.

David Pallman's Azure Storage Explorer application (AzureStorageExplorer.sln) is a Windows Presentation Foundation front-end for displaying table, blob, and queue values in Azure local and cloud storage. You can download the app's binary files and source code from http://bit.ly/ErrGT, www.codeplex.com/azurestorageexplorer.

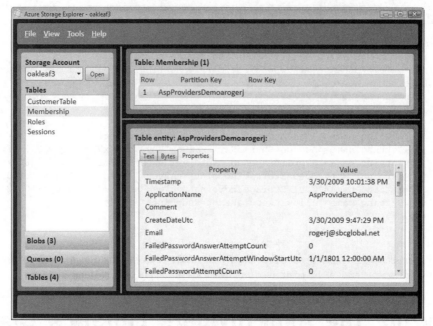

Figure 6-8: Azure Storage Explorer displaying part of the author's Member table data.

The PartitionKey value, which doesn't appear in Figure 6-8, is the concatenation of ApplicationName, the literal letter a and the UserName with an empty string as the RowKey value; this combination creates a unique partition for each row. This approach ensures the maximum distribution (scalability) of membership data, which could expand to millions of rows for a very popular web application.

The TableStorageMembershipProvider.cs file's class diagram, shown in Figure 6-9, contains Table StorageMembershipProvider, MembershipRow (refer to Figure 6-8), MembershipDataServiceContext, and EmailComparer classes. The EmailComparer class aids testing for a unique e-mail address for each new member.

The TableStorageRoleProvider Class

The Roles table holds a combination Role-name rows and UserInRole rows, as shown in Figure 6-10. The upper Table pane shows three Role-name rows for DbAdmin (1), DbReader (2), and DbWriter (3) role names and one of three UserInRole rows for an administrative user.

The lower pane of Figure 6-10 displays the attribute names and values of the Role entity selected in the upper pane as elements of an XML document. Notice that the PartitionKey property value is the concatenation of ApplicationName and the literal letter a, and the RowKey property value is the RoleName (DbAdmin) with literal 62 inserted, apparently to accommodate potential duplicate names. In this case, a single partition stores all Role rows for a particular web application (service). Listing 6-6 shows the properties of the row for a user (refer to Figure 6-8) who's a member of the DbAdmin group.

MembershipRow
Class
→ TableStorageEntity

⊞ Fields

⊟ Properties
- 🔲 ApplicationName
- 🔲 Comment
- 🔲 CreateDateUtc
- 🔲 Email
- 🔲 FailedPasswordAnswerAttemptCount
- 🔲 FailedPasswordAnswerAttemptWindowSt...
- 🔲 FailedPasswordAttemptCount
- 🔲 FailedPasswordAttemptWindowStartUtc
- 🔲 IsAnonymous
- 🔲 IsApproved
- 🔲 IsLockedOut
- 🔲 LastActivityDateUtc
- 🔲 LastLockoutDateUtc
- 🔲 LastLoginDateUtc
- 🔲 LastPasswordChangedDateUtc
- 🔲 Password
- 🔲 PasswordAnswer
- 🔲 PasswordFormat
- 🔲 PasswordQuestion
- 🔲 PasswordSalt
- 🔲 ProfileBlobName
- 🔲 ProfileIsCreatedByProfileProvider
- 🔲 ProfileLastUpdatedUtc
- 🔲 ProfileSize
- 🔲 UserId
- 🔲 UserName

⊟ Methods
- ⍐ CompareTo
- ⍐ MembershipRow (+ 1 overload)

MembershipDataServiceContext
Class
→ TableStorageDataServiceContext

⊟ Properties
- 🔲 Membership

EmailComparer
Class

⊟ Methods
- ⍐ Compare

TableStorageMembershipProvider
Class
→ MembershipProvider

⊞ Fields

⊟ Properties
- 🔲 ApplicationName
- 🔲 EnablePasswordReset
- 🔲 EnablePasswordRetrieval
- 🔲 MaxInvalidPasswordAttempts
- 🔲 MinRequiredNonAlphanumericCharacters
- 🔲 MinRequiredPasswordLength
- 🔲 PasswordAttemptWindow
- 🔲 PasswordFormat
- 🔲 PasswordStrengthRegularExpression
- 🔲 RequiresQuestionAndAnswer
- 🔲 RequiresUniqueEmail

⊟ Methods
- ⍐ ChangePassword
- ⍐ ChangePasswordQuestionAndAnswer
- ⍐ CheckPassword (+ 2 overloads)
- ⍐ CreateDataServiceContext
- ⍐ CreateUser
- ⍐ DeleteUser
- ⍐ EncodePassword
- ⍐ EvaluatePasswordRequirements
- ⍐ FindUsersByEmail
- ⍐ FindUsersByName
- ⍐ GeneratePassword
- ⍐ GenerateSalt
- ⍐ GetAllUsers
- ⍐ GetNumberOfUsersOnline
- ⍐ GetPassword
- ⍐ GetUser (+ 1 overload)
- ⍐ GetUserFromTable
- ⍐ GetUserNameByEmail
- ⍐ Initialize
- ⍐ IsUniqueEmail (+ 1 overload)
- ⍐ PasswordAttemptWindowAsTimeSpan
- ⍐ ProcessGetUserQuery
- ⍐ ResetPassword
- ⍐ UnEncodePassword
- ⍐ UnlockUser
- ⍐ UpdateUser
- ⍐ ValidateUser

Figure 6-9: The TableStorageMembershipProvider's class diagram.

Listing 6-6: Properties for an AspProvidersDemo user's DbAdmin role assignment

```
<entity>
  <PartitionKey>AspProvidersDemoarogerj</PartitionKey>
  <RowKey>Db62Admin</RowKey>
```

Continued

Listing 6-6: Properties for an AspProvidersDemo user's DbAdmin role assignment
(continued)

```
    <Timestamp>3/30/2009 9:47:05 PM</Timestamp>
    <ApplicationName>AspProvidersDemo</ApplicationName>
    <RoleName>DbAdmin</RoleName>
    <UserName>rogerj</UserName>
<entity>
```

Appending the UserName *to the* PartitionKey *value increases scalability.*

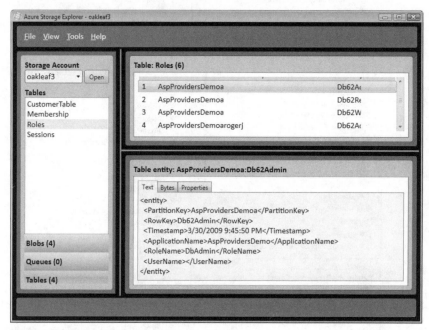

Figure 6-10: Four of the six rows for three Role names and one user in the three roles.

The TableStorageRoleProvider.cs file's class diagram defines classes — TableStorageRoleProvider, RoleRow, and RoleDataServiceContext — that correspond to those of the TableStorageMember-Provider.cs file. Figure 6-11 shows the properties and methods of these three classes.

The TableStorageProfileProvider Class

Blobs in the profileprovidercontainer store profile names in plain text and values as encrypted byte arrays; each user can have zero or one profile, so no Profiles table is required. The Membership table's ProfileBlobName, ProfileIsCreatedByProfileProvider, ProfileLastUpdatedUtc, and ProfileSize attribute-value pairs store profile management details. Figure 6-12 shows the profile content that generates the entries of Figure 6-13.

Forms in the \WROX\Chapter06\AspProvidersDemo\AspProvidersDemo.sln sample project are reformatted to match the colors of the \WROX\Chapter06\AzureTableTestHarnessSSL\AzureTableTest Harness.sln project's form.

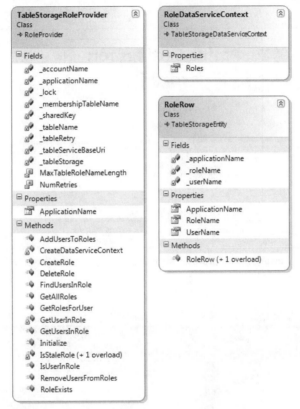

Figure 6-11: The TableStorageRoleProvider's class diagram.

In Figure 6-13, the 0 argument in the Age:S:0:2 segment represents the start position of the Age value (21) in the string; 2 represents the length. Similarly, the Gender value (Male) starts at position 2 and is 4 characters long. Finally, the Country value (USA) starts at position 6 and is 3 characters long.

Figure 6-14 combines the TableStorageProfileProvider.cs and TableStorageSessionProvider.cs files' class diagrams.

The TableStorageSessionProvider Class

In the case of session state, HTTP requests from a single user are likely to be forwarded to different machines in the data center if you specify two or more service instances in the ServiceConfig-uration.cscfg file. The session state provider in this sample stores session data in a blob of the sessionprovidercontainer container. A Sessions table row stores the blob name and other session management data, as shown in Figure 6-15. Regardless whether the load balancer routes requests from the same user address to different machines in the Azure Fabric, session state is retrieved from the storage services and thus kept consistent across the entire session.

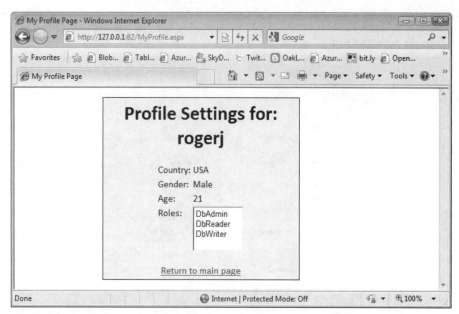

Figure 6-12: Viewing a user profile's attribute-value pairs and assigned roles in the MyProfile.aspx page.

Figure 6-13: Plain text attribute names (Country, Gender, and Age) and encoded values in a profile blob.

Storing session state that contains unencrypted personally identifiable information in persistent blobs probably violates the governmental regulations and industry rules discussed in Chapter 5's "Gaining and Auditing Regulatory Compliance" section and related sections.

Figure 6-14: The TableStorageProfileProvider and TableStorageSessionProvider class diagrams.

Session state converts the session dictionary's contents to a binary blob by a custom serialization process and stores the blob to the `sessionprovidercontainer` container. Serialization and deserialization supports .NET primitive types, including String, Boolean, DateTime, TimeSpan, Int16, Int32, Int64, Byte, Char, Single, Double, Decimal, SByte, UInt16, UInt32, UInt64, Guid, and IntPtr, and writes these types directly to the blob. BinaryFormatter serializes object types and is slower than that for primitive types. Figure 6-16 shows the Base64Binary-encoded representation of the opaque byte array from a serialized session dictionary with only a few string values.

Figure 6-15: Sessions row attribute-value management pairs for a session blob.

Figure 6-16: Part of the Base64Binary-encoded representation of a session-state blob.

*The "Fast, Scalable, and Secure Session State Management for Your Web Applications" MSDN Magazine article by Michael Volodarsky (*http://bit.ly/DIMCS, http://msdn.microsoft.com/en-us/ magazine/cc163730.aspx*) provides more details about ASP.NET session state management, including an explanation of ASP.NET 2.0 session partitioning.*

Moving the AspProvidersDemo's Data Source to the Cloud

Listing 6-7 shows the ServiceConfiguration.cscfg file's settings for secure HTTPS transport of Azure Tables and Blobs for the AspProvidersDemo service.

It's a recommended practice to verify connectivity with Azure Data Services before attempting to integrate membership services with an existing Azure service's WebRole project.

Listing 6-7: Service configuration settings for secure remote storage endpoints

```xml
<?xml version="1.0"?>
<ServiceConfiguration serviceName="AspProvidersDemo"
xmlns="http://schemas.microsoft.com/ServiceHosting/2008/10/ServiceConfiguration">
  <Role name="WebRole">
    <Instances count="2" />
    <ConfigurationSettings>
     <! — For cloud storage — >
     <Setting name="AccountName" value="oakleaf3"/>
     <Setting name="AccountSharedKey"      value="gVIpq7XHK+4t0iivSTP .." />
     <Setting name="BlobStorageEndpoint" value="https://blob.core.windows.net" />
     <Setting name="QueueStorageEndpoint" value="https://queue.core.windows.net" />
     <Setting name="TableStorageEndpoint" value="https://table.core.windows.net" />
     <Setting name="allowInsecureRemoteEndpoints" value="false"/>
    </ConfigurationSettings>
  </Role>
</ServiceConfiguration>
```

The `allowInsecureRemoteEndpoints` setting, which is emphasized for cloud storage in Listing 6-7, requires SSL/TLS (secure HTTPS) connections to Storage Services by default (`value=""` or `value="false"`).

See Chapter 5's "Enabling TLS for Azure Data Services" for more information about using TLS with Azure Tables and Blobs.

If you're running your service on the Azure Fabric in the same data center as your storage services and don't want to incur the TLS overhead, set `value="true"`.

Substitute your `AccountName` *and* `AccountSharedKey` *values for those shown for cloud storage in Listing 6-7.*

Integrating Membership Services with an Azure Service

Integrating ASP.NET Membership Services with an existing WebRole project would be a major problem if it weren't possible to customize your own version of the AspProviderDemo.sln project and then import its files. However, importing and modifying the files is a somewhat complex project because of the large number of files that must be copied from the Asp-ProviderDemo_WebRole to the *ExistingProjectName*_WebRole folder and integrated into the final solution.

Copying and Integrating Membership-Related Files

The \WROX\Azure\Chapter06\AzureTableTestHarnessSSL folder contains Chapter 5's AzureTableTestHarnessSSL.sln project upgraded with most of the AspProviderDemo_WebRole's *.aspx, *.aspx.cs, and *.aspx.designer.cs files and all the AspProvider class library's files. The strategy used to integrate the two projects was as follows:

1. Copy the \WROX\Azure\Chapter05\AzureTableTestHarnessSSL folder to \WROX\Chapter06.

2. Compile and run the destination project to verify operability with remote Azure Data Services in the new location.

3. Rename the destination project's Web.config file to Web.config.bak or the like.

4. Copy the \WROX\Azure\Chapter05\AzureTableTestHarnessSSL\StorageClient and … \Common projects to \WROX\Azure\Chapter06\AzureTableTestHarnessSSL. Add the two projects to the destination solution.

5. Copy the \WROX\Azure\Chapter06\ChangePassword.aspx, CreateNewWiz-ard.aspx, Login.aspx, ManageRoles.aspx, MyProfile.aspx, and MySession.aspx with their *.aspx.cs and *.aspx.designer.cs files as well as the Web.config file to the \WROX\Azure\Chapter06\AzureTableTestHarnessSSL\AzureTableTestHarness_WebRole folder.

6. Add each copied *.aspx and the Web.config file items to the AzureTableTestHarness_Web-Role project.

7. Right-click the AzureTableTestHarness_WebRole's References node, click the Projects tab, select AspProviders, Common, and StorageClient class libraries, and click OK to add the three references (see Figure 6-17).

8. Open the copied Web.config file and change all instances of `applicationName="AspProviderDemo"` to `applicationName="AzureTableTestHarness"`.

9. Open the ServiceConfiguration.cscfg file and add the `<Setting name="allowInsecure RemoteEndpoints" value="false"/>` element.

10. Open the ServiceDescription.cscfg file and add the `<Setting name="allowInsecureRemote Endpoints" />` element.

11. Right-click the Login.aspx page's node and choose Set as Start Page.

12. Press F5 and cross your fingers while waiting for the Login form to appear.

13. Previously entered user names and passwords aren't applicable to the new AzureTableTest Harness application, so click Create a New User to open the CreateNewUserWizard, and create a temporary account with a fictitious user name.

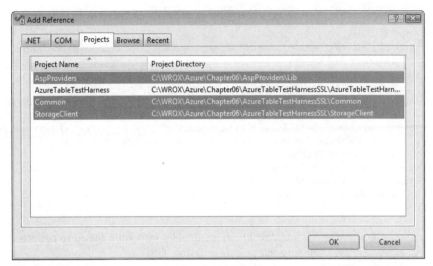

Figure 6-17: Adding references to the AspProviders, Common, and StorageClient class libraries.

Customizing the AzureTableTestHarness Project's Default.aspx Page

Emulate the login/logout behavior of the AspProviderDemo project's Default.aspx page by adding the following to the end of the text in the `<div>` at the top of the page:

```
(<asp:LoginStatus ID="LoginStatus2" runat="server" /> 
<asp:LoginName ID="LoginName1" runat="server" />)
```

Emulating links on the AspProviderDemo project's Default.aspx page simplifies the integration process for initial testing, so add a `<div>` to the bottom of the page with the LinkButton controls shown in Listing 6-8.

Listing 6-8: LinkButtons to emulate those on the AspProviderDemo project's Default.aspx

```
<div style="font-family: Calibri, Arial, Helvetica, sans-serif;"
id="divManageAccts">
    Manage <b><asp:LoginName ID="LoginName2" runat="server" /></b> Account:
    <asp:LinkButton ID="lbProfile" runat="server"
PostBackUrl="~/MyProfile.aspx">View
<b>
    <asp:LoginName ID="LoginName3" runat="server" /> </b>Profile</asp:LinkButton>
```

Continued

Listing 6-8: LinkButtons to emulate those on the AspProviderDemo project's Default.aspx *(continued)*

```
           
    <asp:LinkButton ID="lbSession" runat="server"
PostBackUrl="~/MySession.aspx">View
<b>
    <asp:LoginName ID="LoginName4" runat="server" /> </b>Session</asp:LinkButton>
           
    <asp:LinkButton ID="lbChangePassword" runat="server"
        PostBackUrl="~/ChangePassword.aspx">Change <b>
    <asp:LoginName ID="LoginName5" runat="server" /> </b>Password</asp:LinkButton>
           
    <asp:LinkButton ID="lbRoles" runat="server" PostBackUrl="~/ManageRoles.aspx"
        Enabled="False">Manage User Roles</asp:LinkButton>
           
    <asp:LinkButton ID="lbNewAccount" runat="server"
PostBackUrl="~/CreateNewWizard.aspx"
        Enabled="False">Create New Account</asp:LinkButton>
</div>
```

The lbRoles *and* lbNewAccount *LinkButtons are disabled by default; these two controls are enabled only for members of the DbAdmins role by code in Listing 6-9.*

Figure 6-18 shows the page with the preceding modification and controls enabled for a member of the DbAdmins account.

Listing 6-9: Enabling special controls for members of the DbAdmins and DbWriters roles

```
// Enable adding, deleting and recreating Customers for DbAdmins and DbWriters
bool isWriter = false;
if (Page.User.IsInRole("DbAdmin") || Page.User.IsInRole("DbWriter"))
{
    frmAdd.Enabled = true;

    // Enable adding roles and new accounts for DbAdmins
    bool isAdmin = false;
    if (Page.User.IsInRole("DbAdmin"))
        isAdmin = true;

    LinkButton lbRoles = Page.Form.FindControl("lbRoles") as LinkButton;
    if (lbRoles != null)
        lbRoles.Enabled = isAdmin;
    LinkButton lbNewAccount =
        Page.Form.FindControl("lbNewAccount") as LinkButton;
    if (lbNewAccount != null)
        lbNewAccount.Enabled = isAdmin;
    isWriter = true;
}
if (!isWriter)
{
```

```
    // Disable Customer updates for DbReaders
    Button delCusts = Page.Form.FindControl("btnDeleteAll") as Button;
    if (delCusts != null)
        delCusts.Enabled = false;
    Button createCusts = Page.Form.FindControl("btnCreateCustomers") as Button;
    if (createCusts != null)
        createCusts.Enabled = false;
    Button updateCusts = Page.Form.FindControl("btnUpdateCusts") as Button;
    if (updateCusts != null)
        updateCusts.Enabled = false;
}
```

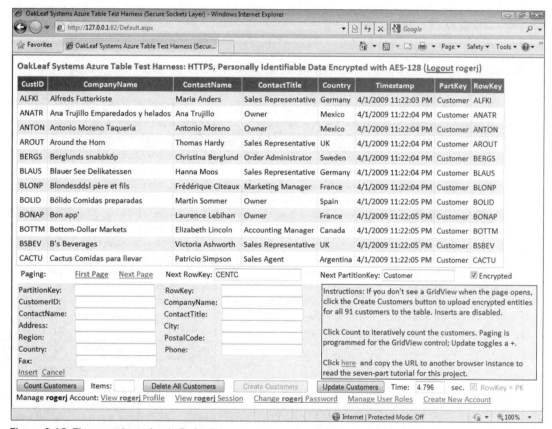

Figure 6-18: The sample project's Default.aspx page with LoginStatus, LoginName, and LinkButton controls as it appears to a member of the DbAdmins role.

Figure 6-19 shows the Default.aspx page after logging out a member of the DbAdmins role. The same controls are enabled and disabled for a member of the DbReader role only.

The Production web server in later CTPs might behave differently from the Developer Fabric with respect to start pages. Login.aspx is specified as the start page in step 11 of the preceding section's instructions and the Developer web server issues `http://127.0.0.1:81/Login.aspx` as the startup URL. However, the Production Fabric might issue `http://ServiceName.CloudApp.net/Default.aspx` regardless of the start page setting. Removing the `Default.aspx` page name doesn't solve the problem. To force Login.aspx as the start page, add the element shown in Listing 6-10 to Web.config's `<webServer>` group:

Listing 6-10: Specifying Login.aspx as the default page in IIS 7.0

```
<defaultDocument enabled="true">
    <files>
        <clear />
        <add value="Login.aspx" />
    </files>
</defaultDocument>
```

A minor change to the `_Default` *class's* `Page_Prerender` *event handler can prevent displaying the GridView as the result of explicit calls to* `../Default.aspx`. *See the sample project's Default.aspx.cs file for details.*

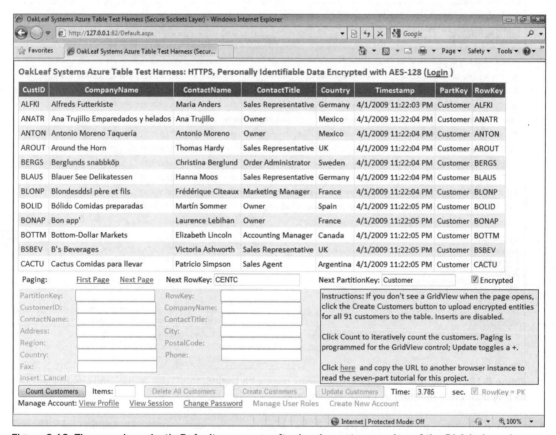

Figure 6-19: The sample project's Default.aspx page after logging out a member of the DbAdmins role.

Figure 6-20 shows the truncated page without the GridView for a user who hasn't logged in.

You can run the finished version of the upgraded AzureTableTestHarness service on Windows Azure at `http://oakleaf4.cloudapp.net/Login.aspx`.

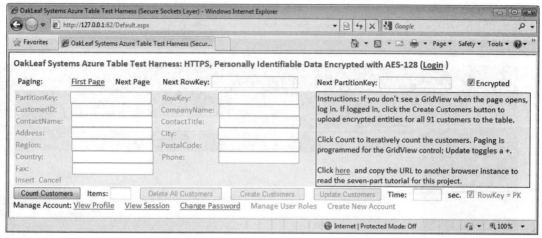

Figure 6-20: The Default.aspx page hiding data from unauthenticated users.

Authenticating Users with Windows Live ID

Most Windows users have at least one WLID for logging in to Microsoft and other online services that require user authentication. As noted at the beginning of this chapter, a May 2009 update to the Azure Services Developer Portal decoupled Live ID authentication from Hosted Services. Doing this removed the Live Services and Active Directory Federation section and Application ID field from the Hosted Service page. This section moved to a new Live Services: Existing APIs project that specifies the Hosted Service's domain, points to its URL, and provides Application ID and Secret Key values. The portal adds this new project and assigns it the same name as the corresponding Hosted Service (see Figure 6-21).

> *All web applications, not just Azure projects, use Live Services: Existing APIs projects that you create in the Azure Services Developer Portal to register with the WLID service.*

The WLID service assigns the Application ID value and uses it to look up the Return URL for the Hosted Services project's page and to generate a unique Personal User IDentifier (PUID) for the user and the site. The PUID can act as primary key for additional registration data provided by the user. The Secret Key value encrypts and signs the security token provided by the WLID service and corresponds to a password for the project.

> *WLID requires the requesting client's browser to support cookies.*

Downloading and Installing the WLID Web Authentication SDK 1.2

Microsoft describes the Windows Live ID Web Authentication SDK 1.2 (http://bit.ly/Z9KKG, www.microsoft.com/downloads/details.aspx?FamilyID=E565FC92-D5F6-4F5F-8713-4DD1C90DE19F& displaylang=en) as a "platform-independent interface for implementing Windows Live ID sign-in on Web sites of all kinds" and an "HTTP-based, platform-neutral interface for implementing Windows Live ID authentication in your existing site, even if it is hosted by a third-party." It's available for individual download in ASP.NET (C# and VB), Java, Perl, PHP, Python, and Ruby.

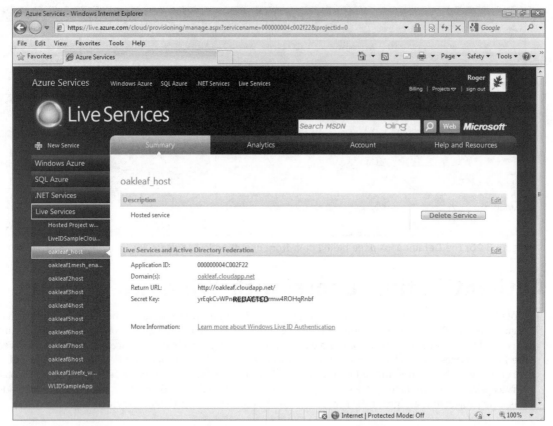

Figure 6-21: The Live Services: Existing APIs project added for a Hosted Service by the Azure Services Developer Portal.

The C# and VB SDKs contain a sample file-system web site named WebAuth. After you download and run webauth-cs-1.2.msi, webauth-vb-1.2.msi or both, copy the lowest-level WebAuth folder and its contents to your \inetpub\wwwroot folder. Launch Vista's IIS 7 or Windows 7's IIS 7.5 Manager, navigate to and right-click the Web Auth Folder and choose Convert to Application (or click the Convert to Application link in the Actions pane) to activate the web site (see Figure 6-22).

The WebAuth site's Web.config file contains a special set of Application ID (`wll_appid`) and Secret Key (`wll_secret`) values in the `<configuration>` section that point to `http://localhost/webauth/sample/default.aspx` as the ReturnURL value, as shown in Listing 6-11.

Listing 6-11: Web.config settings for WLID's default Application ID and SecretKey settings for authenticating web sites.

```
<appSettings>
  <add key="wll_appid" value="00163FFF80003301" />
  <add key="wll_secret" value="ApplicationKey123"/>
  <add key="wll_securityalgorithm" value="wsignin1.0"/>
</appSettings>
```

Test the web site by typing the preceding URL into your browser to display a page similar to that shown in Figure 6-23.

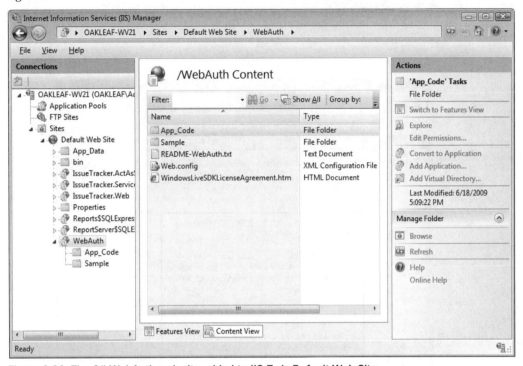

Figure 6-22: The C# WebAuth web site added to IIS 7.x's Default Web Site.

A border has been added to the table cell and font-family specifications changed in Figure 6-23.

Click the Sign In link to open the WLID sign-in page, which offers the alternative of creating an Information Card for sign-in (see Figure 6-24).

Sign in with your WLID to display the WLID sign-out page, which displays your PUID for the application (see Figure 6-25).

You import code from the WebAuth.sln project's WindowsLiveLogin.cs class as well as the Default.aspx and webauth_handler.aspx pages to the LiveIDSampleCloudService.sln project, which you create later in the chapter.

The \WROX\Azure\Chapter06\LiveIDSampleCloudService folder contains a working version of the sample project that runs on the Development Fabric. You must register the project with the Return URL for the webauth_handler.aspx page (`http://localhost:##/webauth-handler.aspx`, where `##` is the port number, usually 81) and substitute your values for `wll_appid` and `wll_secret` in Web.config.

Installing the Windows Live Tools for Visual Studio

Installing Windows Live Tools for Microsoft Visual Studio 2008+ is optional because WebAuth's code in the Default.aspx page imports a WebAuth.htm login control to an IFRAME from http://login.live.com/controls/. Windows Live Tools adds a Windows Live group to the VS Toolbox that includes IDLoginStatus and IDLoginView ASP.NET server controls, as well as MessengerChat, SilverlightStreamMedia and Contacts controls, and a Virtual Earth group, none of which are related to WLID. Installation also adds a Windows Live ID Web Role template to VS's New Project dialog (see Figure 6-26).

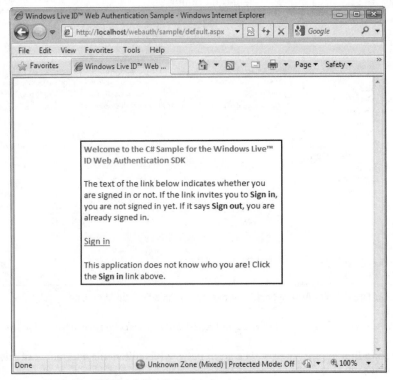

Figure 6-23: The C# WebAuth site's sign-in status.

To download and install the latest release of the Windows Live Tools for VS 2008+, go to dev.live.com/tools/ and click the Download link.

IDLoginStatus Control

The IDLoginStatus control (http://bit.ly/Q3Cew, http://msdn.microsoft.com/en-us/library/cc305086.aspx) substitutes for the imported WebAuth.htm control used by the WebAuth sample project. The control presents users with a link to log in; clicking the link takes them to the WLID login page where they log in with their WLID. After the WLID service has authenticated them, they are redirected to the page you specify as the Return URL value when you register your project in the Azure Services Developer Portal. The following table lists and describes the IDLoginStatus control's parameters.

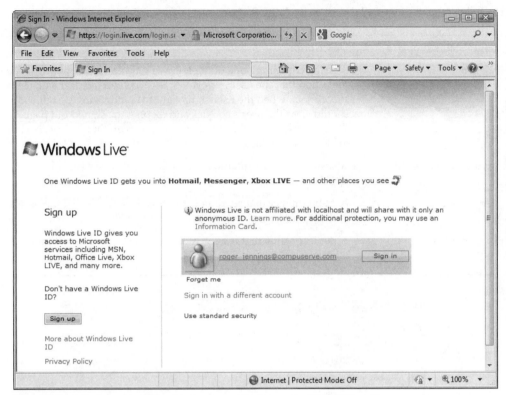

Figure 6-24: Windows Live ID's sign-in page called from the WebAuth page.

LoginStatus Parameter	Description
ID	Required. The unique identifier for the control (default value = IDLoginStatus1).
ApplicationContext	Optional. A string containing state information (not used in the sample project)
ApplicationID ConfigKey	Required. A string specifying the name of the <appSettings> key that contains the value of the Application ID (default value = wll_appid).
ApplicationSecret ConfigKey	Required. A string specifying the name of the <appSettings> key that contains the value of the secret key (default value = wll_secret).
Automatically Convert Authentication	Optional. Set True to automatically log in a user who has logged in with a Windows Live ID and who has previously associated that ID with an ASP.NET profile on the Web page (default value = True).

The following table lists and describes the LoginStatus control's properties.

LoginStatus Property	Description
Action	A string containing one of the following three values, which specifies the action that the user performed: Login when the user signs into the site. Logout when the user signs out of Windows Live. Your code should clear the user's cookies and display the signed out page. Clearcookie when the Windows Live ID Sign Out page calls your site to clear user cookies.
ApplicationUserID	A string containing a unique identifier for the user signed into this application or service.
TimeStamp	A 32-bit integer that represents the time in seconds that the user last authenticated, measured from January 1, 1970 GMT.
LoggedInLiveID	A Boolean value that is true if the user has signed into Windows Live; otherwise false.

Figure 6-25: The C# WebAuth site's sign-out status.

The IDLoginStatus control requires a ScriptManger control on the page, which the Windows Live ID Web Role template adds for you. This control supports obtaining wll_appid *and* wll_secret *values only from the Web.config file; unlike the it doesn't support obtaining these values from the*

ServiceConfiguration.cscfg file. According to members of the Azure team, ASP.NET 4.0 will permit editing Web.config files in the Azure Services Development Portal. For more information about this issue, see `http://bit.ly/vIVlh, http://oakleafblog.blogspot.com/2009/06/problems-deploying -webrole-with-windows.html.`

IDLoginStatus also raises server-side and client-side events.

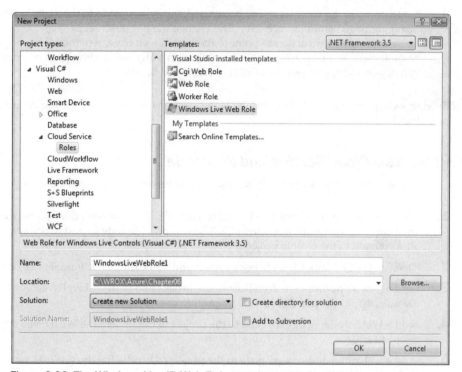

Figure 6-26: The Windows Live ID Web Role template added by Windows Live Tools for VS.

IDLoginView Control

The IDLoginView control (`http://bit.ly/AMkLh, http://msdn.microsoft.com/en-us/library/ cc305081.aspx`) is an alternative to enable WLID authentication. It supports associating a Windows Live ID with an ASP.NET membership profile on a web page and provides six templates for content applicable to anonymous or logged-on users.

Creating and Testing the Initial LiveIDSampleCloudService

Implementing WLID authentication for an existing web site consists of five basic steps:

1. Create a new Blank Cloud Service with a Windows Live Web Role and Default.aspx page, an empty WindowsLiveLogin.cs class and empty webauth_handler.aspx page.

2. Copy code from the WebAuth.sln web site sample to Default.aspx, WindowsLiveLogin.cs and webauth_handler.aspx, replace Default.aspx's IFRAME code with a LoginStatus control, and test with default w11_appid and w11_secret values in the Developer Fabric.

3. Use the Azure Services Developer Portal to register http://localhost:81/webauthhandler .aspx (or similar) with the WLID service, change the Res.Redirect(LoginPage) instruction to an existing Azure Hosted Service landing page, such as http://oakleaf.cloudapp.net, and test the authorization handler page.

4. Copy or move the web page(s) to be secured and related code to the sample project, changing page names as necessary, and change the Res.Redirect(http://oakleaf .cloudapp.net) instruction to point to the copied web page, renamed if the original was Default.aspx. At this point, your web application's original landing page is secure, so you can deploy the application as a Production Hosted Service.

The following sections provide detailed, step-by-step directions to secure an existing Azure Hosted Service (oakleaf_host).

Creating the New Cloud Service and Web Role

Follow these steps to create the sample web application and its empty pages and class file:

1. Download and run webauth-cs-1.2.msi or later file, if you haven't done so previously, and then open the WebAuth web site in VS 2008+ to provide code to past to web pages and class files you add to the sample project.

2. Open a new C# Blank Cloud Service project and name it LiveIDCloudService or the like.

3. Add a new Windows Live Web Role to the project and name it LiveIDWebRole; accept Default.aspx as the name of its web page.

4. Add a WindowsLiveLogin.cs class to the project to implement the WLID web authentication protocol in C#.

5. Add a webauth-handler.aspx page to the project to handle the three WLID authentication actions and display the secured web page.

6. Press F5 to compile and run the project in the Development Fabric and display an empty page. Make a note of its URL, which usually is http://127.0.0.1:81/Default.aspx.

Copying Code from the WebAuth Sample

The WebAuth sample web site contains most of the code you need to get a sample web application with WLID authentication up and running in the Developer Fabric. Here's the drill for copying and modifying the code from the WebAuth site:

1. Open WebAuth from its file-system location, open webauth_handler.aspx.cs, copy all its code, and paste it to the sample app's webauth_handler.aspx.cs code-behind file replacing the default source code stub.

2. Open WebAuth's webauth_handler.aspx, copy its Page directive, and overwrite the same directive in the sample app's webauth_handler.aspx file. Replace the Page directive's CodeFile= with CodeBehind=. Remove the default source code stub.

3. Open WebAuth's \WebCode\WindowsLiveLogin.cs class file, copy all its code, and paste it to the sample app's WindowsLiveLogin.cs file.

4. Open WebAuth's Default.aspx.cs file, copy all its code, and paste it to the sample app's Default.aspx.cs file replacing the default source code stub.

5. Open WebAuth's Default.aspx file, copy all its code, including its `Page` directive, and replace all source in the sample app's Default.aspx file. Replace the `Page` directive's `CodeFile=` with `CodeBehind=` and `Inherits="WindowsLiveWebRole.webauth_handler"` with `Inherits="HandlerPage"`.

6. Open the AJAX Extensions group, and add a ScriptManager control above the opening `<table>` tag. IDLoginStatus requires a ScriptManager control on the page.

7. Wrap the SciptManager control and the table in a pair of `<form runat="server">` ... `</form>` tags.

8. Right-click the Default.aspx icon and choose Set as Start Page.

9. Press F5 to build and run the sample app.

10. If you receive a "Value cannot be null. Parameter name: value" run-time error, open the sample app's Web.config file, and replace the `<appSettings />` element with the following default `<appSettings>` group for the WebAuth site:

```
<appSettings>
    <add key="wll_appid" value="00163FFF80003301" />
    <add key="wll_secret" value="ApplicationKey123" />
</appSettings>
```

11. Press F5 again to compile and run the sample, and display the login table cell (refer to Figure 6-23).

Optionally, change the `<title>` and `<h1>` elements' text to reflect the new application's name and add a `font-size="Small"` attribute to the IDLoginStatus control's definition.

Registering the webauth_handler Page's ReturnURL in the Development Fabric

The webauth_handler.aspx page processes handles state for the three different `Action` values so its URL must registered as the ReturnURL for the sample application. Debugging webauth_handler.aspx.cs's `Page_Load` event handler requires running the sample app in the Development Fabric. Follow these steps to temporarily register `http://localhost:81/webauth_handler.aspx` (or the like) as the return URL, modify the Web.config file to point to the new WLID registration, add a redirect to an unsecured Azure Hosted Application, and test the handler's response, do the following:

1. Log into the Azure Services Developer Portal (`http://bit.ly/12kdPb`, `http://lx.azure.microsoft.com/Cloud/Provisioning/Default.aspx`), click the New Project link, and click the Live Services: Existing API button to open the Create a Project: Project properties page.

2. Type a short name for the project, such as WLIDSampleApp in the Project Label text box, a brief description in the Project Description text box, leave the Domain text box empty, and type the handler page's Developer Fabric URL in the Return URL text box (see Figure 6-27).

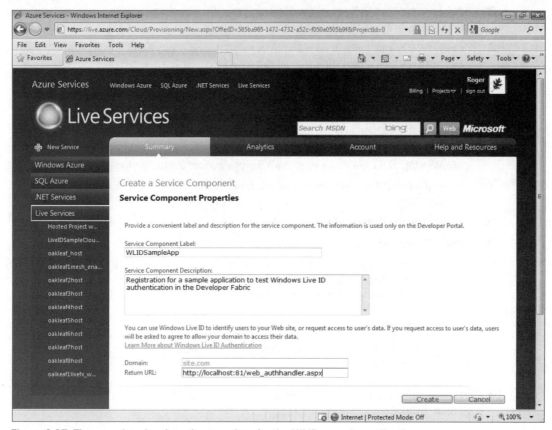

Figure 6-27: The completed registration template for the WLID sample application.

3. Click Create to register the Return URL and open the page that WLID returns with unique Application ID and Secret Key values (see Figure 6-28).

4. Open the sample app's Web.config file and replace the `wll_appid` and `wll_secret` values with the Application ID and Secret Key values from step 3.

5. Open the sample app's webauth_handler.aspx.cs code-behind file and replace the `res.Redirect(LoginPage);` instruction on line 85 with `res.Redirect("http://oakleaf .cloudapp.net");` or substitute the URL for the landing page of an unsecured Hosted Application you've uploaded to the Azure Production Fabric.

6. Press F5 to build and run the sample app, log in with your WLID, and verify that the Hosted Application appears as expected.

7. Perform a few operations that result in a post-back to verify that the WLID authentication cookie works as expected.

8. Navigate back to the sign-in page and verify that the Sign Out link substitutes for Sign In.

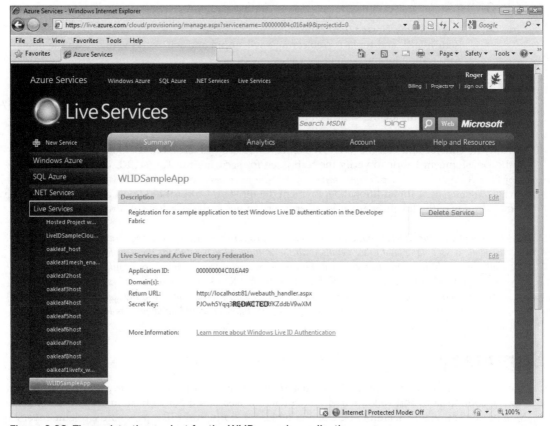

Figure 6-28: The registration project for the WLID sample application.

At this point, you've verified that WLID authentication is working but you haven't secured the target Hosted Project running in the Production fabric. Unauthenticated users can continue to open the application at `http://oakleaf.cloudapp.net` with no difficulty.

Securing a Hosted Project in the Azure Production Fabric

The most practical method to require WLID authentication for an existing Hosted Project is to incorporate its components in the project containing the webauth_handler.aspx page or vice-versa, depending on the project's complexity. Following are the generic steps to integrate, test, and promote a combined project to the Azure Production Fabric:

1. Add the original app's page, code-behind, class and library files to the sample app, either by importing them or copying their contents as in the preceding sections.

2. If the original app uses cloud storage, add the required `TableStorageEndpoint` or `BlobStorageEndpoint` and `AccountSharedKey` elements to the ServiceDefinition.csdef and ServiceConfiguration.cscfg files.

3. Test the project in the Development Fabric with cloud storage.

4. Create a new Hosted Service with `http://ProjectURL/webauth_handler.aspx` as the Return URL and replace Web.config's wll_appid and wll_secret values with the new Application ID and Secret Key values.

5. Change the `res.Redirect()` URL to the new Return URL.

6. Publish the project to the new Hosted Service, promote it to Production status, and verify your results are the same as for the preceding section's test.

Review the code of and run the \WROX\Azure\Chapter06\LiveIDSampleCloudService project in the Development Fabric to verify the technique for securing the TargetURL page and see the `http://bit.ly/vIVlh, http://oakleafblog.blogspot.com/2009/06/problems-deploying-webrole -with-windows.html` for additional deployment details. This OakLeaf blog post contains a link to a live demonstration of the LiveIDSampleCloudService running on the Windows Azure Production Fabric.

For simplicity, the LiveIDSampleCloudService.sln project doesn't include a registration page or code to associate a user name and other details with the unique ID generated for the user for each application that's shown in the sign-out message of Figure 6-25. A real world application would require a registration page to add rows to a RegisteredUsers table with a RowKey value of the unique ID and a Status attribute indicating whether the user was logged in or not. As users log in to the application, code would test for the existence of a row for the user. If present, the user would be flagged as logged in; if not, the user would be asked to register.

Summary

ASP.NET Membership Services in .NET 2.0 and later eliminate the need for developers to write and rewrite code to store and validate user credentials for web-based authentication and authorization. Membership providers default to SQL Server tables for storing user IDs, passwords, role membership, profiles, and session state. The Windows Azure SDK includes a sample AspProviders.dll class library and an AspProviderDemo.sln web application that demonstrate techniques for adding authentication and authorization features to Windows Azure web applications without the need to use the .NET Access Control Service (ACS).

The AspProviderDemo.sln web application offers a Default.aspx page with links to six membership-related forms: Login.aspx, ChangePassword.aspx, CreateNewWizard.aspx, ManageRoles.aspx, MyProfile.aspx, and MySession.aspx. AspProviderDemo's forms don't have a consistent theme, but it's not difficult to add Cascading Style Sheet (CSS) styles to enforce conformity with existing pages' appearance.

After you've styled AspProviderDemo to your satisfaction, you can import the AspProvider library and AspProviderDemo's forms, as well as Web.config to an existing Azure web application, such as Chapter 5's AzureTableTestHarnessSSL. Adding references to StorageClient and AspProvider, as well as making a few tweaks to Web.config and ServiceConfiguration.cscfg/ServiceDefinition.csdef, lets you authorize members of DbReader, DbWriter, and DbAdmin classes to run increasingly authoritative features of the original AzureTableTestHarnessSSL page.

Many organizations will prefer single sign-on with WLID authentication. Implementing WLID authentication requires copying code from the WLID Web Authentication SDK 1.2 or later WebAuth sample web site project and, optionally, the LoginStatus control from the Windows Live Tools for Microsoft Visual Studio 2008 or later. The chapter ends with step-by-step instructions for writing, deploying, and testing basic WLID authentication in the Azure Developer and Production Fabrics.

7

Optimizing the Scalability and Performance of Azure Tables

SQL Azure Database (SADB) offers most of the relational database management features of SQL Server 2008 Enterprise, but Azure Tables come to the fore when scalability is the criterion. The SDS team classified SDS v1 as suitable for most "departmental" database applications in its "First round of Questions and Answers" blog post of March 12, 2009 (http://bit.ly/cTWjP, http://blogs.msdn.com/ssds/archive/2009/03/12/9471765.aspx), and SDS architect Nigel Ellis announced at the MIX 09 conference (http://bit.ly/4v0B2y, http://videos.visitmix.com/MIX09/T06F) that database size will be capped at 5GB to 10GB. SDS is a premium service; therefore, users can expect a significant surcharge to hourly instance, data storage, and, potentially, data ingress and egress fees. These limitations and, especially, surcharges mean that financial executives will require .NET architects and developers designing and writing Azure application to justify substituting SDS for plain-old Azure tables (POATs).

Earlier chapters discussed how tables based on the Entity-Attribute-Value (EAV) data model, such as Azure, Amazon SimpleDB, and Google App Engine (GAE) tables, differ from their relational cousins. This chapter concentrates on helping .NET architects and developers get the most out of Azure tables' scalability benefits and maximize their performance in enterprise-scale applications.

Assigning Primary Key Values to Entities

Azure tables' composite primary key, which consists of concatenated PartitionKey and RowKey property value strings, provides a unique entity ID, also called an object ID, to identify and sort entities within an Azure table. PartitionKey values identify table partitions for load balancing across storage nodes.

Brewer's conjecture, commonly called the *CAP theorem*, states:

> When designing distributed web services, there are three properties that are commonly desired: consistency, availability, and partition tolerance. *It is impossible to achieve all three.*

Windows Azure stores entities with the same `PartitionKey` value in a single location, typically a virtual server node running on the Azure Fabric. Azure stores a master and at least two replica versions of each node in different failure domains. Entities in a table having the same `PartitionKey` value are said to be in a *locality*, which is the unit of consistency for Azure Tables. A locality has no partition tolerance, so it's possible, at least theoretically, to achieve consistency and availability for the entities in the locality.

If a table contains multiple entities with the same `PartitionKey` value, unique `RowKey` values are required to provide a unique entity ID; otherwise, `RowKey` values can be empty strings or a value indicating the entity's type or kind, such as `Customer`, `Order`, or `OrderDetail`. The flexible properties feature of Azure tables permits storing entities of different types in the same table.

Following is the ranking of query performance with the `$filter` query operator (a lower number is faster):

1. Query by `PartitionKey` and `RowKey` values.
2. Query by `PartitionKey` and some other property value.
3. Query by `RowKey` only or any other property value.

If you don't include the `PartitionKey` *value, the server-side query engine will scan all partitions for* `RowKey` *or other property value matches.*

You must include valid `PartitionKey` and `RowKey` values, which include the `String.Empty` value, for every insert, update, or delete operation you execute.

Choosing Partition Keys

`PartitionKey` values can be strings having a `Length` property value of 0KB to 32KB and cannot contain any of the following characters:

❑ Forward slash (`/`)
❑ Backslash (`\`)
❑ Number sign (`#`)
❑ Question mark (`?`)

If you expect that your table could ultimately contain more entities than a single Azure node can reasonably be expected to hold, you should plan on assigning the `PartitionKey` value on an individual parent entity basis, such as by `UserID`, `CustomerID`, `CreditCardID`, `OrderID`, or `ProductID`. Assigning the same `PartitionKey` value to parent and child entities ensures that they are maintained in the same locality, which speeds processing.

The documentation for Azure tables doesn't include a recommended or absolute maximum partition size to fit in a single Azure node. For example, if you're writing a social networking service similar to

Twitter, which might have had about four million users when this book was written, then user profile entities with a 2KB image and 1KB of text would total 12GB in size. A site as successful as Facebook, with about 150 million users in the same time frame, would generate a 750GB table.

Child entities, such as `Orders` and `LineItems` for `Customers` can be identified by natural `RowKey` values of `OrderID` and `OrderID + LineItemID`, respectively.

Natural key values derive from an entity key value. Alternatives are a GUID or an auto-generated or programmatically assigned sequential surrogate key value, which is similar to SQL Server's `identity` column property.

`Customer` entities with `CustomerID` as the `PartitionKey` and `Orders` and `LineItems` as child entities in the same table might provide optimum partitioning, especially when later Azure releases provide more granular geolocation services. Tables containing records for particular countries or regions could be assigned to the closest data center, such as NorthwestUS (Quincy, WA) or SouthwestUS (San Antonio, TX).

This chapter's sample project is \WROX\Azure\Chapter07\UploadOrderEntitiesWinform.sln. Its `Orders` and `OrderDetails` tables are based on the Northwind Sample database's Orders and Order Details tables, which are expected to be found in a .\SQLEXPRESS instance. The Azure Tables have a computed unique `PartitionKey` value, which delivers `Order` entities in descending `Order` sequence. An `(int.MaxValue – OrderID).ToString().PadLeft(10, '0')` expression generates the 10-character fixed-width, left-zero-padded string required to maintain consistent sorting as `OrderID` values reach more than nine digits. `RowKey` values are set to `String.Empty`. Figure 7-1 shows the sample project's form after adding 100 `Order` and 282 `OrderDetail` entities to separate `OrderTable` and `DetailTable` tables.

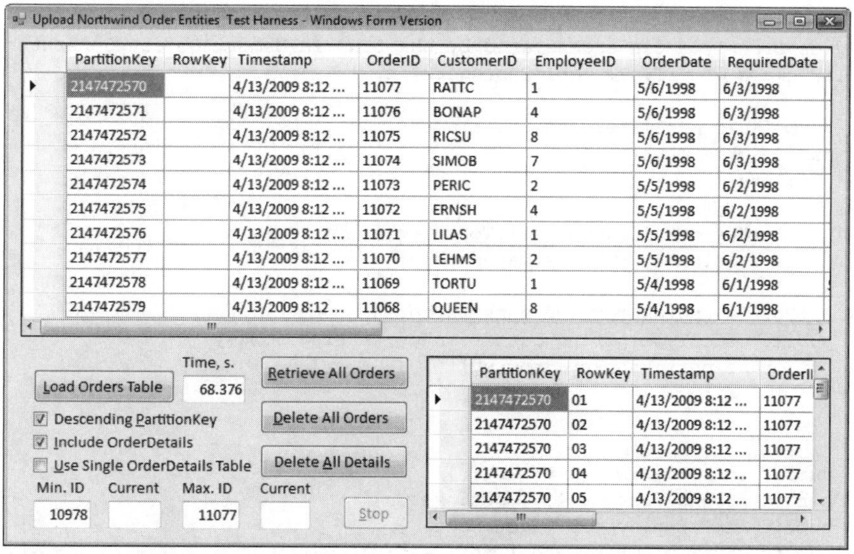

Figure 7-1: The Windows-form test harness after uploading data from a client-side SQL Server instance to OrderTable and DetailTable Azure Tables in the cloud.

The descending sequence allows applying the `Take(n)` LINQ Standard Query Operator (SQO) to return the n most recent orders in a query such as `(from c in ordContext.OrderTable select c).Take(10)`.

Adding Row Keys

Multiple child entities, such as `OrderDetails`, can occur for a single parent entity ID value (`OrderID`), so they require `RowKey` values to maintain uniqueness. The relational Order Details table has a composite primary key, which consists of `OrderID + ProductID` values. Therefore, natural `RowKey` values could be created from a `ProductID.ToString().PadLeft(6, '0')` expression for ProductID values < 1000000.

An alternative is a surrogate sequential item number converted to a left-padded string by an expression such as `ItemNumber.ToString().PadLeft(2, '0')` for services with a maximum of 99 different items. This chapter's sample project's `DetailTable` uses the alternative expression to compute `RowKey` values.

Handling Associated Entities

Azure Tables don't support entity associations (relationships), although ADO.NET Data Services and the AtomPub wire format support 1:*n*, 1:1, and *n*:1 associations with the `$expand` query option, which returns links to associated entities inline, and AtomPub `<link rel=... />` elements. If your child entities have a property value equal to the parent entity's `PartitionKey` value (or `PartitionKey` plus `RowKey` value) you can use the LINQ `join` SQO in queries against in-memory sequences that implement `IEnumerable` or `IQueryable` to perform the approximate equivalent of the `$expand` option.

The initial version of the sample project stored parent and child entities in separate tables to simplify displaying associated `DetailTable` entities in DataGridView controls. The code in Listings 7-1 and 7-2 from the OrderClasses.cs file define the structure of the `OrderTable` and `DetailTable`:

Listing 7-1: Code to define the `OrderDataModel` class for the `OrderTable` parent table

```
#region OrderType class generated by the LINQ In-Memory Object Generator (LIMOG) v2
public class OrderType: TableStorageEntity
{
    // Default parameterless constructor
    public OrderType()
       : base()
    {
        RowKey = Guid.NewGuid().ToString();
        PartitionKey = "OrderDataModel";
    }
    // Partial parameterized constructor
    public OrderType(string partitionKey, string rowKey)
       : base(partitionKey, rowKey)
    {
    }

    public int OrderID { get; set; }
    public string CustomerID { get; set; }
    public int? EmployeeID { get; set; }
    public DateTime OrderDate { get; set; }
    public DateTime? RequiredDate { get; set; }
    public DateTime? ShippedDate { get; set; }
    public int? ShipVia { get; set; }
    public double? Freight { get; set; }
```

```
        public string ShipName { get; set; }
        public string ShipAddress { get; set; }
        public string ShipCity { get; set; }
        public string ShipRegion { get; set; }
        public string ShipPostalCode { get; set; }
        public string ShipCountry { get; set; }
}
#endregion
```

Listing 7-2: Code to define the `OrderDetailDataModel` class for the `OrderDetailTable` child table

```
#region DetailType class generated by the LINQ In-Memory Object Generator
(LIMOG) v2
public class DetailType: TableStorageEntity
{
    // Default parameterless constructor
    public DetailType()
        : base()
    {
        RowKey = Guid.NewGuid().ToString();
        PartitionKey = "OrderDetailDataModel";
    }
    // Partial parameterized constructor
    public DetailType(string partitionKey, string rowKey)
        : base(partitionKey, rowKey)
    {
    }

    public int OrderID { get; set; }
    public int ProductID { get; set; }
    public double UnitPrice { get; set; }
    public int Quantity { get; set; }
    public double Discount { get; set; }
}
#endregion
```

Server-side code adds the `Timestamp` system property value as rows add to the tables.

The sample project was then updated to take advantage of Azure Tables' flexible properties and store parent and child entities in the same table. Listing 7-3 is the definition of the combined `OrderDetailType`, which is the union of `OrderType` and `DetailType`, for the `OrderDetailTable`.

Listing 7-3: Code to define the `OrderDetailType` class for the `OrderDetailTable` child table

```
#region OrderDetailType class (union of OrderType and DetailType)
public class OrderDetailType: TableStorageEntity
{
    // Default parameterless constructor
    public OrderDetailType()
        : base()
```

Continued

```
    {
        RowKey = Guid.NewGuid().ToString();
        PartitionKey = "OrderDetailType";
    }
    // Partial parameterized constructor
    public OrderDetailType(string partitionKey, string rowKey)
        : base(partitionKey, rowKey)
    {
    }

    public int OrderID { get; set; } // Shared with Detail

    // OrderType with additional nullable value types
    public string CustomerID { get; set; }
    public int? EmployeeID { get; set; }
    public DateTime? OrderDate { get; set; }
    public DateTime? RequiredDate { get; set; }
    public DateTime? ShippedDate { get; set; }
    public int? ShipVia { get; set; }
    public double? Freight { get; set; }
    public string ShipName { get; set; }
    public string ShipAddress { get; set; }
    public string ShipCity { get; set; }
    public string ShipRegion { get; set; }
    public string ShipPostalCode { get; set; }
    public string ShipCountry { get; set; }

    // DetailType; all properties nullable
    public int? ProductID { get; set; }
    public double? UnitPrice { get; set; }
    public int? Quantity { get; set; }
    public double? Discount { get; set; }

    // Classes; private setter prevents storing the types
    public OrderType orderType { get; private set; }
    public DetailType detailType { get; private set; }
}
#endregion
```

The `orderType` and `detailType` setters are private to prevent them from being stored in the table.

Substituting the class name, such as `OrderType`, for the parent table's `RowKey` value, and the class name followed by a numeric suffix for the child table's unique `RowKey` value is common practice. For example, when the Use Single OrderDetails Table check box is marked, `OrderType` entities added to the `OrderDetailTable` have `OrderType` as the `RowKey` value. `DetailType` entities added to the `OrderDetailTable` have `DetailType_##` as the `RowKey` value, where ## is the two-digit item sequence number. Figure 7-2 shows the sample project's form after adding 100 `OrderType` and 282 `DetailType` entities to the single `Order DetailTable`.

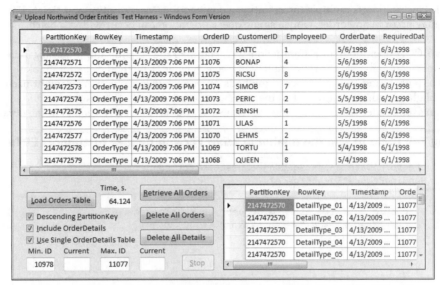

Figure 7-2: The Windows-form test harness after uploading data from a client-side SQL Server instance to an Azure OrderDetailTable in the cloud.

Taking Advantage of Entity Group Transactions

Early Azure Table versions provided support for ACID (atomic, consistent, isolated, and durable) transactions for single entity types with a common `PartitionKey` only. More recent table versions (the May 2009 CTP's v 2009–04–14 and later) support *Entity-Group Transactions* (EGTs). EGTs support ACID transactions for create, update, and delete operations on batches of parent and child entities with the same `PartitionKey` value. Following are the requirements for EGTs from the Table Service API's "Performing Entity Group Transactions" topic (`http://bit.ly/kfWtD`, `http://msdn.microsoft.com/en-us/library/dd894038.aspx`):

❏ All entities subject to operations as part of the transaction must have the same PartitionKey value.

❏ An entity can appear only once in the transaction, and only one operation may be performed against it.

❏ The transaction can include at most 100 entities, and its total payload may be no more than 4 MB in size.

❏ The Table Service doesn't support linking operations in a change set.

The ADO.NET Data Services specification's "Batch Requests" topic (`http://bit.ly/14mlEO`, `http://msdn.microsoft.com/en-us/library/cc668802.aspx`) defines a batch as a "container of create, update, and delete (CUD) operations called changesets, as well as a query operation, which is a retrieval operation within a batch." A changeset represents "one or more CUD operations."

A single batch supports multiple Insert Entity, Update Entity, Merge Entity, and Delete Entity operations, which may occur in any order. Only a single query operation can occur within a batch.

To wrap CUD operations in a transaction with the `StorageClient` sample library, add a `SaveChangesOptions.Batch` argument to your `SaveChanges()` method call after invoking `AddObject()`, `UpdateObject()`, and `DeleteObject()` methods on your `Context` object. You might need to add the highlighted code in Listing 7-4 to the `StorageClient` library's TableStorage.cs file to add the `x-ms-version` header when processing the request, if you have an early version of the library:

Listing 7-4: Code to add the minimum table version header to support EGTs

```
private void DataContextSendingRequest(object sender,
    SendingRequestEventArgs e)
{
    HttpWebRequest request = e.Request as HttpWebRequest;
    request.Headers.Add("x-ms-version", "2009-04-14");
    . . .

}
```

Steve Marx's "Sample Code for Batch Transactions in Windows Azure Tables" blog post (http://bit.ly/j2VXy, http://blog.smarx.com/posts/sample-code-for-batch-transactions-in-windows-azure-tables) *offers an EGT example with simple tables.*

Uploading Table Data

As you learned in earlier chapters, Azure Data Services use the HTTP POST method to insert entities into tables. Listing 7-5 is an example of the AtomPub POST request message produced by the Windows Azure SDK's sample StorageClient library's classes in the TableStorage.cs file to add a row from the Northwind sample database's Orders table to an `OrderType` entity in an Azure `OrderTable`:

Listing 7-5: The HTTP POST request to insert an entity from the Northwind Orders table

```
POST /OrderTable HTTP/1.1
User-Agent: Microsoft ADO.NET Data Services
x-ms-date: Wed, 08 Apr 2009 22:49:49 GMT
Authorization: SharedKeyLite oakleaf3:f3o42— -RedactedKey— -6qT6r9AiYnkRS80=
Accept: application/atom+xml,application/xml
Accept-Charset: UTF-8
DataServiceVersion: 1.0;NetFx
MaxDataServiceVersion: 1.0;NetFx
Content-Type: application/atom+xml
Host: oakleaf3.table.core.windows.net
Content-Length: 1383
Expect: 100-continue

<?xml version="1.0" encoding="utf-8" standalone="yes"?>
   <entry xmlns:d="http://schemas.microsoft.com/ado/2007/08/dataservices"
     xmlns:m="http://schemas.microsoft.com/ado/2007/08/dataservices/metadata"
     xmlns="http://www.w3.org/2005/Atom">
   <title />
```

```
<updated>2009-04-08T22:49:49.8086948Z</updated>
<author>
  <name />
</author>
<id />
<content type="application/xml">
  <m:properties>
    <d:CustomerID>BSBEV</d:CustomerID>
    <d:EmployeeID m:type="Edm.Int32">4</d:EmployeeID>
    <d:Freight m:type="Edm.Double">2.17</d:Freight>
    <d:OrderDate m:type="Edm.DateTime">1998-03-11T00:00:00</d:OrderDate>
    <d:OrderID m:type="Edm.Int32">10943</d:OrderID>
    <d:PartitionKey>2147472704</d:PartitionKey>
    <d:RequiredDate m:type="Edm.DateTime">1998-04-08T00:00:00</d:RequiredDate>
    <d:RowKey m:null="false" />
    <d:ShipAddress>Fauntleroy Circus</d:ShipAddress>
    <d:ShipCity>London</d:ShipCity>
    <d:ShipCountry>UK</d:ShipCountry>
    <d:ShipName>B's Beverages</d:ShipName>
    <d:ShipPostalCode>EC2 5NT</d:ShipPostalCode>
    <d:ShipRegion m:null="true" />
    <d:ShipVia m:type="Edm.Int32">2</d:ShipVia>
    <d:ShippedDate m:type="Edm.DateTime">1998-03-19T00:00:00</d:ShippedDate>
    <d:Timestamp m:type="Edm.DateTime">0001-01-01T00:00:00</d:Timestamp>
  </m:properties>
</content>
</entry>
```

The `SharedKeyLite`*'s Base64Binary-encoded signature shown partially redacted in the preceding example isn't the* `AccountSharedKey` *value from the Service Configuration.cscfg or App.config file. The* `SharedKeyLite` *signature consists of several concatenated headers encoded with the HMAC-SHA256 algorithm.*

Azure Tables support a simplified version of the ADO.NET Data Services (formerly the "Astoria Project") client API for create, retrieve, update, and delete (CRUD) operations by means of the `ClientServices` library. The create operation with the POST method returns a confirmation of the data inserted, such as that shown in Listing 7-6:

Listing 7-6: The HTTP POST response after uploading an entity from the Northwind Orders table

```
HTTP/1.1 201 Created
Cache-Control: no-cache
Content-Type: application/atom+xml;charset=utf-8
ETag: W/"datetime'2009-04-08T22%3A48%3A37.9913381Z'"
Location:
http://oakleaf3.table.core.windows.net/OrderTable(PartitionKey='2147472704'
,RowKey='')
Server: Table Service Version 1.0 Microsoft-HTTPAPI/2.0
x-ms-request-id: 05b91086-1747-42d6-98ed-1ad6c85537bd
Date: Wed, 08 Apr 2009 22:48:37 GMT
Content-Length: 1774
```

Continued

Listing 7-6: The HTTP POST response after uploading an entity from the Northwind Orders table *(continued)*

```xml
<?xml version="1.0" encoding="utf-8" standalone="yes"?>
<entry xml:base="http://oakleaf3.table.core.windows.net/"
xmlns:d="http://schemas.microsoft.com/ado/2007/08/dataservices"
xmlns:m="http://schemas.microsoft.com/ado/2007/08/dataservices/metadata"
m:etag="W/&quot;datetime'2009-04-08T22%3A48%3A37.9913381Z'&quot;"
xmlns="http://www.w3.org/2005/Atom">
  <id>http://oakleaf3.table.core.windows.net/OrderTable(PartitionKey='2147472
704',RowKey='')</id>
  <title type="text"></title>
  <updated>2009-04-08T22:48:38Z</updated>
  <author>
    <name />
  </author>
  <link rel="edit" title="OrderTable"
href="OrderTable(PartitionKey='2147472704',RowKey='')" />
  <category term="oakleaf3.OrderTable"
scheme="http://schemas.microsoft.com/ado/2007/08/dataservices/scheme" />
  <content type="application/xml">
    <m:properties>
      <d:PartitionKey>2147472704</d:PartitionKey>
      <d:RowKey></d:RowKey>
      <d:Timestamp m:type="Edm.DateTime">2009-04-08T22:48:37.9913381Z</d:Timestamp>
      <d:CustomerID>BSBEV</d:CustomerID>
      <d:EmployeeID m:type="Edm.Int32">4</d:EmployeeID>
      <d:Freight m:type="Edm.Double">2.17</d:Freight>
      <d:OrderDate m:type="Edm.DateTime">1998-03-11T00:00:00</d:OrderDate>
      <d:OrderID m:type="Edm.Int32">10943</d:OrderID>
      <d:RequiredDate m:type="Edm.DateTime">1998-04-08T00:00:00</d:RequiredDate>
      <d:ShipAddress>Fauntleroy Circus</d:ShipAddress>
      <d:ShipCity>London</d:ShipCity>
      <d:ShipCountry>UK</d:ShipCountry>
      <d:ShipName>B's Beverages</d:ShipName>
      <d:ShipPostalCode>EC2 5NT</d:ShipPostalCode>
      <d:ShipVia m:type="Edm.Int32">2</d:ShipVia>
      <d:ShippedDate m:type="Edm.DateTime">1998-03-19T00:00:00</d:ShippedDate>
    </m:properties>
  </content>
</entry>
```

It's clear from the POST request and response messages that the vast majority of the bytes on the wire are the data overhead inherent in RESTful data operations with the AtomPub wire format. The payload for the HTTP 201 response message is about 1.3 times the size of the request message's payload. The combined size of the two payloads is 3,157 plus 973 header bytes for a relational table record with a UTF-8 size of about 159 bytes. The insert messages are (4130 − 159) * 100/4130 = 96.2% overhead, assuming that the return payload is discarded. In other words, the request and response messages are about 26 times the size of uncompressed relational data. The added overhead contributes significantly to increased data ingress charges, so it's important that you measure the expected message sizes before finalizing a budget for moving your relational data to Azure Tables.

Comparing Code for Uploading Data to Individual or Heterogeneous Tables

Listing 7-7 is the btnLoadOrders_Click event handler that updates individual or combined parent and child entities, depending on the state of the Use Single OrderDetails Table check box (chkSingleTable). Only minor changes are required to accommodate both OrderType and DetailType entities in an OrderDetailTable; these changes are emphasized in the following listing.

Listing 7-7: Code to selectively upload OrderType and DetailType or OrderDetailType entities to Azure Table(s)

```
private void btnLoadOrders_Click(object sender, EventArgs e)
{
    Stopwatch timer = new Stopwatch();
    timer.Start();
    try
    {
        // Set cursor, clear text boxes and enable Stop button
        this.Cursor = Cursors.WaitCursor;
        txtCurOrderID.Text = "";
        txtDelOrderID.Text = "";
        txtCurOrderID.Text = "";
        txtTime.Text = "";
        btnStop.Enabled = true;
        Application.DoEvents();

        // Order and Detail contexts
        ordContext = new OrderDataServiceContext(account);
        ordContext.RetryPolicy = RetryPolicies.RetryN(3, TimeSpan.FromSeconds(1));
        ordContext.SendingRequest
            += new
EventHandler<SendingRequestEventArgs>(OrderSendingRequestHandler);

        SqlCommand dtlCmd = null;
        if (chkIncludeDetails.Checked)
        {
            // Set up required objects
            dtlContext = new DetailDataServiceContext(account);
            dtlContext.RetryPolicy = RetryPolicies.RetryN(3,
TimeSpan.FromSeconds(1));
            dtlContext.SendingRequest
                += new
EventHandler<SendingRequestEventArgs>(DetailSendingRequestHandler);
            // Details command
            dtlConn = new SqlConnection(@"Data Source=.\SQLEXPRESS; Integrated
                Security=True; Initial Catalog=Northwind");
            dtlConn.Open();
            dtlCmd = new SqlCommand(" ", dtlConn);
        }
```

Continued

197

Listing 7-7: Code to selectively upload `OrderType` **and** `DetailType` **or** `OrderDetailType` **entities to Azure Table(s)** *(continued)*

```
        // Open Orders connection and specify query
        ordConn.Open();
        string query = "SELECT * FROM Orders WHERE OrderID BETWEEN " +
txtMinOrderID.Text
            + " AND " + txtMaxOrderID.Text + " ORDER BY OrderID ";
        if (chkDescOrderID.Checked)
            query += "DESC";

        // Set up Order SqlCommand and SqlDataReader
        SqlCommand ordCmd = new SqlCommand(query, ordConn);
        SqlDataReader ordRdr = ordCmd.ExecuteReader();
        while (ordRdr.Read())
        {
            OrderType newOrder = new OrderType();

            // Create and add PartitionKey, empty or kind (OrderType) RowKey
            int partitionKey = int.MaxValue - (int)ordRdr[0];
            int length = int.MaxValue.ToString().Length; // Length is 10
            newOrder.PartitionKey = partitionKey.ToString().PadLeft(10, '0');
            if (chkSingleTable.Checked)
                newOrder.RowKey = "OrderType"; //type or kind
            else
                newOrder.RowKey = String.Empty;

            // Process Order properties
            newOrder.OrderID = (int)ordRdr[0];
            newOrder.CustomerID = (string)ordRdr[1];
            newOrder.EmployeeID = (int)ordRdr[2];
            newOrder.OrderDate = (DateTime)ordRdr[3];
            newOrder.RequiredDate = (DateTime?)ordRdr[4];
            if (ordRdr[5] != DBNull.Value)
                newOrder.ShippedDate = (DateTime?)ordRdr[5];
            if (ordRdr[6] != DBNull.Value)
                newOrder.ShipVia = (int)ordRdr[6];
            if (ordRdr[7] != DBNull.Value)
            {
                // Direct cast throws exception
                string freight = ordRdr[7].ToString();
                newOrder.Freight = double.Parse(freight);
            }
            newOrder.ShipName = (string)ordRdr[8];
            newOrder.ShipAddress = (string)ordRdr[9];
            newOrder.ShipCity = (string)ordRdr[10];
            // Ireland (no postal codes except Dublin)
            if (ordRdr[11] != DBNull.Value)
                newOrder.ShipRegion = (string)ordRdr[11];
            // Most of Europe
            if (ordRdr[12] != DBNull.Value)
                newOrder.ShipPostalCode = (string)ordRdr[12];
            newOrder.ShipCountry = (string)ordRdr[13];
```

```
                    // Add and save the Order entity with retries
                    if (chkSingleTable.Checked)
                    ordContext.AddObject(OrderDetailDataServiceContext.
                        OrderDetailTableName, newOrder);
                    else
                        ordContext.AddObject(OrderDataServiceContext.
                            OrderTableName, newOrder);

                    // Test HTTP Response
                    DataServiceResponse ordResponse =
                        ordContext.SaveChangesWithRetries(SaveChangesOptions.None);
                    List<OperationResponse> ordRespList = ordResponse.ToList();
                    if (ordRespList.Count() > 0)
                        foreach (OperationResponse opResp in ordRespList)
                        {
                            if (opResp.StatusCode != 201)
                            {
                                // Log an error
                            }
                        }

                    if (chkIncludeDetails.Checked)
                    {
                        // Add Details for Order
                        string dtlQuery = "SELECT * FROM [Order Details] WHERE
OrderID = " +
                        newOrder.OrderID.ToString();
                        dtlCmd.CommandText = dtlQuery;
                        SqlDataReader dtlRdr = dtlCmd.ExecuteReader();
                        int detailNumber = 1;
                        while (dtlRdr.Read())
                        {
                            // Use Order's partition key and item number as row key
                            DetailType newDetail = new DetailType();
                            newDetail.PartitionKey = newOrder.PartitionKey;
                            if (chkSingleTable.Checked)
                            newDetail.RowKey = "DetailType_" +
                                detailNumber.ToString().PadLeft(2, '0');
                            else
                                newDetail.RowKey = detailNumber.ToString().PadLeft(2, '0');
                            newDetail.OrderID = newOrder.OrderID;
                            newDetail.ProductID = (int)dtlRdr[1];

                            // Direct casts throw exception; use string intermediary
                            string price = dtlRdr[2].ToString();
                            newDetail.UnitPrice = double.Parse(price);
                            string quan = dtlRdr[3].ToString();
                            newDetail.Quantity = int.Parse(quan);
                            string disc = dtlRdr[4].ToString();
                            newDetail.Discount = double.Parse(disc);

                            // Add and save the Detail entity
                            if (chkSingleTable.Checked)
```

Continued

199

Listing 7-7: Code to selectively upload `OrderType` **and** `DetailType` **or** `OrderDetailType`
entities to Azure Table(s) *(continued)*

```
                    dtlContext.AddObject(OrderDetailDataServiceContext.
                        OrderDetailTableName, newDetail);
                else
                    dtlContext.AddObject(DetailDataServiceContext.
                        DetailTableName, newDetail);

                DataServiceResponse dtlResponse =
                    dtlContext.SaveChangesWithRetries(SaveChangesOptions.None);

                // Test HTTP Response
                List<OperationResponse> dtlRespList = dtlResponse.ToList();
                if (dtlRespList.Count() > 0)
                    foreach (OperationResponse opResp in dtlRespList)
                    {
                        if (opResp.StatusCode != 201)
                        {
                            // Log an error
                        }
                    }
                detailNumber += 1;
            }
            dtlRdr.Close();
        }
        txtCurOrderID.Text = newOrder.OrderID.ToString();
        if (isStop)
        {
            isStop = false;
            break;
        }
        Application.DoEvents();
    }
    timer.Stop();
    FillDataGridView(10);
}
catch (Exception exc)
{
    MessageBox.Show(exc.Message + "\r\n\r\n" + exc.InnerException,
        "Exception Adding Order to Azure Table");
}
finally
{
    if (ordConn.State == ConnectionState.Open)
        ordConn.Close();
    if (dtlConn != null && dtlConn.State == ConnectionState.Open)
        dtlConn.Close();
    this.Cursor = Cursors.Default;
    isStop = false;
}
txtTime.Text = (timer.ElapsedMilliseconds / 1000D).ToString("0.000");
btnLoadOrders.Enabled = false;
btnDeleteAllOrders.Enabled = true;
}
```

Code in the event-handler for the Use Single OrderDetails Table check box's CheckChanged *event marks the Include OrderDetails check box when a single table is selected.*

Comparing Performance of Homogeneous and Heterogeneous Table Operations

The following table compares the time in seconds to upload and delete 100 OrderType entities with and without 232 DetailType entities in two homogeneous or one heterogeneous (OrderDetailTable) using plain-text HTTP or secure HTTP with Transport Layer Security (TLS).

Number of Tables, Protocol	Upload Orders Only	Delete Orders Only	Upload Orders with Details	Delete Orders with Details
Two tables, HTTP	18.86	13.55	67.75	70.92
Two tables, HTTPS (TLS)	20.80	13.57	69.18	74.40
One table, HTTP	19.15	13.64	69.17	48.75
One table, HTTPS (TLS)	21.44	13.91	70.57	49.53

Differences in upload times for OrderType entities in one or two-table scenarios are insignificant. However, deleting DetailType entities is much faster with a single table because the lookup operation that instantiates the child entities for deletion isn't necessary.

It's safe to infer that updating DetailType *entities would share a similar performance gain because the update operation requires the same lookup process as the deletion.*

Listing 7-8 is the btnDeleteAll_Click event handler code with the lookup operation's lines highlighted.

Listing 7-8: Code to selectively delete OrderTable **and** DetailTable **or** OrderDetailTable **entities**

```
private void btnDeleteAllOrders_Click(object sender, EventArgs e)
{
    // Delete all orders (with Details, if specified)
    // It's faster to delete and recreate the tables

    this.Cursor = Cursors.WaitCursor;
    btnStop.Enabled = true;
    Stopwatch timer = new Stopwatch();
    timer.Start();
    isDeleting = true;

    if (chkSingleTable.Checked)
    {
        // OrderDetail contexts with retry policies
        ordDtlContext = new OrderDetailDataServiceContext(account);
```

Continued

Listing 7-8: Code to selectively delete `OrderTable` **and** `DetailTable` **or** `OrderDetailTable` **entities** *(continued)*

```
        ordDtlContext.RetryPolicy = RetryPolicies.RetryN(3,
TimeSpan.FromSeconds(1));
        ordDtlContext.SendingRequest +=
            new EventHandler<SendingRequestEventArgs>(OrderSendingRequestHandler);
        var ordDtls = from c in ordDtlContext.OrderDetailTable
                    select c;
        TableStorageDataServiceQuery<OrderDetailType> query =
            new TableStorageDataServiceQuery<OrderDetailType>
            (ordDtls as DataServiceQuery<OrderDetailType>);
        IEnumerable<OrderDetailType> queryResults = query.ExecuteAllWithRetries();

        try
        {
            foreach (OrderDetailType orderDetail in ordDtls)
            {
                // Delete the Order
                Application.DoEvents();
                txtDelOrderID.Text = orderDetail.OrderID.ToString();
                ordDtlContext.DeleteObject(orderDetail);

                // Save changes for each Detail
                DataServiceResponse ordResponse =
                    ordDtlContext.SaveChangesWithRetries(SaveChangesOptions.None);
            }
            // Confirm all Orders are gone
            FillDataGridView(10);
        }
        catch (Exception exc)
        {
            this.Cursor = Cursors.Default;
            MessageBox.Show(exc.Message + "\r\n\r\n" + exc.InnerException,
                "Exception Deleting OrderDetail record from Azure Table");
        }
        finally
        {
            btnLoadOrders.Enabled = true;
            txtTime.Text = (timer.ElapsedMilliseconds / 1000D).ToString("0.000");
            this.Cursor = Cursors.Default;
            isStop = false;
            isDeleting = false;
        }
    }
    else
    {
        // Order and Order_Detail contexts with retry policies
        ordContext = new OrderDataServiceContext(account);
        ordContext.RetryPolicy = RetryPolicies.RetryN(3, TimeSpan.FromSeconds(1));
        ordContext.SendingRequest +=
            new EventHandler<SendingRequestEventArgs>(OrderSendingRequestHandler);

        if (chkIncludeDetails.Checked)
        {
```

```
            dtlContext = new DetailDataServiceContext(account);
            dtlContext.RetryPolicy = RetryPolicies.RetryN(3,
TimeSpan.FromSeconds(1));
            dtlContext.SendingRequest +=
                new
EventHandler<SendingRequestEventArgs>(DetailSendingRequestHandler);
        }
        var orders = from c in ordContext.OrderTable
                    select c;
        TableStorageDataServiceQuery<OrderType> query =
            new TableStorageDataServiceQuery<OrderType>
            (orders as DataServiceQuery<OrderType>);
        IEnumerable<OrderType> queryResults = query.ExecuteAllWithRetries();
        try
        {
        foreach (var order in orders)
        {
            bool usePartitionKey = true;
            if (chkIncludeDetails.Checked)
            {
                // Delete the Order's Order Details entities first
                if (usePartitionKey)
                {
                    // Partition key property is indexed, so should be faster
                    var details = from c in dtlContext.DetailTable
                                where c.PartitionKey == order.PartitionKey
                                select c;
                    foreach (var detail in details)
                        dtlContext.DeleteObject(detail);
                }
                else
                {
                    // OrderID property isn't indexed
                    var details = from c in dtlContext.DetailTable
                                where c.OrderID == order.OrderID
                                select c;
                    foreach (var detail in details)
                        dtlContext.DeleteObject(detail);
                }

                // Test response code and headers for error tracking
                DataServiceResponse dtlResponse =
                    dtlContext.SaveChangesWithRetries(SaveChangesOptions.None);
                List<OperationResponse> dtlRespList = dtlResponse.ToList();
                if (dtlRespList.Count() > 0)
                    foreach (OperationResponse opResp in dtlRespList)
                    {
                        if (opResp.StatusCode != 204)
                        {
                            IDictionary<string, string> opRespStr =
opResp.Headers;

                            // Log an error
                        }
                    }
            }
```

Continued

203

Listing 7-8: Code to selectively delete `OrderTable` **and** `DetailTable` **or** `OrderDetailTable` **entities** *(continued)*

```
                    }
                    // Delete the Order
                    txtDelOrderID.Text = order.OrderID.ToString();
                    ordContext.DeleteObject(order);

                    // Save changes for each Detail
                    DataServiceResponse ordResponse =
                        ordContext.SaveChangesWithRetries(SaveChangesOptions.None);

                    // Test HTTP Response
                    List<OperationResponse> ordRespList = ordResponse.ToList();
                    if (ordRespList.Count() > 0)
                    {
                        foreach (OperationResponse opResp in ordRespList)
                        {
                            if (opResp.StatusCode != 204)
                            {
                                IDictionary<string, string> opRespStr = opResp.Headers;
                                // Log an error
                            }
                        }
                    }
                    Application.DoEvents();
                    if (isStop)
                    {
                        isStop = false;
                        break;
                    }
                }
                // Confirm all Orders are gone
                FillDataGridView(10);
            }
            catch (Exception exc)
            {
                this.Cursor = Cursors.Default;
                MessageBox.Show(exc.Message + "\r\n\r\n" + exc.InnerException,
                    "Exception Deleting Order or Order Detail from Azure Table");
            }
            finally
            {
                btnLoadOrders.Enabled = true;
                txtTime.Text = (timer.ElapsedMilliseconds / 1000D).ToString("0.000");
                this.Cursor = Cursors.Default;
                isStop = false;
                isDeleting = false;
            }
        }
    }
```

Differences in `DetailType` *lookup time as the result of substituting an indexed* `RowKey` *value for a scanned* `OrderID` *value aren't significant for the maximum number of entities (2,155) available from the Order Details table.*

Displaying Data from Heterogeneous Tables in Grids

The ascending index on `PartitionKey` and `RowKey` causes parent and child entities in the `OrderDetailTable` to appear with child `DetailType` entities followed by their parent `OrderType` entity, as shown in Figure 7-3.

Figure 7-3: David Pallman's Azure Storage Explorer displaying a DetailType entity.

Displaying Parent Entities

As is the case for data uploads, downloading data from heterogeneous tables requires only a minor change to the LINQ to REST query to filter out unwanted entities. Listing 7-9 is the code to fill the Orders DataGridView control with the most recent `OrderType` entities from the `OrderDetailTable` or `OrderTable`. The `OrderType` filter operator for the query is shaded.

Listing 7-9: Filling a DataGridView control with a specified number of the most recent parent entities

```
private void FillDataGridView(int numberOfOrders)
{
```

Continued

205

Listing 7-9: Filling a DataGridView control with a specified number of the most recent parent entities *(continued)*

```
        try
        {

            // Fill the Order DataGridView
            this.Cursor = Cursors.WaitCursor;
            Stopwatch timer = new Stopwatch();
            timer.Start();
            if (chkSingleTable.Checked)
            {
                dgvOrders.Columns[1].Width = 75;
                dgvDetails.Columns[1].Width = 100;
                dgvDetails.Columns[2].Width = 90;
                var orders = (from c in ordDtlContext.OrderDetailTable
                        where c.RowKey == "OrderType"
                              select c).Take(numberOfOrders);
                TableStorageDataServiceQuery<OrderDetailType> query =
                    new TableStorageDataServiceQuery<OrderDetailType>
                    (orders as DataServiceQuery<OrderDetailType>);
                IEnumerable<OrderDetailType> queryResults = query.ExecuteWithRetries();
                OrderBindingSource.DataSource = queryResults;
            }
            else
            {
                dgvOrders.Columns[1].Width = 60;
                dgvDetails.Columns[1].Width = 60;
                dgvDetails.Columns[2].Width = 120;
                var orders = (from c in ordContext.OrderTable
                            select c).Take(numberOfOrders);
                TableStorageDataServiceQuery<OrderType> query =
                    new TableStorageDataServiceQuery<OrderType>
                    (orders as DataServiceQuery<OrderType>);
                IEnumerable<OrderType> queryResults = query.ExecuteWithRetries();
                OrderBindingSource.DataSource = queryResults;
            }
            isLoaded = true;
            OrderBindingSource_CurrentChanged(null, null);
            txtTime.Text = (timer.ElapsedMilliseconds / 1000D).ToString("0.000");
            Application.DoEvents();
            this.Cursor = Cursors.Default;
        }
        catch (Exception exc)
        {
            this.Cursor = Cursors.Default;
            MessageBox.Show(exc.Message + "\r\n\r\n" + exc.InnerException,
                "Exception filling Order DataGridView");
        }
    }
```

Displaying 100 `OrderType` entities from the `OrderTable` is slightly faster (3.22 versus 3.47 seconds) than from the `OrderTable` table because the homogeneous table scan covers only 30 percent of the entities of the heterogeneous table.

Displaying Child Entities

The lower DataGridView control displays part of the DetailType entities for the DetailType entity that the user selects in the upper Order DataGridView by executing the code of Listing 7-10. In this case, the filter is the inverse of that for OrderType entities.

Listing 7-10: Filling a DataGridView control with the child entities of a selected parent entity

```
private void OrderBindingSource_CurrentChanged(object sender, EventArgs e)
{
    if (isLoaded)
    {
        // Load the Details DataGridView with Details entities for selected
Order entity
        this.Cursor = Cursors.WaitCursor;
        Stopwatch timer = new Stopwatch();
        // Application.DoEvents();

        if (chkSingleTable.Checked)
        {
            OrderDetailType currentRow = OrderBindingSource.Current as
OrderDetailType;
            if (currentRow != null)
            {
                var details = (from d in ordDtlContext.OrderDetailTable
                               where d.PartitionKey == currentRow.PartitionKey
                               && d.RowKey != "OrderType"
                               select d);
                TableStorageDataServiceQuery<OrderDetailType> query =
                    new TableStorageDataServiceQuery<OrderDetailType>
                    (details as DataServiceQuery<OrderDetailType>);
                IEnumerable<OrderDetailType> queryResults =
query.ExecuteWithRetries();
                DetailBindingSource.DataSource = queryResults;
            }
        }
        else
        {
            OrderType currentRow = OrderBindingSource.Current as OrderType;
            if (currentRow != null)
            {
                var details = (from d in dtlContext.DetailTable
                               where d.PartitionKey == currentRow.PartitionKey
                               select d);
                TableStorageDataServiceQuery<DetailType> query =
                    new TableStorageDataServiceQuery<DetailType>
                    (details as DataServiceQuery<DetailType>);
                IEnumerable<DetailType> queryResults = query.ExecuteWithRetries();
                DetailBindingSource.DataSource = queryResults;
            }
        }
    }
```

Continued

Listing 7-10: Filling a DataGridView control with the child entities of a selected parent entity (continued)

```
            dgvDetails.DataSource = DetailBindingSource;
            if (txtTime.Text.Length > 0)
            {
                // Add current to existing elapsed time
                double ordersTime = double.Parse(txtTime.Text);
                txtTime.Text = ((timer.ElapsedMilliseconds / 1000D) +
                    ordersTime).ToString("0.000");
            }
            else
                // Report current elapsed time
                txtTime.Text = (timer.ElapsedMilliseconds / 1000D).ToString();
            this.Cursor = Cursors.Default;
        }
```

Summary

One of the primary incentives for moving data from on-premises relational databases to Azure Tables in the cloud is to maximize scalability under fluctuating demand and deliver peak performance from WebRole and WorkerRole projects. Maximizing scalability requires paying close attention to the current and potential storage size of table partitions, which should not exceed the storage capacity of a single Azure computing node. You implement a partition strategy for load balancing by choosing a set of PartitionKey values to result in table partition (locality) sizes that are comfortable for the Azure Fabric's clusters. Flexible properties permit Azure Tables to store multiple entity types with varying properties. Storing a single parent and multiple descendent (child) entries in a partition is an effective approach to controlling ultimate partition storage size. It's up to the Azure Fabric to provide applications fast access to multiple related partitions in individual tables.

Unique RowKey values within a single partition provide the equivalent of a composite primary key for entity identifiers and order entities within the partition. Many applications will require or prefer entities sorted in descending order, which requires calculating the PartitionKey and, potentially, RowKey values from *NumericType*.MaxValue – *NumericPropertyValue* calculations. This technique sorts OrderType entities in descending OrderID sequence to permit applying LINQ's Take(*n*) Standard Query Operator to return the last *n* OrderType entities.

Substituting a table containing parent and child entities for separate parent and child tables demonstrates substantial improvement in the performance of deletion and, by inference, update operations on child entities. The chapter's sample project reduces the time required to delete parent and child entities uploaded from the Northwind database's Orders and Order Details tables by about one-third. The sample project also demonstrates how to write queries to separate the parent and child entities for display in individual databound grid controls.

8

Messaging with
Azure Queues

Azure Queues provide reliable, asynchronous message delivery between components of a cloud-based service. Dispatching computing operations of WorkerRole projects to improve service scalability is the most common use for Azure Queues, which also can assist the Azure Fabric's load-balancing features by engaging extra nodes in computing-intensive tasks. Offloading computation to a WorkerRole can speed the response of cloud-based WebRole pages to user requests. This chapter will show you how to combine a WebRole, WorkerRole and Queue to create what's called an Azure-hosted composite application.

Queues are the simplest of the three Azure data models. A single `http://servicename.queue.core.windows.net` service account supports an unlimited number of uniquely named queues. Also, a queue can contain an unlimited number of messages, each of which can hold up to 8MB of string or binary payload. Your application can assign an additional 8MB maximum of custom metadata to a queue in the form of name/value pairs. Individual messages don't support custom metadata but have a maximum lifespan (time-to-live or TTL) of seven days. Like Azure Tables and Blobs, Queues offer a RESTful application programming interface (API) for enabling multiple platforms and programming languages to manipulate them when running on the Development and Azure Fabrics. Queues support both HTTP and HTTPS (secure HTTP with Transport Layer Security, TLS) protocols.

Figure 8-1 illustrates a simple workflow with a single queue for offloading computing services to a pair of WorkerRoles from a cloud web application (WebRole) that processes web requests and an on-premises Windows client. The WebRole and client apps enqueue work request messages that either of the two WorkerRoles starts processing. As the two WorkerRoles complete their work, they add a new blob to the appropriate container or an entity to a table. The WebRole and client then process and display the new blob or entity.

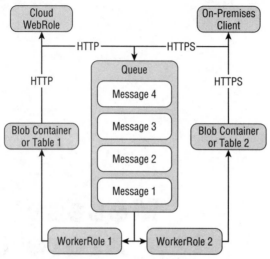

Figure 8-1: Diagram of an Azure Queue for dispatching similar compute requests from a cloud WebRole and on-premises Windows client.

Creating and Processing Azure Queues and Messages

The `StorageClient` class library includes a Queue.cs file, which defines the queue-related .NET classes and event handler described in the following table:

Class or Event Handler	Description
QueueStorage	A factory method for `QueueStorage`.
MessageQueue	Instances of this class represent a queue in a user's storage account.
QueueProperties	Default properties of a `MessageQueue`.
Message	Instances of this class represent a single message in the queue.
MessageReceivedEventHandler delegate and `EventArgs`	Listens for incoming messages by periodically polling for incoming messages.

Figure 8-2 is a class diagram of the preceding queue-related classes and the event handler delegate and its EventArgs.

`QueueStorageRest` and `QueueRest` classes in the RestQueue.cs file inherit from Queue.cs's `QueueStorage` and `MessageQueue` classes, respectively.

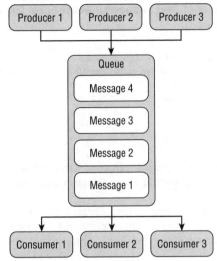

Figure 8-2: The StorageClient **class library's queue-related classes and event handler delegate.**

Listing a Storage Account's Queues

There's only one queue-related StorageClient method at the storage account level: ListQueues(). To list the queues for a specific *storageaccount* (oakleaf3 for this example), invoke the HTTP GET method with http://oakleaf3.core.windows.net?comp=list as the URI. Listing 8-1 contains the HTTP request and response messages for the MessageQueue.ListQueues() method.

Listing 8-1: The HTTP request and response messages for a list of the oakleaf3 account's queues

```
GET /?comp=list&maxresults=50&timeout=30 HTTP/1.1
x-ms-date: Thu, 16 Apr 2009 21:22:11 GMT
Authorization: SharedKey oakleaf3: fs7sL9ZDPkbDQTM5If1fImxKxzRG9TicIfl01io1tbk=
Host: oakleaf3.queue.core.windows.net

HTTP/1.1 200 OK
Content-Type: application/xml
Server: Queue Service Version 1.0 Microsoft-HTTPAPI/2.0
x-ms-request-id: a652d4ac-e750-419e-80e5-d30c9feda67a
Date: Thu, 16 Apr 2009 21:21:05 GMT
Content-Length: 310

<?xml version="1.0" encoding="utf-8"?>
<EnumerationResults AccountName="http://oakleaf3.queue.core.windows.net/">
  <MaxResults>50</MaxResults>
  <Queues>
    <Queue>
```

Continued

Listing 8-1: The HTTP request and response messages for a list of the oakleaf3 account's queues *(continued)*

```
        <QueueName>thumbnailmaker</QueueName>
        <Url>http://oakleaf3.queue.core.windows.net/thumbnailmaker</Url>
      </Queue>
      <! - .. Additional <Queue> groups, if present - >
    </Queues>
    <NextMarker />
  </EnumerationResults>
```

SharedKey values aren't redacted because the Base64Binary-encoded HMACSHA256 hash is valid only for a single request at a specific instant in x-ms-date *date and time.*

Listing 8-2 is sample code for the `StorageClient` library's `QueueStorage.ListQueues()` method that's defined in Queue.cs. The default `timeout` value for `GET` and `POST` operations is 30 seconds with no retries. To specify a different `timeout` value and `RetryPolicy` for operations on the queue, add the emphasized commands.

Listing 8-2: Code to list queues in the storage account specified in the ServiceConfiguraton.cscfg file

```
QueueStorage queueStorage = QueueStorage.
    Create(StorageAccountInfo.GetDefaultQueueStorageAccountFromConfiguration());
queueStorage.Timeout = TimeSpan.FromSeconds(60);
queueStorage.RetryPolicy = RetryPolicies.RetryN(3, TimeSpan.FromSeconds(1));

IEnumerable<MessageQueue> queueList = queueStorage.ListQueues();
```

Issuing HTTP/REST Requests at the Queue Level

Following are the three methods that issue HTTP/REST requests at the queue level:

❑ `GetQueue()` creates a queue with a specified storage account.

❑ `DeleteQueue()` deletes an instantiated queue object.

❑ `SetProperties()` adds or overwrites optional custom metadata for the specified queue instance.

Create a Queue with a Specified Storage Account

To create a queue with the specified storage account, invoke the HTTP `PUT` method with `http://oakleaf3.queue.core.windows.net/myqueue` as the URI. Listings 8-3 and 8-4 show a typical REST and `StorageClient`-based request.

Listing 8-3: The HTTP PUT request and response messages to create a queue named "thumbnailmaker"

```
PUT /thumbnailmaker?timeout=30 HTTP/1.1
x-ms-date: Thu, 16 Apr 2009 22:01:26 GMT
```

```
Authorization: SharedKey oakleaf3: fkySK4GsmjFxK72dX3SiqA1iYCnjsrLv3jEWeqzSBpc=
Host: oakleaf3.queue.core.windows.net
Content-Length: 0

HTTP/1.1 201 Created
Transfer-Encoding: chunked
Server: Queue Service Version 1.0 Microsoft-HTTPAPI/2.0
x-ms-request-id: a8a6c17d-2ab1-439b-b886-2cc54b04c93b
Date: Thu, 16 Apr 2009 22:00:04 GMT


0
```

Listing 8-4 is the `StorageClient` code to add a `thumbnailmaker` queue to the account specified in the ServiceConfiguration.cscfg file (`oakleaf3`).

Listing 8-4: Code to create a queue named "thumbnailmaker"

```
QueueStorage queueStorage = QueueStorage.
    Create(StorageAccountInfo.GetDefaultQueueStorageAccountFromConfiguration());
MessageQueue queue = queueStorage.GetQueue("thumbnailmaker");
```

The `thumbnailmaker` *queue is a component of the Thumbnails.sln sample project of the Windows Azure SDK (March 2009 CTP).*

According to the SDK documentation, the `MessageQueue.Name` property value must be a valid Domain Name System (DNS) name, conforming to the following naming rules:

❑   A queue name must start with a letter or number, and may contain only letters, numbers, and the dash (-) character.

❑   The first and last letters in the queue name must be alphanumeric. The dash (-) character may not be the first or last letter.

❑   All letters in a queue name must be lowercase.

❑   A queue name must be from 3 to 63 characters long.

Delete the Specified Queue and Its Contents Permanently

Listing 8-5 contains the HTTP request and response messages to delete a queue from the `oakleaf3` storage account.

Listing 8-5: The HTTP request and response messages to delete a queue named "thumbnailmaker"

```
DELETE /thumbnailmaker?timeout=30 HTTP/1.1
x-ms-date: Thu, 16 Apr 2009 21:51:06 GMT
Authorization: SharedKey oakleaf3: RaZ3H1vpCVWfgqejwmtD4SuYIf/9vWzgbNvteOpw2go=
Host: oakleaf3.queue.core.windows.net
Content-Length: 0
Connection: Keep-Alive
```

Continued

Listing 8-5: The HTTP request and response messages to delete a queue named "thumbnailmaker" *(continued)*

```
HTTP/1.1 204 No Content
Content-Length: 0
Server: Queue Service Version 1.0 Microsoft-HTTPAPI/2.0
x-ms-request-id: 3983249f-9d63-4f3a-8c45-c5c99408aced
Date: Thu, 16 Apr 2009 21:50:06 GMT
```

Listing 8-6 is the .NET code to delete the queue.

Listing 8-6: Code to delete a queue named "thumbnailmaker"

```
QueueStorage queueStorage = QueueStorage.
    Create(StorageAccountInfo.GetDefaultQueueStorageAccountFromConfiguration());
MessageQueue queue = queueStorage.GetQueue("thumbnailmaker");
queue.DeleteQueue();
```

Notice that you must create an instance of the queue to delete it.

Set or Update the User-Defined Metadata for the Queue

Custom metadata is associated with the queue as name-value pairs, which requires a reference to the System.Collections.Specialized namespace. The request of Listing 8-7 adds or overwrites three metadata items and their string values.

Listing 8-7: The HTTP request and response messages to add three metadata properties to the "thumbnailmaker" queue

```
PUT /thumbnailmaker?comp=metadata&timeout=30 HTTP/1.1
x-ms-date: Thu, 16 Apr 2009 23:34:56 GMT
x-ms-meta-prop1: value1
x-ms-meta-prop2: value2
x-ms-meta-prop3: value3
Authorization: SharedKey oakleaf3: rkff+mq0vD7HLcFuIbr10yHH3msD2HSBtLvtwckm/6uo=
Host: oakleaf3.queue.core.windows.net
Content-Length: 0
Connection: Keep-Alive

HTTP/1.1 204 No Content
Content-Length: 0
Server: Queue Service Version 1.0 Microsoft-HTTPAPI/2.0
x-ms-request-id: 08a829e2-96a8-4c08-a846-6c34909b04a0
Date: Thu, 16 Apr 2009 23:34:28 GMT
```

Creating and adding the name/value metadata pairs follows the obscure pattern shown in Listing 8-8.

Listing 8-8: Code to add three metadata properties to the "thumbnailmaker" queue

```
QueueProperties queueProps = new QueueProperties();
NameValueCollection propsColl = new NameValueCollection();
propsColl.Add("prop1", "value1");
propsColl.Add("prop2", "value2");
propsColl.Add("prop3", "value3");
queueProps.Metadata = propsColl;
queue.SetProperties(queueProps);
```

Working with HTTP/REST at the Message Level

The following table lists the five most important message-level methods of the MessageQueue object for the Windows Azure SDK (March 2009 CTP).

MessageQueue.Method()	Description
MessageQueue.PutMessage (Message, MessageTTL)	Adds a new message to the queue's tail. MessageTTL specifies the time-to-live interval for the message. The message can be stored in text or binary (byte array) format but message content returns in Base64Binary-encoded format only.
MessageQueue.ApproximateCount()	Retrieves the approximate number of messages in the queue and other optional queue metadata, if present.
MessageQueue.GetMessage[s] ([NumOfMessages, VisibilityTimeout])	Retrieves one or more NumOfMessages messages from the head of the queue and optionally makes these messages invisible for the given VisibilityTimeout in seconds, which defaults to 30 seconds and has a maximum of two hours. This method returns a PopReceipt. There is no guaranteed return order of the messages from a queue, and a message may be returned more than once.
MessageQueue.PeekMessage[s] ([NumOfMessages])	Retrieves one or more NumOfMessages messages from the head of the queue without making the messages invisible to other callers. This operation returns a PopReceipt for each of the message returned.
MessageQueue.DeleteMessage (PopReceipt)	Deletes the message associated with the PopReceipt which is returned from an earlier GetMessage call. A message that's not deleted reappears on the queue after its VisibilityTimeout period.
MessageQueue.Clear()	Deletes all the messages from the queue instance. The caller should retry this operation until it returns true to ensure that no messages remain in the queue.

Add a Message to the Queue

Listing 8-9 contains the request and response messages to add a brief string message (Test message 1) having TTL = 20 seconds to the thumbnailmaker queue.

Listing 8-9: The HTTP request and response messages to add a simple string message to the "thumbnailmaker" queue

```
POST /thumbnailmaker/messages?messagettl=20&timeout=30 HTTP/1.1
x-ms-date: Fri, 17 Apr 2009 19:07:03 GMT
Authorization: SharedKey oakleaf3:oWF+mq0vD7HLcFuIbr10yHH3msD2HSBtLvtwckm/6uo=
Host: oakleaf3.queue.core.windows.net
Content-Length: 76
Expect: 100-continue
<QueueMessage>
  <MessageText>VGVzdCBtZXNzYWdlIDE=</MessageText>
</QueueMessage>

HTTP/1.1 201 Created
Transfer-Encoding: chunked
Server: Queue Service Version 1.0 Microsoft-HTTPAPI/2.0
x-ms-request-id: 4938b0ff-7628-45e3-8bff-40c1b13af513
Date: Fri, 17 Apr 2009 19:06:11 GMT
0
```

The code of Listing 8-10 creates a new queue and adds three brief messages to it.

Listing 8-10: Code to create a queue and add three simple string messages to it

```
QueueStorage queueStorage = QueueStorage.Create(StorageAccountInfo.
    GetDefaultQueueStorageAccountFromConfiguration());
MessageQueue queue = queueStorage.GetQueue("thumbnailmaker");
Message testMsg = new Message("Test message 1");
bool putMsg = queue.PutMessage(testMsg, 20);
testMsg = new Message("Test message 2");
putMsg = queue.PutMessage(testMsg, 20);
testMsg = new Message("Test message 3");
putMsg = queue.PutMessage(testMsg, 20);
```

Get the Approximate Number of Messages in the Queue

To determine whether your WorkerRole process is keeping up with requests, it's a good practice to periodically test the length of the queue to verify that it's not growing to an inordinate length. Listing 8-11 shows the request and response messages for a queue containing 18 messages and three sample metadata properties.

Listing 8-11: The HTTP request and response messages to retrieve the approximate number of messages in a queue (emphasized), along with any other custom metadata added to it

```
GET /thumbnailmaker?comp=metadata&timeout=30 HTTP/1.1
x-ms-date: Fri, 17 Apr 2009 19:53:35 GMT
```

```
Authorization: SharedKey oakleaf3:8umeUClWuRyCcP9lE+LDkmF1vv+TjIDvkZTPhuqhMJY=
Host: oakleaf3.queue.core.windows.net

HTTP/1.1 200 OK
Transfer-Encoding: chunked
Server: Queue Service Version 1.0 Microsoft-HTTPAPI/2.0
x-ms-request-id: 3f86938f-6d00-4f42-9b3a-05f86a9de42b
x-ms-approximate-messages-count: 18

x-ms-meta-prop1: value1
x-ms-meta-prop2: value2
x-ms-meta-prop3: value3
Date: Fri, 17 Apr 2009 19:52:34 GMT

0
```

Listing 8-12 shows the `StorageClient` code to perform the same task as Listing 8-11.

Listing 8-12: Code to retrieve the approximate number of messages in a specified queue as an integer

```
int ApproxNum = queue.ApproximateCount();
```

Future Azure versions will include APIs for service manager tasks, so you'll be able to add nodes to scale up your WorkerRole as the queue increases in length and reduce nodes as demand subsides.

Get a Message from the Queue

Listing 8-13 contains the HTTP request and response messages for retrieving a single message from a queue. Retrieving more than one message at a time from the queue is relatively uncommon.

Listing 8-13: The HTTP request and response messages to retrieve a single message from the selected queue

```
GET /thumbnailmaker/messages?numofmessages=1&timeout=30 HTTP/1.1
x-ms-date: Fri, 17 Apr 2009 19:07:13 GMT
Authorization: SharedKey oakleaf3:RaZ3H1vpCVWfgqejwmtD4SuYIf/9vWzgbNvteOpw2go=
Host: oakleaf3.queue.core.windows.net

HTTP/1.1 200 OK
Transfer-Encoding: chunked
Content-Type: application/xml
Server: Queue Service Version 1.0 Microsoft-HTTPAPI/2.0
x-ms-request-id: 380bfd79-0073-456e-9b06-72e28bbd75ab
Date: Fri, 17 Apr 2009 19:06:17 GMT

1BA
<?xml version="1.0" encoding="utf-8"?>
<QueueMessagesList>
  <QueueMessage>
    <MessageId>7e74cf00-bf24-4aad-aa18-04d719a18821</MessageId>
```

Continued

Listing 8-13: The HTTP request and response messages to retrieve a single message from the selected queue *(continued)*

```
        <InsertionTime>Fri, 17 Apr 2009 19:06:48 GMT</InsertionTime>
        <ExpirationTime>Fri, 17 Apr 2009 19:06:31 GMT</ExpirationTime>
        <PopReceipt>AQAAALBGaaiPv8kB</PopReceipt>
        <TimeNextVisible>Fri, 17 Apr 2009 19:06:48 GMT</TimeNextVisible>
        <MessageText>VGVzdCBtZXNzYWdlIDE=</MessageText>
    </QueueMessage>
</QueueMessagesList>
0
```

You should treat the PopReceipt *value as opaque because the Azure team warns that its format might change without notice.*

Listing 8-14 is the code to retrieve a single message from the queue.

Listing 8-14: Code to retrieve a single message from a designated queue

```
Message getMsg = queue.GetMessage();
```

The getMsg variable receives the PopReceipt value. Retrieving and processing messages in a while loop, such as that in Listing 8-15, is a common practice:

Listing 8-15: Typical code loop to retrieve and process a single message as it arrives in the queue

```
// ..
while (true)
{
    try
    {
        Message msg = queue.GetMessage();
        if (msg != null) // Test for PopReceipt presence
        {
            string content = msg.ContentAsString();

            // Call processing procedures here

            // If processing is successful
            queue.DeleteMessage(msg);
        }
        else
        {
            // Wait 1000 milliseconds
            Thread.Sleep(1000);
        }
    }
    catch (StorageException e)
```

```
    {
        // Write details of StorageExceptions to the log
        // Successive tries might recover from the problem
        // after message regains visibility

        RoleManager.WriteToLog("Error",
            string.Format("Exception when processing queue message: '{0}'",
            e.Message));
    }
}
```

Your code must delete the message after processing the message successfully to prevent it from being processed again after it becomes visible.

Peek at a Message in the Queue

Listing 8-16's request and response messages let your code inspect a message without setting it invisible:

Listing 8-16: The HTTP request and response messages to inspect, rather than process, a single message

```
GET /thumbnailmaker/messages?numofmessages=1&peekonly=True&timeout=30 HTTP/1.1
x-ms-date: Fri, 17 Apr 2009 19:03:24 GMT
Authorization: SharedKey oakleaf3:fs7sL9ZDPkbDQTM5If1fImxKxzRG9TicIfl01io1tbk=
Host: oakleaf3.queue.core.windows.net

HTTP/1.1 200 OK
Transfer-Encoding: chunked
Content-Type: application/xml
Server: Queue Service Version 1.0 Microsoft-HTTPAPI/2.0
x-ms-request-id: 0eaa5187-355c-4875-91b4-f100001dbc33
Date: Fri, 17 Apr 2009 19:02:29 GMT

151
<?xml version="1.0" encoding="utf-8"?>
<QueueMessagesList>
  <QueueMessage>
    <MessageId>8f423dbe-29c7-4131-801d-6ad36949e216</MessageId>
    <InsertionTime>Fri, 17 Apr 2009 19:02:12 GMT</InsertionTime>
    <ExpirationTime>Fri, 17 Apr 2009 19:02:32 GMT</ExpirationTime>
    <MessageText>VGVzdCBtZXNzYWdlIDM=</MessageText>
  </QueueMessage>
</QueueMessagesList>
0
```

The code of Listing 8-17 enables inspecting a message without setting it invisible:

Listing 8-17: Code to inspect a single message in a designated queue

```
Message peekMsg = queue.PeekMessage();
```

Delete a Message from the Queue

As mentioned in and after Listing 8-15, you must delete messages from the queue after processing them. Listing 8-18 contains the HTTP request and response messages to delete a message with the designated `PopReceipt` value.

Listing 8-18: The HTTP request and response messages to delete a single message having the designated PopReceipt value

```
DELETE /thumbnailmaker/messages/04178ce6-254b-4fb8-bc5b-
7641eb70a089?popreceipt=AQAAAJCmmh6Pv8kB&timeout=30 HTTP/1.1
x-ms-date: Fri, 17 Apr 2009 19:03:25 GMT
Authorization: SharedKey oakleaf3:fkySK4GsmjFxK72dX3SiqA1iYCnjsrLv3jEWeqzSBpc=
Host: oakleaf3.queue.core.windows.net
Content-Length: 0

HTTP/1.1 204 No Content
Content-Length: 0
Server: Queue Service Version 1.0 Microsoft-HTTPAPI/2.0
x-ms-request-id: f54a6398-6132-4cc1-9104-ca2bde5f8717
Date: Fri, 17 Apr 2009 19:02:30 GMT
```

For completeness, Listing 8-19 is the command to delete a single message and return `true` if deletion succeeds.

Listing 8-19: Code to delete a single message with the specified PopReceipt value (highlighted) in a designated queue

```
bool delMsg = queue.DeleteMessage(getMsg);
```

Clearing All Messages from the Queue

Listing 8-20 shows the HTTP request and response messages for removing all messages from the queue without processing them.

Listing 8-20: The HTTP request and response messages to clear all messages from the queue

```
DELETE /thumbnailmaker/messages?timeout=30 HTTP/1.1
x-ms-date: Fri, 17 Apr 2009 21:46:15 GMT
Authorization: SharedKey oakleaf3:DTUJNwdPOI16nR/Pdmb9dWO+QdimgHtp9Nmr9Tgpk9k=
Host: oakleaf3.queue.core.windows.net
Content-Length: 0

HTTP/1.1 204 No Content
Content-Length: 0
Server: Queue Service Version 1.0 Microsoft-HTTPAPI/2.0
x-ms-request-id: 307c7487-a4f4-4f4a-8c4e-6545cf3b1270
Date: Fri, 17 Apr 2009 21:45:09 GMT
```

Listing 8-21 illustrates a loop to ensure that all messages are cleared:

Listing 8-21: Code to ensure clearing all messages from a queue

```
while (!queue.Clear())
{
    Thread.Sleep(250);
}
```

The preceding loop will attempt to clear remaining messages at quarter-second intervals.

Enhancing the Thumbnails.sln Sample Solution

Real-world services that rely on Azure Queues usually combine a WorkerRole and WebRole in a single project. The Thumbnails folder in the \Program Files\Windows Azure SDK\v1.0\samples.zip archive contains the source code for the sample Thumbnails.sln service. Thumbnails.sln combines Web and WorkerRoles to upload graphics files from the user's local file system into Azure Blobs and display in a bound ListView control thumbnail images from blobs created from the file versions. A WorkerRole handles the thumbnail generation process asynchronously by polling the "thumbnailmaker" queue at one-second intervals. A ScriptManager control manages client script for AJAX-enabled ASP.NET Web pages. An AJAX UpdatePanel contains the ListView to partially render the page asynchronously and minimize UI flashing on postbacks.

Figure 8-3 shows the \WROX\Azure\Chapter08\Thumbnails2\Thumbnails.sln project's page with 15 added thumbnails of images used in OakLeafBlog posts during 2009 and earlier.

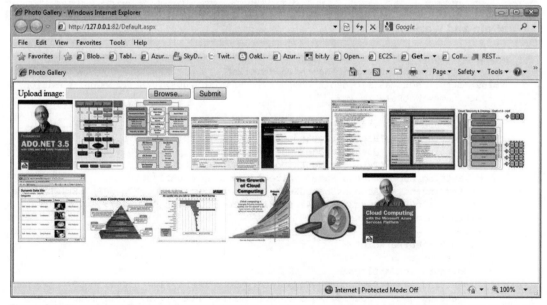

Figure 8-3: The original Thumbnails.sln project's page after the addition of 15 thumbnails of images from OakLeaf blog posts.

Thumbnails2 includes AJAX modifications by Steve Marx, a Microsoft developer evangelist, to reduce network traffic generated by polling for recently added thumbnails. The later "Moving to Client-Side Detection of Added Thumbnail Images" section describes the changes.

Understanding the Interaction Between WebRoles and WorkerRoles

Interaction between WebRole and WorkerRole projects in the same solution usually is limited to instructions in the form of messages in queues with state contained in persistent blobs or tables. This convention, which discourages sharing state with static classes' static properties, provides a very disconnected relationship between the UI and background processes and enhances scalability.

The WorkerRole and its MessageQueue *object is the only means of communicating instructions to and from Azure services by programs outside the Azure Fabric. Blobs and tables only communicate state.*

The Azure team wrote the original Thumbnails.sln project to demonstrate the recommended Web/Queue/Worker pattern. In the spirit of "one picture is worth 1,000 words," Figure 8-4 is a flow diagram that shows the MessageQueue interconnection between the Thumbnails_WebRole project's code in Default.aspx.cs and the Thumbnails_WorkerRole code in WorkerRole.cs.

The ServiceConfiguration.cscfg file contains <Role> groups for both roles. Listing 8-22 contains the default document for the Thumbnails Cloud Service project for local storage; values in this file prevail over those in Web.config and App.config files.

Listing 8-22: The default ServiceConfigure.cscfg document for a project containing a WebRole and WorkerRole

```xml
<?xml version="1.0"?>
<ServiceConfiguration serviceName="Thumbnails"
xmlns="http://schemas.microsoft.com/ServiceHosting/2008/10/ServiceConfiguration">
  <Role name="WebRole">
    <Instances count="1"/>
    <ConfigurationSettings>
      <Setting name="BlobStorageEndpoint" value="http://127.0.0.1:10000/" />
      <Setting name="QueueStorageEndpoint" value="http://127.0.0.1:10001/" />
      <Setting name="TableStorageEndpoint" value="http://127.0.0.1:10002/" />
      <Setting name="AccountName" value="devstoreaccount1"/>
      <Setting name="AccountSharedKey" value="Eby8vdM02xNOcqFlqUwJPLlmEtlCDXJ1OUz
        FT50uSRZ6IFsuFq2UVErCz4I6tq/K1SZFPTOtr/KBHBeksoGMGw=="/>
    </ConfigurationSettings>
  </Role>
  <Role name="WorkerRole">
    <Instances count="1"/>
    <ConfigurationSettings>
      <Setting name="BlobStorageEndpoint" value="http://127.0.0.1:10000/" />
      <Setting name="QueueStorageEndpoint" value="http://127.0.0.1:10001/" />
      <Setting name="TableStorageEndpoint" value="http://127.0.0.1:10002/" />
      <Setting name="AccountName" value="devstoreaccount1"/>
```

```
<Setting name="AccountSharedKey" value="Eby8vdM02xNOcqFlqUwJPLlmEtlCDXJ1OUz
    FT50uSRZ6IFsuFq2UVErCz4I6tq/K1SZFPTOtr/KBHBeksoGMGw=="/>
    </ConfigurationSettings>
  </Role>
</ServiceConfiguration>
```

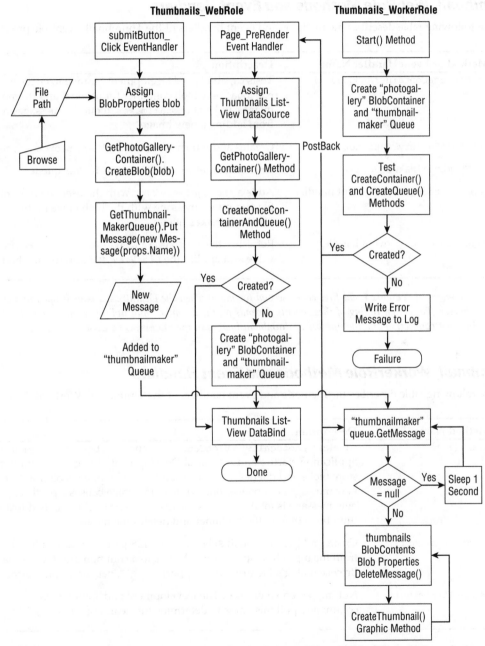

Figure 8-4: Flow Diagram for the Thumbnails_WebRole and Thumbnails_WorkerRole projects in the Thumbnails.sln solution.

The ServiceDefinition.csdef file has duplicate <Role> sections for WebRole and WorkerRole also.

Specifying twice the initial number of instances of WorkerRoles as WebRoles for worker processes that require substantial computing resources is a common practice.

Thumbnail_WebRole Methods and Event Handlers

The following table describes the methods and event handlers of the Thumbnail_WebRole project.

Method or Event Handler Name	Description
CreateOnceContainerAndQueue()	Tests capability of Development Storage to create a photogallery blob container for original and thumbnail images and a thumbnailmaker queue for messages resulting from adding a new image
GetPhotoGalleryContainer()	Creates and returns the photogallery BlobContainer
GetThumbnailMakerQueue()	Creates and returns the thumbnailmaker queue
submitButton_Click() event handler	Adds a photogallery blob with the user-selected image file and puts a message with the blob name on the thumbnailmaker queue
Page_PreRender() event handler	Refreshes the thumbnails ListView.DataSource property value and applies the ListView.DataBind() method

The Page_Prerender event fires every second (or more) when the Default.aspx page is open in a client browser. The actual timing of these events depends on the download and upload speeds of the client's Internet connection and the number of thumbnail images in the thumbnails BlobContainer.

Thumbnail_WorkerRole Methods and Event Handlers

The following table describes the methods and event handlers of the Thumbnail_WorkerRole project.

Method Name	Description
Start()	Creates a photogallery BlobContainer and thumbnailmaker Queue on application startup and tests local Development Storage's capability to store blobs and queues in a five-second while loop; if successful, tests for new messages is a one-second while loop, which causes a postback. If a new message is found, invokes the CreateThumbnail() method to add a thumbnail blob to the container and deletes the message.
CreateThumbnail()	Creates a *.jpg thumbnail Stream with a 128-px maximum width or height from the input bitmap Stream, which is in a common graphics format. The Browse dialog's Pictures type supports *.jpg, *.jpeg, and *.png formats.
GetHealthStatus()	Not implemented or used. The Development and Azure Fabrics continually poll this value to determine the health of a role.

The preceding `Start()` method overrides the default `System.Threading.Start()` method.

The `CreateThumbnail()` *method uses* `HighQualityBicubic` *interpolation,* `AntiAlias` *smoothing mode, and* `HighQuality` *pixel-offset mode, which is the highest quality and most computing-intensive combination.*

Analyzing Network Traffic Implications of Polling for Blob Updates

The Thumbnails_WebRole project's default design attempts to transmit large HTTP request and response messages to clients every second because the `Page_PreRender` event handler updates the `thumbnails` ListView control each time the Thumbnails_WorkerRole project polls the message queue. Listing 8-23 is the HTTP request message, which contains the partial `ViewState` for the `thumbnails` ListView control with 10 thumbnail images.

Listing 8-23: The Thumbnails_WebRole project's HTTP request message with 10 thumbnail images with partial ViewState contents

```
POST /Default.aspx HTTP/1.1
Accept: */*
Accept-Language: en-us
Referer: http://oakleaf6.cloudapp.net/Default.aspx
x-microsoftajax: Delta=true
Content-Type: application/x-www-form-urlencoded; charset=utf-8
Cache-Control: no-cache
Accept-Encoding: gzip, deflate
User-Agent: Mozilla/4.0 (compatible; MSIE 8.0; Windows NT 6.0; Trident/4.0;
GTB6; SLCC1; .NET CLR 2.0.50727; Media Center PC 5.0; .NET CLR 3.5.21022;
.NET CLR 3.5.30428; .NET CLR 3.5.30729; .NET CLR 3.0.30618; MS-RTC LM 8;
InfoPath.2; OfficeLiveConnector.1.3; OfficeLivePatch.1.3)
Host: oakleaf6.cloudapp.net
Content-Length: 2206
Connection: Keep-Alive
Pragma: no-cache

sm1=up1%7Ctimer1&_EVENTTARGET=timer1&_EVENTARGUMENT=&_VIEWSTATE=%2FwEPDw
UJOTA5OTI0ODEyD2QWAgIDDxYCHgdlbmN0eXBlBRNtdWx0aXBhcnQvZm9ybS1kYXRhFgICBw9kF
gJmD2QWAgIBDxQrAAIPFgQeC18hR..
W1ibmFpbHMvMTYzMzc1ODQ4NDU0MTI4Mzc1MF82ZDAzYTEwNy1kZmM3LTQ1NTEtODIwMS04MDUy
ZGRiOWVjMjNkZBgBBQp0aHVtYm5haWxzDzwrAAoCBzwrAAoACAIKZEurQMs6U2KWVZfJSazWYOc
Au%2BBU&_EVENTVALIDATION=%2FwEWAgKOvLC7AQKSuuDUC%2Flfv0QnrZPAfITZ19v9fSgx%
2BFOG&_ASYNCPOST=true&
```

The size of the request headers is 702 bytes and the request payload is 2,206 bytes for a total message size of 2,908 bytes.

Listing 8-24 is the HTTP response message, which contains the partial `ViewState` for the `thumbnails` ListView control with ListView data for 3 of the 10 thumbnail images.

Listing 8-24: The Thumbnails_WebRole project's HTTP request message with 10 thumbnail images with partial ViewState contents

```
HTTP/1.1 200 OK
Cache-Control: private
Content-Type: text/plain; charset=utf-8
Server: Microsoft-IIS/7.0
X-AspNet-Version: 2.0.50727
X-Powered-By: ASP.NET
Date: Wed, 22 Apr 2009 22:24:21 GMT
Content-Length: 5189

2368|updatePanel|up1|


                        <img id="thumbnails_ctrl0_photoImage"
src="http://oakleaf3.blob.core.windows.net/photogallery/thumbnails/16337574
40636206298_114f3d2f-4fbc-4d83-9831-954ae0693734" style="border-width:0px;"
/>


                        <img id="thumbnails_ctrl1_photoImage"
src="http://oakleaf3.blob.core.windows.net/photogallery/thumbnails/16337584
73471680000_549f111f-f1e4-4652-b886-d1b703740797" style="border-width:0px;"
/>

..

                        <img id="thumbnails_ctrl9_photoImage"
src="http://oakleaf3.blob.core.windows.net/photogallery/thumbnails/16337584
84541283750_6d03a107-dfc7-4551-8201-8052ddb9ec23" style="border-width:0px;"
/>


                        <span id="timer1"
style="visibility:hidden;display:none;"></span>
|0|hiddenField|_EVENTTARGET||0|hiddenField|_EVENTARGUMENT||2044|hiddenFie
ld|_VIEWSTATE|/wEPDwUJOTA5OTI0ODEyD2QWAgIDDxYCHgdlbmN0eXBlRWxlRW5tdWx0aXBhcnQPv
Zm9ybS1kYXRhFgICBw9kFgJmD2QWAgIBDxQrAAIPFgQeC18hRGF0YUJvdW5kZx4LXyFJdGVtQ29
1bnQCCmRkFgJmD2QWFAIBD2QWAgIBDw8WAh4ISW1hZ
..
S04MDUyZGRiOWVjMjNkZBgBBQp0aHVtYm5haWxzDzwrAAoCBzwrAAoACAIKZEurQMs6U2KWVZfJ
SazWYOcAu+BU|48|hiddenField|_EVENTVALIDATION|/wEWAgKOvLC7AQKSuuDUC/lfv0Qnr
ZPAfITZ19v9fSgx+FOG|0|asyncPostBackControlIDs|||0|postBackControlIDs|||4|up
datePanelIDs||tup1|0|childUpdatePanelIDs|||3|panelsToRefreshIDs||up1|2|asyn
cPostBackTimeout||90|12|formAction||Default.aspx|13|pageTitle||Photo
Gallery|149|scriptBlock|ScriptPath|/ScriptResource.axd?d=9YtLxwU-
nmRnm7oJ9nOfEaztduuiriMqe964NLCEARKknzUa7EJGulUSq-
QKJyN3_XQG98ij_ElfezvDJkF-
OgjZtff28LO1U1_MHbdocg1&t=ffffffff9a77c993|155|scriptStartupBlock|ScriptCon
tentNoTags|Sys.Application.add_init(function() {
    $create(Sys.UI._Timer,
{"enabled":true,"interval":1000,"uniqueID":"timer1"}, null, null,
```

```
$get("timer1"));
});
|
```

Calculating Cloud Data Egress and Ingress Costs

The size of the response headers is 221 bytes and the response payload is 5,981 bytes for a total message size of 6,202 bytes. The total size of the request and response message is 2,908 + 6,202 = 9,110 bytes. A single user with a browser permanently connected to the service will generate 9.11KB/s of traffic or (9.11 * 60 * 60 * 24 * 30) = 23,613,120 KB/month = 23,613 GB/month. Microsoft hadn't published data ingress and egress charges when this book was written but Amazon Web Services' EC2 or S3 would cost an average of about ((2,908 * $0.10) + (6,202 * $0.15))/9,110 = $0.134/GB, so a single continuously connected user would cost 23,613 * $0.139 = *$3,165.48 per month in bandwidth charges.*

> *When this book was written, Microsoft charged US$ 0.10/GB for data ingress (uploaded request messages) and $0.15/GB for data egress (downloaded response messages).*

Obviously, passing large chunks of ViewState in both directions would be unjustified if it isn't required to keep clients up to date with added thumbnails. The remaining sections of this chapter discuss techniques for minimizing polling message size and frequency.

Testing the Effect of Disabling ViewState for the GridView

To disable the thumbnails GridView's `ViewState` property, launch the SDK's version of Thumbnails.sln, open Default.aspx in Design View, right-click the `thumbnails` GridView, and set the `EnableViewState` property value to False.

> *The \WROX\Azure\Chapter08\Thumbnails2\Thumbnails2.sln project's* `EnableViewState` *property is False for the GridView.*

Change the ServiceConfiguration.cscfg file to point to Azure Storage Services, deploy the modified project to Azure Staging, start Fiddler2 or another HTTP proxy, and add a thumbnail for a new image. The HTTP request and response messages will be similar to those shown in Listing 8-25.

Listing 8-25: HTTP request and partial response messages for adding a thumbnail image with the GridView's ViewState turned off

```
POST /Default.aspx HTTP/1.1
Accept: */*
Accept-Language: en-us
Referer: http://c1529552-0b46-4cdb-94ca-c57afb3454e4.cloudapp.net/Default.aspx
x-microsoftajax: Delta=true
Content-Type: application/x-www-form-urlencoded; charset=utf-8
Cache-Control: no-cache
```

Continued

Listing 8-25: HTTP request and partial response messages for adding a thumbnail image with the GridView's ViewState turned off *(continued)*

```
Accept-Encoding: gzip, deflate
User-Agent: Mozilla/4.0 (compatible; MSIE 8.0; Windows NT 6.0; Trident/4.0;
GTB6; SLCC1; .NET CLR 2.0.50727; Media Center PC 5.0; .NET CLR 3.5.21022;
.NET CLR 3.5.30428; .NET CLR 3.5.30729; .NET CLR 3.0.30618; MS-RTC LM 8;
InfoPath.2; OfficeLiveConnector.1.3; OfficeLivePatch.1.3)
Host: c1529552-0b46-4cdb-94ca-c57afb3454e4.cloudapp.net
Content-Length: 384
Connection: Keep-Alive
Pragma: no-cache

sm1=up1%7Cup1&_EVENTTARGET=up1&_EVENTARGUMENT=&_VIEWSTATE=%2FwEPDwUKMTg5
Mzc1MTYwNA9kFgICAQ8WAh4HZW5jdHlwZQUTbXVsdGlwYXJ0L2Zvcm0tZGF0YWQYAQUKdGh1bWJ
uYWlscw88KwAKAgc8KwALAAgCC2SFWZDKhqAaOPzva5eASsIza%2FKThg%3D%3D&_EVENTVALI
DATION=%2FwEWAwKm5OL7CgKSuuDUCwLiscFWTsrhGkwLuRvDmUJ036ugm2zSSFA%3D&uploade
dBlobName=1633760951352592276_5d79389a-0f12-491d-981e-
132d55fa48b7&_ASYNCPOST=true

HTTP/1.1 200 OK
Cache-Control: private
Content-Type: text/plain; charset=utf-8
Server: Microsoft-IIS/7.0
X-AspNet-Version: 2.0.50727
X-Powered-By: ASP.NET
Date: Thu, 23 Apr 2009 14:52:16 GMT
Content-Length: 3442

2950|updatePanel|up1|


                    <img id="thumbnails_ctrl0_photoImage"
src="http://oakleaf3.blob.core.windows.net/photogallery/thumbnails/16337574
40636206298_114f3d2f-4fbc-4d83-9831-954ae0693734" style="border-width:0px;"
/>
..

                    <img id="thumbnails_ctrl9_photoImage"
src="http://oakleaf3.blob.core.windows.net/photogallery/thumbnails/16337584
84541283750_6d03a107-dfc7-4551-8201-8052ddb9ec23" style="border-width:0px;"
/>

                    <img id="thumbnails_ctrl10_photoImage"
src="http://oakleaf3.blob.core.windows.net/photogallery/thumbnails/16337609
49623206208_d1326fb8-ad84-4ec3-9511-7e3548ff0920" style="border-width:0px;"
/>

|144|hiddenField|_VIEWSTATE|/wEPDwUKMTg5Mzc1MTYwNA9kFgICAQ8WAh4HZW5jdHlwZQ
UTbXVsdGlwYXJ0L2Zvcm0tZGF0YWQYAQUKdGh1bWJuYWlscw88KwAKAgc8KwAMAAgCDGGQUSzBhE
R/hxlgzwh8QwLLIHdcqqw==|56|hiddenField|_EVENTVALIDATION|/wEWAwLOjelaApK64N
QLAuKxwVbbg55vMN4DLmfvx0sGaYOQZhZgLg==|0|asyncPostBackControlIDs|||0|postBa
ckControlIDs|||4|updatePanelIDs||tup1|0|childUpdatePanelIDs|||3|panelsToRef
reshIDs||up1|2|asyncPostBackTimeout||90|12|formAction||Default.aspx|13|page
Title||Photo Gallery|
```

The request header is 702 bytes and payload is 384 bytes for a total of 1,086 bytes. The response header is 221 bytes and payload is 3,442 bytes for a total of 3,663 bytes. The traffic saving by eliminating View-State data is 9110 − (1086 + 3663) = 4,361 bytes or about 48% of the original traffic. Although this is a worthwhile saving, potential bandwidth cost of $1,500 or more per user remains unacceptable.

Moving to Client-Side Detection of Added Thumbnail Images

Steve Marx recommended changes to my enhanced PhotoGallery version of the original Thumbnails project in a comment to the "Scalability and Cost Issues with Windows Azure Web and WorkerRole Projects – Live Demo" OakLeaf blog post (http://oakleafblog.blogspot.com/2009/04/scalability-issues-with-windows-azure.html) of April 22, 2009. Marx suggested using a Remote Procedure Call (RPC, not HTTP) method with AJAX to call the web server and ask whether the blob that was just uploaded has a thumbnail yet. After it has a thumbnail, trigger an UpdatePanel asynchronous post-back, and then stop any polling after that. This approach makes a new thumbnail immediately visible to the user who uploads it but not to other users. Other users must manually refresh their browser to see added thumbnails.

Here are the steps that Marx suggested:

1. Add a HiddenField below the FileUpload and Button controls to store the name of the new blob:

   ```
   <asp:HiddenField ID="uploadedBlobName" runat="server" />
   ```

2. Add code to set the uploadBlobName value in the submitButton_Click event handler:

   ```
   uploadedBlobName.Value = props.Name
   ```

3. Add a static method to handle the polling:

   ```
   [WebMethod]
   public static bool IsThumbnailReady(string name)
   {
       return BlobStorage.Create(StorageAccountInfo.

   GetDefaultBlobStorageAccountFromConfiguration()).
       GetBlobContainer("photogallery").
       DoesBlobExist(string.Format("thumbnails/{0}", name));
   }
   ```

4. Add EnablePageMethods="true" to the ScriptManager to enable the static method:

   ```
   <asp:ScriptManager ID="sm1" runat="server" EnablePageMethods="true" />
   ```

5. Add client-side script after the </body> element to perform the poll:

   ```
   <script type="text/javascript">
       Sys.WebForms.PageRequestManager.getInstance()
   ```

```
                        .add_pageLoaded(function(sender,
        args) {
                if (args.get_panelsUpdated() == '') {
                    var blobname = $get('<%= uploadedBlobName.ClientID %>').value;
                    if (blobname != '') {
                        checkReady(blobname);
                    }
                }
            });
            function checkReady(blobname) {
                PageMethods.IsThumbnailReady(blobname, function(result) {
                    if (result) {
                        doPostBack('<%= up1.ClientID %>', '');
                    }
                    else {
                        setTimeout(function() { checkReady(blobname) }, 1000);
                    }
                });
            }
        </script>
```

Adding the preceding code results in a poll every second with a lightweight "is the thumbnail ready" ping after submitting a new source image blob. The operation consists of 67 bytes of posted data and a 10-byte response and might need to be done two or more times, depending on the time that the CreateThumbnail() method requires to generate thumbnails. When complete, an UpdatePanel refresh occurs, which requires the 4,749 bytes calculated in the previous section.

In mixed mode, with the project running in the Development Fabric connecting to Azure cloud-based Data Storage, Fiddler2 displays the HTTP request and response messages shown in Listing 8-26 every second.

Listing 8-26: HTTP request and response messages generated by WorkerRole polling

```
GET /thumbnailmaker/messages?numofmessages=1&timeout=30 HTTP/1.1
x-ms-date: Thu, 23 Apr 2009 18:28:29 GMT
Authorization: SharedKey
oakleaf3:rH4IzA7B+XpZL2O0jqxjJRK4QiYyIIztUTb+FVeR5MQ=
Host: oakleaf3.queue.core.windows.net

HTTP/1.1 200 OK
Transfer-Encoding: chunked
Content-Type: application/xml
Server: Queue Service Version 1.0 Microsoft-HTTPAPI/2.0
x-ms-request-id: addaaadd-61a9-4667-a5f9-11bf8c6fde68
Date: Thu, 23 Apr 2009 18:26:48 GMT

3E
<?xml version="1.0" encoding="utf-8"?><QueueMessagesList />
0
```

To prevent one-second postbacks from the WorkerRole refreshing the DataSource property value of the thumbnails ListView every second, add an if (!Page.IsPostBack) block to wrap the Page_PreRender event handler's code. Opening the page in the browser sets the DataSource property value, but subsequent Browse operations cause the ListView to disappear. To prevent the disappearance, do the following:

1. Add a `private static bool refreshData = true;` variable to the `_Default` class.

2. Wrap the `Page_PreRender` event handler with the emphasized `if` block:

```
protected void Page_PreRender(object sender, EventArgs e)
{
    if (refreshData || !Page.IsPostBack)
    {
        thumbnails.DataSource = from o in GetPhotoGalleryContainer().
                                    ListBlobs("thumbnails/", false)
                               select new { Url = ((BlobProperties)o).Uri };
        thumbnails.DataBind();
        if (!Page.IsPostBack)
            refreshData = false;
    }
}
```

3. Add a `refreshData = true;` statement after the close of the `submitButton_Click` event handler's `if (upload.HasFile)` block:

Figure 8-5 shows the changes made to the original Thumbnails.sln project by the Thumbnails2.sln project as shaded elements.

The \WROX\Azure\Chapter08\Thumbnails2\Thumbnails2.sln project has the preceding modifications applied. To test the project in Mixed mode, change the ServiceConfiguration.cscfg file's <Role> sections to correspond to your `AccountName` and `AccountSharedKey` values.

Enabling Thumbnail Deletion

The original Thumbnails.sln and modified Thumbnails2.sln solutions enable adding thumbnails to the containers but don't support deleting them. The \WROX\Azure\Chapter08\PhotoGallery\ PhotoGallery.sln project adds a `gvBlobs` GridView that lists the thumbnail blobs and lets users delete the thumbnail and the associated original image blob. Figure 8-6 shows the PhotoGallery service running in the Production Fabric with 11 thumbnails loaded.

Adding the `gvBlobs` GridView to the Thumbnails2.sln project is a relatively straightforward process:

1. Add the GridView to the update panel under the ListView and specify column properties. The blobs' `Content-Language` and `Content-Encoding` attributes are empty, so those columns aren't displayed.

2. Add a `Delete` command field with a `HeaderText` property of `Blobs`.

3. Add the following instructions to the `Page_PreRender` event handler after the `thumbnails.DataBind` instruction:

```
gvBlobs.DataSource = GetPhotoGalleryContainer().ListBlobs("thumbnails/",
```

```
                false);
            gvBlobs.DataBind();
```

4. Add a `gvBlobs_RowDeleting` event handler with the code of Listing 8-27:

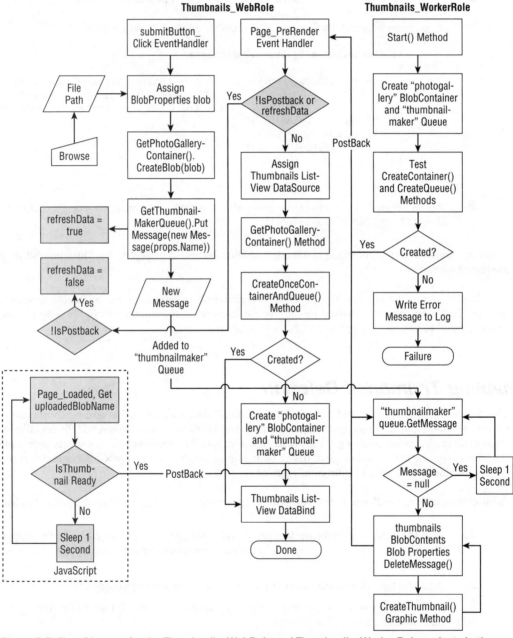

Figure 8-5: Flow Diagram for the Thumbnails_WebRole and Thumbnails_WorkerRole projects in the Thumbnails2.sln solution.

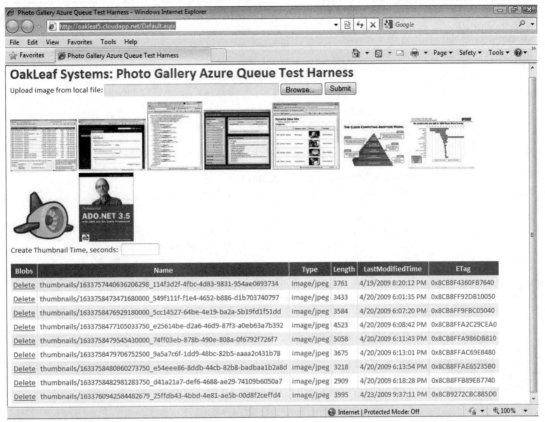

Figure 8-6: A GridView added to the Thumbnails2 page to display a list of thumbnail blobs and enable deletion of thumbnail and source image blobs.

Listing 8-27: HTTP request and response messages generated by WorkerRole polling

```
protected void gvBlobs_RowDeleting(object sender,
    System.Web.UI.WebControls.GridViewDeleteEventArgs e)
{
    // Delete the specified thumbnail blob
    int index = e.RowIndex;
    if (index < gvBlobs.DataKeys.Count)
    {
        // Keep a minimun of three thumbnails
        if (gvBlobs.DataKeys.Count > 3)
        {
            // Delete the thumbnail
            string blobName = (string)gvBlobs.DataKeys[index].Value;
            BlobContainer blobContainer = GetPhotoGalleryContainer();
            if (blobContainer.DoesBlobExist(blobName))
            {
                blobContainer.DeleteBlob(blobName);
                RoleManager.WriteToLog("Information",
```

Continued

```
                    string.Format("Deleted '{0}'", blobName));
        }
        else
            RoleManager.WriteToLog("Information",
                string.Format("Failed to delete '{0}'", blobName));

        // Delete the original image blob (without thumbnails/
        // prefix)
        blobName = blobName.Substring(11);
        if (blobContainer.DoesBlobExist(blobName))
        {
            blobContainer.DeleteBlob(blobName);
            RoleManager.WriteToLog("Information",
                string.Format("Deleted '{0}'", blobName));
        }
        else
            RoleManager.WriteToLog("Information",
                string.Format("Failed to delete '{0}'", blobName));

        // Set the refreshData flag
        refreshData = true;
    }
    else
        statusMessage.Text = "Please leave at least 3 thumbnails
            for other users.";
    }
}
```

A live demonstration of the PhotoGallery.sln project is at http://oakleaf5.cloudapp.net/.

Summary

Azure Queues provide a reliable message delivery system to support dispatching asynchronous computing work. Queues are the only method offered by the Azure Storage Services for persisting interactive instructions with Azure Services; tables and blobs only persist state.

A single StorageAccount accommodates an unlimited number of MessageQueues and each MessageQueue can persist an unlimited number of Messages, which can store up to 8KB of content. You can store Messages larger than 8KB in blobs and substitute the blobs' Name property values for the content. Queue programming semantics ensure that a message can be processed at least once. Azure Queues have a REST API, which enables applications written in any language access the queue over the Internet or intranets with HTTP or HTTPS request and response messages. The StorageClient library lets developers treat Azure Queues as .NET objects.

The Windows Azure SDK (March 2009 CTP) includes a sample application, Thumbnails.sln, which demonstrates how to program interaction between a WebRole, which provides a user interface for creating a collection of thumbnail images from source graphic files from users' local file system, and a WorkerRole, which handles the computing process to generate a thumbnail image of 124 px maximum width or height. A single `BlobContainer` persists source and thumbnail files in blobs having related names.

Real-world tests of Thumbnails.sln demonstrate that its design would result in extremely high bandwidth consumption in even moderately scaled environments. Reducing the bandwidth by disabling ViewState of the ListView that stores the thumbnail images doesn't reduce the bandwidth sufficiently to produce an economically viable service.

Part III

Tackling Advanced Azure Services Techniques

9

Authenticating Users with .NET Access Control Services

.NET Access Control Services (ACS) is one of three .NET Services for Windows Azure Platform. ACS is a customizable, cloud-based Security Token Service (STS) that supports user authentication by any of the following credentials:

❑ User (solution) name and password

❑ Windows Live ID

❑ Windows CardSpace

❑ X.509 certificate

❑ Security Assertion Markup Language (SAML) tokens issued by third-party STSs

> *Wikipedia describes SAML as "an XML-based standard for exchanging authentication and authorization data between security domains, that is, between an identity provider (a producer of assertions) and a service provider (a consumer of assertions)." SAML "is a product of the OASIS Security Services Technical Committee [and] has become the definitive standard underlying many web Single Sign-On solutions in the enterprise identity management problem space." Additional information about the SAML Technical Committee (TC) is at* `http://bit.ly/Xsv31,www.oasis-open.org/committees/tc_ home.php?wg_abbrev=security`. *The saml.xml.org site (`http://saml.xml.org/`) is the primary source of SAML resources for developers.*

ACS is an STS infrastructure hosted in Windows Azure that authenticates credentials and issues tokens. Each .NET Services solution has a private, isolated STS at its disposal. ACS also provides a role-based authorization framework that relies on claims-based rules. Integrating ACS with an Azure WebRole or other .NET applications requires installing the Windows Identity Foundation (WIF, formerly "Geneva" Framework), which was available in a Beta 2 version when this book was written. WIF implements the `System.IdentityModel` namespace to simplify claims-based applications. It builds on the Windows Communication Foundation (WCF) infrastructure to implement WS-Trust and comes with an HttpModule called the WS-Federation Authentication Module (FAM) that simplifies implementing WS-Federation in browser-based applications.

As mentioned later in this chapter, the `System.IdentityModel` *namespace wasn't compatible with Windows Azure when this book was written.*

WS-Federation is the web services (WS-*) specification for federating identities from a variety of sources (domains) to simplify sharing services from secure web sites and SOAP-based services. This chapter demonstrates how features of Microsoft's current WS-Federation implementation are used by WCF-based SOAP clients and web services. WS-Federation also defines syntax for expressing the WS-Trust protocol and WS-Federation extensions in a browser-based environment. This syntax provides a common approach to federating identity operations for web services and browser-based applications.

Although ACS currently has a credentials store for name/password, Windows CardSpace v1 self-issued information cards, and X.509 certificates, the .NET Services team has no plans for ACS to be an Identity Provider in the long term. ACS will use Windows Live Identity Services (WLID) in the future.

Sections later in this chapter describe how to create federated CardSpace credentials for testing with ACS. ACS has built-in support for Windows Live ID (WLID) credentials.

Creating a .NET Services Solution

You must create a .NET Services solution before you can take advantage of ACS and "Geneva" Framework features. A .NET Services solution provisions all three .NET Services — ACS, ServiceBus, and Workflow Services other than ACS are the subject of later chapters. .NET Services gained a RESTful API with HTTP/HTTPS request and response messages for most operations in the March 2009 Community Technical Preview (CTP).

To provision a set of .NET Services go to `http://portal.ex.azure.microsoft.com/` and accept the Terms of Use to open the My Subscriptions page. Click the Add Solution link to open the Create Solution page, type a unique name for the solution (similar to `oakleaf-acs` for this example) in the text box, click the Validate Name link to test for uniqueness (see Figure 9-1), and click OK to add the solution to the My Subscriptions page and start the provisioning process (see Figure 9-2).

.NET Service solution names become part of a DNS name and thus must follow DNS naming rules. Solution names must start with a letter followed by a combination of letters and numbers, but starting with xn, Xn, xN, or XN prefixes is prohibited. Dashes (-) are the only special character permitted. Solution names must be unique, so you can't create an `oakleaf-acs` *solution; substitute your own solution name to prevent conflicts.*

The empty space in the Status column between Access Control Service and Service Bus Registry will be filled with a Workflow Service link when Workflow Services are restored by the release of .NET Framework 4. Workflow Services were temporarily removed from the .NET Services July 2009 CTP and later.

Click the Access Control Service link to open the Manage the Microsoft .NET Access Control page (see Figure 9-3).

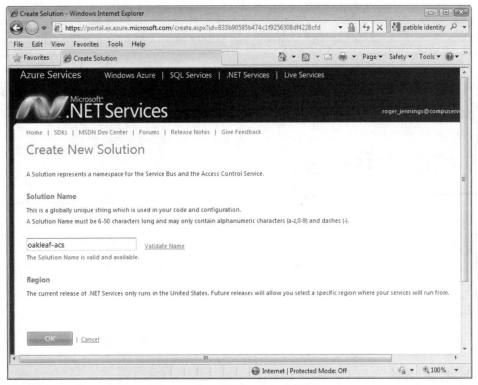

Figure 9-1: Assign a unique name for the .NET Services solution.

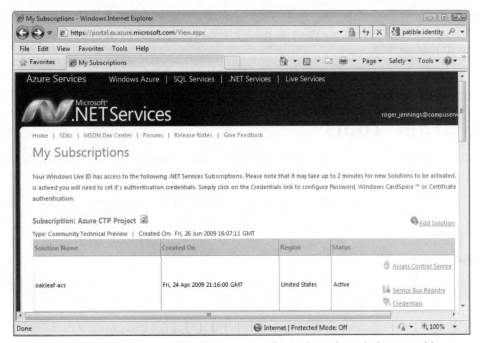

Figure 9-2: The Create Solution page displays a row for each service solution you add.

Figure 9-3: After a short time, the Windows Azure Platform provisions the .NET Solution you specified and opens its management page.

Installing the .NET Services SDK, and Other Tools

Downloading and installing the .NET Services SDK is required to enable ACS samples that use the ServiceBus or Workflow services.

The Azure Management Tools and the Azure Service Training Kit are optional but you'll find they have content that will help you learn more about identity management for .NET Services and Azure web applications.

.NET Services SDK

The latest version of the .NET Services SDK was the July 2009 Community Technical Preview (CTP) when this book was written. The SDK includes the Microsoft.ServiceBus assembly, C# and VB sample code, and preliminary ACS documentation. You can install the latest version of the SDK, which creates a program group, from `http://bit.ly/bL2xY`, `http://go.microsoft.com/fwlink/?LinkID=129448`. The .NET Services Development Center is at `http://bit.ly/bhAKT`, `http://msdn.microsoft.com/en-us/azure/netservices.aspx` and the .NET Services – Technical Discussions forum is at `http://bit.ly/2T98wb`, `http://social.msdn.microsoft.com/Forums/en-US/netservices/threads`.

Java and Ruby versions of the .NET Services SDK are available at `http://bit.ly/ZjLwx`, `www.schakra.com/stuff-we-do/jdotnetservices.html` *and* `http://bit.ly/Ms1YE`, `www.dotnetservicesruby.com/`, *respectively.*

Azure Management Tools (Optional)

The Azure Services Management Tools provide a Microsoft Management Console (MMC) SnapIn and Windows PowerShell cmdlets that enable users to configure and manage .NET Access Control Services, and the .NET Workflow Service. These tools let you view and change .NET Access Control Scopes and Rules in an MMC GUI, rather than pages of the .NET Services portal, and deploy and view workflows. You can download the current Azure Services Management Tools from the MSDN Code Gallery at `http://bit.ly/gKlP0`, `http://code.msdn.microsoft.com/AzureManagementTools`.

Vittorio Bertocci's January 2008 blog post, "A visual tour of the .NET Access Control service via Azure Services Management Console" (`http://bit.ly/2LV411`, `http://blogs.msdn.com/vbertocci/archive/2009/01/08/a-visual-tour-of-the-net-access-control-service-via-azure-services-management-console.aspx`) *shows you how to substitute the snap-in's GUI for the arduous process of configuring scopes and roles with the Azure portal's Manage the Microsoft .NET Access Control Service pages.*

Azure Services Training Kit (Optional)

The Azure Services Training Kit includes hands-on labs (HOLs), PowerPoint presentations, and demonstrations that are designed to help you learn how to use the Windows Azure Platform. An IntroAccessControlService HOL, as well as IntroNetServices and IndentityAccessControlServices presentations are applicable to this chapter's content. You can download the latest Azure Services Training Kit from `http://bit.ly/DAZKt`, `http://go.microsoft.com/fwlink/?LinkID=130354`.

Microsoft "Geneva" Beta 2 (Verify Compatibility Before Installing)

The Beta 2 version of Microsoft "Geneva" was released in June 2009 and is available for download from `http://bit.ly/4xUgjs`, `www.microsoft.com/downloads/details.aspx?displaylang=en&FamilyID=118c3588-9070-426a-b655-6cec0a92c10b`. "Geneva" consists of the following three components:

❑ Windows Identity Foundation ("Geneva" Framework) for building .NET applications that use claims to make user access decisions

❑ Active Directory Federation Services ("Geneva" Server) security token service (STS) for issuing and transforming claims, enabling federations, and managing user access

❑ Windows CardSpace (Windows CardSpace "Geneva") for helping users navigate access decisions and for developers to build customer authentication experiences for users

You can download the preceding components, as well as "Geneva" whitepapers and overviews from `http://bit.ly/qseXe`, `https://connect.microsoft.com/site/sitehome.aspx?SiteID=642`. The Claims Based Access Platform (CBA), Code-Named "Geneva" forum is at `http://bit.ly/ADmws`, `http://social.msdn.microsoft.com/Forums/en-US/Geneva/threads/` and the infrequently updated MSDN "Geneva" Team blog is at `http://bit.ly/xcK6h`, `http://blogs.msdn.com/card/default.aspx`. Channel 9's "The Id Element" show at `http://bit.ly/14hig7`, `http://channel9.msdn.com/identity/` offers interviews with Microsoft product group members and others about identity, ACS, and "Geneva."

Microsoft "Geneva" Beta 1 was incompatible with the Windows Azure Platform (March 2009 CTP) and WebRole applications using the "Geneva" Framework would not run in the Azure Production Fabric. For more information on this issue, see Vittorio Bertocci's, "Claims and Cloud: Pardon our Dust" blog post of April 1, 2009 (`http://bit.ly/CTUf4`, `http://blogs.msdn.com/vbertocci/archive/2009/04/01/claims-and-cloud-pardon-our-dust.aspx`).

A Microsoft technical support representative reported in the Windows Azure Forum that Windows CardSpace "Geneva" is not compatible with the Windows CardSpace applet included with Windows Vista and Windows 7. Uninstalling the "Geneva" Framework reverts to the original Windows CardSpace applet. See the "Windows Cardspace "Geneva" (Beta 2) is Incompatible with Windows Cardspace (Default) Control Panel Applet" bug report at `http://bit.ly/e408T`, `https://connect.microsoft.com/feedback/ViewFeedback.aspx?FeedbackID=453987&SiteID=642`. When this book was written the preceding warnings had not been retracted for "Geneva" Beta 2.

Microsoft announced a change to the names of "Geneva" components on July 13, 2009: "Geneva" Server is now Active Directory Federation Services (ADFS), "Geneva" Framework is Windows Identity Foundation, and Windows CardSpace "Geneva" is Windows CardSpace.

Creating CardSpace Credentials at FederatedIdentity.net

Microsoft's Identity Lab (Identity Protocols Security Token Service, `ipsts`) is a set of hosted security token services to support testing of Identity Protocols. The goal of the lab is to provide a set of custom test endpoints to evaluate the interoperability of Identity Protocols, including Microsoft CardSpace, among multiple partners and vendors. Microsoft promotes its CardSpace credentials as an industry-standard, SAML v1.1-compliant source of identity information. Vista was the first Windows version to include a CardSpace Control Panel applet. You use CardSpace credentials to test federation of third-party CardSpace and LiveID identity services in later sections of this chapter.

You can learn more about the Windows CardSpace protocol from its main MSDN page (`http://bit.ly/nxmph`, `http://msdn.microsoft.com/en-us/windows/aa663320.aspx`), the "Geneva" Team Blog (`http://bit.ly/1a0YwJ`, `http://blogs.msdn.com/card/`) and the Windows

CardSpace ('InfoCard') Forum (http://bit.ly/12MnJr, http://social.msdn.microsoft.com/forums/en-US/windowscardspace/threads/).

To obtain a managed CardSpace information card, browse to the Microsoft Identity Lab's Microsoft Identity Interop Sts Logon page (http://bit.ly/3oJeO, https://ipsts.federatedidentity.net/MgmtConsole/Login.aspx) and click the Sign Up button to open the Registration page. Type a fictitious name in the UserName text box, a password in the Password and Confirm Password text boxes, and mark the Accept Terms of Use check box (see Figure 9-4).

Figure 9-4: The Identity Lab's Registration page warns you not to disclose confidential information in this CardSpace credential.

Click Submit to open the Claims Configuration page. Accept the default (marked) setting for the By Default, Release the Following Claims to Any Relying Party check box. These are the minimum claims required by most relying parties. Type fictitious names in the First Name and LastName text boxes and accept the referring party's Email Address (*UserName*@ipsts.federatedidentity.net), as shown in Figure 9-5.

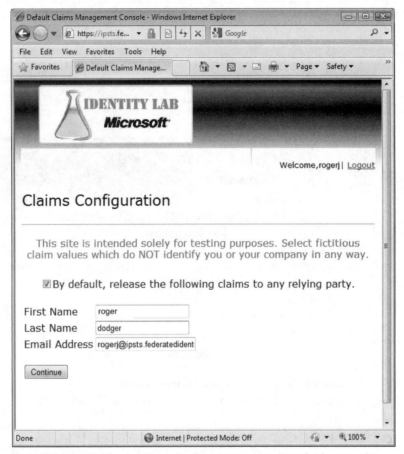

Figure 9-5: The Claims Configuration Page generates the referring party's e-mail address for you.

Click Continue to open the Edit Profile Information/Manage Relying Party Policies page (see Figure 9-6.) The Edit Profile Information link opens a page that lets you add to and edit the information you entered previously; the Manage Relying Party Policies page enables selecting the profile information you release to relying parties.

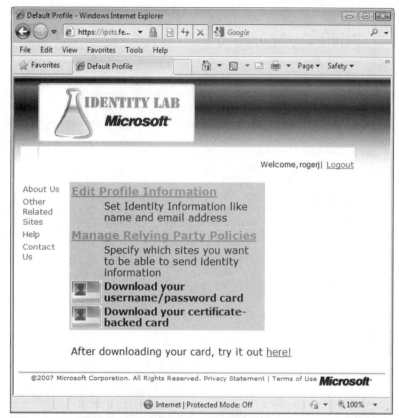

Figure 9-6: The Edit Profile Information/Manage Relying Party Policies page has links for editing and downloading CardSpace credentials.

Click the Edit Profile Information Link to open an expanded version of the Claims Configuration page. Add fictitious information to the First Name and Last Name text boxes, accept the default Email Address, and type Domain Users in the Group text box. Mark their selection for your default profile by marking the four associated check boxes (see Figure 9-7).

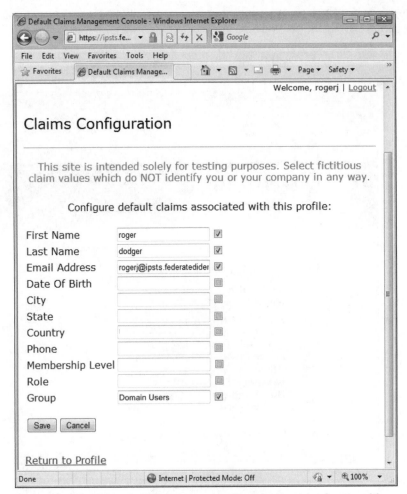

Figure 9-7: The Claims Configuration page with default entries for use with the Azure Services Training Kit's Federation.sln HOL.

The following table relates the Claims Configurati on page's friendly names to SOAP WS-* `identity/claims` URIs. The page uses friendly names to avoid disclosing information about your personal or your company's identity.

Friendly Name	Claim Type URI
Site Specific ID	`'http://schemas.xmlsoap.org/ws/2005/05/identity/claims/` `privatepersonalidentifier'`
First Name	`'http://schemas.xmlsoap.org/ws/2005/05/identity/claims/givenname'`

Friendly Name	Claim Type URI
Last Name	'http://schemas.xmlsoap.org/ws/2005/05/identity/claims/surname'
Email Address	'http://schemas.xmlsoap.org/ws/2005/05/identity/claims/emailaddress'
Date Of Birth	'http://schemas.xmlsoap.org/ws/2005/05/identity/claims/dateofbirth'
City	'http://schemas.xmlsoap.org/ws/2005/05/identity/claims/locality'
State	'http://schemas.xmlsoap.org/ws/2005/05/identity/claims/stateorprovince
Country	'http://schemas.xmlsoap.org/ws/2005/05/identity/claims/country'
Phone	'http://schemas.xmlsoap.org/ws/2005/05/identity/claims/mobilephone'
Group	'http://schemas.xmlsoap.org/claims/Group'
Role	'http://ipsts.federatedidentity.net/role'
Membership Level	'http://ipsts.federatedidentity.net/membershiplevel'

Click Submit to return to the Edit Profile Information/Manage Relying Party Policies page, click Save to return to the Manage Relying Party Policies, and click the Manage Relying Party Policies link to open the Relying Parties page, which contains Edit/View buttons for HTTPS and HTTP policies. Click the EditView button for the unsecured http://relyingparty.federatedidentity.net party to open the Edit a Policy page. Mark the check boxes for the profile items you want to release, click Browse, and navigate to the public key file for ACS that's included in the Azure Services Toolkit (see Figure 9-8, which shows only the first five items).

The certificate is located at \AzureServicesKit\Labs\IntroAccessControlService\Assets\ accesscontrol.windows.net.cer.

Click Save to save your changes and return to the Edit Profile Information/Manage Relying Party Policies page. Click the Download Your Username/Password card button to open the File Download dialog for the InformationCard.crd file, and click Yes when asked whether you want to save the card with Windows CardSpace on your local computer. This adds the CardSpace Information Card credential to the Windows CardSpace Control Panel tool (see Figure 9-9).

Repeat the preceding step for the Certificate-Backed card, which requires you to click a link to generate and download the FederatedIdentity.pfx certificate and click Open to start the Certificate Import Wizard. Click Next, accept the default File Name, click Next, type **1234** as the password, and click Next to download and add the certificate-backed card to the Windows CardSpace Control Panel tool.

Exploring the HTTP Request and Response Messages of the CardSpace Information Card

The http://ipsts.federatedidentity.net/ URI's Edit Profile Information/Manage Relying Party Policies page's Download Your Username/Password card button sends the HTTP request message shown in Listing 9–1 to your computer, which adds an item to the LocalCardStore1.5001.crds credential store located in the \Users*UserName.DomainName*\AppData\Local\Microsoft\CardspaceV2 folder, which opens with the Microsoft IdentityManager (also known as the Windows CardSpace applet). Listing 9–1 shows the content (with binary data truncated) of the request message for the rogerj Identity Card with the three claims shown in Figure 9-8.

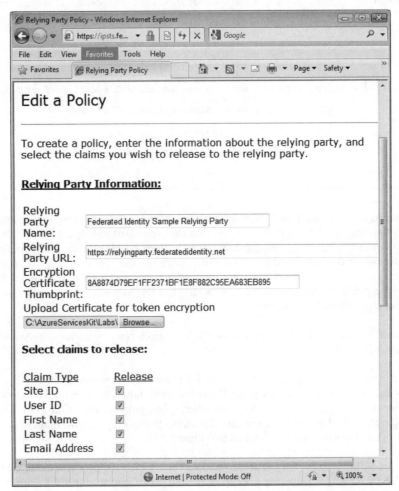

Figure 9-8: Creating a policy for the sample Federated Identity Http Sample Relying Party.

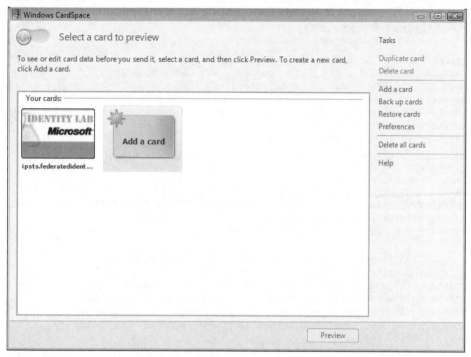

Figure 9-9: Vista and later Windows operating systems have a Windows CardSpace applet for selecting CardSpace credentials to use with applications that support this identity protocol.

Listing 9-1: HTTP request message for creating the CardSpace credentials for the policy of Figure 9-8

```
POST /MgmtConsole/UserProfile.aspx HTTP/1.1
Accept: image/gif, image/jpeg, image/pjpeg, application/x-ms-
application, application/vnd.ms-xpsdocument,
application/xaml+xml, application/x-ms-xbap,
application/vnd.ms-excel, application/vnd.ms-powerpoint,
application/x-shockwave-flash, application/x-silverlight-2-b2,
application/x-silverlight, application/msword, */*
Referer:
https://ipsts.federatedidentity.net/MgmtConsole/UserProfile.aspx
Accept-Language: en-us
User-Agent: Mozilla/4.0 (compatible; MSIE 8.0; Windows NT 6.0;
```

Continued

251

Listing 9-1: HTTP request message for creating the CardSpace credentials for the policy of Figure 9-8 *(continued)*

```
Trident/4.0; GTB6; SLCC1; .NET CLR 2.0.50727; Media Center PC 5.0;
.NET CLR 3.5.21022; .NET CLR 3.5.30428; .NET CLR 3.5.30729;
.NET CLR 3.0.30618; MS-RTC LM 8; InfoPath.2;
OfficeLiveConnector.1.3; OfficeLivePatch.1.3)
Content-Type: application/x-www-form-urlencoded
Accept-Encoding: gzip, deflate
Host: ipsts.federatedidentity.net
Content-Length: 399
Connection: Keep-Alive
Cache-Control: no-cache
Cookie: ASP.NET_SessionId=c3qfhfjsvznt1g55fiz0kamd;
.ASPXAUTH=C5AA499D1D055CE8072092ECEDA418E4598C89C7B05DB127720
8B472E254623DF2FCD982F7084A0B4E8B4279763CBBF95207A54C958593B8
47D8C12E5BAFA0B03C17657ACCCE5ED47FA7FBBE05C7AB7C

__EVENTTARGET=&__EVENTARGUMENT=&__VIEWSTATE=%2FwEPDwUKMTUzMjgw
MDIxNWQYAQUeX19Db250cm9sc1JlcXVpcmVVQb3N0QmFja0tleV9fFgQFEkxvZ2l
uU3RhdHVzMSRjdGwwMQUSTG9naW5TdGdF0dXMxJGN0bDAzBQVjdGwwNwUMSW1hZ2
VCdXR0b24yK3zW1NJzQ9rHBuQIlifR5JFLlxM%3D&__PREVIOUSPAGE=4NPldbO
FJaNjq31q4SSNo1oBM5xQci6E8YDLyrH2srk1&__EVENTVALIDATION=%2FwEWB
ALGkJvgBgK%2B3vvOCQKkwImNCwLSwtXkAsHGA9QzJH4lHeSdXMPXSnU%2F9GGE
&ctl07.x=34&ctl07.y=18
```

As of the March 2009 CTP, ACS and related identity services had RESTful APIs. Listing 9–2 is the HTTP response message returned by the Windows CardSpace applet when you elect to store the Information Card or when interchanging credentials to request user (Requester) access to an application (Relying Party) that uses ACS for authorization.

Listing 9-2: HTTP response message containing the CardSpace credentials created by Listing 9-1 with items shown in Figure 9-8 highlighted and encrypted content truncated

```
HTTP/1.1 200 OK
Cache-Control: private
Content-Type: application/x-informationCardFile
Server: Microsoft-IIS/7.0
Content-Disposition: attachment; filename=InformationCard.crd
X-AspNet-Version: 2.0.50727
X-Powered-By: ASP.NET
Date: Mon, 27 Apr 2009 21:47:57 GMT
Content-Length: 26838

<ds:Signature xmlns:ds="http://www.w3.org/2000/09/xmldsig#">
  <ds:SignedInfo>
    <ds:CanonicalizationMethod
      Algorithm="http://www.w3.org/2001/10/xml-exc-c14n#"/>
    <ds:SignatureMethod
      Algorithm="http://www.w3.org/2000/09/xmldsig#rsa-sha1"/>
    <ds:Reference URI="#_Object_InformationCard">
```

```
      <ds:Transforms>
        <ds:Transform Algorithm="http://www.w3.org/2001/10/xml-exc-c14n#"/>
      </ds:Transforms>
      <ds:DigestMethod Algorithm="http://www.w3.org/2000/09/xmldsig#sha1"/>
      <ds:DigestValue>bL+zolLfpZdzmfG0C2DbMiwhzxs=</ds:DigestValue>
   </ds:Reference>
</ds:SignedInfo>
<ds:SignatureValue>hSb4hICvKaHlYKfkcYhrcvWQyblOhayFijcOFtXjVgQ6Dfat
   PM40bx2h2X/KW4W7zyZs
   ..
   TJWfzTO59HSymfCw5jdzZ1IO3I58d3qwXU/1F3BWLD2IABQSWGW78o/Lc95GY300
   gIzWdQTwbOToRLdZoIo=
</ds:SignatureValue>
<KeyInfo xmlns="http://www.w3.org/2000/09/xmldsig#">
   <X509Data>
      <X509Certificate>
         MIIF+jCCBOKgAwIBAgIKfaH88AAFAADqAjANBgkqhkiG9w0BAQ
         izETMBEGCgm
         ..
         jkwdWg1zNXz+xdq8RjFg6kWtK2tzVqs+T1+R26ciJRqMvuowqUvwSpng
         OUHbwVoc7nbVQ==
      </X509Certificate>
   </X509Data>
</KeyInfo>
<ds:Object Id="_Object_InformationCard">
   <i:InformationCard xml:lang="en"
      xmlns:i="http://schemas.xmlsoap.org/ws/2005/05/identity">
   <i:InformationCardReference>
      <i:CardId>
         urn:uuid:559d0b9e-05f2-4dac-ac31-c572fb456af4
      </i:CardId>
      <i:CardVersion>2</i:CardVersion></i:InformationCardReference>
      <i:CardName>ipsts.federatedidentity.net</i:CardName>
      <i:CardImage MimeType="image/jpeg">
         /9j/4AAQSkZJRgABAQEAYABgAAD/2wBDAAgGBgcGBQgHBwcJCQgKDBQNDAs
         LDBkSEw8UHRofHh0aHBwgJ
         ..
         FFABRRRQAUUUUAFFFFABRRRQAUUUUAFFFFABRRRQAUUUUAFFFFABRRRQB//
         2Q==
      </i:CardImage>
      <i:Issuer>http://ipsts.federatedidentity.net</i:Issuer>
      <i:TimeIssued>2009-04-27T21:47:57.837Z</i:TimeIssued>
      <i:TimeExpires>2009-05-04T21:47:57.837Z</i:TimeExpires>
      <i:TokenServiceList>
         <i:TokenService>
            <EndpointReference
               xmlns="http://www.w3.org/2005/08/addressing">
            <Address>
               https://ipsts.federatedidentity.net/SecurityTokenService/
                  InteropSts.svc/Sts
            </Address>
            <Metadata>
               <Metadata xmlns="http://schemas.xmlsoap.org/ws/2004/09/mex"
                  xmlns:xsi="http://www.w3.org/2001/XMLSchema-instance"
```

Continued

253

Listing 9-2: HTTP response message containing the CardSpace credentials created by Listing 9-1 with items shown in Figure 9-8 highlighted and encrypted content truncated (continued)

```
                    xmlns:xsd="http://www.w3.org/2001/XMLSchema"
                    xmlns:wsx="http://schemas.xmlsoap.org/ws/2004/09/mex">
                    <wsx:MetadataSection
                      Dialect="http://schemas.xmlsoap.org/ws/2004/09/mex"
                      xmlns="">
                      <wsx:MetadataReference>
                      <Address xmlns="http://www.w3.org/2005/08/addressing">
                        https://ipsts.federatedidentity.net/
                        SecurityTokenService/InteropSts.svc/mex
                      </Address>
                      </wsx:MetadataReference>
                    </wsx:MetadataSection>
                </Metadata>
              </Metadata>
              <Identity xmlns="http://schemas.xmlsoap.org/ws/
                    2006/02/addressingidentity">
                <KeyInfo xmlns="http://www.w3.org/2000/09/xmldsig#">
                  <X509Data>
                      <X509Certificate>
                        KfaH88AAFAADqAjANBgkqhkiG9w0BAQUFADCBizETMBEGCgmSJ
                        ..
                        kWtK2tzVqs+T1+R26ciJRqMvuowqUvwSpngOUHbwVoc7nbVQ==
                      </X509Certificate>
                  </X509Data>
                </KeyInfo>
              </Identity>
            </EndpointReference>
            <i:UserCredential>
              <i:UsernamePasswordCredential>
                <i:Username>rogerj</i:Username>
              </i:UsernamePasswordCredential>
            </i:UserCredential>
          </i:TokenService>
        </i:TokenServiceList>
        <i:SupportedTokenTypeList>
          <t:TokenType xmlns:t="http://schemas.xmlsoap.org/ws/
              2005/02/trust">
           http://docs.oasis-open.org/wss/oasis-wss-saml-token-profile-
           1.1#SAMLV1.1
          </t:TokenType>
          <t:TokenType xmlns:t="http://schemas.xmlsoap.org/ws/
              2005/02/trust">
            http://docs.oasis-open.org/wss/oasis-wss-saml-token-profile-
            1.1#SAMLV2.0
          </t:TokenType>
```

```
<t:TokenType xmlns:t="http://schemas.xmlsoap.org/ws/
  2005/02/trust">
   http://schemas.microsoft.com/ws/2006/05/identitymodel/
     tokens/Kerberos
</t:TokenType>
<t:TokenType
  xmlns:t="http://schemas.xmlsoap.org/ws/2005/02/trust">
  http://schemas.microsoft.com/ws/
    2006/05/identitymodel/tokens/Rsa
</t:TokenType>
<t:TokenType xmlns:t="http://schemas.xmlsoap.org/ws/
  2005/02/trust">
  http://schemas.microsoft.com/2008/08/sessiontoken
</t:TokenType>
<t:TokenType xmlns:t="http://schemas.xmlsoap.org/ws/
  2005/02/trust">
  http://schemas.microsoft.com/ws/
    2006/05/identitymodel/tokens/UserName
</t:TokenType>
<t:TokenType xmlns:t="http://schemas.xmlsoap.org/ws/
  2005/02/trust">
  http://schemas.microsoft.com/ws/2006/05/
    identitymodel/tokens/X509Certificate
</t:TokenType>
<t:TokenType xmlns:t="http://schemas.xmlsoap.org/ws/
  2005/02/trust">
  urn:oasis:names:tc:SAML:1.0:assertion
</t:TokenType>
</i:SupportedTokenTypeList>
<i:SupportedClaimTypeList>
<i:SupportedClaimType
  Uri="http://schemas.xmlsoap.org/ws/
    2005/05/identity/claims/givenname">
  <i:DisplayTag>First Name</i:DisplayTag>
  <i:Description>
    A person's name which is not their surname nor middle name
  </i:Description>
</i:SupportedClaimType>
<i:SupportedClaimType
  Uri="http://schemas.xmlsoap.org/ws/
    2005/05/identity/claims/surname">
  <i:DisplayTag>Last Name</i:DisplayTag>
  <i:Description>The family name of a person</i:Description>
</i:SupportedClaimType>
<i:SupportedClaimType
  Uri="http://schemas.xmlsoap.org/ws/
    2005/05/identity/claims/emailaddress">
```

Continued

255

Listing 9-2: HTTP response message containing the CardSpace credentials created by Listing 9-1 with items shown in Figure 9-8 highlighted and encrypted content truncated (continued)

```
      <i:DisplayTag>Email Address</i:DisplayTag>
      <i:Description>
        an electronic mailbox address of a person
      </i:Description>
  </i:SupportedClaimType>
  <i:SupportedClaimType
    Uri="http://schemas.xmlsoap.org/ws/
      2005/05/identity/claims/dateofbirth">
      <i:DisplayTag>Date Of Birth</i:DisplayTag>
      <i:Description>The date of birth of a person</i:Description>
  </i:SupportedClaimType><i:SupportedClaimType
    Uri="http://schemas.xmlsoap.org/ws/
      2005/05/identity/claims/locality">
      <i:DisplayTag>City</i:DisplayTag>
      <i:Description>
        The name of a locality, such as a city, county or
          other geographic region
      </i:Description>
  </i:SupportedClaimType>
  <i:SupportedClaimType
    Uri="http://schemas.xmlsoap.org/ws/
      2005/05/identity/claims/stateorprovince">
      <i:DisplayTag>State</i:DisplayTag>
      <i:Description>
        Abbreviation for state or province name of a physical address
      </i:Description>
  </i:SupportedClaimType>
  <i:SupportedClaimType
    Uri="http://schemas.xmlsoap.org/ws/
      2005/05/identity/claims/country">
      <i:DisplayTag>Country</i:DisplayTag>
      <i:Description>Country of a physical address</i:Description>
  </i:SupportedClaimType>
  <i:SupportedClaimType
    Uri="http://schemas.xmlsoap.org/ws/
      2005/05/identity/claims/mobilephone">
      <i:DisplayTag>Phone</i:DisplayTag>
      <i:Description>
        Mobile telephone number of a person
      </i:Description>
  </i:SupportedClaimType>
      <i:SupportedClaimType
        Uri="http://schemas.xmlsoap.org/ws/
          2005/05/identity/claims/privatepersonalidentifier">
      <i:DisplayTag>Site ID</i:DisplayTag>
      <i:Description>A private personal identifier</i:Description>
  </i:SupportedClaimType>
  <i:SupportedClaimType Uri="http://ipsts.federatedidentity.net/
      membershiplevel">
      <i:DisplayTag>Membership Level</i:DisplayTag>
```

```
            </i:SupportedClaimType>
            <i:SupportedClaimType
                Uri="http://ipsts.federatedidentity.net/role">
                <i:DisplayTag>Role</i:DisplayTag>
            </i:SupportedClaimType>
            <i:SupportedClaimType
                Uri="http://ipsts.federatedidentity.net/group">
                <i:DisplayTag>Group</i:DisplayTag>
        </i:SupportedClaimType>
```

```
            <i:SupportedClaimType
              Uri="http://schemas.xmlsoap.org/ws/
                2005/05/identity/claims/name">
              <i:DisplayTag>User ID</i:DisplayTag>
              <i:Description>Name</i:Description>
            </i:SupportedClaimType>
          </i:SupportedClaimTypeList>
          <i:RequireAppliesTo Optional="false"/>
          <i:PrivacyNotice Version="1">
            http://www.federatedidentity.net/Privacy.txt
          </i:PrivacyNotice>
          <ic07:IssuerInformation
              xmlns:ic07="http://schemas.xmlsoap.org/ws/
              2007/01/identity">
            <ic07:IssuerInformationEntry>
              <ic07:EntryName>Contact Us</ic07:EntryName>
              <ic07:EntryValue>FedId@microsoft.com</ic07:EntryValue>
            </ic07:IssuerInformationEntry>
            <ic07:IssuerInformationEntry>
              <ic07:EntryName>Web Page</ic07:EntryName>
              <ic07:EntryValue>
                  www.FederatedIdentity.net
              </ic07:EntryValue>
            </ic07:IssuerInformationEntry>
          </ic07:IssuerInformation>
          <ic07:RequireStrongRecipientIdentity
              xmlns:ic07="http://schemas.xmlsoap.org/ws/2007/01/identity"/>
        </i:InformationCard>
      </ds:Object>
    </ds:Signature>
```

Non-sensitive information, such as supported claim types, appears in clear text. The highlighted lines in Listing 9–2 include all custom claim types. Data, such as claim values, is encrypted; encrypted data is truncated for brevity.

Standardizing Information Card Terminology

The `http://bit.ly/119HbZ`, `http://schemas.xmlsoap.org/ws/2005/05/identity/` and `http://bit.ly/hBfz6`, `http://docs.oasis-open.org/imi/ns/identity-200810` URI redirect to Oasis's Identity Metasystem Interoperability (IMI) 1.0 namespace (`http://bit.ly/hBfz6`, `http://docs.oasis-open.org/imi/ns/identity-200810`), which also contains a directory of links to related resources using the Resource Directory Description Language (RDDL) 2.0

(`http://bit.ly/fPzsL`, `www.openhealth.org/RDDL/20040118/rddl-20040118.html`). The IMI 1.0 specification is related to the WS-Trust, WS-SecurityPolicy, and WS-Addressing specifications.

The IMI 1.0 namespace's Committee Draft 02 of February 19, 2009 defines the terms related to the Information Card Model and Information Card listed in the following table.

Term	Definition
Information Card Model	Refers to the use of Information Cards containing metadata for obtaining Digital Identity claims from Identity Providers and then conveying them to Relying Parties under user control.
Information Card	Provides a visual representation of a Digital Identity for the end user. Information Cards contain a reference to an IP/STS that issues Security Tokens containing the Claims for that Digital Identity.
Digital Identity	A set of Claims made by one party about another party.
Claim	A piece of information about a Subject that an Identity Provider asserts about that Subject.
Subject	An individual or entity about whom claims are made by an Identity Provider.
Service Requester	Software acting on behalf of a party who wants to obtain a service through a digital network.
Relying Party (RP)	A network entity providing the desired service, and relying upon Digital Identity.
Identity Provider (IP)	A network entity providing the Digital Identity claims used by a Relying Party.
Security Token Service	A WS-Trust endpoint.
Identity Provider Security Token Service (IP/STS)	The Security Token Service run by an Identity Provider to issue tokens.
Relying Party Security Token Service (RP/STS	A Security Token Service run by a Relying Party to accept and issue tokens.
Identity Selector (IS)	A software component available to the Service Requester through which the user controls and dispatches her Digital Identities (for example, CardSpace "Geneva").
Trust Identity	A verifiable claim about a principal (for example, name, identity, key, group, privilege, capability, and so on).
Security Token	Represents a collection of claims.
Signed Security Token	A security token that is asserted and cryptographically endorsed by a specific authority (for example an X.509 certificate, a Kerberos ticket, or a self-issued Information Card).
Unsigned Security Token	A security token that is not cryptographically endorsed by a specific authority (for example, a security token backed by shared secrets such as usernames and passwords).

Term	Definition
Proof-of-Possession	Data that is used in a proof process to demonstrate the sender's knowledge of information that SHOULD only be known to the claiming sender of a security token.
Integrity	The process by which it is guaranteed that information is not modified in transit.
Confidentiality	The process by which data is protected such that only authorized actors or security token owners can view the data.
Digest	A cryptographic checksum of an octet stream.
Signature	A cryptographic binding of a proof-of-possession and a digest. (This covers both symmetric key-based and public key-based signatures; consequently, non-repudiation is not always achieved.)

You'll find most of these terms used throughout the rest of this chapter.

Using a Managed CardSpace Credential with ACS

Figure 9-10 shows the seven primary interactions between Service Requesters, Access Control solutions and Relying Parties when using managed CardSpace Information Cards issued by a third-party IP.

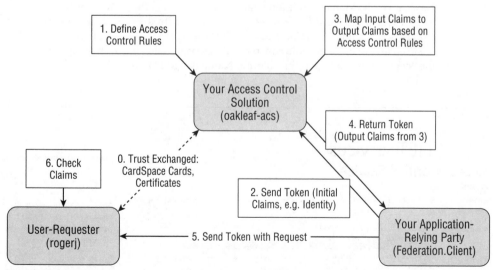

Figure 9-10: The seven primary interactions between Service Requesters, Access Control solutions and Relying Parties with managed CardSpacecredentials.

The `ipsts.FederatedIdentity.net` CardSpace Information Card you created and added to the local Information Card store in the preceding section is the same as that needed by the Azure Services Training Kit's IntroAccessControlServices HOL. This HOL includes the final version of the Federation.sln solution in the \AzureServicesKit\Labs\IntroAccessControlServices\Ex01FederatedIdentity\end folder. Federation.sln contains two simple ServiceBus projects: Client and Service; Service is the setup project.

See the earlier "Azure Services Training Kit (Optional)" section for details about downloading the Training Kit. You don't need to run the setup operations or add code snippets to the projects. The solution in the . . .\end folder has all required source code.

Setting Up FederatedIdentity.net for Use with the oakleaf-acs Solution

The following sections are based on instructions contained in the IntroAccessControlServices HOL. You can access the HOL instructions in HTML format from \AzureServicesKit\Labs\IntroAccessControl-Services\Lab.html\html\DocSet_Default.html, which contains links to HOL components in sequence. The following two sections' content is from Task 2 of "Exercise 1: Using Managed Cards with the .NET Access Control Service."

Configuring FederatedIdentity.net as a Recognized Token Issuer

Federating IPs requires your ACS solution to trust each IP you don't create yourself with the solution. Configuring a third-party IP as a recognized token issuer is one of the elements of Step 0 in Figure 9-13. Do the following to configure FederatedIdentity.net as a Recognized Issuer for the oakleaf-acs RP/STS solution's ServiceBus service:

1. Navigate to the Manage Solution page (`http://bit.ly/1wGpH`, `https://accesscontrol.ex.azure.microsoft.com/` for this example), sign in with the credential you used to create the `oakleaf-acs` solution, navigate to and click the `oakleaf-acs` solution's `Access Control Service` link to open the Solution: oakleaf-acs page., click the Manage Scopes button to open the Scopes page, and open the Solution Name list (see Figure 9-11).

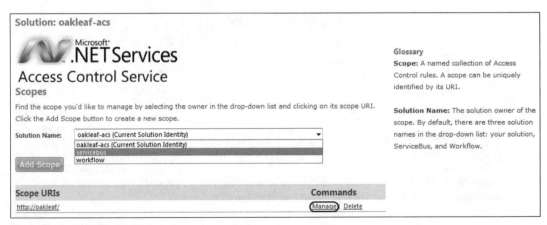

Figure 9-11: Creating the `http://oakleaf-acs.servicebus.windows.net` **scope.**

Scopes are named collections of ACS rules. Scopes make it simpler to manage rules for a particular solution or project.

2. Select servicebus in the Solution Name list to add a new `http://oakleaf-acs.servicebus.windows.net` scope for the ServiceBus project and click the `Manage` link to open the Scope Management: Rules page (see Figure 9-12).

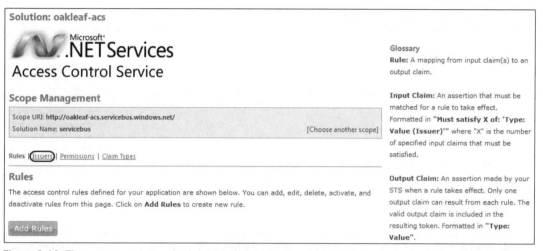

Figure 9-12: The management and rules page for the `http://oakleaf-acs.servicebus.windows.net` **scope.**

3. Click the `Issuers` link to open the Scope Management: Issuers page and click the Add Issuer button to open the Scope Management: Add Issuers page.

4. Type a friendly name, FederatedIdentityNet for this example, in the DisplayName text box, and the URI for the issuer, `https://ipsts.federatedidentity.net/MgmtConsole/`, in the Issuer URI and Certificate URL text boxes (see Figure 9-13).

    You can't add a new issuer with the same URI as an existing issuer. Thus, if you added clear text and secure versions of the `ipsts.federatedidentity.net` *IP to your Windows CardSpace store, you must select and delete the unsecure (HTTP) version from the store before continuing to step 5.*

5. Click Save to recognize the new token issuer and return to the Scope Management: Issuers page.

6. Click the `Rules` link to open the Scope Management: Rules page (see Figure 9-14).

Setting Up Claims Transformation Rules

ACS basic capability is as a claims transformation engine, which generates output claims from input clams. An *input claim* is an assertion that must be matched for a rule to take effect. The format for an input claim is "Must satisfy *n* of: 'Type: Value (Issuer)'" where *n* is the number of specified input claims that must be satisfied, Any or All. An *output claim* is an assertion made by the STS when a rule takes effect. (Only one output claim can result from each rule.) The valid output claim is included in the resulting token. Output claims are formatted as "Type: Value" pairs, such as Action: Send.

Figure 9-13: Adding the entries required to configure FederatedIdentity.net as a recognized token issuer.

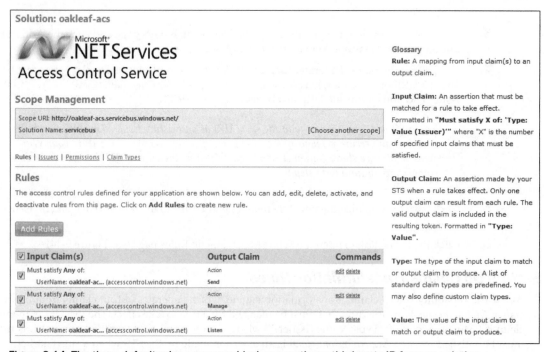

Figure 9-14: The three default rules you can add when creating a third-party IP for your solution.

In the earlier "Creating CardSpace Credentials at FederatedIdentity.net" section, you accepted the By Default, Release the Following Claims to Any Relying Party check box option, which generated the three rules shown in Figure 9-14. To understand how rules work, click the Edit link of the first input claim to display the Scope Management: Edit Rule page (see Figure 9-15).

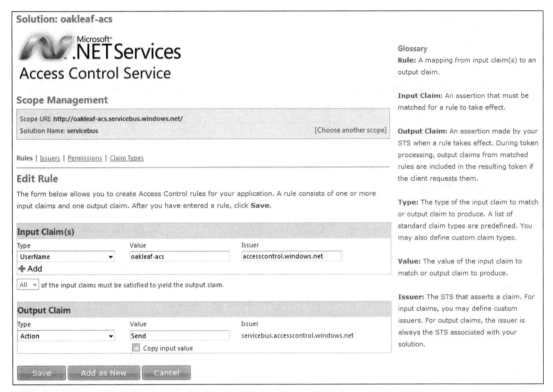

Figure 9-15: One of the three default rules for ServiceBus or Workflow scopes.

Following is an explanation of the entries for a claim transformation:

❑　The Input Claim(s): Type list lets you select one of the eight custom claim types; UserName for this example.

❑　The Input Claim(s): Value text box contains the value to be matched for the rule to take effect; oakleaf-sys for this example.

❑　The Input Claim(s): Issuer text box contains the scope name, accesscontrol.windows.net, for oakleaf-sys as the Input Claim.

❑　The Output Claim(s): Type list contains the same eight choices as the Input Claims(s): Type list, but Action is the most common selection.

❑　The Output Claim(s): Value text box for the Action type contains Send to send the Input to the Output Claim.

❑　The Input Claim(s): Issuer text box contains the scope name to which the input claim is sent; servicebus.accesscontrol.windows.net for this example.

The Group special claim type doesn't appear in Figure 9-15's list and is required by the following line in the Federation.sln solution's Client project's Program class's Main() method:

```
behavior.Credentials.FederationViaCardSpace.ClaimTypeRequirements.Add(
    new ClaimTypeRequirement("http://ipsts.federatedidentity.net/group"));
```

To add the required Group claim to the scope, you must substitute the Group claim type from FederatedIdentityNet for AccessControl's default Group claim type. To do this, click the Claim Types link to open the Claim Types list, click the delete link, and click OK to confirm the deletion.

Click Add Claim Types to open the Add Claim Type form, type **Group** in the Display Name text box, **http://ipsts.federatedidentity.net/group** in the Claim Type text box (see Figure 9-16), and click Save to save your substitution.

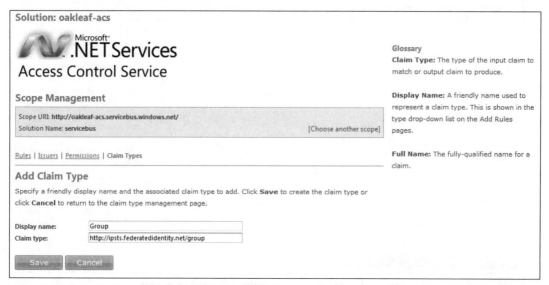

Figure 9-16: Substituting a Group custom claim in the `http://oakleaf-acs.servicebus.windows.net/` **scope.**

Click Save to save the changes and return to the Scope Management: Claim Types page.

Click the Rules link and click Add Rules to open the Add Rules form. In the Input Rules group, select Group from the Type list, type **Domain Users** in the Value text box and **FederatedIdentityNet** in the Issuer text box (see Figure 9-17). Click Save to save your changes.

Your Rules form appears as shown in Figure 9-18.

Registering with FederatedIdentity.net as a Relying Party

The ipsts.federatedidentity.net IP is an auditing STS and maintains a list of the RPs to which it's willing to send tokens. To add the new claim to the IP-STS, log in to https://ipsts.federatedidentity. net/MgmtConsole, click the Manage Relying Parties button to open the Relying Parties Policy page, click Edit/View and verify that at least the default and Group claims check boxes are marked in the Select Claims to Release list for each Policy (see Figure 9-19).

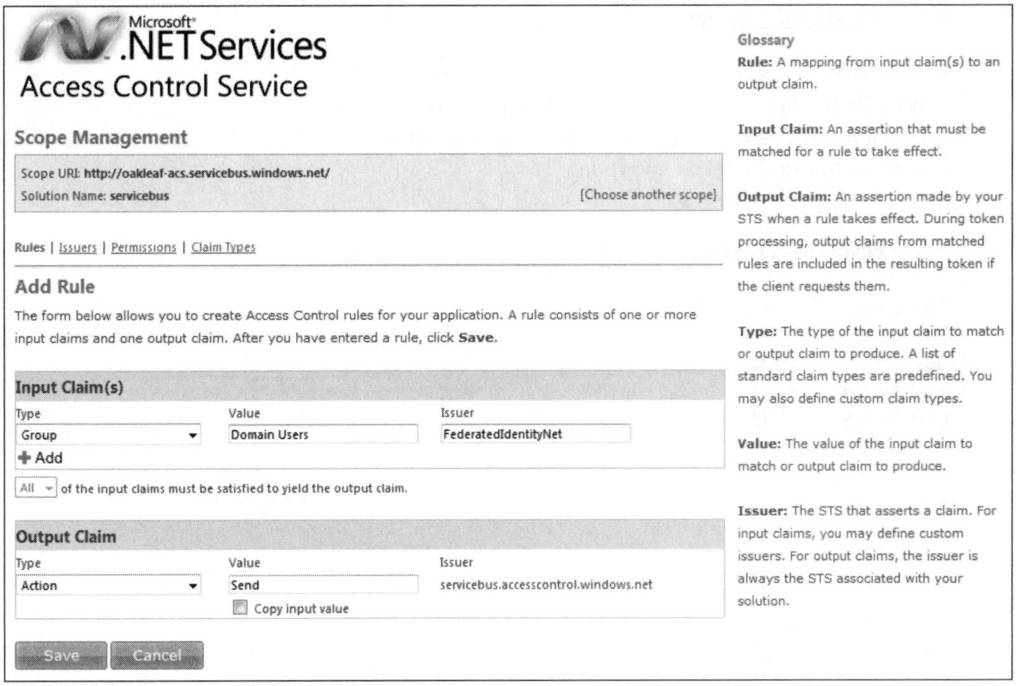

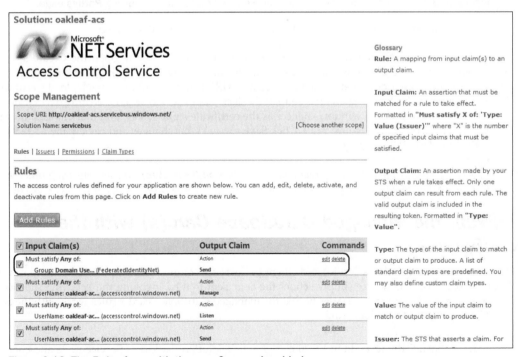

Figure 9-17: Adding the Group rule to the `http://oakleaf-acs.servicebus.windows.net/` **scope.**

Figure 9-18: The Rules form with the new Group rule added.

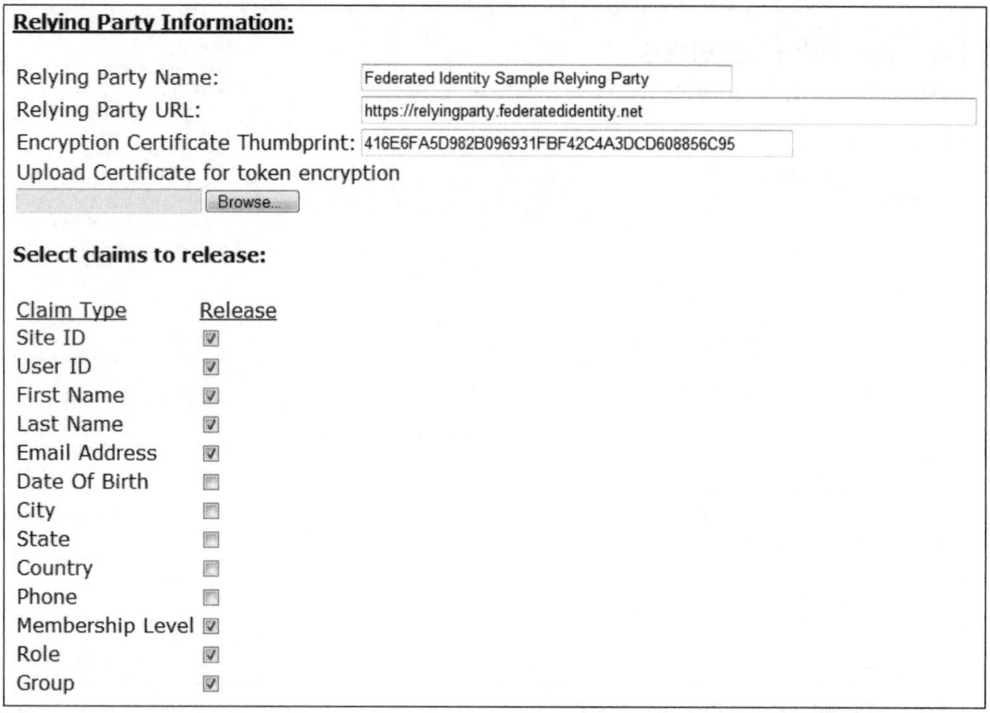

Relying Party Information:

Relying Party Name: `Federated Identity Sample Relying Party`

Relying Party URL: `https://relyingparty.federatedidentity.net`

Encryption Certificate Thumbprint: `416E6FA5D982B096931FBF42C4A3DCD608856C95`

Upload Certificate for token encryption

[Browse...]

Select claims to release:

Claim Type	Release
Site ID	☑
User ID	☑
First Name	☑
Last Name	☑
Email Address	☑
Date Of Birth	☐
City	☐
State	☐
Country	☐
Phone	☐
Membership Level	☑
Role	☑
Group	☑

Figure 9-19: Verifying the presence of required Selected Claims in the Relying Parties page.

If Group isn't marked, mark it before returning to the Relying Parties Policy page.

Return to the Relying Party Policies page and click Add a New Policy to open the Create a New Policy form, type **accesscontrol.windows.net** in the Relying Party Name text box, type **http://accesscontrol.windows.net** in the Relying Party URL text box, and mark the Upload Certificate for Token Encryption check box. Then browse to and select \AzureServicesKit\Labs\IntroAccessControl-Service\Assets\accesscontrol.windows.net.cer as the certificate's public key, and mark at least the Site ID and Group check boxes (see Figure 9-20). Click Save to save your changes and review the added policy in the Relying Party Policies page.

Saving a copy of the individual InformationCard.crd files on the local machine for importing into the CardSpace store when necessary is a good practice.

Verifying the Managed CardSpace Card(s) with the EchoService

The Federation.sln solution's Service and Client projects are command-line applications for a sample WCF EchoService. The service simply echoes the text sent to it by invoking the Echo(string text) method (OperationContract). To verify that the managed CardSpace card's rules work with the Service and Client projects, do the following:

1. Open Federation.sln in VS 2008, right-click Solution Explorer's Service node and choose Debug, Start New Instance to start the WCF service and open the console window. Type

the ACS solution name (`oakleaf-acs`, for this example), press Enter, type your solution's password, and press Enter. The Service returns the fully qualified service address and the console appears as shown in Figure 9-21.

Relying Party Information:

Relying Party Name: accesscontrol.windows.net

Relying Party URL: http://accesscontrol.windows.net

Upload Certificate for token encryption

sscontrol.windows.net.cer Browse...

Select claims to release:

Claim Type	Release
Site ID	☑
User ID	☐
First Name	☐
Last Name	☐
Email Address	☐
Date Of Birth	☐
City	☐
State	☐
Country	☐
Phone	☐
Membership Level	☐
Role	☐
Group	☑

Save   Cancel

Figure 9-20: Mark the Site ID and Group check boxes on the Create a New Policy form.

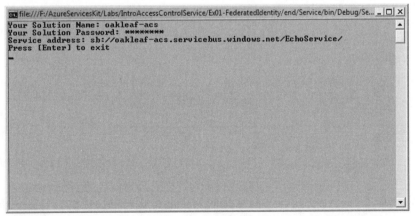

```
file:///F:/AzureServicesKit/Labs/IntroAccessControlService/Ex01-FederatedIdentity/end/Service/bin/Debug/Se... _ □ ×
Your Solution Name: oakleaf-acs
Your Solution Password: ********
Service address: sb://oakleaf-acs.servicebus.windows.net/EchoService/
Press [Enter] to exit
```

Figure 9-21: Start the WCF service by typing the solution name and password when requested.

2. Start the Client project by right-click the Client Node and choose Debug, Start New Instance. Type the solution name, and press Enter (see Figure 9-22).

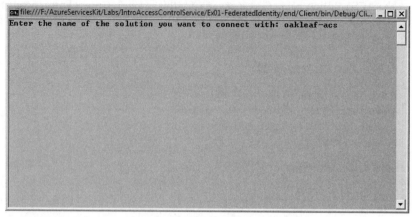

Figure 9-22: Start the WCF Client project by typing the solution name.

3. After a few seconds, Windows CardSpace's Do You Want to Send a Card to This Site dialog opens to let you select the managed card to send to the accesscontrol.windows.net site (see Figure 9-23).

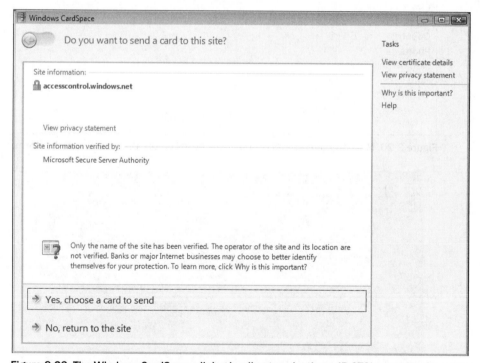

Figure 9-23: The Windows CardSpace dialog leading to selecting a IP-STS's card for the service.

4. Click the Yes, Choose a Card to Send link to open the Choose a Card to Send to: accesscontrol.windows.net dialog (see Figure 9-24).

5. Select the ipsts.federatedidentity.net card and click the Preview button to open a Do You Want to Send This Card to: accesscontrol.windows.net dialog (see Figure 9-25). Group is colored red and marked with an asterisk to indicate that the required value is missing.

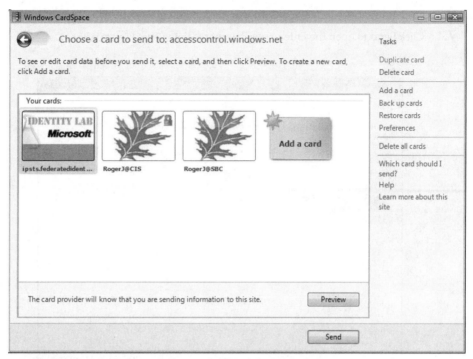

Figure 9-24: The CardSpace dialog for selecting the card to retrieve.

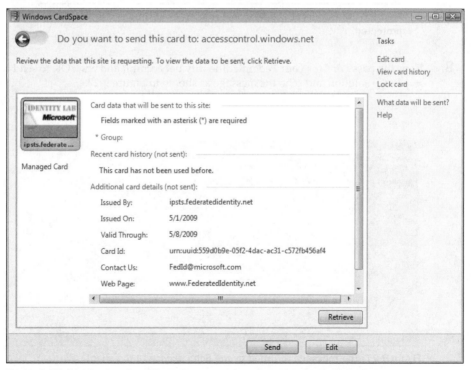

Figure 9-25: Previewing the selected managed card and its required field(s).

6. Click Retrieve to update the CardSpace credential with recently modified data.

7. Click Send to open the Enter Your Password dialog (see Figure 9-26).

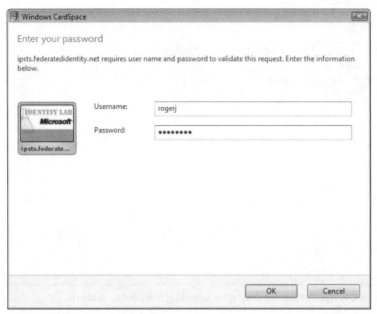

Figure 9-26: The `ipsts.federatedidentity.net` **card is password protected.**

8. Type the password for your FederatedIdentity.net account and click OK to send the token to your ACS solution and echo the message as shown in Figure 9-27.

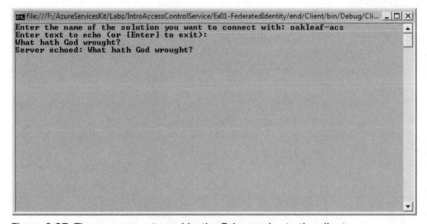

Figure 9-27: The message returned by the Echo service to the client.

Summary

Microsoft .NET Services are a set of three highly scalable services hosted in Windows Azure for .NET developers: The .NET Access Control Service, .NET Service Bus and .NET Workflow Service. ACS interacts with the .NET Service Bus to minimize the need for complex programming to secure services that users external to your organization must access. The .NET Workflow Service had been temporarily removed from the .NET Services SDK when this book was written; it will be reinstated in the Windows Azure Platform when Microsoft releases .NET 4.0 and its improved Workflow implementation.

ACS is a Security Token Service that supports claim-based user authentication and authorization by several methods, including username/password combinations, Windows Live ID, Windows CardSpace, X.509 certificates, or SAML security tokens issued by third parties. ACS's recognition of third-party STSs enables federation of authentication and authorization operations for external users. This chapter's sample project takes advantage of Microsoft's Identity Lab to emulate a commercial third-party federated STS.

The chapter began with instructions for provisioning a .NET Services solution from the Windows Azure Developer Portal as well as downloading the required .NET Services SDK and optional Azure Management Tools and Training Kit. Beta versions of Windows Identity Foundation and Active Directory Federation Service, which formerly were two of the three components of a framework that was code-named "Geneva," aren't used in this chapter's example because they weren't compatible with Windows CardSpace and Windows Azure WebRole and other applications when this book was written.

The chapter concludes with detailed instructions for creating a Windows CardSpace information card sample with help from the Identity Lab and then using the card to implement a simple ACS/Service Bus federated identity application based on the Azure Services Training Kit's IntroAccessControlServices hands-on lab. The chapter concludes with instructions for testing the Service Bus project's federated authentication and authorization features.

10

Interconnecting Services with the .NET Service Bus

Chapter 9 introduced you to the .NET Service Bus (SB) in the context of the .NET Access Control Service (ACS). This chapter concentrates on using the SB and its various messaging patterns for traversing firewalls and Network Address Translation (NAT) devices while interconnecting Windows Azure and other applications via the Internet.

> *The .NET Service Bus was formerly known as the Internet Service Bus when it was in Biz Talk Services' beta testing stage. Biz Talk Services was part of the Biz Talk Labs (http://labs.biztalk.net) incubation project and was renamed as the .NET Service Bus in 2008.*

SB enhances the industry-standard Enterprise Service Bus (ESB) pattern by integrating enterprise applications with a bidirectional messaging fabric or bus designed specifically for service integration over the Internet (see Figure 10-1).

SB provides the following features or services:

❑   Federated identity and access control with .NET Access Control Services (ACS), Windows CardSpace and, optionally, the Windows Identity Foundation (WIF) and Active Directory Federation Services (ADFS)*

❑   Consistent service and endpoint naming to simplify relaying or routing of messages

❑   Service registry to simplify discovery by NAT clients behind firewalls and other users

❑   A common messaging fabric, which offers multiple communication options, including publish/subscribe (pub/sub) or send/listen features

❑   Messaging with RESTful HTTP Request/Response, SOAP, WS-*, and Windows Communication Framework (WCF) protocols

---

*When this book was written, "Geneva" Framework Beta 2 (WIF's predecessor) wasn't compatible with the Windows Azure Fabric because of its use of the Data Protection Application Programming Interface (DPAPI). "Geneva" Framework Beta 2's Windows CardSpace "Geneva" Control Panel applet wasn't compatible with Windows Vista's and Windows 2010's default Windows CardSpace applet.

❑ Integration with service orchestration by .NET Services Workflow Service (WFS) for processing messages in accordance with a predefined business process or workflow

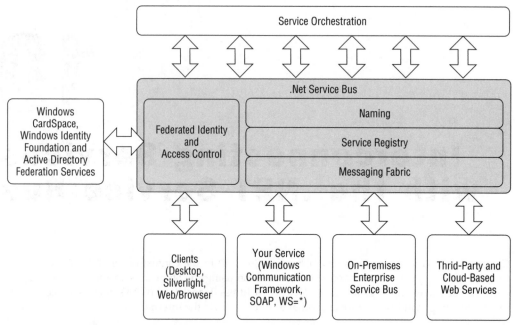

Figure 10-1: .NET Services' Service Bus extends the traditional Enterprise Service Bus pattern with federated security and access control features.

SB brokers differences of identity management, naming conventions, message formats, and communication protocols across services. After a service joins the bus, any other client or service on the bus can connect to it over the Internet, regardless of its ability to communicate with other services or clients directly.

This chapter requires familiarity with the concepts of ASP.NET web services and WCF but doesn't expect readers to have WCF development expertise.

Creating a .NET Services Solution and Installing Prerequisites

Follow Chapter 9's "Creating a .NET Services Solution" section except for the solution name; Chapter 9's Access Control Service solution name is `oakleaf-acs`; for this example, the solution name is `oakleaf-sb`.

You won't be able to use `oakleaf-sb` *as your solution name because all solution names must be globally unique.*

When you click the Service Bus button on the Manage Services page, the Microsoft .NET Service Bus Overview page displays an Endpoint Quick Reference section with examples of typical SB endpoint URIs for the solution name you chose (see Figure 10-2).

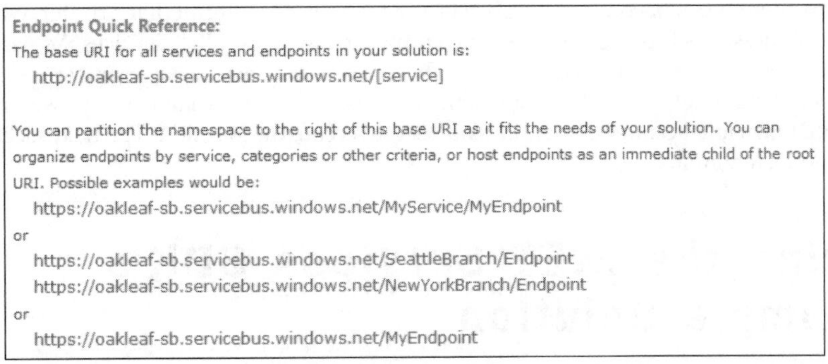

Endpoint Quick Reference:

The base URI for all services and endpoints in your solution is:

http://oakleaf-sb.servicebus.windows.net/[service]

You can partition the namespace to the right of this base URI as it fits the needs of your solution. You can organize endpoints by service, categories or other criteria, or host endpoints as an immediate child of the root URI. Possible examples would be:

https://oakleaf-sb.servicebus.windows.net/MyService/MyEndpoint

or

https://oakleaf-sb.servicebus.windows.net/SeattleBranch/Endpoint
https://oakleaf-sb.servicebus.windows.net/NewYorkBranch/Endpoint

or

https://oakleaf-sb.servicebus.windows.net/MyEndpoint

Figure 10-2: The Microsoft .NET Service Bus Overview page's Endpoint Quick Reference section provides endpoint URI examples.

The `oakleaf-sb` solution owns the DNS root namespaces `sb://oakleaf-sb.servicebus.windows.net` for traditional SOAP (TCP/IP) transport and `http[s]://oakleaf-sb.servicebus.windows.net` for the RESTful HTTP API. You're free to extend the root URI with a hierarchy of your choosing, as illustrated by the examples in Figure 10-2.

If you haven't done so already, you must install the current .NET Services SDK CTP as described in Chapter 9's "Installing the .NET Services SDK and Other Tools" section.

Relaying Messages with SB

The basic SB messaging fabric supplies a centralized, load-balanced relay service, which supports multiple transport protocols and web-service standards, specifically REST, SOAP, and WS-*. The relay service provides several connectivity options and can help negotiate direct peer-to-peer connections when feasible.

SB is designed to be platform agnostic, but is optimized for .NET 3.5 and WCF for usability and performance. SB, ACS, and WFS provide support for SOAP and REST interfaces, so it's possible for other SOAP or REST-compliant programming environments to integrate with these .NET Services. The .NET Services SDK, introduced in Chapter 9, provides support for C# and VB. Java and Ruby SDKs also support these two popular programming languages. The .NET Services SDK sets up WCF relay bindings and their channel components, and integrates them with SB automatically.

SB's relay bindings provide service endpoints with secure, Internet-accessible addresses regardless of the actual network location of the machine hosting the service, such as the following location types:

❑   Computers connecting through the Network Address Translation (NAT) service whose primary IP (v4) address is in a private range that's not normally Internet addressable, such as 10.*x.x.x*, 192.168.*x.x*, or 172.16.*x.x*-172.31.*x.x*

❑   Computers residing behind one or more firewalls that ordinarily prevent incoming connections

❑   Computers without permanently assigned IP addresses under publically registered domain names

To overcome these types of constraints, SB acts as a web service intermediary router, which doesn't affect the content of messages it passes between the endpoints. SB uses .NET Services Access Control Service (ACS) to authenticate server and client users. The `Microsoft.ServiceBus` namespace includes a set of ACS client credential helpers that automatically acquire default username and password security tokens from the .NET Services account credential you used to create the solution. The next section describes how to enable these credentials.

Analyzing the .NET Services SDK's EchoSample Solution

The Microsoft .NET Services SDK (March 2009 CTP) includes several sample projects under the \Program Files\Microsoft .NET Services SDK ... \Samples\ServiceBus folder. The \GettingStarted folder contains an Echo folder with subfolders for C# and VB versions of an Echo service. The Echo service is a simple WCF solution with Server and Client console projects in an EchoSample.sln solution. The service accepts a string from the client and echoes it back (see Figure 10-3).

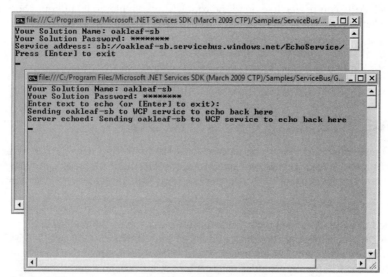

Figure 10-3: This simple web service (upper) and client (lower) console authenticate their user with the SB solution name and password, and then echo a string between the client and service.

Inspecting the Service Project's EchoContract.cs, EchoService.cs, and Program.cs Files

The EchoService.sln's Service C# project has a reference to \Program Files\Microsoft .NET Services SDK (March 2009 CTP)\Assemblies\Microsoft.ServiceBus.dll and contains three class files: EchoContract.cs, EchoService.cs, and Program.cs. Listing 10-1 shows the contents of EchoContract.cs, which defines IEchoContract and IEchoChannel interfaces.

Listing 10-1: The content of the Service\EchoContract.cs class file

```
namespace Microsoft.ServiceBus.Samples
{
    using System;
    using System.ServiceModel;

    [ServiceContract(Name = "IEchoContract",
        Namespace = "http://samples.microsoft.com/ServiceModel/Relay/")]
        public interface IEchoContract
    {
        [OperationContract]
        string Echo(string text);
    }

    public interface IEchoChannel : IEchoContract, IClientChannel { }
}
```

The EchoContract.cs file is identical for the Service and Client projects.

Listing 10-2 defines the `EchoService` WCF service, which inherits `IEchoContract` and specifies the action performed, returning the `text` string to the client.

Listing 10-2: The content of the Service\EchoService.cs class file

```
namespace Microsoft.ServiceBus.Samples
{
    using System;
    using System.ServiceModel;

    [ServiceBehavior(Name = "EchoService",
        Namespace = "http://samples.microsoft.com/ServiceModel/Relay/")]
    class EchoService : IEchoContract
    {
        public string Echo(string text)
        {
            Console.WriteLine("Echoing: {0}", text);
            return text;
        }
    }
}
```

The Service project's App.config file is identical to that for a WCF Service Application project except for the `netTcpRelayBinding` attribute value that specifies the relay service and is highlighted in Listing 10-3.

Listing 10-3: The contents of the Service\App.config file; the attribute value that specifies the RelayService is highlighted

```
<?xml version="1.0" encoding="utf-8" ?>
<configuration>
  <system.serviceModel>
    <services>
```

Continued

277

Listing 10-3: The contents of the Service\App.config file; the attribute value that specifies the RelayService is highlighted *(continued)*

```
        <!-- Application Service -->
        <service name="Microsoft.ServiceBus.Samples.EchoService">
          <endpoint contract="Microsoft.ServiceBus.Samples.IEchoContract"
                    binding="netTcpRelayBinding" />
        </service>
      </services>
    </system.serviceModel>
  </configuration>
```

According to the .NET Services Library documentation, `Microsoft.ServiceBus.NetTcpRelayBinding` generates a run-time communication stack by default, which uses transport security, TCP for message delivery, and a binary message encoding. This binding is the appropriate .NET Services system-provided choice for communicating over an Intranet.

The Client project's App.config file is identical to that of the Server project except for substitution of `<client>` for `<services>`, `Endpoint` for `Service`, and the addition of a `name="RelayEndpoint"` attribute value pair, as highlighted in Listing 10-4.

Listing 10-4: The contents of the Client\App.config file with differences from the Service\App.config file highlighted

```
<?xml version="1.0" encoding="utf-8" ?>
<configuration>
  <system.serviceModel>
    <client>
      <!-- Application Endpoint -->
      <endpoint name="RelayEndpoint"
                contract="Microsoft.ServiceBus.Samples.IEchoContract"
                binding="netTcpRelayBinding"/>
    </client>
  </system.serviceModel>
</configuration>
```

Verifying the Service User's Credentials with Code in Program.cs

The Program.cs file contains code that requests the user to enter at the command prompt the solution name and the password for the .NET Services account that hosts the solution. When you run the solution with F5, the Service project's `Main()` method shown in Listing 10-5 requests the user to supply the solution name and account password, requests the Azure Services Portal's certificate for the user account under which the solution runs, and then verifies the password supplied. If the solution name is found and the password matches, the service opens.

Listing 10-5: Code to obtain and verify the Service project's SolutionName and Password and start the service

```
namespace Microsoft.ServiceBus.Samples
{
    using System;
    using System.ServiceModel;
    using System.ServiceModel.Description;
    using Microsoft.ServiceBus;
    using Microsoft.ServiceBus.Description;
    using System.Text;

    class Program
    {
        static void Main(string[] args)
        {
            // Determine the system connectivity mode based on the command line
            // arguments: -http, -tcp or -auto   (defaults to auto)
            ServiceBusEnvironment.SystemConnectivity.Mode =
                GetConnectivityMode(args);

    Console.Write("Your Solution Name: ");
            string solutionName = Console.ReadLine();
            Console.Write("Your Solution Password: ");
            string solutionPassword = ReadPassword();

            // create a well-formed endpoint address in the solution's
            //      namespace
            Uri address = ServiceBusEnvironment.CreateServiceUri("sb",
                solutionName, "EchoService");

            // create the credentials object for the endpoint
            TransportClientEndpointBehavior
                userNamePasswordServiceBusCredential =
                new TransportClientEndpointBehavior();
            userNamePasswordServiceBusCredential.CredentialType =
                TransportClientCredentialType.UserNamePassword;
            userNamePasswordServiceBusCredential.Credentials.UserName.
                UserName =                    solutionName;
            userNamePasswordServiceBusCredential.Credentials.
                UserName.Password =                    solutionPassword;

            // create the service host reading the configuration
            ServiceHost host =
                new ServiceHost(typeof(EchoService), address);

            // add the Service Bus credentials to all endpoints
            //      specified in config
            foreach (ServiceEndpoint endpoint in
```

Continued

279

```
                        host.Description.Endpoints)
            {
                    endpoint.Behaviors.
                        Add(userNamePasswordServiceBusCredential);
            }

            // open the service
            host.Open();

            Console.WriteLine("Service address: " + address);
            Console.WriteLine("Press [Enter] to exit");
            Console.ReadLine();

            // close the service
            host.Close();
        }
    }
}
```

The SDK Utilities region at the end of the file contains the code for the GetConnectivityMode() method that sets the SystemConnectivity.Mode property to one of the following ConnectivityMode enumeration values:

❑ ConnectivityMode.Tcp is the default and causes all one-way and event listeners to create independent connections through port 808 (unsecured) or 828 (secured by SSL/TLS).

❑ ConnectivityMode.Http specifies an alternate HTTP polling mode through outbound-only port 80 (unsecured) or port 443 (secure by SSL/TLS).

❑ ConnectivityMode.AutoDetect probes the connections to auto-detect the mode to use; TCP is the preferred mode.

In the absence of an /auto, -auto, /tcp, or -tcp command-line argument, the GetConnectivityMode() method returns ConnectivityMode.AutoDetect.

Invoking the ServiceBusEnvironment.CreateServiceUri() method with the arguments shown in Listing 10-5 generates the sb://oakleaf-sb.servicebus.windows.net/EchoService URI as the service endpoint location, as shown in Figure 10-3's upper console window.

Invoking the host.Open() method POSTs a request to ACS http:servicebus.accesscontrol.windows.net/sts/username_for_certificate, which is one of the six solution endpoints. It takes a second or two to process the request, which has a payload of about 9KB of a mostly encrypted SOAP envelope; the response is a mostly encrypted SOAP response envelope that's nearly 20KB in size. Message encryption uses the WS-Security standard, rather than SSL/TLS transport encryption, to maintain data confidentiality. Figure 10-4 shows the SOAP response envelope open in IE8.

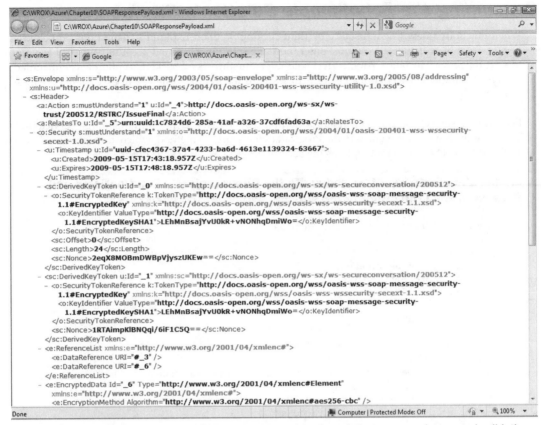

Figure 10-4: IE8 displaying a sample SOAP response envelope for solution name and password validation.

The \WROX\Azure\Chapter10 folder contains a pair of typical SOAP request and response headers (*.txt) and message payload (*.xml) for validating the solution name and account password. The complexity of the SOAP messages required to enable the wss-soap-message-security (also known as, ws-security), ws-secureconversation, and ws-trust standards led to widespread adoption of simpler RESTful Web services. However, ws-* standards are essential for establishing enterprise-level security for cloud computing environments and federation of trust across domains.

If you type an invalid `solutionName`, you receive an "EndpointNotFoundException; No DNS entries exist for host oakleaf-sx.servicebus.windows.net" message when invoking the `host.Open()` method. An incorrect `solutionPassword` throws a "Fault exception was unhandled; authN failed: 'oakleaf-sb' of PasswordCredential (#a5566db9-4a5a-52f7-edea-64a000a3cb08)" or similar exception.

The variable name `solutionPassword` is somewhat misleading because the password required is that for the WLID you used to sign in to the .NET Services/SQL Services Portal to add the SB solution. Similarly, `userNamePassword` is a misnomer because the name element is the solution name.

Consuming the EchoSample Solution's Service

When you start a new Client instance by right-clicking Solution Explorer's Client node and choosing Debug, Start New Instance, you must enter the same solution name and account password as you did to start the Service instance. An incorrect solution name throws a "SocketException was unhandled; No such host is known" exception; an incorrect password throws the same "Fault exception ... " message as the Service.

EchoSample.sln's Client project contains a Contract.cs file that's identical to that of the Service project. There are only minor differences in the Program.cs file's `Main()` method, which are highlighted in Listing 10-6. An `IEchoChannel` object replaces the Service project's `ServiceHost` object.

Listing 10-6: Code to obtain and verify the Client project's SolutionName and Password, send the string to the service, and await the echoed text

```
namespace Microsoft.ServiceBus.Samples
{
    using System;
    using System.ServiceModel;
    using Microsoft.ServiceBus;
    using System.Text;

    class Program
    {
        static void Main(string[] args)
        {
            // Determine the system connectivity mode based on the
            // arguments: -http, -tcp or -auto   (defaults to auto)
            ServiceBusEnvironment.SystemConnectivity.Mode =
                GetConnectivityMode(args);

            Console.Write("Your Solution Name: ");
            string solutionName = Console.ReadLine();
            Console.Write("Your Solution Password: ");
            string solutionPassword = ReadPassword();

            // create the service URI based on the solution name
            Uri serviceUri =
                ServiceBusEnvironment.CreateServiceUri("sb",
                solutionName, "EchoService");

            // create the credentials object for the endpoint
            TransportClientEndpointBehavior
                userNamePasswordServiceBusCredential =
                new TransportClientEndpointBehavior();
            userNamePasswordServiceBusCredential.CredentialType =
                TransportClientCredentialType.UserNamePassword;
            userNamePasswordServiceBusCredential.Credentials.
                UserName.UserName = solutionName;
            userNamePasswordServiceBusCredential.Credentials.
                UserName.Password = solutionPassword;
```

```
// create the channel factory loading the configuration
ChannelFactory<IEchoChannel> channelFactory =
    new ChannelFactory<IEchoChannel>("RelayEndpoint",
    new EndpointAddress(serviceUri));

// apply the Service Bus credentials
            channelFactory.Endpoint.Behaviors.
    Add(userNamePasswordServiceBusCredential);

// create and open the client channel
```

```
IEchoChannel channel = channelFactory.CreateChannel();
channel.Open();

Console.WriteLine("Enter text to echo (or [Enter] to
    exit):");
string input = Console.ReadLine();
while (input != String.Empty)
{
    try
    {
        Console.WriteLine("Server echoed: {0}",
            channel.Echo(input));
    }
    catch (Exception e)
    {
        Console.WriteLine("Error: " + e.Message);
    }
    input = Console.ReadLine();
}

channel.Close();
channelFactory.Close();
```

```
        }
    }
}
```

Making Services Publicly Discoverable

Each solution generates an Atom 1.0 channel feed with an item group for each listening (running) service that's been added to the Service Bus Registry. IE8 detects the feed at the solution's URI, http[s]://oakleaf-sb.servicebus.windows.net for this example. .NET Services CTPs earlier than March 2009 automatically registered all services for the solution. Subsequent CTPs require code to add ServiceRegistrySettings.DiscoveryMode = DiscoveryType.Public and, optionally, ServiceRegistrySettings.DisplayName = "FriendlyName", to each endpoint, as shown in Listing 10-7.

Listing 10-7: Code to add the solution to the Service Bus Registry and display DiscoveryMode and DisplayName for each service in the solution's Atom feed

```
ServiceRegistrySettings settings = new ServiceRegistrySettings();
settings.DiscoveryMode = DiscoveryType.Public;
settings.DisplayName = "OakLeaf-ServiceBus";

// Add the Service Bus credentials to all endpoints specified in the
//     configuration
foreach (ServiceEndpoint endpoint in host.Description.Endpoints)
{
    endpoint.Behaviors.Add(userNamePasswordServiceBusCredential);
    endpoint.Behaviors.Add(settings);
}
```

Figure 10-5 shows IE8 detecting the Atom feed for the EchoService example with the code of Listing 10-7 added and the service listening.

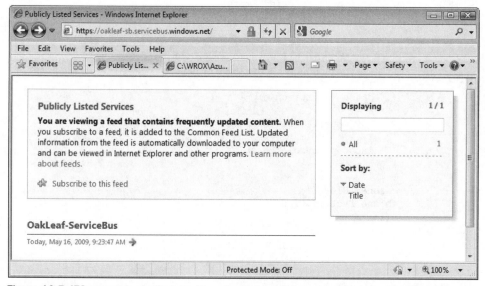

Figure 10-5: IE8 responds similarly to Atom feeds from SB services, blogs, and other web content.

If you don't add a `ServiceRegistrySettings.DisplayName` *value,* items *are named for the first level of the service name hierarchy;* EchoService *for this example.*

Figure 10-6 shows IE8 displaying the content of a file, oakleaf-sb.servicebus.windows.net.xml, created by saving the Atom feed document's with IE8's Page, View Source command.

The \WROX\Azure\Chapter10 folder contains a NetTcpRelaySample folder with the EchoSample solution modified to be publicly discoverable.

Figure 10-6: The Atom feed document content for the publicly discoverable `oakleaf-sb` solution.

Using the Configuration File to Specify WSHttpRelayBinding

.NET Services adds several new HTTP bindings that the relay service supports: `WebHttpRelayBinding`, `BasicHttpRelayBinding`, `WSHttpRelayBinding`, and `WS2007HttpRelayBinding`. These bindings enable clients that don't use WCF to connect to the SB and underlying services. `WebHttpRelayBinding` is based on a simple RESTful HTTP implementation for compatibility with the widest range of client platforms and web service client capabilities. `BasicHttpRelayBinding` is a very simple SOAP implementation with limited security features. `WSHttpRelayBinding` requires clients to support the same suite of WS-* protocols that the endpoint uses. `WS2007HttpRelayBinding` supports updated versions of the Security, ReliableSession, and TransactionFlow binding elements, as well as SOAP 1.2 messaging.

As you would expect, HTTP relay bindings carry more processing overhead than their TCP counterparts.

The \Program Files\Microsoft .NET Services SDK ... \Samples\ServiceBus\ExploringFeatures \Bindings\WSHttp\Simple\CS35 folder contains a WSHttpRelayEchoSample.sln that demonstrates several SB features:

❑ Substituting the `WSHttpRelayBinding` for the `NetTcpRelayBinding` to avoid the need to open client TCP port 808 or 828 (secure) for connecting to the service

❑ Using the configuration file (App.config for this example) to specify endpoint behaviors, and other endpoint properties

❑ Refactoring the service name from `EchoService` to `EchoHttpService` to prevent conflicts with `EchoService` names from other samples running simultaneously

❑ Specifying the client credential type and substituting a CardSpace information card for the `UserNamePassword` in the configuration file

The Service and Client projects' EchoContract.cs files, as well as the Service project's Service.cs file are identical to those of the preceding EchoService example, with the exception of the service name. The Service project's App.config file, shown in Listing 10-8, contains the principal difference between two solutions with the additions highlighted.

Listing 10-8: The EchoHttpService's Service project moves specification of credentials and binding type from the Project.cs file's `Main()` method to the App.config file

```xml
<?xml version="1.0" encoding="utf-8" ?>
<configuration>
  <system.serviceModel>


    <behaviors>
      <endpointBehaviors>
        <behavior name="cardSpaceClientCredentials">
          <transportClientEndpointBehavior credentialType="CardSpace" />
        </behavior>
      </endpointBehaviors>
    </behaviors>

    <bindings>
      <!-- Application Binding -->
      <wsHttpRelayBinding>
        <binding name="default">
          <security mode="None"/>
        </binding>
      </wsHttpRelayBinding>
    </bindings>


    <services>
      <!-- Application Service -->
      <service name="Microsoft.ServiceBus.Samples.EchoHttpService">
        <endpoint name="RelayEndpoint"
                  contract="Microsoft.ServiceBus.Samples.IEchoContract"
                  binding="wsHttpRelayBinding"
```

```
                        bindingConfiguration="default"
                        behaviorConfiguration="cardSpaceClientCredentials"
                        address="" />

     </service>
    </services>

   </system.serviceModel>
  </configuration>
```

The following table describes valid values of the `credentialType` attribute supplied by the `TransportClientCredentialType` enum as provided by the `Microsoft.ServiceBus` class library documentation:

Member name	Description
AutomaticRenewal	A self-issued Windows CardSpace information card that is registered with the Access Control service through the Access Control portal's account management page. This option requires no further settings on the `Credentials` property. The difference between the `CardSpace` and `AutomaticRenewal` credentials is that a credential configured with this type will cause the access token to be automatically renewed as needed.
CardSpace	A self-issued Windows CardSpace information card that is registered with the Access Control service through the Access Control portal's account management page. This option requires no further settings on the `Credentials` property.
FederationViaCardSpace	A managed Windows CardSpace information card issued by and backed by an identity provider that is trusted by the Access Control service.
Unauthenticated	No client credential provided. This option avoids acquiring and sending a token altogether and is required for all clients that are not required to authenticate per their service binding's policy.
UserNamePassword	The username/password credential for the Service Bus solution registered with the Access Control service. The credential is set on the nested `UserName.UserName` and `UserName.Password` properties of the `Credentials` property.
X509Certificate	An X.509 certificate for the Service Bus solution that has been registered with the Access Control service through the Access Control portal's account management page. The certificate (which must contain a private key) is specified on the nested `ClientCertificate` property of the `Credentials` property.

Associating a Self-Issued Card Space Identity Card with the Current Solution

The <behaviors> group requires the client to have a self-issued CardSpace credential associated with the oakleaf-sb solution. For this example, the ipsts.federatedidentity.net (FedId) information cards you created in Chapter 9 aren't valid as the default credential for the oakleaf-sb solution, but one of them will be selected as the default card for the solution. To enable establishing a new self-issued card as the default, open Control Panel's Windows CardSpace applet (see Figure 10-7).

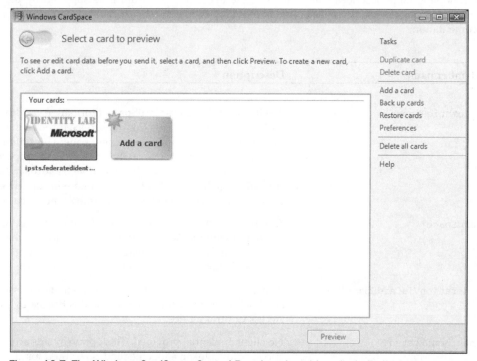

Figure 10-7: The Windows CardSpace Control Panel applet with a single FedId card present.

To create a new self-issued CardSpace credential, click the Add a Card button to open the Add a Card dialog (see Figure 10-8), and click the Create a Personal Card button to open the Edit a New Card dialog and type a name for the card; oakleaf_sb for this example (see Figure 10-9).

Card names can only contain letters ([a–z A–Z]), digits ([0–9]), and underscore (_) and must begin with letters or an underscore.

Click the Save button to save your changes and close the applet.

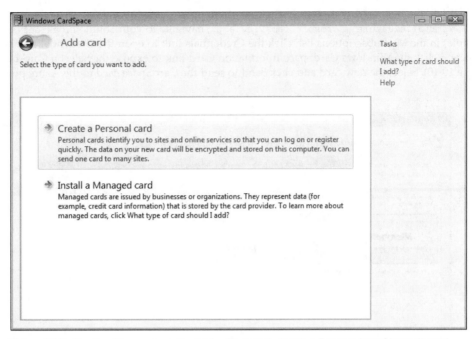

Figure 10-8: The CardSpace applet's Add a Card dialog with a Personal (self-issued) card selected.

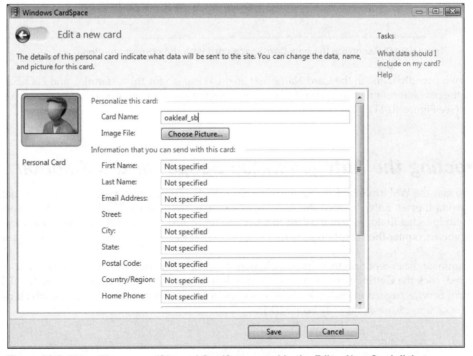

Figure 10-9: Name the new self-issued CardSpace card in the Edit a New Card dialog.

To associate the new card with your current solution, open the Solution: *Your Solution* page at `http://portal.ex.azure.microsoft.com/View.aspx`, navigate to your solution (`oakleaf-sb` for this example) in the My Subscriptions list, click the Credentials link to open the Credential Management page, and click the Windows CardSpace Information Card link to expose the Select a Card button (see Figure 10-10). Select the new card and click Send to send the CardSpace card to the Azure portal.

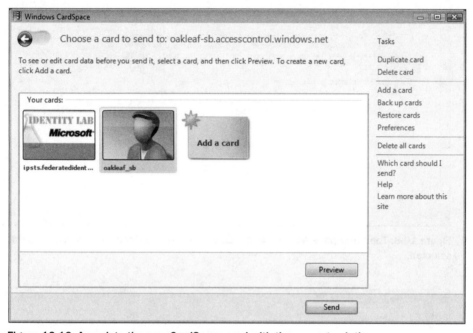

Figure 10-10: Associate the new CardSpace card with the current solution.

Assign a friendly name in the Card Name text box (oakleaf_sb for this example), and click Save to associate the new information card with the currently selected solution and open the Credential Management Page (see Figure 10-11).

Correcting the Autogenerated Scope for the Solution

If you run the WSHttpRelayEchoSample.sln solution's Service project, type your solution name at the prompt, press Enter to open the Windows CardSpace's Choose a Card to Send to: accesscontrol.windows.net dialog, select the card to use (see Figure 10-12), and click Send to authenticate the service, you encounter the exception shown in Figure 10-13 at the `Main()` method's `host.Open()` instruction.

To eliminate the exception, close the console window and, with your version of the `oakleaf-sb` solution selected, click the Getting Started: Access Control link to open the Manage the Microsoft .NET Access Control Service page, and click the Manage Scopes button to open the Scopes page, which displays `http://echoservice` as the only Scope URI.

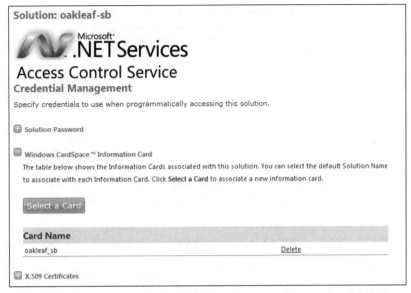

Figure 10-11: Confirm that the selected CardSpace card is associated with the current solution.

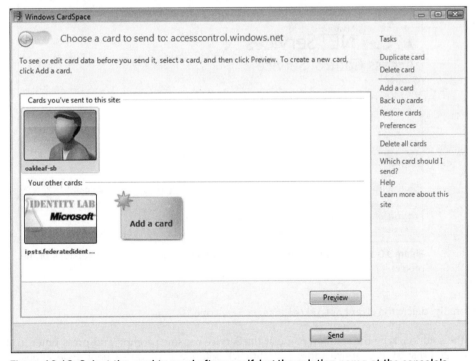

Figure 10-12: Select the card to send after specifying the solution name at the console's prompt.

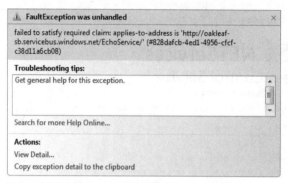

Figure 10-13: The autogenerated `http://echoservice` **scope URI isn't valid for the** `oakleaf-sb` **solution.**

Click Add Scope to open the Add Scope page, type the service address URI requested in Figure 10-12 (`http://oakleaf-sb.servicebus.windows.net/EchoService/`) in the Scope URI text box and click Save. To accommodate the refactored version in the ... \Chapter 10 folder, repeat this process with `http://oakleaf-sb.servicebus.windows.net/EchoHttpService/` as the scope, as shown in Figure 10-14.

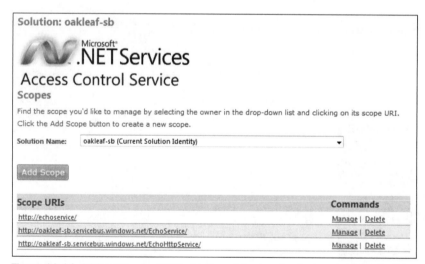

Figure 10-14: Add well-formed URIs for the original and refactored versions of the project.

Optionally, delete the errant `http://echoservice/` scope.

Run the solution, type the solution name at the Service console prompt, and press Enter to start the service and display the service address. Right-click Solution Explorer's Client node, choose Debug, Start a New Instance, type some text to echo, press Enter, and select and send the CardSpace card again.

Specifying Binding Details in App.config

The `<bindings>` group and the emphasized attribute/value pairs in the `<endpoint>` element's `binding` attribute shown earlier in Listing 10-8 specify the binding element used to specify an HTTP transport for transmitting messages on the Service Bus relay.

The \WROX\Azure\Chapter10\WSHttpRelaySample folder includes RawHTTPClientRequestFile.txt and RawHTTPClientResponseFile.txt files captured by Fiddler2. Notice that the `<body>` group at the end of both files contains the text you typed in clear text because `<security mode="None"/>` is specified. The following table describes members of the `SecurityMode` enum:

SecurityMode Member Name	Description
None	Security is disabled.
Transport	Security is provided using a secure transport (for example, HTTPS).
Message	Security is provided using SOAP message security.
TransportWithMessageCredential	A secure transport (for example, HTTPS) provides integrity, confidentiality, and authentication while SOAP message security provides client authentication.

Listing 10-9 shows the EchoHttpService's `Main()` method with behavior and binding settings specified in App.config.

Listing 10-9: The EchoHttpService's `Main()` method with behavior and binding settings specified in App.config

```
namespace Microsoft.ServiceBus.Samples
{
    using System;
    using System.ServiceModel;
    using System.ServiceModel.Description;
    using Microsoft.ServiceBus;
    using Microsoft.ServiceBus.Description;

    class Program
    {
        static void Main(string[] args)
        {
            string serviceBusSolutionName =
                GetServiceBusSolutionName();

            Uri address =
                ServiceBusEnvironment.CreateServiceUri("http",
                serviceBusSolutionName, "EchoHttpService");
```

Continued

Listing 10-9: The EchoHttpService's `Main()` method with behavior and binding settings specified in App.config (continued)

```
ServiceHost host =
    new ServiceHost(typeof(EchoService), address);
host.Open();

Console.WriteLine("Service address: " + address);
Console.WriteLine("Press [Enter] to exit");
Console.ReadLine();

host.Close();
        }
    }
}
```

Summary

The .NET Service Bus is an implementation of the Enterprise Service Bus (ESB) model. SB enhances connectivity between WCF clients, as well as clients running on other platforms, and WCF services running the in Windows Azure Fabric. SB enables client and service communication to traverse firewalls and Network Address Translation (NAT) devices that otherwise would not be possible. SB acts as a web service intermediary router, which doesn't affect the content of messages it passes between the endpoints. SB uses .NET Services Access Control Service (ACS) to authenticate server and client users. You can create as many .NET Service accounts (called *solutions*) as you want with an Azure CTP. A CTP account gives you access to SB, as well as ACS, Workflow, and SQL Azure Database.

This chapter dives deeply into two of the many sample SB applications from the .NET Services SDK (March 2009 CTP). The first, EchoService.sln in the \Program Files\Microsoft .NET Services SDK ... \Samples\ServiceBus\GettingStarted\Echo\CS35 folder, demonstrates a message relay service between a WCF client and service that uses username/password security for a TCP transport. The simple service does nothing more than echo text typed in a client console window back to the client. A modified version of the EchoService.sln in the \WROX\Azure\Chapter10\NetTcpRelay folder demonstrates how to make services publicly discoverable with Item entries of an Atom feed. Code in the Service and Client projects' Program.cs file handles most configuration chores.

The second example, WSHttpRelayEchoSample.sln in the \Program Files\Microsoft .NET Services SDK ... \Samples\ServiceBus\ExploringFeatures\Bindings\WSHttp\Simple\CS35 folder, substitutes the WSHttpRelayBinding for TcpRelayBinding. WSHttpRelayBinding enables clients that don't support WCF or are on networks that don't allow inbound TCP traffic to consume WCF services. This sample also demonstrates use of self-issued CardSpace information cards for service and client authentication. The Service and Client projects' App.config file specifies configuration of bindings and services.

11

Exploring .NET Service Bus Queues and Routers

Microsoft .NET Services and the .NET Service Bus deliver the following three additional components that this book hasn't covered yet:

❑ *.NET Workflow Service* (WFS) provide a highly scalable and reliable cloud-based host for Windows Workflow Foundation (WF) running as .NET code in the Azure Fabric.

❑ *Service Bus Queues* (SBQs) provide a durable first-in, first-out (FIFO) data structure to which senders can add and from which listeners can retrieve messages.

❑ *Service Bus Routers* (SBRs) handle delivery of durable messages to all (multicast) or individual subscribers. Listeners, including queues, can subscribe to these messages.

The .NET Services SDK (March 2009 CTP) introduced SBQs and SBRs.

The .NET Services Team announced on June 12, 2008 that they "would hold off further releases of the Workflow Service until after .NET Framework 4 ships" to enable building the Workflow Service on .NET Framework 4's workflow engine. The team took down Windows Azure's Workflow Service runtime in July 2008 and removed Workflow Service elements from the SDK for .NET Services July 2009 CTP. An updated electronic version of this chapter that includes a sample Workflow Service project for VS 2010 will be posted to the Wrox Website for this book as soon as possible after the team ships the first CTP of Workflow Services for .NET 4.0.

This chapter describes basic features and implementations of SBQ and SBR components and provides simple C# demonstration projects based on the .NET Services SDK's sample solutions. All examples use .NET Access Control Services (ACS) and Service Bus (SB) techniques you learned in Chapters 9 and 10.

You can learn more about the basics of WF at the MSDN .NET Framework Developer's landing page for WF (http://bit.ly/SGfsG, http://msdn.microsoft.com/en-us/netframework/aa663328.aspx). *"A Developer's Guide to the Microsoft .NET Service Bus" whitepaper describes SBQs and SBRs, which the .NET Services SDK (March 2009 CTP) introduced* (http://bit.ly/3o9Bmz).

Persisting Messages in Service Bus Queues

The primary application for the SB is acting as a transient relay between senders and active listeners. If the listener isn't active when the sender issues a message, the message is lost. Message loss also occurs if the sender issues messages faster than the listener can process them. To overcome these issues, the .NET Services team introduced SB Queues and SB Routers in the .NET Services SDK's March 2009 CTP. SBQs and SBRs are discoverable, persisted SB objects that are independent of listeners' lifetimes. Figure 11-1 illustrates an SBQ's components and their relationships; later sections describe SBRs, which can also use SBQs.

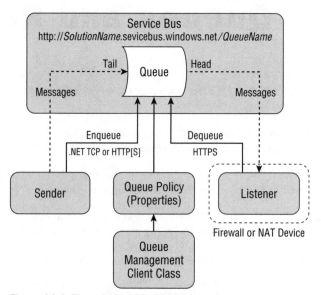

Figure 11-1: The relationship of SBQ components.

This chapter uses the terms listener and receiver interchangeably.

Creating SBQs with the QueueManagementClient Class

Like the other .NET Services, the basic API is REST with HTTP GET and POST methods and Atom-Pub extensions to define SBQs. The .NET Services SDK's Microsoft.ServiceBus namespace (Microsoft.ServiceBus.dll) provides the wrapper classes described in the following table to simplify creating SBQs with a specific set of policies and accessing queues with clients.

Queue Class	Description
QueueClient	Provides client access to an SBQ
QueuePolicy	Specifies the set of rules and constraints for an SBQ
QueueManagementClient	Enables clients to manage SBQs

Listing 11-1 shows the skeleton C# code for using the preceding classes.

Listing 11-1: Skeleton C# code for the QueueMangementClient class's methods

```csharp
public static class QueueManagementClient
{
    public static QueueClient CreateQueue(TransportClientEndpointBehavior
        credential, Uri queueUri, QueuePolicy queuePolicy);
    public static void DeleteQueue(TransportClientEndpointBehavior credential,
        Uri queueUri);
    public static QueueClient GetQueue(TransportClientEndpointBehavior
        credential, Uri queueUri);
    public static QueuePolicy GetQueuePolicy(TransportClientEndpointBehavior
        credential, Uri queueUri);
    public static DateTime RenewQueue(TransportClientEndpointBehavior credential,
        Uri queueUri, TimeSpan requestedExpiration);
}
```

Following are the steps to create a new queue based on the Readme.htm file for the .NET Services SDK's Queue sample projects:

1. Create a QueuePolicy instance and define the name and desired properties of the queue. The `<QueuePolicy>` element is defined in the namespace http://schemas.microsoft.com/ws /2007/08/connect.

2. Obtain a security token for the SB solution from the AccessControlService (see Listing 11-2).

3. Test for the existence of a queue of the same name in the solution (see Listing 11-3, which indicates existence of the specified queue).

4. If the specified queue doesn't exist, embed the serialized QueuePolicy into an ATOM 1.0 `<atom:entry>` as an extension and POST the entry to the designated queue URI with the content-type application/atom+xml;type=entry. The request must carry an X-MS-Identity-Token header and the respective identity must have Manage permission on for the scope that covers the queue's URI (see Listing 11-4).

If the queue was successfully created, the POST request returns with a 201 (created) status code along with a Location header. The location header contains the queue's management URI that you need to retain in your application state to have access to the queue's metadata and management functions. If the queue could not be created successfully, the request may yield one of the HTTP status codes described in the table following Listing 11-4.

297

Listing 11-2: HTTP request and response headers to obtain the security token for an SBQ as the response payload

```
GET /issuetoken.aspx?u=oakleaf-sb&p=safegate HTTP/1.1
Host: accesscontrol.windows.net
Connection: Keep-Alive

HTTP/1.1 200 OK
Cache-Control: private
Content-Length: 40
Content-Type: text/plain
Server: Microsoft-IIS/7.0
X-AspNet-Version: 2.0.50727
Set-Cookie: ASP.NET_SessionId=jjqlyg45u4xxeo55u3mec1r3; path=/; HttpOnly
X-Powered-By: ASP.NET
Date: Tue, 26 May 2009 21:11:30 GMT

LMT8pPDDy0j2aen5qDFWxCfL+2pcosiBAvQlRg==
```

Listing 11-3: The Atom payload returned by a GET request for an active queue using the security token returned by Listing 11-5

```
GET / HTTP/1.1
X-MS-Identity-Token: LMT8pPDDy0j2aen5qDFWxCfL+2pcosiBAvQlRg==
Host: oakleaf-sb.servicebus.windows.net

HTTP/1.1 200 OK
Transfer-Encoding: chunked
Content-Type: application/atom+xml;type=feed;charset=utf-8
Server: Microsoft-HTTPAPI/2.0
Date: Tue, 26 May 2009 21:11:31 GMT

164
<feed xmlns="http://www.w3.org/2005/Atom">
  <title type="text">Publicly Listed Services</title>
  <subtitle type="text">
    This is the list of publicly-listed services currently available
  </subtitle>
  <id>uuid:88f27a0c-6adb-49fe-8494-baefebfd041a;id=3123</id>
  <updated>2009-05-26T21:11:31Z</updated>
  <generator>Microsoft® .NET Services - Service Bus</generator>
</feed>
0
```

Listing 11-4: The Atom payload to create a new queue with a lifetime of one hour using the security token returned by Listing 11-5

```
POST /MyHttpQueue/ HTTP/1.1
X-MS-Identity-Token: quCHs/PDy0gmodPM4qfOf1XjT/chwcczGIaTUQ==
```

```
Content-Type: application/atom+xml;type=entry;charset=utf-8
Host: oakleaf-sb.servicebus.windows.net
Content-Length: 371
Expect: 100-continue

<entry xmlns="http://www.w3.org/2005/Atom">
  <id>uuid:e1a20be8-2fec-4b65-88df-82656feade09;id=1</id>
  <title type="text" />
  <updated>2009-05-26T21:33:25Z</updated>
  <QueuePolicy xmlns:i="http://www.w3.org/2001/XMLSchema-instance"
               xmlns="http://schemas.microsoft.com/ws/2007/08/connect">
    <ExpirationInstant>2009-05-26T22:33:25.1328918Z</ExpirationInstant>
  </QueuePolicy>
</entry>

HTTP/1.1 201 Created
Transfer-Encoding: chunked
Content-Type: application/atom+xml;type=entry;charset=utf-8
Expires: Tue, 26 May 2009 22:33:25 GMT
Location: https://oakleaf-sb.servicebus.windows.net/MyHttpQueue/!(queue)
Server: Microsoft-HTTPAPI/2.0
Date: Tue, 26 May 2009 21:33:25 GMT

300
<entry xmlns="http://www.w3.org/2005/Atom">
  <id>uuid:61006d59-4ea2-4e16-82d1-6dfea136bb15;id=12865</id>
  <title type="text">myhttpqueue</title>
  <updated>2009-05-26T21:33:25Z</updated>
  <link rel="alternate" href="https://oakleaf-sb.servicebus.windows.net/
      MyHttpQueue/"/>
  <link rel="self" href="https://oakleaf-
    sb.servicebus.windows.net/MyHttpQueue/!(queue)"/>
  <link rel="queuehead" href="https://oakleaf-
    sb.servicebus.windows.net/MyHttpQueue/!(queue/head)"/>
  <link rel="queuecontrol" href="https://oakleaf-
    sb.servicebus.windows.net/MyHttpQueue/!(queue/control)"/>
  <QueuePolicy xmlns="http://schemas.microsoft.com/ws/2007/08/connect"
    xmlns:i="http://www.w3.org/2001/XMLSchema-instance">
```

```
    <Discoverability>Public</Discoverability>
```

```
    <ExpirationInstant>2009-05-26T22:33:25.1328918Z</ExpirationInstant>
  </QueuePolicy>
</entry>
0
```

Code	Name	HTTP Status Description
400	Bad Request	The policy was malformed or invalid.
403	Forbidden	The client did not provide an X-MS-Identity-Token header, the provided token is no longer valid for use, or the provided identity is not authorized to create a queue at this location.
409	Conflict	There is already a queue with an incompatible policy at the given location or the location is occupied by a router or a Service Bus listener.
415	Unsupported Media Type	The request did not carry the required content-type header.
500	Internal Server Error	The processing failed on a condition internal to the Service Bus service.

One of the reasons for selecting the HttpQueueSample for analysis in this chapter is the ability of a web debugger, such as Fiddler2, to capture and display most or all traffic between the client and service.

Test-Driving the HttpQueueSample Solution

The . . .\HttpMessages\C#35\HttpQueueSample.sln solution is one of six sample projects in the \Program Files\.NET Services SDK (July 2009 CTP)\Samples\ServiceBus\ExploringFeatures\Queues\ and \WROX\Azure\Chapter11\Queues folders. According to the Readme.htm file:

> This sample demonstrates how to use the Microsoft .NET Services Service Bus Queue feature using plain HTTP requests.
>
> This sample shows a simple message producer (sender) and two types of message consumers that leverage the Service Bus REST protocols to discover existing or new create Queues and shows how to send messages into a Queue and retrieve messages from a Queue with destructive and non-destructive (peek/lock) reads.
>
> Queues in the Service Bus are free-format message queues that can accept, store, and allow for retrieval of plain HTTP request messages with any HTTP method except GET (and HEAD). Because Queues are one-way messaging primitives that provide decoupling of sender and receiver, GET is not a meaningful operation for Queues, since the queue does not have access to the resource representation of the recipient(s) of the messages it carries.

The HttpQueueSample solution consists of the following three projects:

❑ **Sender** requests the SB solution name and account password from the user, creates a new queue at https://SolutionName.servicebus.windows.net/MyHttpQueue/ if it doesn't exist, and lets the user enter a text message to enqueue.

❑ **Consumer** discovers or creates the MyHttpQueue queue and polls it for messages in a loop with destructive reads, which dequeue the message.

❑ PeekLockConsumer discovers or creates the `MyHttpQueue` queue and polls it for messages; it ran-domly decides whether to dequeue a locked message or place a lock on an unlocked message.

As of the July 2009 CTP, the maximum permissible message size is constrained to 60KB. The message size limit for later versions is expected to be subject to system configuration and metadata available on the customer's service plan.

You can run the three projects in any sequence. The most common sequence is Sender, Consumer, which enqueues a message that the Consumer reads after it starts. To execute this sequence, follow these steps:

1. Open \WROX\Azure\Chapter11\Queues\HttpMessages\C#35\HttpQueueSample.sln in VS 2008 SP1 or later and press F5 to build and run the solution with Sender as the Startup Project.

2. Type your solution name, press Enter, type your service account password, and press Enter to obtain a security token from ACS.

3. If a client or network firewall requests permission for the application to pass a TCP request through a port, grant the permission, close the console window, press F5 and redo step 2.

4. When the Sender console requests text to enqueue, type a brief message and press Enter.

5. Right-click the Consumer project's Solution Explorer node and choose Debug, Start a New Instance to open the Consumer console window.

6. If a client or network firewall requests permission for the application to pass a TCP request through a port, grant the permission, close the console window, press F5 and redo step 5.

7. Observe that the message you typed in step 4 appears in the last line of the Consumer console window (see Figure 11-2).

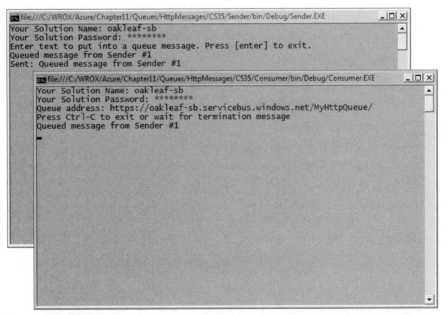

Figure 11-2: The Consumer project's console window displaying the queued message.

Spelunking the HttpQueueSample Solution's Code

Both console projects obtain a username/password authentication token from ACS, test for the existence of a persistent object (queue or workflow), create and persist a message-oriented object, and send a message to a queue or workflow. Listing 11-5 shows the code for the Sender project's Main() method.

Listing 11-5: The Sender project's Main() method code

```
namespace Microsoft.Samples.ServiceBus
{
    using System;
    using System.Linq;
    using System.ServiceModel;
    using Microsoft.ServiceBus;
    using System.Text;
    using System.ServiceModel.Channels;
    using System.Net;
    using System.Xml;
    using System.ServiceModel.Syndication;
    using System.IO;

    class Program
    {
        static void Main(string[] args)
        {
            // Get UserNamePassword credentials


            Console.Write("Your Solution Name: ");
            string solutionName = Console.ReadLine();
            Console.Write("Your Solution Password: ");
            string solutionPassword = ReadPassword();


            // Create the service URI based on the solution name

            Uri queueUri =
                ServiceBusEnvironment.CreateServiceUri(Uri.UriSchemeHttps,
solutionName,
                "/MyHttpQueue/");
            Uri queueManageUri;
            Uri queueHeadUri;
            // Get the existing queue or create a new one

            string token = HttpGetAuthenticationToken(solutionName,
                solutionPassword);
            QueuePolicy queuePolicy = HttpGetQueue(token, queueUri,
                out queueHeadUri);
            if (queuePolicy == null)
            {

                // Create a new queue policy with an expiration time of 1 hour


                queuePolicy = new QueuePolicy();
```

```
        queuePolicy.ExpirationInstant = DateTime.UtcNow +
            TimeSpan.FromHours(1);
```

```
        // Added to make queue publicly discoverable
```

```
        queuePolicy.Discoverability = DiscoverabilityPolicy.Public;
        queueManageUri = HttpCreateQueue(token, queueUri, queuePolicy);
    }
```

```
    // Added: Inspect the default QueuePolicy property values if set
```

```
var authorization = queuePolicy.Authorization;
var enqueueTimeout = queuePolicy.EnqueueTimeout;
var maxConcurrentReaders = queuePolicy.MaxConcurrentReaders;
var maxDequeueRetries = queuePolicy.MaxDequeueRetries;
var maxMessageAge = queuePolicy.MaxMessageAge;
var maxMessageSize = queuePolicy.MaxMessageSize;
var maxQueueCapacity = queuePolicy.MaxQueueCapacity;
var maxQueueLength = queuePolicy.MaxQueueLength;
var overflow = queuePolicy.Overflow;
var poisonMessageDrop = queuePolicy.PoisonMessageDrop;
var transportPolicy = queuePolicy.TransportProtection;

Console.WriteLine("Enter text to put into a queue message.
    Press [enter] to exit.");
string input = Console.ReadLine();
while (input != String.Empty)
{
    try
    {
```

```
        // Send message
```

```
        HttpWebRequest sendRequest =
            HttpWebRequest.Create(queueUri) as
            HttpWebRequest;
        sendRequest.Method = "POST";
        sendRequest.Headers.Add("X-MS-Identity-Token",
            token);
        sendRequest.ContentType =
            "text/plain;charset=utf-8";
        using (var sendStream =
            sendRequest.GetRequestStream())
        {
            using (var writer = new StreamWriter(sendStream,
                Encoding.UTF8))
            {
                writer.Write(input);
                writer.Flush();
            }
        }
        sendRequest.GetResponse().Close();

        Console.WriteLine("Sent: {0}", input);
```

Continued

Listing 11-5: The Sender project's `Main()` method code *(continued)*

```
        }
        catch (Exception e)
        {
            Console.WriteLine("Error: " + e.Message);
        }
        input = Console.ReadLine();
    }

    // Exit and leave the queue persisted for the consumer.

}
// HttpGetAuthenticationToken() method
// HttpGetQueue() method
// GetParentUri() method
// HttpCreateQueue() method
// SDK Utility methods
    }
}
```

A queue is an instance of a `QueuePolicy`. The following table lists members of the `QueuePolicy` class and their default values. Default values of `2,147,483,647` (`int32.MaxValue`) represent an unlimited value.

Property Name	Description	Default Value
`Authorization`	Gets or sets the authorization policy for the current instance. (Inherited from `JunctionPolicy`).	`Required`
`Discoverability`	Determines whether and under what circumstances the junction is discoverable using the Atom feed. (Inherited from `JunctionPolicy`)	`Managers`
`EnqueueTimeout`	Gets or sets the enqueue timeout.	`10 seconds`
`ExpirationInstant`	Gets or sets the expiration instant. (Inherited from `JunctionPolicy`)	`24 hours later`
`MaxConcurrent-Readers`	Gets or sets the maximum number of concurrent readers.	`2,147,483,647`
`MaxDequeueRetries`	Gets or sets the maximum number of dequeue retries.	`2,147,483,647`
`MaxMessageAge`	Gets or sets the maximum message age.	`10 minutes`
`MaxMessageSize`	Gets or sets the max message size. (Inherited from `JunctionPolicy`)	`61,440`
`MaxQueueCapacity`	Gets or sets the maximum queue capacity.	`2,097,152`
`MaxQueueLength`	Gets or sets the maximum queue length.	`2,147,483,647`

Overflow	Gets or sets the overflow policy, which indicates the handling of messages in case the buffer reached capacity and the `BufferTimeout` expired.	`RejectIncoming-Message`
PoisonMessageDrop	Gets or sets the poison message drop endpoint address.	`null`
TransportProtection	Gets or sets the type of transport protection. (Inherited from `JunctionPolicy`)	`AllPaths`

Only `QueuePolicy` property values set explicitly by code appear in the `<QueuePolicy>` group of the Atom discovery `<feed>`'s `<entry>` for the instance, as shown emphasized in Listing 11-6.

Listing 11-6: The Atom 1.0 feed for the `https://oakleaf-sb.servicebus.windows.net/` **endpoint**

```
<feed xmlns="http://www.w3.org/2005/Atom">
  <title type="text">Publicly Listed Services</title>
  <subtitle type="text">
    This is the list of publicly-listed services currently available
  </subtitle>
  <id>uuid:ff9bc499-19aa-49e4-a1da-d8c2afb349ea;id=340</id>
  <updated>2009-05-27T19:46:45Z</updated>
  <generator>Microsoft® .NET Services - Service Bus</generator>
  <entry>
    <id>uuid:ff9bc499-19aa-49e4-a1da-d8c2afb349ea;id=341</id>
    <title type="text">myhttpqueue</title>
    <updated>2009-05-27T19:46:45Z</updated>
    <link rel="alternate" href="https://oakleaf-sb.servicebus.windows.net/
        MyHttpQueue/"/>
    <link rel="self"
      href="https://oakleaf-sb.servicebus.windows.net/
      MyHttpQueue/!(queue)"/>
    <link rel="queuehead"
      href="https://oakleaf-sb.servicebus.windows.net/
      MyHttpQueue/!(queue/head)"/>
    <link rel="queuecontrol"
      href="https://oakleaf-sb.servicebus.windows.net/
      MyHttpQueue/!(queue/control)"/>

    <QueuePolicy xmlns="http://schemas.microsoft.com/ws/2007/08/connect"
        xmlns:i="http://www.w3.org/2001/XMLSchema-instance">
        <Discoverability>
          Public
        </Discoverability>
        <ExpirationInstant>2009-05-27T20:08:25.2308651Z</ExpirationInstant>
      </QueuePolicy>
```

Continued

```
        </entry>
    </feed>
```

The `<link rel="alternate"...>` link points to the queue's tail, to which clients submit messages, and
`<link rel="queuehead"...>` points to the head from which consumers receive messages.

Delivering Messages with Service Bus Routers

Routers forward messages from one or more publishers to one or more subscribers to create a pub/sub
messaging model with optional multicasting to all subscribers. Publishers send messages using HTTP,
HTTPS, or the SB's "NetOneway" protocol as plain HTTP messages or SOAP 1.1/1.2 envelopes, but
neither publishers nor subscribers can invoke the HTTP GET method on one-way messages. Subscribers
can subscribe to a router either using a `NetOnewayBinding` listener or listen to any publicly reachable
HTTP endpoint.

The ...\HttpRouter\C#35\HttpRouter.sln solution is one of two sample projects in the \Program
Files\.NET Services SDK (March 2009 CTP)\Samples\ServiceBus\ExploringFeatures\Routers\ and
\WROX\Azure\Chapter11\Routers folders. HttpRouter corresponds to the HttpQueueSample solution
and uses the RESTful HTTP protocol; the other sample solution, SoapRouter.sln, wraps messages in
SOAP 1.2 envelopes. According to the Readme.htm file, "This sample shows a simple message publisher
(sender) and two types of subscribers that leverage the Service Bus REST protocols to discover existing
or create new Routers and shows how to send messages into a Router and how to subscribe to and
receive messages via Routers." Figure 11-3 is a diagram of a router with an optional queue.

Queues can subscribe to routers in the same way that listeners do.

The HttpRouter.sln solution contains the following three projects:

❑ **Publisher** requests the SB solution name and account password from the user, creates a new
router at `https://SolutionName.servicebus.windows.net/MyHttpRouter/` if it doesn't exist
and lets the user enter a text message to route.

❑ **QueueSubscriber** requests the SB solution name and account password from the user, creates a
new queue at `https://SolutionName.servicebus.windows.net/MyHttpRouter/` if it doesn't
exist and waits for a publisher to place messages in the queue. QueueSubscriber's `Main()`
method code is almost identical to that in Listing 11-5.

❑ **HttpPushSubscriber** creates a uniquely named, Internet-facing HTTPS Web Service endpoint
on the SB with the WS2007HttpRelayBinding. The endpoint emulates a SOAP 1.2 endpoint that
might already exist in the Azure Fabric. Push subscriber endpoints aren't required to use the SB.

Router and queue architecture is quite similar; therefore, HttpRouter's Publisher project code, partially shown in Listing 11-7, is very similar to HttpQueueSample's Sender code. The Router API offers
`RouterClient`, `RouterManagementClient`, `RouterPolicy`, `RouterSubscription`, and other `Router`...
helper classes; all but `RouterSubscription` have corresponding `Queue`... classes.

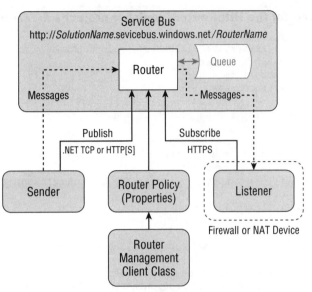

Figure 11-3: The relationship of SBR components, including an optional SBQ.

Listing 11-7: Code for the HttpRouter.Publisher project's `Main()` method

```
namespace Microsoft.Samples.ServiceBus
{
    using System;
    using System.Linq;
    using System.Net;
    using System.ServiceModel.Syndication;
    using System.Text;
    using System.Xml;
    using Microsoft.ServiceBus;

    class Program
    {
        static void Main(string[] args)
        {

        // Get solution name and service account password

            Console.Write("Your Solution Name: ");
            string solutionName = Console.ReadLine();
            Console.Write("Your Solution Password: ");
            string solutionPassword = ReadPassword();

        // Create the service URI based on the solution name

            Uri routerUri = ServiceBusEnvironment.
```

Continued

Listing 11-7: Code for the HttpRouter.Publisher project's `Main()` **method** *(continued)*

```
            CreateServiceUri("https", solutionName,
            "/MyHttpRouter/");
    Uri subscriptionsUri;
    Uri routerManageUri;

    // Get the existing router or create a new one

    string token = HttpGetAuthenticationToken(solutionName,
        solutionPassword);
    RouterPolicy routerPolicy = HttpGetRouter(token, routerUri,
        out subscriptionsUri);
    if (routerPolicy == null)
    {

        // Create a new router policy with an expiration of 1 hour

        routerPolicy = new RouterPolicy();
        routerPolicy.ExpirationInstant = DateTime.UtcNow +
            TimeSpan.FromHours(1);

        routerPolicy.MaxSubscribers = int.MaxValue;
        routerPolicy.MessageDistribution =
            MessageDistributionPolicy.AllSubscribers;

        routerPolicy.TransportProtection =
            TransportProtectionPolicy.None;
        routerPolicy.Discoverability =
            DiscoverabilityPolicy.Public;
        routerManageUri = HttpCreateRouter(token, routerUri,
            routerPolicy);
    }

    Console.WriteLine("Enter some text to put into a router
        message. Press [enter] to exit.");
    string input = Console.ReadLine();
    while (input != String.Empty)
    {
        try
        {

            // Send the message

            HttpWebRequest sendRequest =
                HttpWebRequest.Create(routerUri+"?status="+
                Uri.EscapeDataString(input)) as HttpWebRequest;
            sendRequest.Method = "POST";
            sendRequest.Headers.Add("X-MS-Identity-Token",
                token);
            sendRequest.ContentLength = 0;
            sendRequest.GetResponse().Close();

            Console.WriteLine("Sent: {0}", input);
        }
```

```
            catch (Exception e)
            {
                Console.WriteLine("Error: " + e.Message);
            }
            input = Console.ReadLine();
        }


        // Exit and leave the router alive until it expires


    }
    // HttpGetAuthenticationToken() method
    // HttpGetRouter() method
    // GetParentUri() method
    // HttpCreateRouter() method
    // ReadPassword() method
}
}
```

Notice that the `RouterPolicy` instance has several router-specific property values (emphasized) set explicitly, as well as `TransportProtection`, which also is a `QueuePolicy` member. The `MessageDistributionPolicy.AllSubscribers` enumeration member specifies multicast delivery.

Running the HttpRouter.sln solution is similar to running HttpQueueSample.sln. Pressing F5 builds the solution and runs the Publisher project. Typing a message and then starting the QueueSubscriber project doesn't display the message because QueueSubscriber creates the listener's queue. Figure 11-4 shows the result of sending router message #1 before opening the QueueSubscriber console window and sending router message #2 after.

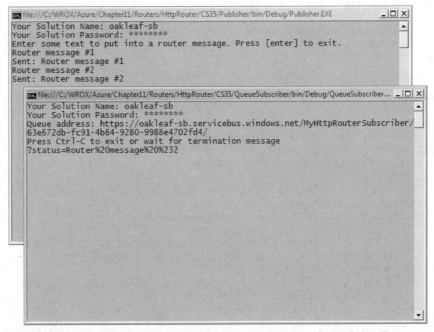

Figure 11-4: Router message #1 was sent before opening the QueueSubscriber console; router message #2 (URL-encoded) was sent after.

As you would expect, HTTP POST headers and Atom-formatted payload for a new RouterPolicy, as shown in Listing 11-8, are quite similar to those for a new QueuePolicy (refer to Listing 11-6).

Listing 11-8: HTTP POST request and response messages for creating a new RouterPolicy instance

```
POST /MyHttpRouter/ HTTP/1.1
X-MS-Identity-Token: +SytR77Ey0jdTLeDXmuxlg/6jzMy5SG6RA/+yQ==
Content-Type: application/atom+xml;type=entry;charset=utf-8
Host: oakleaf-sb.servicebus.windows.net
Content-Length: 561
Expect: 100-continue

<entry xmlns="http://www.w3.org/2005/Atom">
  <id>uuid:a38eb5a6-7319-4b12-9624-4c226e0f25d9;id=1</id>
  <title type="text" />
  <updated>2009-05-27T21:43:33Z</updated>
  <RouterPolicy xmlns:i="http://www.w3.org/2001/XMLSchema-instance"
      xmlns="http://schemas.microsoft.com/ws/2007/08/connect">
    <Discoverability>Public</Discoverability>
    <ExpirationInstant>2009-05-27T22:43:33.7426466Z</ExpirationInstant>
    <TransportProtection>None</TransportProtection>
    <MaxSubscribers>2147483647</MaxSubscribers>
    <MessageDistribution>AllSubscribers</MessageDistribution>
  </RouterPolicy>
</entry>

HTTP/1.1 201 Created
Transfer-Encoding: chunked
Content-Type: application/atom+xml;type=entry;charset=utf-8
Expires: Wed, 27 May 2009 22:43:33 GMT
Location: https://oakleaf-sb.servicebus.windows.net/MyHttpRouter/!(router)
Server: Microsoft-HTTPAPI/2.0
Date: Wed, 27 May 2009 21:43:34 GMT

35C
<entry xmlns="http://www.w3.org/2005/Atom">
  <id>uuid:b1be1f1f-70da-49eb-8ca7-6e43b2988517;id=2317</id>
  <title type="text">myhttprouter</title>
  <updated>2009-05-27T21:43:34Z</updated>
  <link rel="alternate" href="https://oakleaf-
    sb.servicebus.windows.net/MyHttpRouter/"/>
  <link rel="self"
    href="https://oakleaf-sb.servicebus.windows.net/MyHttpRouter/!(router)"/>
  <link rel="subscriptions"
    href="https://oakleaf-sb.servicebus.windows.net/
      MyHttpRouter/!(router/subscriptions)"/>
  <RouterPolicy xmlns="http://schemas.microsoft.com/ws/2007/08/connect"
      xmlns:i="http://www.w3.org/2001/XMLSchema-instance">
    <Discoverability>Public</Discoverability>
    <ExpirationInstant>2009-05-27T22:43:33.7426466Z</ExpirationInstant>
    <TransportProtection>None</TransportProtection>
    <MaxSubscribers>50</MaxSubscribers>
```

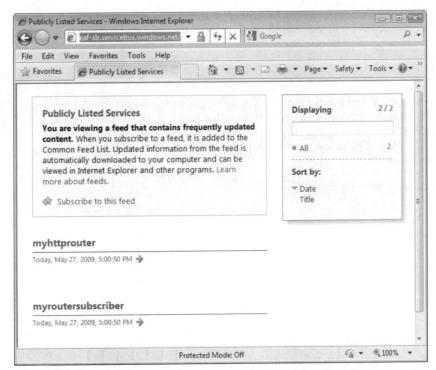

**Figure 11-5: IE8 displaying the Atom 1.0 feed after running the HttpRouter
solution's Publisher and QueueSubscriber projects.**

```
    <MessageDistribution>AllSubscribers</MessageDistribution>
  </RouterPolicy>
</entry>
0
```

Figure 11-5 shows IE8 displaying the `https://oakleaf-sb.servicebus.windows.net/` Atom feed after
running the Publisher and QueueSubscriber projects.

Summary

.NET Services supports three features that persist objects programmatically in the Azure Fabric: the .NET
Workflow Service and the .NET Service Bus's queues and routers. .NET Services also provides .NET
Services Portal pages to manage workflow types and instances of types; queues and routers don't have a
management UI as of the March 2009 CTP.

The Windows Azure Platform's Workflow Service (WFS) page describes the service: "The Workflow
Service is a high-scale host for running workflows in the cloud. It provides a set of activities optimized
for sending, receiving, and manipulating HTTP and Service Bus messages; a set of hosted tools to deploy,
manage and track the execution of workflow instances; and a set of management APIs. Workflows (WFs)
can be constructed using the familiar Visual Studio 2008 Workflow Designer." The electronic version

of the chapter will demonstrate how to create and run WFS solutions, as well as analyze the code and messages to create WFs with the workflow management APIs.

As developers began testing the SB, it became apparent that two additional features were required to adapt the SB to the Windows Azure environment: Service Bus Queues (SBQs) to persist messages for asynchronous delivery and Service Bus Routers (SBRs) to enable message routing to more than one listener and even. Routers implement a composable publish/subscribe model for messages from selected senders. Subscribers can add a queue to ensure that messages aren't lost when a listener goes offline temporarily. The last half of this chapter demonstrated SBQs and SBRs with RESTful HTTP messaging. The .NET Services SDK installs queue and router sample solutions that wrap messages in SOAP 1.1/1.2 envelopes also.

Index

Entity Group Transactions (EGTs), 85, 109, 193–194. *See also* ACID
ACID *v.*, 193
code to add the minimum table version header to support EGTs (Listing 7–4), 194
requirements for, 193
Entity-Attribute-Value tables. *See* EAV tables
Errors.cs, 72
ESB (Enterprise Service Bus) model, 39, 273–274, 294. *See also* Service Bus
EU Directive 95/46/EC, 120, 123
EU Safe Harbor regulations, 149
Everex, 9
Everything as a Service (EaaS), 11–13, 18
cloud computing and, 11–13, 18
defined, 13
HP and, 13
Execute . . . () methods, 90
Exodus Communications, 11
"Exploiting SQL Azure Database's Relational Features" (online chapter), xxii, xxv, xxvi, 41, 48, 63

F

FaaS (Files as a Service), 11, 12, 13, 14, 18, 40
Fabric. *See* Cloud Fabric; Development Fabric
Fabric Controller (FC, Azure Fabric Controller), 57–58
availability, 57–58
diagram, 57
load balancing and, 49, 50, 51, 53, 60, 209
role of, 49, 50–51, 60
Failure Domains, 51, 52, 53, 60, 63, 111, 188
"Fast, Scalable, and Secure Session State Management for Your Web Applications" article, 169
fate sharing/ reputation, 116
Fault Domains. *See* Failure Domains
FC. *See* Fabric Controller
FC Core, 57
Federal Cloud Infrastructure, 17
Federal Information Processing Standard (FIPS), 118, 135

FederatedIdentity.net. *See also* CardSpace information card; Identity Lab
claims transformation rules and, 261–264
oakleaf-acs solution and, 260–266
as Recognized Token Issuer, 260–261
Relying Party and, 247, 250, 264–266
FederatedIdentity.pfx certificate, 249
Fiddler2, 68–71, 79, 128, 141, 227, 230, 293, 300
Files as a Service (FaaS), 11, 12, 13, 14, 18, 40
FIPS (Federal Information Processing Standard), 118, 135
firewalls, 18, 54, 116, 124, 273, 275, 294, 296, 301, 307
Firmware as a Service. *See* HaaS
Firmware/Hardware layer, 14, 15
FISMA, 18, 119, 149
500 (Internal Server Error), 300
five-layer cloud computing model, 14–15
flexible properties feature (Azure tables), 188, 191, 208
Flexiscale, 12
flow diagrams, Thumbnails_WebRole and Thumbnails_WorkerRole projects
Thumbnails2.sln (modified project), 231, 232
Thumbnails.sln (original project), 222, 223, 231, 232
Force.com. *See* Salesforce.com
Foreign Corrupt Practices Act, 120
400 (Bad Request), 300
403 (Forbidden), 300
409 (Conflict), 300
415 (Unsupported Media Type), 300
Fratto, Mike, 16

G

GAE. *See* Google App Engine
Gartner, 3, 8, 9, 13
"Geneva" Beta 2, 239, 243–244, 273
Geneva CardSpace. *See* CardSpace
Geneva Framework. *See* Windows Identity Foundation

Geneva Server. *See* Active Directory Federation Services
"Geneva" Team Blog, 244
geolocation services, 21, 27, 118, 153, 189
Get Blob, 109–110
GET method. *See* HTTP GET
GetHealthStatus(), 224
GetMessages (Message-Queue.GetMessage[s]), 215
GetPhotoGalleryContainer(), 224
GetQueue(), 212
GetThumbnailMakerQueue(), 224
GLBA. *See* Gramm-Leach-Bliley Act
GoGrid, 12, 18
Golden, Bernard, 117
Google App Engine (GAE)
Azure *v.*, 47, 51, 115
BigTable storage system and, 13, 29
Cloud Application Layer and, 14
Cloud Status and, 12
DataStore, 12, 111
Django framework and, 13
EAV tables and, 13, 29, 111, 187
Google Trends service and, 4
Java and, xxi
outages, 117
PaaS, xxi, 18
Python and, xxi, 13, 14, 15, 59
SLAs, 117
as specialty ASP, 10
TaaS and, 13
virtualized runtime application platform and, 13
webapp framework and, 13
Google.com
CAP Theorem and, 30
Chrome, 9
Schmidt and, 3, 4
Trends service, 4
governance, cloud, 16–18. *See also* obstacles
government agencies, cloud computing and, 119, 150
Gramm-Leach-Bliley Act (GLBA), 119, 120, 148, 149, 150
Grance, Tim, 118
Green, Frederick, 148
grids
displaying child entities, 207–208
displaying data from heterogeneous tables in, 205–208
displaying parent entities, 205–206